Schriften zum Recht der Digitalisierung

Edited by

Florian Möslein, Sebastian Omlor and Martin Will

30

ARTIBUS INGENUIS J. C. B. M. 1801

Decentralised Autonomous Organisation (DAO) Regulation

Principles and Perspectives for the Future

Edited by

Madalena Perestrelo de Oliveira
and António Garcia Rolo

Mohr Siebeck

Madalena Perestrelo de Oliveira is Professor at the Faculty of Law of the University of Lisbon.
orcid.org/0000-0002-8908-2991

António Garcia Rolo is Guest Academic Assistant at the Faculty of Law of the University of Lisbon.
orcid.org/0000-0002-6406-6207

ISBN 978-3-16-163700-1 / eISBN 978-3-16-163701-8
DOI 10.1628/978-3-16-163701-8

ISSN 2700-1288 / eISSN 2700-1296 (Schriften zum Recht der Digitalisierung)

Die Deutsche Nationalbibliothek lists this publication in the German National Bibliography; detailed bibliographic data is available at *https://dnb.dnb.de.*

Published by Mohr Siebeck Tübingen 2024. www.mohrsiebeck.com

The book was typeset by using Stempel Garamond typeface and printed on non-aging paper by Laupp & Göbel in Gomaringen, and bound by Buchbinderei Nädele in Nehren.

Printed in Germany.

Foreword

Clearing the Way for an Informed Discussion on the Future of DAO Regulation

Madalena Perestrelo de Oliveira and António Garcia Rolo

I. About the Project and its Interim Conclusions

Decentralised autonomous organisations ("DAO"s) – as well as similarly decentralised arrangements based on the blockchain – are one of the most challenging phenomena emerging from the blockchain revolution, presenting unprecedented legal challenges to lawyers and academics. The emergence of DAOs has the potential to be *the* transformative event for corporate law in the 21st century, putting into question tenets we have had for granted and forcing corporate lawyers to rethink what they hold as immutable and to adapt many corporate law rules to the new reality.

At the Lisbon DAO Observatory, a research project set up within the Lisbon Research Centre for Private Law (CIDP – *Centro de Investigação de Direito Privado*) of the Faculty of Law of the University of Lisbon, we are seeking to find answers for these deeply enthralling and exciting challenges. The objective of this Research Project is to try to find legal answers to the current legal challenges posed by DAOs and similar arrangements in order to help shaping future legislative action.

Law and technology do not always make the best bedfellows. While it is true that legal certainty and the need to protect those involved in blockchain business arrangements often require the definition of a legal framework, there have been instances where the law is ill-suited to technology (such as the General Data Protection Regulation and the difficulty of reconciling the right to be forgotten with the use of blockchain technology). The law (or its interpretation) should not restrain technological innovation. On the contrary, it should create an environment conducive to its development and, where necessary, ensure adequate protection for markets and investors. Of course, this does not mean that technology should develop without any external control, regardless of the risks it may pose. Furthermore, DAOs are evolving rapidly and differ in purpose, structure, function and risks they pose for participants, which makes it particularly challenging to draw a one size fits all framework. We recognise that it is not easy to regulate DAOs without losing the key features that make them special and attractive to market participants. At the Lisbon DAO Observatory we are trying to find legal answers that do not jeopardise the core DAO concept and philosophy.

The achievement of this objective is made possible by consecutive steps – the first step was the organisation of the 1st Lisbon DAO Legal Structure Workshop (on March 17th, 2022). We believe in the importance of freely discussing challenging and controversial issues, in constant articulation with relevant stakeholders and the DAO ecosystem. The legal system cannot be based on solutions or regulations that ignore social reality and practical experiences. This is why the Lisbon DAO Observatory's research project is based on the dialogue with the DAO ecosystem. Having that in mind, in the 1st Workshop we gathered representatives from seven DAOs of all shapes and sizes in order to ascertain their structure, the legal challenges they face and how they deal with them. On the 25th of May 2022, we organised a follow-up event – the 2nd Lisbon DAO Legal Structure Workshop – where we hosted legal scholars and practitioners explaining: (i) how most DAOs would be qualified under major European jurisdictions (Portugal, Germany, France and the UK); and (ii) how they are already being dealt with in more forward-looking jurisdictions, such as Malta, Wyoming and the Marshall Islands, with the latter three jurisdictions having explicitly recognised DAOs in their corporate law.

The outputs of this event can be consulted in our first publication *Decentralised Autonomous Organisations (DAOs) in Various Jurisdictions: from Old Rules to Innovative Approaches*, published by AAFDL Editora (Lisbon, Portugal) on 2023 and freely available online at https://lisbondaoobservatory.cidp.pt/publication/decentralised-autonomous-organisations-daos-in-various-jurisdictions-from-old-rules-to-innovative-approaches/8.

This 2nd Lisbon DAO Legal Structure Workshop and the resulting publication made clear the current legal status of DAOs in most jurisdictions. Our contributors concluded that in most major jurisdictions (Portugal, Germany, France and the UK in particular were addressed) most DAOs, even if their members do not want to, will be considered partnerships or other similar forms of business organisation and their members would be unlimitedly liable for the actions of the DAO. As we saw, more forward-looking jurisdictions (Malta, Wyoming and the Marshall Islands were addressed in our first publication) try to offer some respite from this consequence by providing different mechanisms of legal recognition of DAOs (which is explicit in the Wyoming and Marshall Island cases).

II. The *Status Quo*

As we have mentioned in our previous publications, DAOs are difficult to define with precision and there are various definitions in articles, textbooks or glossaries. We will work on the basis of a narrow definition of DAO as a form of human organisation based on blockchain technology, in which various members pool funds or assets (usually, but not necessarily, cryptoassets) to undertake a given activity (not necessarily for profit). They are partially or mostly governed by a bundle of smart contracts, deployed on a given blockchain. As the name indicates, DAOs are simultaneously decentralised and autonomous: *(i)* decentralised because most DAOs seek to have no centralised management, instead placing important decisions in the hands of associates, seeking to mitigate the traditional agency problem between shareholders and management; and *(ii)* autonomous because many decision-making powers traditionally held by the management can be entrusted to a smart contract, that defines the rules of the organisation and usually holds the DAO's treasury.

As concluded in the 2nd Lisbon DAO Legal Structure Workshop and the resulting ebook published in 2023, regardless of the will of the members of a DAO, arrangements falling within this definition of DAOs (and other arrangements classified as DAOs) would be considered partnerships (or the equivalent "civil societies" in civil law jurisdictions) in most jurisdictions if the DAO is indeed a collective form of carrying out an activity with proceeds directly or indirectly split between its members. Such frameworks usually require the presence of a personal element (members who exercise varying degrees of control), a teleological element (carrying out an activity which can be more or less profit-oriented) and a material-economic element (pooled resources and splitting of proceeds).

In most jurisdictions, judges will emphasise the usefulness of a non-strict definition of partnership. The purpose of the framework is to apply to as many situations as possible and is usually not dependent on the will of the members.

The consequences of being classified as a partnership or similar arrangement, which will usually not have legal personality, is the unlimited liability of all members as partners, which is highly undesirable for participants in any form of economic activity.

Therefore, if DAOs fulfil these conditions (and many do), they will not escape the law (at least theoretically). They thus live in this legal limbo whereby they seek not to be legally analysed or find legal wrappers to try to insulate some legal risks in some aspects of their governance.

However, this legal uncertainty is not sustainable in the long term.

III. Thinking About Regulation

Since the legal uncertainty surrounding DAOs is not sustainable, as it subjects them to the framework applicable to partnerships regardless of their say on the matter and likely dissuades other actors of participating in or interacting with a DAO, the Lisbon DAO Observatory takes the next step and starts thinking about possible avenues to address this situation.

Therefore, on the 20th April, 2023, the Lisbon DAO Observatory organised an International Conference on DAO Regulation (https://lisbondaoobservatory.cidp.pt/Archive/Docs/f163312187242.pdf) that gathered top-tier scholars, industry players and practitioners from all over the world in order to discuss how should any future legislative intervention, recognition or regulation of DAOs be crafted.

In this conference, there were discussions and interventions on the shape of any future DAO Regulation and on major topics such as mandatory decentralisation, legal personality, governance structures, limited liability and on crucial sectorial issues, including dispute resolution, civil liability, tax law or conflict of laws.

It is worth noting that any discussion on future regulation of DAOs must consider a preliminary question – should DAOs even be specifically regulated? One must bear in mind that any legislator can choose between a holistic regulation of DAOs (creating a specific law addressing all legal aspects of DAOs) or sectorial (only addressing specific issues, be it liability, judicial standing or tax status).

Another interesting question is whether any regulation should be imposed by public authorities or if self-regulation is enough. This is a contentious issue which was hotly debated in our first roundtable in the International Conference on DAO Regulation – while there was a consensus around the need to have more clarity, there were differing perspectives on whether the industry itself can adhere to self-regulation instruments (for instance the COALA model law)[1] or if it should be entirely up to public legislators to address the issue, without prejudice of combining both approaches in a hybrid approach in which certain central tenets are determined by legislators and other aspects dealt with through self-regulation.

In the event that one determines that public legislative intervention is needed, if one is thinking from a European perspective, it is pertinent to ponder whether this initiative should come from the European Union legislator. Indeed, if each of the 27 Member States goes its own way, there will be significant problems in

[1] Coalition of Automated Legal Applications, *Model Law for Decentralised Autonomous Organisations (DAOs)*, 2021, available at https://coala.global/wp-content/uploads/2022/03/DAO-Model-Law.pdf (accessed 10 October 2023).

mutual recognition and freedom of movement of DAOs within the European Union. However, DAOs, by their nature, are a bit everywhere and usually comprise people from various nationalities and locations. Addressing them on a purely national basis in a space which can benefit from common legislation would unnecessarily complicate their already fickle legal security. Therefore, it is our interim position that any legislative initiative in Europe should come from the European Union, either through Directive-led harmonisation or through uniform law such as a Regulation (to which there is a precedent, though not a very successful one, in the European Company Regulation). In future outputs, we will dwell more on how this could be done.

These are the major and transversal topics of how to regulate DAOs, vividly discussed in our Conference's first roundtable and incidentally mentioned in several of our chapters. The preceding paragraphs aimed at merely giving the reader a heads-up on where the regulation of DAOs we are discussing could come from.

IV. Presentation of the Works

Our first three works will present differing perspectives on the relationship between the degree of decentralisation present in a DAO and its regulation. When is a DAO decentralised? Should any future regulation require a certain degree of decentralisation in order to apply to DAOs? Should any future regulation impose any governance structures to ensure such decentralisation?

Thereafter, other three chapters will provide us with insights on major issues on the application of company law principles to DAOs, which should be kept in mind of any prospective regulator – should DAOs be granted legal personality? Should they enjoy a limited liability comparable to companies and how would such framework operate? Should any regulation of DAOs provide for some minimum governance requirements?

Having addressed these nuclear issues, we will see how any future regulation should approach the relationship between DAOs and the off-chain world – can a DAO stand before a State court? How should civil liability be applied, do classical models still work? How can we know that a DAO *knows* something, an issue highly relevant for civil liability? And how should regulation further address transaction costs and security risks for DAOs?

Finally, the two concluding chapters will address how DAOs intersect with two particularly important fields of law – tax law and private international law. It is indeed crucial to understand how and if DAOs should be taxed, and how future regulation can provide clear paths to help determine the law applicable to DAOs.

With these insightful chapters we hope to have contributed to the on-going discussion about the content of any future DAO regulation and how key issues should be addressed, giving prospective legislators or academics material to reflect upon and to contribute to a truly informed discussion on the issues that come with regulating DAOs. Universities have a responsibility to challenge the legal *status quo* and provide strong theoretical foundations that can be used as a basis for thinking about the future regulation of DAOs and inspire practitioners, policy makers and community members to try out new solutions. In the Lisbon DAO Observatory, we will carry on our work and attempt to conclude on what we view as the most balanced path to take. As in all things, a balance must be struck. If DAOs continue to grow we cannot continue leaving them completely devoid of a particular framework other than partnership law, which is created for small and flexible business arrangements between parties with a high degree of mutual trust and may be inadequate for the big operations DAOs often undertake. However, to subject DAOs to the existing rules of company law would be antithetical to their purpose – the law should not impose traditional and rigid governance models and membership requirements for DAOs and should allow a certain degree of freedom and flexibility for their members. After all, the whole point of DAOs is to experiment with different governance models – that are more decentralised and which can function autonomously – that do away with traditional corporate structures and the agency problems related thereto.

Table of Contents

DAOs and Mandatory Decentralisation: How to assess decentralisation when shaping regulation for DAOs*

Madalena Perestrelo de Oliveira and Marta Boura

ABSTRACT Despite being defined as decentralised arrangements, the question on how to assess the required level of decentralisation when regulating DAOs is not obvious or simple. On the contrary, its analysis relies on the perception of decentralisation as a spectrum which is recognised at different levels. It's on this basis that this paper is construed.

I. Introduction: DAOs as decentralised arrangements

1) DAOs are decentralised autonomous organisations and it is based on these three elements that this concept is construed.[1] In simple terms, DAOs are (i) decentralised as they are collectively owned and lack a centralised management, (ii) autonomous due to the automatic execution of decision-making powers through smart contracts and (iii) organisations as, ultimately, they are merely a form of human organisation. Therefore, in order to analyse DAOs (and how to draft a future regulation that is adequate, if needed) one must start by determining which organisations fall within the scope of a DAO and which do not.

Autonomy in a DAO is achieved through smart contracts, which can be defined as "a computer program that operates based on distributed ledger technology, namely the blockchain, and which allows the automatic performance of certain obligations when certain facts occur".[2] These self-executing agreements define the rules on which the DAO operates. Besides, all associates' rights result from smart contracts whose content is defined by the community, therefore

---

* This article was prepared in the context of the International Conference on DAO Regulation 2023 organised by the Lisbon DAO Observatory on 20 April 2023.

[1] *Jentzsch*, Decentralized Autonomous Organization to Automate Governance: Final Draft (2016). Available at: https://download.slock.it/public/DAO/WhitePaper.pdf (19.07.2023). Providing further analysis on the rise of DAOs, *Rolo*, RDT 1-1 (2019), 33–87.

[2] *Lima Pinheiro*, Laws Applicable to International Smart Contracts and Decentralized Autonomous Organizations (DAOS), 2023, 1. Available at: https://ssrn.com/abstract=4467408 or http://dx.doi.org/10.2139/ssrn.4467408 (19.07.2023).

there is no one who centrally decides the future of a DAO. In that sense, "a DAO is a *smart contract conceptualised as an organisation*".[3/4]

In general, smart contracts bring the promise of (i) elimination of ambiguity, (ii) prevention of non-performance and fraud, as they do not rely or depend on any human intervention, (iii) transparency, as the entire community is duly aware of the terms on which the smart contract is created, (iv) disintermediation, (v) no litigation, as a result of the autonomation of compliance and (vi) irreversibility of its terms. However, this model is not without its challenges. While the irrevocability offered by a smart contract grants the "advantage of eliminating or reducing the risk of non-performance"[5], doubts arise as to how the codification is carried out in relation to operational and non-operational aspects and/or mandatory legal rules, the applicable law[6] and the inclusion of off-chain information. It is also difficult to determine how subsequent events or changes in applicable law are considered in the code, or whether the obligations codified are lawful or unlawful. Changes to the blockchain may affect the performance of a smart contract, and the impact of insolvency events or consumer's rights are yet to be determined. There is also some uncertainty about how smart contracts implement vague or indeterminate ideas or concepts, such as best efforts obligations, market practice standards, or reasonable performance or execution that is contrary to the parties' intention (for example, due to errors in coding or execution of a code that is different from what the parties expected).[7] In addition, in most civil law jurisdictions, it could also be discussed how immutability or irrevocability affect remedies for non-performance of *off-chain* obligations that cannot be automated. This comes to show that execution of smart contracts can, in practice, indeed lead to litigation and entail difficulties around its enforceability.

As to the organisational element, DAOs can be generally defined as a vehicle through which its members pursue a common purpose (which may or not be profitable). This only requires a certain structure through which a DAO can

---

[3] *Rolo* (fn. 2), 56.

[4] On how smart contracts are implemented, see *Jentzsch* (fn. 2).

[5] *Lima Pinheiro* (fn. 3), 2.

[6] *Lima Pinheiro* (fn. 3); *Perestrelo de Oliveira/Rolo/Santos/Teixeira*, Decentralised Autonomous Organisations (DAO): Conceito, Enquadramento Legal e Desafios, 2022. Available at: https://boletim.oa.pt/decentralised-autonomous-organisations-dao-conceito-enquadramento-legal-e-desafios1/ (19.07.2023).

[7] Addressing these issues, see *Ana Perestrelo de Oliveira*, Smart Contracts, Risco e Codificação da Desvinculação ou Modificação Negocial – Os Falsos Dilemas da Inter-relação Lei-código nos Contratos Empresariais, Almedina, 2023; *Freire*, Blockchain e Smart Contracts – Implicações Jurídicas, Almedina, 2022 (reprint); Thematic report prepared by the European Union Blockchain Observatory Forum entitled Legal and Regulatory Framework of Blockchains and Smart Contracts, 2019. Available at: https://www.eublockchainforum.eu/sites/default/files/reports/report_legal_v1.0.pdf (19.07.2023).

aggregate its members and provide a sense of community.[8] Although it is possible to find traditional corporate features within a DAO, such as governance rights granted to token holders, assets and a treasury, the fundamental differences between a DAO and a traditional corporation make it difficult to determine its legal nature or qualification. In fact, DAOs aim to create a community where there are no top-down decision-making processes, and which is based on full transparency and democracy. Therefore, the culture of a DAO is inherently different from that of a corporation.

Generally, under Portuguese Law, a DAO would be considered a civil partnership, in the sense that, under the Portuguese Civil Code, such partnership will exist if two or more partners undertake to contribute assets or services towards the joint exercise of an economic activity and agree to distribute the profits arising therefrom. This is a classical legal framework, which was designed to frame the typical joint exercise of economic activities and has just begun to be applied to DAOs. There is a level of uncertainty regarding the applicability of this legal framework to DAOs, although the legal response to the questions typically raised by the functioning and operation of DAOs tend to rely on an analogy between the participation, by token holders, in DAOs and the joint pursuit of an economic activity. However, the level of decentralisation of the DAO may impact how these entities are qualified under different jurisdictions. In fact, if a DAO is sufficiently decentralised in the sense that there is no coordinated effort of its participants, it might be argued that there is no joint exercise of an economic activity, rendering it harder to qualify a DAO as a civil partnership. However, under Portuguese law there is little development by legal scholars regarding what should be considered a "joint exercise of an economic activity", which makes it difficult to evaluate how greater decentralisation would impact any DAO's qualification. However, one should note that the mere fact that participants undertake decisions through voting could be sufficient to identify a "joint exercise" of an economic activity. Moreover, even if a DAO is not qualified as a civil partnership, we believe that a court of law, under Portuguese law, would likely apply civil partnership rules by analogy to such contractual relationship.

2) Decentralisation is not binary as an element: the market is not divided into completely decentralised organisations (or structures) and others completely centralised. As a fact, decentralisation moves on a spectrum that is particularly difficult to achieve conceptually.[9] However, we believe that decentralisation is

---

[8] *Boss*, ALSRP 2023, 15. According to the Author, "(...) this element does not cause much debate: it can be understood as the requirement that the DAO should have somewhat of a structure. This does not necessarily imply a specific (legal) form, but it mostly focuses on whether the DAO in question is more than just a spontaneous group of individuals".

[9] *Veas*, DeFi and MiCA: How much decentralisation is enough?, Lexology, 2023. Available at https://www.lexology.com/library/detail.aspx?g=ada74ccc-c1aa-4dfd-bdbc-93fcda62bdb2

the key element on which not only the qualification of a blockchain arrangement as a DAO depends on, but also as the cornerstone for future regulation of DAOs. However, the difficulty remains as to how we can pursue a draft regulation for DAOs without establishing criteria to assess decentralisation or its different levels.

II. The spectrum of decentralisation: from centralisation to absolute decentralisation

1. Are (pure) DAOs a myth?

1) Decentralisation is not a univocal concept, nor a legal one; yet DAOs depend on decentralisation to define themselves as DAOs.

DAOs first emerged as an alternative to traditional organisation models.[10] Their development is linked to the advancement of blockchain technology but, at its core, it intends to provide for cheaper and easier solutions of pursuing collective purposes.[11] In fact, DAOs represent the so-called emergence of "platform cooperatives", which consist in "a governance model that centres on digital tools and is underpinned by the cooperative principles of democratic decision-making and shared ownership of the platform by workers and users".[12] This new concept is governed by seven principles, which were established in 2017 by the International Co-operative Alliance. Those are (i) voluntary and

(28.06.2023); *Boiron*, Sufficient decentralization: a playbook for web3 builders and lawyers, 6 ss. Available at: https://variant.fund/wp-content/uploads/2022/08/Sufficient-Decentralization-by-Marc-Boiron.docx.pdf (28.06.2023).

[10] DAOs' model also differs from other strucutres as crowdfunding or ICOs, see *Bellavitis/Fisch/Momtaz*, The rise of decentralised autonomous organizations (DAOs): a first empirical glimpse, Venture Capital, 2022, 3 ss. Available at SSRN: https://ssrn.com/abstract=4074833 or http://dx.doi.org/10.2139/ssrn.4074833 (18.07.2023).

[11] Also, "DAOs have begun to disrupt intermediated business models and industries in which such platforms are dominant through disintermediation. At the core of the movement toward greater disintermediation is the promise of more favorable rent sharing, as entrepreneurs and investors or sellers and buyers get to share the transaction surplus exclusively, without the need to pay for intermediation services thanks to smart contract technology (Momtaz, 2022). In principle, markets, industries, and entire economies could be governed by smart contracts, powered by robotics, and independently regulated by the DAOs' members. Consider the example of Amazon: Today Jeff Bezos is the main shareholder of Amazon, Amazon's CEO is the manager, and Amazon sellers are the service providers. Through a DAO, Amazon sellers could cooperate and share decision-making and a DAO could allow every Amazon seller to be a shareholder, manager, and service provider at the same time", see *Bellavitis/Fisch/Momtaz* (fn. 11), 4.

[12] *Nabben/Puspasari/Kelleher/Sanjay*, Grounding Decentralised Technologies in Cooperative Principles: What Can 'Decentralised Autonomous Organisations' (DAOs) and Platform Cooperatives Learn from Each Other?, 2021, 1. Available at SSRN: https://ssrn.com/abstract=3979223 or http://dx.doi.org/10.2139/ssrn.3979223 (21.07.2023).

open membership, (ii) democratic member control, (iii) member economic participation, (iv) autonomy and independence, (v) education, training and information, (vi) co-operation among co-operatives and (vii) concern for community.[13]

In general, we can say that centralised management structures have been discredited in some sectors of society over the last few years. Participants turn to DAOs hoping to find a system where corporate decisions lie in the hands of associates creating a more democratic organisation and avoiding typical corporate issues which compromise the organisation autonomy and independence (e.g. traditional agency problem between shareholders and management). In DAOs, participants also find a community where their purposes are most likely to be achieved considering that no human interference is allowed in the management of the DAO's treasury, for instance, due to the automatic execution of smart contracts. Ultimately, DAOs are a project to work on that does not depend on any physical infrastructures. Therefore:

> "Because of their decentralized nature, DAOs offer transparent, distributed, and decentralized decision-making that increases disintermediation not only within organizations, but also at the market, industry, and economy levels. The distinction between shareholders, managers, and other stakeholders, such as industry participants, is blurred, giving rise to numerous benefits (and challenges)".[14]

However, from a conceptual point of view, such broad delimitation comprises difficulties. First, it fails to sufficiently define how much decentralisation is required for a DAO to qualify as such. Also, it may be argued that, as a wide concept, it may capture all blockchain systems therefore lacking any conceptual substract.

2) Some state DAOs are, ultimately, DINOs (*Decentralised in Name Only*[15]), meaning decentralisation is nothing more than an illusion[16] or a mirage.[17] Indeed, even in communities that are committed to political decentralisation, based on the idea of "distributed consensus"[18], it is very common for control groups to be formed, i.e., a small number of people who hold the majority of the

---

[13] International Co-operative alliance, *Guidance Notes to the Co-operative Principles.* Available at: https://ica.coop/sites/default/files/basic-page-attachments/guidance-notes-en-221700169.pdf (21.07.2023). Also, see *Nabben/Puspasari/Kelleher/Sanjay* (fn. 13), 3.

[14] *Bellavitis/Fisch/Momtaz* (fn. 11), 6.

[15] *Kerstens*, speech at *I International Conference on DAO Regulation*, organised by *Lisbon DAO Observatory*, at Faculty of Law University of Lisbon (April 2023).

[16] *Omlor/Franke*, Europäische DeFi – Regulierungsperspektiven. Ein- und Ausblick der EU-Kommission, BKR 2022, 682.

[17] Study requested by ECON Committee, European Parliament, entitled "Remaining regulatory challenges in digital finance and crypto-assets after MiCA", 2023, 17. Available at: https://www.europarl.europa.eu/RegData/etudes/STUD/2023/740083/IPOL_STU(2023)740083_EN.pdf (11.07.2023).

[18] *De Filippi/Lavayssière*, Blockchain technology: toward a decentralized governance of digital platforms?, The great awakening, Puctum Books, 2020, 185-222, 201.

governance tokens of a given project, in such a way that they can condition the decisions taken, thus jeopardising decentralisation.[19]

This comes to state decentralisation as a complex concept. In addition to compromising the scalability of the protocol, a bad decision at the wrong time can be ruinous for the organisation and the conflict of interests in a wide community is unavoidable. Added to this is the inevitable community tendency towards the pursuit of short-term goals, which can be an obstacle to making decisions that would favour the community in the long term. Decentralisation can mean chaos, especially when accompanied by a lack of communication. By way of example, if those responsible for marketing do not communicate with other contributors to the protocol, they will not know how it is offered to the public and, in turn, those who develop the software do not have access to the elements to understand the needs of their users.[20] On the other hand, permanent communication flows in most cases mean that there is centralisation comparable to that of a traditional corporate structure, with the associated legal consequences.

Seconding Guilherme Maia and João Vieira dos Santos[21], we believe that only systems built on a decentralised settlement layer (architectural decentralisation), with no control over user assets (decentralisation in the custody of crypto-assets) and in which all aspects of decision-making, responsibility for maintaining the code and rights associated with control and ownership of the protocol belong to the token holders (political decentralisation) should be considered decentralised protocols. To this we would only add that political decentralisation cannot ignore the way in which off chain activities are carried out. The impossibility of translating all the rules into code means that there will be issues that need to be decided outside the protocol. In most blockchain networks, changes relating to the network protocol will need to be made through an off-chain decision-making process, where some level of centralisation can be identified.[22] Off-chain community governance raises delicate questions related to the invisible forces at work behind supposedly decentralised communities.

This means that effective decentralisation is likely to be illusory, as it is generally possible to identify centralised custody or cloud services that allow, at least, centralised analysis of the data collected by the applications.[23] The promised decentralisation of DAO will likely give way to concentration and oligopoly, as decentralised functioning does not prevent the concentration of market

---

[19] *Möslein/Kaulartz/Renning*, RDi 2021, 517, Rn. 37; *Omlor/Franke* (fn. 17) 682.

[20] *Boiron* (fn. 10) 9.

[21] *Maia/Santos*, RED 2, Vol. 28, 2022.

[22] *De Filippi/Lavayssière* (fn. 19), 204 ss. Consider, among other examples, the fork Ethereum decision following a diversion of funds that exploited a flaw in The DAO's code. Community members who did not agree to this fork continue to use an alternative version of the network (the Ethereum Classic).

[23] *Zunzunegui*, Revista de Derecho del Mercado Financiero, WP 1/2022, 10. Available at: https://ssrn.com/abstract=4040930 or http://dx.doi.org/10.2139/ssrn.4040930.

power. Primavera Di Filipi and Xavier Lavayssière[24] predict that, if left to the invisible hand of the market, these blockchain-based applications will, with high probability, evolve into centralized platforms and lead to the emergence of new intermediaries and even new incumbents. It is important to be aware of these risks.

3) In any case, as per our view, a DAO does not live merely within the scope of a complete decentralisation. Should it be the case and DAOs would be anything and nothing at the same time. Our research points in a different direction. Instead, different levels of decentralisation should be recognised.

2. Levels of decentralisation

1) At its core, decentralisation is not a legal concept hence the difficulties on how to assess it. Differently:

> "(...) decentralization has technical, geographic, political, economic and legal dimensions. How technically decentralized a DAO is depends on several factors, such as the kind of blockchain it is deployed on and how many nodes are operating on the network to validate transactions. Geographic decentralization can be understood as the degree to which DAO contributors operate in different jurisdictions. Political decentralization is dependent on how diffuse power is in the organization. (...) Economic decentralization refers to the distribution of resources across the community. (...) Each of these dimensions has implications for how the DAO could be legally categorized. Moreover, these dimensions are rarely static. DAOs may become more centralized or decentralized over time as the community and resources evolve". [25]

This means decentralisation can be assessed at several levels and exists in different degrees, in terms that allow the conclusion that decentralisation develops on a spectrum between total centralisation and absolute decentralisation. We can therefore state centralisation takes place along three axes, all relatively independent of each other: (i) architectural decentralisation (number of physical computers in the system and level of tolerance for their failure, which leads us to the analysis of the settlement layer and to the consideration of the existence of a server or central organisation or, on the contrary, of a public blockchain that allows P2P relationships); (ii) political decentralisation (number of people/organisations that control the system's computers); (iii) logical decentralisation (determine if the interface and data structures are likely to be fractionated without loss of functionality).[26]

---

[24] *De Filippi/Lavayssière* (fn. 19), 204.

[25] World Economic Forum, Decentralized Autonomous Organizations: Beyond the Hype, in collaboration with the Wharton Blockchain and Digital Asset Project, White Paper, 2022, 15. Available at: https://www3.weforum.org/docs/WEF_Decentralized_Autonomous_Organizations_Beyond_the_Hype_2022.pdf (19.07.2023).

[26] *Buterin*, The meaning of decentralization. Available at: https://medium.com/@VitalikButerin/the-meaning-of-decentralization-a0c92b76a274 (30.06.2023).

When considering the specific operation of a DAO, decentralisation may also be achieved under three main criteria: hierarchy, influential mechanisms and keyholder/executor centralisation.[27] While hierarchically we do not find, as a rule, any degree of centralisation in a DAO, in the mechanisms and keyholders we can uncover different levels of (de)centralisation. First of all, it is usual in a DAO to have core members with more influence over the remaining members either derived from social rules (i. e., other members tend to follow core members' decisions) or from specific voting rules (which would grant core members decisive voting rights).[28] Should we reflect on the social perspective and we would conclude there is no absolute decentralisation in a community. Since Aristoteles, principles of governance within democracy models have been explored laying down a rule under which diversity would result in better decisions.[29] However, there is a paradox found in the knowledge of people within a community. People don't have the knowledge to vote on everything, which means that decisions on this model are reached by having some people following other people's vote and influence. These informal mechanisms of influence, which are inevitable in a DAO as in any other community, may compromise the goal of independent member participation. To measure this risk, the diversity of the membership should be assessed, even though confidentiality and anonymity may in some cases constitute an obstacle. This monitoring would be helpful in following voting trends in order to assess the degree of decentralisation within influential mechanisms.

Also, it may be possible to identify a centralised power in the keyholder (i. e., "the person who could execute changes to the smart contracts"[30]) which would compromise the decentralisation governance. In any case, it should be noted that decentralisation is shown differently among DAOs. Many DAOs opt for a mix of centralised and decentralised governance, while others evolve from centralisation management when starting a DAOs aiming to achieve, along DAOs life, moderate or complete decentralisation.[31] In fact, we would say that full decentralisation is impossible to achieve at the deployment of a DAO, which means that decentralisation is necessarily a path that needs to be taken.

II. Apart from the complexity of decentralisation due to its different meanings and manifestations in a DAO, there are also difficulties in defining which

---

[27] For the development of these three concepts, see *Boss* (fn. 9), 10 ss.

[28] *Boss* (fn. 9), 12.

[29] On history of politics and lessons for DAO Governance, see *Ast* (public lecture available online at: https://www.youtube.com/watch?v=TIcZj-Oxcgc).

[30] *Boss* (fn. 9), 12.

[31] On this point, *Axelsen/Jensen/Ross* state that "no DAO can start decentralized, as any project must be initiated by a small core team, bootstrapping development until the project matures and attracts open-source contributors", see, CSIMQ, no. 31, 51–75, 2022, 69. https://doi.org/10.7250/csimq.2022-31.04, Available at SSRN: https://ssrn.com/abstract=4210073 (19.07.2023).

aspects of the DAO's functioning should be assessed in order to determine the level of decentralisation. In fact, decentralisation may be considered on the basis of the structure of a DAO or based on the degree of decentralisation of its activities. The question arises as to whether we should consider only the governance structure of a DAO or also the way in which off-chain activities are carried out.

In respect to decentralisation of off-chain activities it should be noted that decentralisation can be achieved in several different ways. A first hypothesis consists in attributing decision-making powers to each member of the community, another way to consider is the division of the community into subDAOs, which may receive funding from the DAO and be subject or not to the instructions of the community, expressed through voting. Finally, a legal entity – typically a foundation or trust – can be set up to carry out functions on behalf of the community.[32]

III. How can a future regulation address decentralisation?

1. Principles and COALA Model Law

1) The exercise of EU competences should be governed by subsidiarity and proportionality principles.[33] Adequacy should be also assessed when shaping regulation. In fact, "the very function of proportionality is to reconcile the need for uniform rules and for the further integration of the single market with the adaptation of the rules, with proper justification, to realities that are still very different within the internal market, in order to achieve fair and efficient application of the law". [34] When considering the financial sector, "proportionality obliges the Union legislator to strike a balance between all the principles, objectives and interests involved when crafting the Union banking regulations". [35]

---

[32] *Boiron* (fn. 10) 16. Naturally, also in relation to each subDAO, it will be necessary to evaluate the degree of coordination of efforts among its participants, insofar as, with efficient coordination between them, they may be subject to securities regulation. It is also possible to split the subDAOs into "supported subDAos" and "operations subDAOs". The former would dedicate themselves to off-chain tasks that generate value for the protocol, while the latter would assume the role of supporting the former (17). It is not easy to determine which legal entities should be used by subDAOs to carry out off-chain activities without consequent centralisation. If all DAO off-chain activity is performed through a single entity there will certainly be efficiency gains, but also loss of decentralisation. A possible solution is to have a legal entity corresponding to each subDAO and offering some protection to its members (20).

[33] See both Article 5 of TEU and Protocol (no 2) on the Application of the Principles of Subsidiarity and Proportionality.

[34] *Zilioli*, in: Baums/Remsperger/Sachs/Wieland (eds.), Währungsunion und stabiles Finanzsystem (in the honor of Helmut Siekmann), Duncker & Humblot, 2019, 28.

[35] *Zilioli*, (fn. 35) 16.

The right balance between these principles and the interests found within the (more) digital financial sector is not an easy task. Difficulties arise when considering blockchain-based technology underlying the provision of services or the existence of new agents as DAOs. In fact, digital transformation does not solely impact the market and business operators but also the legal field and, consequently, how law is perceived, interpreted, and applied. Digital legal framework currently requires the articulation with both multiple players (and regulators) and different levels of regulation, which include policies, codes and co-regulation. Besides, the legal system is now presented with a "rule as code" approach consisting in creating and publishing rules and regulation in a way that is considered "better suited" for digital service delivery which definitely impacts how regulation is construed. Following this path, legal concepts are increasingly being replaced by technical descriptions of the technology itself, and rules are created taking into account the specific uses of said technology, categorising behaviours according to the potential risk or consequences of the use of the technology. The Recently approved Regulation of the European Parliament and of the Council laying down harmonised rules on artificial intelligence constitutes an example.[36]

2) Stating human-centred legal design as a challenge entails regulators to also consider the application of new principles, such as the functional equivalence and technology-neutrality.

Functional equivalence approach first appeared on the UNCITRAL Model Law on Electronic Commerce[37] as "based on an analysis of the purposes and functions of the traditional paper-based requirement with a view to determining how those purposes or functions could be fulfilled through electronic-commerce techniques".[38] This approach would facilitate regulation of technology if EU institutions were to follow technology developments more closely. Despite

[36] Proposal for a Regulation of the European Parliament and of the Council Laying Down Harmonised Rules on Artificial Intelligence (Artificial Intelligence Act) and Amending Certain Union Legislative Acts, COM(2021) 206 final, 2021/0106 (COD), Brussels, 21.04.2021. Available at: https://eur-lex.europa.eu/legal-content/EN/TXT/?uri=celex%3A52021PC0206 (27.07.2023).

[37] United Nations Commission on International Trade Law (UNCITRAL), Model Law on Electronic Commerce with Guide to Enactment 1996 with additional article 5 *bis* as adopted in 1998 (the "Model Law on Ecommerce"). Available at: https://uncitral.un.org/sites/uncitral.un.org/files/media-documents/uncitral/en/19-04970_ebook.pdf (27.07.2023).

[38] Model Law on Ecommerce, 20. For these purposes, it is clarified that "[the] Model Law does not attempt to define a computer-based equivalent to any kind of paper document. Instead, it singles out basic functions of paper-based form requirements, with a view to providing criteria which, once they are met by data messages, enable such data messages to enjoy the same level of legal recognition as corresponding paper documents performing the same function. It should be noted that the functional-equivalent approach has been taken in articles 6 to 8 of the Model Law with respect to the concepts of "writing", "signature" and "original" but not with respect to other legal concepts dealt with in the Model Law. For example, article 10 does not attempt to create a functional equivalent of existing storage requirements" (21).

the overall theorical merits of functional equivalence as a principle, "the regulator often does not examine the new technology sufficiently enough and the effect of *ex ante* regulation on the use cases of the new technology".[39] This tends to impair the rationale behind functional equivalence as it limits how technology and its uses are perceived. In any case, the functional equivalence principle relies on the analysis of the existing technology, which means that the idea of providing for an equivalence of the digital market (or online reality) in its entirety would always be limited[40]. It must be considered in a case-by-case approach.

Technology-neutrality, on the other hand, refers to the adoption of market neutrality when it comes to regulate technology. Following competition law principles, this means regulators shall not require the use of any particular technology or, in other words, that regulation should not take a part on how the market includes or excludes different types of technology.[41] It is recognised as a principle of European public services as set out in the new European Interoperability Framework[42] and it is defined under the Framework Directive[43] as "it neither imposes nor discriminates in favour of the use of a particular type of technology".[44] This principle has, however, led to difficult discussions on how regulators should contemplate technology, mainly because the idea of not to exclude technology from a regulation scope should not lead to the path of extending existing (inadequate) regulation to emerging technologies.[45] In practice, this tendency can lead to a form of discrimination against new technologies.

3) Both principles of functional equivalence and technology neutrality have also been embedded in the draft UNIDROIT Principles on Digital Assets and Private Law.[46] With a view to facilitate transactions in digital assets, the UNIDROIT Principles have been designed to provide guidance both to the

---

[39] Following Andrej Savin' critics, *Veerpalu*, Baltic Journal of Law & Politics 12(2), 134-162, 2019, 146. Available at: https://www.researchgate.net/publication/339931469_Functional_Equivalence_An_Exploration_Through_Shortcomings_to_Solutions (27.07.2023).

[40] *Veerpalu* (fn. 40) 146.

[41] *Shadikhodjaev*, European Journal of International Law, Vol. 32, Issue 4, 1221–1247, 2021.

[42] Principle 5 of the New European Interoperability Framework. Promoting Seamless Services and Data Flows for European Public Administrators, 2017. Available at: https://ec.europa.eu/isa2/sites/default/files/eif_brochure_final.pdf (27.07.2023).

[43] Directive 2002/21/EC of the European Parliament and of the Council of 7 March 2002 on a common regulatory framework for electronic communications networks and services (the "Framework Directive").

[44] Recital 18 of the Framework Directive.

[45] Exploring this, *Kamecke/Korber*, E.C.L.R, 2008, 331. Available at: https://koerber.jura.uni-koeln.de/sites/koerber/user_upload/Technological_neutrality_in_the_EC...Kamecke-Koerber_ECLR08_29_5__330-339.pdf (27.07.2023).

[46] Draft UNIDROIT Principles on Digital Assets and private Law, Study LXXXII – PC, 2023, Public Consultation (the "UNIDROIT Principles"). Available at: https://www.unidroit.org/wp-content/uploads/2023/01/Draft-Principles-and-Commentary-Public-Consultation.pdf (27.07.2023).

parties to such transactions and to the States so that national legislation may be drafted in a consistent and uniform manner. According to the draft, these principles are "technology and business model neutral".[47] Functional equivalence is also present as an interpretation guideline. Indeed, in the commentary to Principle 6, the draft reads that "[these] requirements contemplate that 'control' assumes a role that is a functional equivalent to that of 'possession' of movables. However, 'possession' in this context is a purely factual matter and not a legal concept. Moreover, because a digital asset is intangible, this functional equivalence to possession involves only the dominion and power over a digital asset but does not involve the physical situs dimension applicable to possession of movables".[48]

4) It is our opinion that the same principles should apply to DAOs. This was the approach followed in the COALA Model Law for DAOs[49], where functional equivalence is used to establish "equivalence between an object already within the realm of a legal rule and another object not yet encompassed by it".[50] This means that when regulating DAOs rules must be considered in accordance with the functions of their object so to ensure uniformity and equal treatment. Further to that, it is presented a concept of regulatory equivalence which intends to identify "the object or the purpose of any given regulation as goal".[51] Therefore, it is important to identify the objective and purpose of a given regulation and then question whether the same objective can be achieved by technological means.

Decentralised financial markets and the transparency obligations imposed on issuers in the traditional system (such as the obligation to publish a prospectus or to disclose ongoing (*ad hoc*) and periodic information) may serve as an example. These information duties are designed to protect the integrity of the markets and thereby protect investors. However, in a truly decentralised system, there are no information asymmetries between participants that justify these transparency obligations[52], nor is there any entity that can be required to provide this information. In other words, any regulatory approach should always start by defining the objectives that the regulation is intended to achieve and, from there, question whether a mechanism (conventional or technological) already exists that adequately fulfils that purpose.

---

47 UNIDROIT Principles, 3.

48 UNIDROIT Principles, 26.

49 Coalition of Automated Legal Applications (COALA), Model Law for Decentralized Autonomous Organizations (DAOs), 2021. Available at: https://coala.global/wp-content/uploads/2022/03/DAO-Model-Law.pdf (3.07.2023).

50 COALA Model Law, 7.

51 COALA Model Law, 8.

52 Following this path, *Maia/Santos* (fn. 22) 77 state, in general terms, that DeFi does not pose particular risks to investor protection, as the phenomena of informational asymmetry typical of traditional markets is not reflected in DeFi environments.

2. *MiCA and DeFi*

1) We have established regulation should be adequate to the reality it intends to cover. This may, however, be a challenge for DAOs: the tendency to cover DAOs within the traditional regulatory framework should be avoided, as (general) compliance requirements do not address the specificities of DAOs.

The European legislator has recently recognised the need to provide for a uniform legal framework in relation to these new digital tools or ways to provide services (in particular, financial services). We can take MiCA[53] as an example. Nonetheless, decentralised arrangements and activities seem to be still off the regulator's radar (yet not completely forgotten). As a fact, pursuant to MiCA's final text, the Regulation is to be applicable to "natural and legal persons and certain other undertakings and to the crypto-asset services and activities performed, provided or controlled, directly or indirectly, by them, including when part of such activities or services is performed in a decentralised manner".[54] It is only to be considered excluded of MiCA's scope of application situations "[where] crypto-asset services are provided in a fully decentralised manner without any intermediary (...)".[55] If a DeFi community is governed by a DAO, which would be, in most civil law jurisdictions, qualified as a civil partnership, then we can ask whether there is an "intermediary" that could render MiCA applicable. MiCA's scope of application if probably flexible enough to cover some decentralised arrangements. This (grey) delimitation of MiCA's scope raises difficult questions: first of all, if we consider total decentralisation to be either a myth or, at least, a rare reality, what is the level of decentralisation that is sufficiently close to absolute decentralisation for MiCA not to be applicable? It is certainly not a simple task to determine with certainty on which axis the total decentralisation that determines the inapplicability of MiCA or traditional financial regulation should be located, but the decentralisation of the protocol of the financial services provided will certainly not be enough.

2) This discussion has been centred around DeFi arrangements and structures. Nevertheless, it also serves, in the context of this paper, the discussion around DAOs and how to configure a framework based on decentralised arrangements.

In this context, there has been some discussion on alternative concepts that may serve as important criteria or tools when shaping future regulation of DAOs, i.e., *sufficient decentralisation* and "TIGER" Assessment Framework. Moreover, decentralisation also raises the question of who is responsible for

---

[53] Regulation (EU) 2023/1114 of the European Parliament and of the Council of 31 May 2023 on markets in crypto-assets, and amending Regulations (EU) No. 1093/2010 and (EU) No. 1095/2010 and Directives 2013/36/EU and (EU) 2019/1937.

[54] Recital 22 of MiCA.

[55] Recital 22 of MiCA.

compliance: it is therefore necessary to assess who is the point of contact between the legal framework and the decentralised arrangements.

3. Governance tokens: how the debate moved from securities to decentralisation

1) As we know, the crypto-asset market has grown rapidly since its first appearance or, more precisely, since Satoshi Nakamoto published the whitepaper on bitcoin in 2008.[56] Since then, the market has faced internal changes in exchanges, trading, valuation and players that would require the market to adapt in the name of financial stability[57] and the need to protect investors and their investments from fraud. This is the overall purpose of securities law: to protect markets and investors by establishing disclosure requirements, supervision and penalties in order to ensure a transparent and safe market in which market participants can make informed investment decisions.

In the US, the legal discussion surrounding the crypto ecosystem, in particular the qualification of tokens has evolved rapidly. If in 2017 the question was whether a crypto asset should be considered a security, shortly DAOs and DeFi have led to discussions about whether decentralisation could change the conclusions reached in the meantime. In fact, in the US, not only stocks and bonds but also investment contracts must be classified as securities. This notion is particularly important as it allows both the federal courts and the SEC to assess whether investments and instruments that are new to the market and unparalleled in previously known figures should qualify as securities.

The concept of an investment contract was densified by the Supreme Court in 1946[58], through the Howey Test, according to which an investment contracts is one that (i) involves an investment (ii) in a common activity (iii) with a reasonable expectation of profit (iv) resulting from the efforts of others. These four criteria are cumulative: failing one, there is no investment contract and therefore no security. The test, which is flexible enough to adapt to new realities, allows for the possibility of classifying some crypto assets as financial instruments, reaffirming the application of the fundamental principles of US securities regulation even to new paradigms. In this regard, the publication of a report by the SEC, on July 25, 2017[59], in which it analysed the DAO tokens[60] and opted for

---

[56] Available at: https://bitcoin.org/bitcoin.pdf (27.07.2023).

[57] See ESMA, *TRV – Risk Analysis, Crypto-assets and their risks for financial stability*, ESMA50-165-2251, 2022. Available at: https://www.esma.europa.eu/sites/default/files/library/esma50-165-2251_crypto_assets_and_financial_stability.pdf (28.07.2023).

[58] See SEC v. W.J. Howey Co., 328 U.S. 293, 301 (1946). Fundamental in an investment contract "is the presence of an investment in a common venture premised on a reasonable expectation of profits to be derived from the entrepreneurial or managerial efforts of others".

[59] Available at: https://www.sec.gov/litigation/investreport/34-81207.pdf.

[60] The DAO ICO was one of the first and most considerable in this industry and aimed to

their qualification as securities, insofar as they fulfilled the assumptions of the Howey Test, was remarkable. As can be read in the conclusions of the SEC report:

"The registration requirements are designed to provide investors with procedural protections and material information necessary to make informed investment decisions. These requirements apply to those who offer and sell securities in the United States, regardless whether the issuing entity is a traditional company or a decentralized autonomous organization, regardless whether those securities are purchased using U.S. dollars or virtual currencies, and regardless whether they are distributed in certificated form or through distributed ledger technology".[61]

2) The Howey Test and its criteria were already a difficult topic before the emergence of crypto assets. In fact, the debate on how to regulate digital assets mainly stems from discussions on their legal qualification, whether as a security or a commodity, so digital assets and blockchain trading platforms have added more complexity to this discussion.[62]

This test is not based on, and is not related to, a specific asset type: therefore, it can be applied to crypto-assets, token offerings and trading platforms. Therefore, "[inconsistent] application of the Howey test to digital assets by the courts, combined with a jurisdictional fight between the SEC and the CFTC as to which is authorized to regulate digital asset spot markets, has left participants in these markets unsure about their rights and protections". [63]

3) The expansion and maturation of decentralised ecosystems, such as DeFi and DAOs has shown that the challenges of regulating tokens do not end with their form of digital representation or their offering and trading on a blockchain network but extend to more complex domains. The creation and offering of tokens in decentralised networks raises new problems, with a more complex solution. Given the impossibility of identifying a central entity that issues the tokens or that could be bound by the transparency duties typically associated with the offering and trading of securities, it has become inevitable to raise the question of the qualification of tokens when they represent active and/or passive legal positions in decentralised communities.

In this context, in June 2018, William Hinman, at the time responsible for the corporation finance division at the SEC, espoused, for the first time, the concept of "sufficient decentralisation". At the time, he did so in connection with the debate around the legal framework for the sale of Ether, but the notion quickly

---

implement a completely decentralised corporate governance system by offering DAO tokens, which grant the possibility to decide and vote on DAO activities.

[61] See https://www.sec.gov/litigation/investreport/34-81207.pdf, 18.

[62] *Devnani*, North Carolina Banking Institute, Vol. 27, Issue 1, Article 18, 2023, 400. Available at: https://scholarship.law.unc.edu/cgi/viewcontent.cgi?article=1572&context=ncbi (28.07.2023).

[63] *Devnani* (fn. 63) 402.

became a central piece for the regulatory framework for DeFi. According to Hinman[64]: "If the network on which the token or coin is to function is sufficiently decentralized – where purchasers would no longer reasonably expect a person or group to carry out essential managerial or entrepreneurial efforts – the assets may not represent an investment contract.". He continues: "[as] a network becomes truly decentralized, the ability to identify an issuer or promoter to make the requisite disclosures becomes difficult, and less meaningful." The focus is therefore placed on the last prong of the Howey Test: in order to be able to identify a security, the expectation of obtaining a profit must result from the efforts of others.

In this sense, determining the applicability of securities law essentially depends on determining whether there is a group of people coordinating efforts to increase the value of crypto-assets. In a sufficiently decentralised protocol, the value of crypto-assets does not result from the coordinated efforts of a group of people, as opposed to what happens if a protocol or network is not sufficiently decentralised. Only if this coordination is identifiable can we consider the fourth prong of the Howey test to be verified.

Hinman's statement was intended to clarify the circumstances in which crypto-assets should be considered securities, and thus delimit the scope of securities regulation. Since then, this part of the speech has been perpetuated by several voices echoing it, although there is still uncertainty about the concept of decentralisation. As Vitalik Buterin notes, although "decentralisation" is the foundational feature of blockchain and is one of the most used words in the crypto-economic ecosystem, it is also the most ill-defined concept.[65] Decentralisation is not, in its genesis, a legal concept, which makes its use as a key concept to delimit the application of certain legal regulations particularly challenging. In an effort to deepen this idea, in 2019, the Hub for Innovation and Financial Technology (FinHub) of the SEC published the Framework for "investment contract" analysis of digital assets.[66] It follows from this document that the fulfilment of the last prong of the Howey test depends on asking whether "essential tasks or responsibilities are performed and expected to be performed by an [active participant], rather than an unaffiliated, dispersed community of network users". Therefore, the idea of an active participant was introduced, as "a promoter, sponsor, or other third party (or affiliated group of third parties)".

64 See *Hinman*, Digital asset transactions: when Howey met Gary (plastic), San Francisco (15.06.2018). Available at: https://www.sec.gov/news/speech/speech-hinman-061418 (28.06.2023).

65 *Buterin* (fn. 27).

66 Available at: https://www.sec.gov/corpfin/framework-investment-contract-analysis-digital-assets (28.06.2023).

In the European context, the US concept of investment contract does not prevail. As is well known, MiFID II[67] considers transferable securities to be "classes of securities which are negotiable on the capital market, with the exception of instruments of payment", namely, shares "and other securities equivalent to shares" and bonds and any other securities giving the right to acquire or sell any such securities or giving rise to a cash settlement, determined by reference to transferable securities, currencies, interest rates or yields, commodities or other indices or measures (article 4/44 of MiFID II). However, the idea of decentralisation is relevant on two different levels. On the one hand, as explained below, we believe that in the EU, as in the US, true decentralisation also implies that tokens should not be considered functionally equivalent to traditional securities, which will determine the inapplicability of securities regulation. On the other hand, in the case of the provision of financial services in a fully decentralised manner, the MiCA Regulation is not applicable.[68] In other words, although the problem of assessing the degree of decentralisation appears under a different guise in the EU, it is no less relevant there than it is in the US.

Governance tokens are commonly equated with shares, due to the expectation that their holders will participate in a cash flow and also because of the typical attribution of social-like rights, such as voting rights. However, what seems clear at first glance can easily be challenged on closer examination. Normally, governance tokens meet the requirements of transferability, tradability, and homogeneity, which would tend to place them in the securities sphere. However, it should be specifically analysed whether governance tokens are functionally comparable to traditional securities.[69] In cases where an entity responsible for issuing and fulfilling the obligations associated with the tokens is identifiable, it may be appropriate to consider their qualification as securities. However, in the DeFi ecosystem, the fact that there is no entity likely to be responsible for fulfilling the duties and obligations associated with qualification as a security constitutes a significant obstacle to such qualification and renders it irrelevant insofar as it makes enforcement particularly challenging.

---

[67] Directive 2014/65/EU of the Parliament and of the Council of 15 May 2014 on markets in financial instruments and amending Directive 2002/92/EC and Directive 2011/61/EU.

[68] As noted by *Maume*, RDi 2022, 461, Rn. 8, although MiCA does not directly regulate DeFi, it may indirectly cover activities that are only partially decentralised. Regarding the small percentage of cases in which there is effective decentralisation and in which the MiCA Regulation is not applicable, it can be said that a calculated risk of favoring innovation was taken. In this regard, see *Machacek*, RDi 2021, 572, Rn. 53.

[69] At European level, the concept of security requires the fulfillment of several criteria: transmissibility, tradability in capital markets and homogeneity. As an implicit criterion, one can also identify the requirement of functional comparability with legally typical securities, that is, a notorious identity must be sought between the characteristics of the securities provided for by law and other legal situations represented by another title different from the typical ones. See *A. Barreto*, Direito dos Valores Mobiliários, Coimbra, 2016, 130; *Rolo* (fn. 2), 288 ss.

More specifically, from an investor's perspective, owning a share and owning a governance token generate diametrically different expectations that cannot be compared. The rights and obligations of a shareholder are derived from the law, in such a way as to identify a social status based on a specific relationship established between the shareholder and the issuing company. In the case of trading on a regulated market, it is possible to go further and identify an investor[70] status that appears as a plus compared to the shareholder position, and that legitimises additional expectations related to increased transparency obligations borne by the issuer and in favour of the integrity of the markets. On the contrary, the content of governance tokens is exclusively determined by a contract, without it being possible to identify a debtor of these obligations. When a token is issued, it appears on the market with a certain content. However, the expectations of its holders are diametrically different from those of a shareholder. In decentralised communities, there is no issuing entity that is bound to fulfil certain obligations towards token holders. All holder rights are derived from smart contracts, the content of which is defined by the community supporting the DeFi project. There is no one who centrally decides the future of a project. Even if the initiators or promoters of the DeFi project could be identified as debtors – which highly questionable in itself – there would always be an insurmountable legal obstacle: the basic principle of the Law of Obligations is that no one can be obliged to do the impossible (*ad impossibilia nemo obligatur*). Now, as it is the community that decides the fate of the DeFi project and the application of its assets, the initiators cannot consider themselves legally bound by any right that may be represented in the content of the tokens offered and traded on the market.[71]

In governance tokens, therefore, the legal relationship (or other equivalent) between investor and issuer that is established with the ownership of a security is not identifiable. The token is just a private cryptographic key that, by itself, does not grant rights to its holder. If the token holder does not get the rights they were promised when they bought the token, there may be a legal problem, but only at a contractual level. Therefore, we believe that the expectations of a holder of securities and a holder of tokens are different and difficult to compare. In the latter case, the typical relationship between investor and issuer, on which the entire archetype of securities regulation is based, is not established.

The application of the securities regime could be considered by arguing that investors also lack protection in the area of offering and trading governance tokens. However, the reason why they need protection stems solely from the

---

[70] Further developed by *Perestrelo de Oliveira*, Tutela do investidor perante o emitente no mercado de capitais. Um modelo dinâmico de proteção, Coimbra, 2021.

[71] This is the conclusion reached by *Kaulartz*, in: Möslein/Omlor (eds.), FinTech-Handbuch, 2nd ed., 2021, Rn. 60.

underlying technology[72] and not specifically from the information asymmetry that characterises capital markets and the elimination of which is the basis for securities regulation. We will return to this topic below. For now, suffice it to say that this route is not enough to determine the functional comparability between a security and a governance token. It should be noted that, to the extent that these instruments are not covered by securities legislation[73], they may be regulated in the abstract by MiCA, which will make the issuance of governance tokens dependent on the existence of a legal entity, unless crypto-asset services are provided in a fully decentralised manner, without an intermediary (recital 22 of the MiCA). This means that decentralisation will also determine the inapplicability of the MiCA Regulation.

Note that the legal nature of tokens does not crystallise over time. A token originally issued by a commercial company may initially qualify as a security, and, as the project follows a decentralisation path, the content of the token may change substantially in ways that imply a change in qualification. This will be the case when a security token begins to confer rights in a sufficiently decentralised and uncoordinated community, which will determine the value of the protocol.

4. Sufficient decentralisation as a criteria

1) The COALA Model Law only applies to DAOs operating on permissionless blockchains. As it is stated, those would "enable a multiplicity of participants to coordinate on a decentralized basis, in which control of the DAO is established among various actors via a Token-based system, and such permissionless participation is the foundational basis of DAOs".[74] However, as a uniform set of rules intended as a model for national legislation, the Model Law does not specify how decentralisation should be assessed.

Recent research, carried out by Henrik Axelsen, Johannes Rude Jensen and Omri Ross, propose "sufficient decentralisation" to be defined as "a verifiable state, where (1) the design of the DAO is collusion resistant and based on long-term equilibrium; (2) its governance processes have unrestricted and transparent access".[75] For such purposes, sufficient decentralisation may be achieved by analysing how a DAO's protocol is intended to become more decentralised over time. In order to achieve this idea, the Authors present TIGER Assessment

[72] *Möslein/Kaulartz/Renning* (fn. 20), Rn. 37.

[73] We do not deny that there are some cases where governance tokens should qualify as securities, see OECD, Why Decentralised Finance (DeFi) Matters and the Policy Implications, 2022. Available at: Why-Decentralised-Finance-DeFi-Matters-and-the-Policy-Implications.htm (4.07.2023), 58. It seems to us, however, that this qualification cannot be stated in general terms, for the reasons explained in the text.

[74] COALA Model Law, 20.

[75] *Axelsen/Jensen/Ross* (fn. 32) 56.

Framework as a useful tool[76] which is based on a score-card methodology. In simple terms, TIGER intends to cover (i) token weighted voting and incentives, (ii) infrastructures, (iii) governance, (iv) escalation and (v) reputation.

In fact, decentralisation may be reflected in (i) the community decision-making power, (ii) the impact of ideological options on project governance, (iii) inexistence of any central control, (iv) non-limited access, or (v) transparency. Trust in intermediaries is replaced by trust in smart contracts, which is ensured by technical audits carried out by the promoters of DeFi applications. Auditors look for programming flaws or errors in the smart contract code and then publish the conclusive report in a way that is accessible to the network of participants, thereby mitigating the technical risks associated with this type of trading.

However, the technology underpinning the protocol and its form of autonomous organisations are not the only relevant elements to assess whether there is sufficient decentralisation. The word decentralisation is often overused as a supposed shield against legal action, but the technical structure of DeFi does not, in itself, lead to the complete decentralisation of financial services. In fact, as we have stated before, total decentralisation is nothing but an illusion, mainly due to the fact that structures such as DAOs, despite their decentralisation in principle, usually form control groups to ensure greater efficiency in terms of decision-making powers and ownership. In Web3 jargon these token holders are called whales or crypto whales and there is debate in the community about the desirability of establishing voting rights ceilings to ensure that decentralisation is not undermined by these controlling groups. However, in terms of governance, while such options are intended to maintain the political decentralisation of the project, it is important to remember that crypto whales are people or entities who believe in the project and for whom any such restriction could be seen as discouraging their participation. In fact, whales will only be harmful to the extent that they act against the interests of the community[77], and in such cases, solutions can be envisaged using web-based mediation. Political decentralisation may well appeal to the principles of platform cooperativism, based on shared ownership and democratic government.[78]

2) In order to assess whether a given service or activity is sufficiently decentralised, it is also relevant to look at off-chain activities, which include protocol or software development, business development activities, marketing, ownership of intellectual property and protocol governance.[79] Depending on the con-

---

[76] *Axelsen/Jensen/Ross* (fn. 32) 61 ss.

[77] The possibility of resorting to flash loans, without the need to provide guarantees, to obtain governance tokens that can be used for a vote provides scenarios for the appearance of malicious control groups, as noted by OECD (fn. 74) 59.

[78] In relation to these principles, see, with references, *De Filippi*/Lavayssière (fn. 19), 218 ss.

[79] *Boiron* (fn. 10) 1 and 5. The Author directs the playbook to web3 founders who wish to

crete functioning of the protocol, the target market and the government mechanisms, it is possible that off-chain activities determine the value of crypto-assets and that, to this extent, it can be said that token holders expect to obtain profits resulting from these activities developed off the grid. This means that, even in the face of a decentralised protocol, the centralisation of off-chain activities can have an impact on the legal framework of the financial services provided. The existence of decentralisation must be assessed on different levels.[80]

The existence of information asymmetries between participants indicates the need for investor protection. There is no need to fear the competitive risks associated with the dissemination of confidential information. On the contrary, it is normal for confidential information, information on the future of the protocol and information about off-chain activities to be discussed in public forums. In this type of protocols, execution is more relevant than information itself. Therefore, in order to ensure true decentralisation, it is recommended that contracts with third parties explicitly state that the information provided is not confidential, so that it can be made available to the entire community.[81/82]

5. *How to regulate decentralised arrangements?*

1) Regulation and supervision at European level should, in our view, relate to the activity provided and not to the entity providing it, i.e. the object of regulation should not be the entities carrying out a particular activity, but the activity itself.[83] This means that further to the decentralisation requirement, we need to address the question of how we can design a framework that sets out rights, compliance requirements and obligations in the context of decentralised systems where there is no central entity or agent that can be held accountable. In fact, as a concept, a DAO is simply based on codes set out in a set of smart contracts which means that in principle there should be no human intervention in the operation of a DAO.

---

decentralize their off-chain activities and ensure compliance with US securities law and web3 lawyers who are advising founders on the decentralisation process. It makes it clear, however, that the strategies presented in the book are not the only possible way to achieve decentralisation.

[80] Following *Boiron* (fn. 10) 5 in a protocol in the early stages of development, which integrates well with others, the protocol development activity will probably be the one that will have the most impact on the creation of crypto-asset value. On the contrary, in communities where protocol development is already stabilized and integration is more difficult, the value of the protocol will tend to be determined through business development, marketing and government.

[81] *Boiron* (fn. 10) 9.

[82] On Boiron recommendations to ensure no information asymmetries between participants, see *Boiron* (fn. 10) 10 ss.

[83] See *European Commission*, European Stability and Integration Review 2022, 62; *Möslein/Kaulartz/Renning* (fn. 20), Rn. 22.

If this statement is correct, we can state that the traditional regulatory and supervisory model is not compatible with a DAO. Indeed, following Josef Bergt's statement, "[regulating] a truly decentralized infrastructure is a questionable task for regulators".[84] For instance, supervisors would not be able to implement mechanisms such as the prohibition of regulated activities without prior authorisation and compliance with certain organisational and transparency requirements. For such reason, we could state that it seems impossible to determine the person legally responsible for meeting these requirements. There is therefore a lack of "access points" for regulation to be applied.

This discussion has common grounds for DAOs and DeFi. However, differently from DeFi, in case of DAOs, the existence of an organisation may facilitate how regulation perpetrates its agents. A DAO does not rely merely on codes; instead, it counts with the participation of members that compose it (the token holders) to whom some decision powers may be entrusted. Furthermore, for the purposes of carrying out its activities, DAOs may rely on contractors to develop products or supply services and/or legal wrappers.

Therefore, and ultimately, it may be possible to identify agents as a bridge to regulation. However, these may vary, depending on the governance model of the DAO.

2) In any case, before discussing how to establish points of contact between decentralised arrangements and regulation, we need to discuss how traditional models of regulation, which impose such points of contact, can be considered adequate for this type of organisation. Indeed, traditional regulatory models have been designed for both non-digital realities and centralised organisations. The emergence of DAOs and disintermediation models has therefore opened the door to alternative models.

Within blockchain forums there are recent discussions on agent-centric business model and generic multi-agent organisation model approaches.

Agent-centric business model has been developed, in case of DAOs, as an alternative to the lack of a legal wrapper.[85] According to such model, "it is possible to use separate legal entities for interaction with counterparties that do not want to interact directly with a DAO, or with smart contracts in general. These dedicated legal entities are considered agents".[86] This approach has the advantage of providing flexibility to the operation of a DAO as it does not determine a specific individual acting as permanent agent. Instead, it addresses decentralisation allowing a DAO to adjust its agents on a case-by-case approach.

Alternatively, organisation-centric models are construed to address blockchain systems. As opposed to agent-centric approaches, the organisational

---

[84] *Bergt*, Decentralized Finance Unmasked. Behavioral Finance and Public Policy Insights on Financial Market Regulation, Nomos, 2023, 105.

[85] *Boss* (fn. 9), 8.

[86] *Boss* (fn. 9), 8.

model "*abstracts away* the internal details (i.e., the cognitive capabilities) of agents, and thus allows for focusing on the structural, organisational and social dimensions of blockchain systems (...)".[87] When applying to DAOs, this would open the door to a regulatory approach based on the technology or DAO structure rather than its members. Provided there are regulatory requirements to comply with, this model would fail to properly address the bridge between regulators and DAOs.

A third solution is found in the generic multi-agent organisational model as proposed by Hector Roussille, Önder Gürcan and Fabien Michel[88] which is, as we understand, a middle ground between these two perspectives. In fact, by using an Agent/Group/Role approach (AGR)[89], the Authors consider a model for blockchain systems (AGR4BS) in a way that allows "for a clear division of the different building blocks of blockchain systems, while leaving the possibility to explore behavioural divergence in a well-defined framework".[90]

IV. Regulatory opportunities

DAOs constitute an opportunity to explore and test the implementation of both regulatory technology and supervisory technology (also known as RegTech and SupTech).

Following the European Commission's definition, "Regulatory Technology is a sub-set of FinTech that focuses on technologies that may facilitate the delivery of regulatory requirements more efficiently and effectively than existing capabilities"[91], while "Supervisory Technology is a sub-set of FinTech that uses of innovative technology to support supervision. It helps supervisory authorities to digitise reporting and regulatory processes".[92] The underlying rationale would be to bring simplification and efficiency to legislation and supervisory levels in line with the smart regulation guidelines.[93]

---

87 *Roussille / Gürcan / Michel*, Big Data Cogn. Comput. 6, 1, 2022. Available at: https://www.mdpi.com/2504-2289/6/1/1 (27.07.2023).

88 *Roussille / Gürcan / Michel* (fn. 88).

89 *Roussille / Gürcan / Michel* (fn. 88). Following the Authors, roles are "abstract representations of functional positions of agents in a group", groups "identify context for patterns of activities (i.e., roles) that can be shared by sets of agents" and agents are "active, communicating entities playing roles within groups".

90 *Roussille / Gürcan / Michel* (fn. 88).

91 Communication from the Commission to the European Parliament, the Council, the European Economic and Social Committee and the Committee of the Regions on a Digital Finance Strategy for the EU. COM(2020) 591 final, Brussels, 24.09.2020, 7, fn. 16. Available at: https://eur-lex.europa.eu/legal-content/EN/TXT/PDF/?uri=CELEX:52020DC0591 (07.07.2023).

92 COM(2020) 591 final, 15.

93 Communication from the Commission to the European Parliament, the Council, the

Both RegTech and SupTech are now presented as part of a transformation movement of traditional financial institutions. It follows both the need to ensure adequacy of regulation to new digital forms of business operation and to readjust the entire financial market to the challenges of complex regulation and increasing use of technology. Indeed, technologies as RegTech and SupTech have the advantage of providing[94] (i) automate solutions for applicability of complex legal regulations and ensuring implementation of reporting and compliance obligations which are now presented as a burden to agents, (ii) efficiency at lower costs, (iii) transformative market solutions that are more adequate to the increased digitalized and data-driven financial services and "increased volume of information need to monitor".[95]

In case of DAOs, RegTech and SupTech may also facilitate technical implementation of regulatory requirements in smart contracts.[96] It is the idea of law as code or embedded supervision.[97] This approach entails the creation of a technological solution that allows supervisors to automatically monitor compliance with the regulatory framework by analysing transaction information on the blockchain, thereby reducing the need for market participants to collect, verify and make information available to supervisors.[98] Therefore, RegTech and SupTech may be indeed an opportunity to change the whole financial sector.

The European Commission has been particularly attentive to the challenges and opportunities that digitalisation presents for regulation. Alongside the defi-

---

European Economic and Social Committee and the Committee of the Regions. Smart Regulation in the European Union. Com(2010) 543 final, Brussels, 08.10.2010. Available at: https://eur-lex.europa.eu/LexUriServ/LexUriServ.do?uri=COM:2010:0543:FIN:EN:PDF (27.07.2023).

[94] Financial innovation. RegTech and SupTech – change for markets and authorities, ESMA Report on Trends, Risks and Vulnerabilities, No. 1, 2019, 43. Available at: https://www.esma.europa.eu/sites/default/files/trv_2019_1-regtech_and_suptech_change_for_markets_and_authorities.pdf (27.07.2023).

[95] See Financial Stability Board, "The use of supervisory and regulatory technology by authorities and regulated institutions. Market developments and financial stability implications", 9.10.2020. Available at: https://www.fsb.org/wp-content/uploads/P091020.pdf (27.07.2023), 43.

[96] *Möslein/Kaulartz/Renning* (fn. 20), Rn 40. Following this line, see *Omlor/Franke* (fn. 17) 683 and 684.

[97] The European Commission (fn. 84) 63, considers this strategy a sensible regulatory option and points out that the implementation of Regulation (EU) 2022/858 of the European Parliament and of the Council of 30 May 2022 on a pilot scheme for market infrastructures based on distributed ledger technology and amending Regulation (EU) no. 600/2014 and (EU) no. 909/2014 and Directive 2014/65/EU ("DLT Pilot Scheme") will be a good opportunity to assess the benefits of using the DLT technology for reporting purposes and for testing the technology under controlled conditions.

[98] As highlighted in the Digital Finance Strategy for the EU, by 2024, the EU the EU aims to put in place the necessary conditions to enable the use of innovative technologies, including RegTech and SupTech tools, for supervisory reporting by regulated entities and supervision by authorities – see COM(2020) 591 13.

nition of a set of digital goals for 2030[99], which aim to pursue digital policies that empower people and businesses to take advantage of a sustainable, more prosperous and human-centred digital future, the Commission recognises the importance of improving data access and sharing.[100] In particular, it recognises the importance of the data that needs to be reported by financial market participants and its necessity for EU and national supervisors to oversee financial entities and markets. This is the only way to monitor risks, ensure financial stability and market integrity, and protect investors and consumers of financial services in the EU.[101]

The Commission wants more availability, better quality and technical portability of information. To this end, it recognises that "[in] financial markets, distributed ledger technologies (DLT) have the potential to enable supervisors to monitor transactions in real time and allow them to extract transaction reports directly from trading systems (rather than wait for the transaction parties to send reports)".[102] In addition, at the request of the European Parliament, the Commission is planning a pilot project on the technical underpinnings of DLT-based supervision. Without prejudice to the risks and challenges posed by RegTech and SupTech, which should be duly addressed[103], it seems to us that this is undoubtedly the way forward: compliance with applicable regulations by the decentralised financial system will only be possible through decentralised data collection that can be used by the regulator.

All things considered, DAOs may definitely lead to the discovery of more innovative regulatory solutions.

---

99 See Communication from the Commission to the European Parliament, the Council, the European Economic and Social Committee and the Committee of the Regions. 2030 Digital Compass: the European way for the Digital Decade, in COM(2021) 118 final, Brussels, 09.03.2021. Available at: https://eur-lex.europa.eu/legal-content/EN/TXT/?uri=CELEX:52021DC0118 (27.07.2023).

100 See Communication from the Commission to the European Parliament, the Council, the European Economic and Social Committee and the Committee of the Regions. A European strategy for data, COM(2020), 66 final, Brussels, 19.02.2020. Available at: https://eur-lex.europa.eu/legal-content/EN/TXT/PDF/?uri=CELEX:52020DC0066 (27.07.2023).

101 See Communication from the Commission to the European Parliament, the Council, the European Economic and Social Committee and the Committee of the Regions. Strategy on supervisory data in EU financial services, COM(2021) 798 final, Brussels, 15.12.2021. Available at: https://eur-lex.europa.eu/legal-content/EN/TXT/PDF/?uri=CELEX:52021DC0798 (27.07.2023).

102 COM(2021) 798 final 14.

103 Among such risks, it should be considered the risks and challenges in relation to data standardisation and data quality, cyber-risk and data security, third-party dependences (such as cloud service providers), need for both recruitment of experts and training in regulatory and supervisory disciplines, data localisation regarding risks on storage of data within the borders of a certain territory), regulatory arbitrage, risk that expensive or complex regulatory systems become an entry barrier for SupTech and RegTech service providers or reputational risks. See Financial Stability Board (fn. 96), 9-10.

Progressive Decentralization requires Progressive Regulation: Do DAOs require direct legislative intervention, self-regulation or no regulation?

Nathan Vandy

ABSTRACT As DAOs transition from theoretical concepts to prominent entities in the blockchain ecosystem, global regulators recognize their potential to disrupt traditional platforms and create multi-stakeholder digital platforms.[1] A combination of enforcement actions by securities and other regulators whilst balancing product-market-fit, necessitates DAOs adopt a strategy of progressive decentralization – attempting compliance while steadily distributing control and decision-making to the community. DAOs progressively transition towards sufficient decentralization despite this end state being both unclear and unlegislated. To lower this regulatory burdens and foster innovation, it is posited whether DAOs require direct legislative intervention, self-regulation or no regulation.

By discussing the three dimensions of decentralization (technical, economic and legal) and the historical context of progressive and sufficient decentralization, the article uses this framing to analyze an inexhaustive list of regulatory tensions from a US and EU perspective. It concludes with recommendations to foster a more progressive regulatory environment for DAOs. These insights contribute to the evolving discourse on DAOs' potential to enhance operational efficiencies when coordinating online and additionally highlight the potential of blockchain as a regulatory tool.

I. Introduction

The emergence of Bitcoin marked a transformative moment not only in the sphere of finance and technology but also in governance. It introduced a groundbreaking concept – blockchain governance. The ability to operate autonomously, and leverage blockchain technology to govern without centralized authority.[2] Bitcoin's development journey from its transparent and open-source peer-to-peer protocol to the cryptographically rewarded proof-of-work mechanism exemplifies the possibilities of decentralized governance and operations. It offered

[1] *Miller*, A Tale of Two Regulators: Antitrust Implications of Progressive Decentralization in Blockchain Platforms, 77 WASH. & LEE L. REV. ONLINE 387 (2021).

[2] *Axelsen/Jensen/Ross*, When is a DAO Decentralized? Complex Systems Informatics and Modeling Quarterly, no. 31, pp. 51–75, 2022.

accessibility to anyone willing to participate, created a self-sustaining economic ecosystem, and introduced a mathematically scarce digital store of value.[3]

Due to the blockchain being such a nascent technology at the time, there was limited legal or regulatory scrutiny, and Bitcoin was able to reach sufficient decentralization: a protocol developed by a group of distributed developers and operations run by a group of decentralized miners network.[4] With these principles of decentralization, transparency, and efficient management, Bitcoin left as a template: a fluid organization or loosely organized communities, self-directed and governed through smart contracts without the presence of central authority or a managerial hierarchy. [5] It was this revolutionary shift in governance which transcended into a broader movement, the advent of Decentralized Autonomous Organizations (DAOs).

DAOs presented unique opportunities for internet-based collaboration and community-driven initiatives in numerous verticals including financial, consumer applications, and more; however there were clear challenges in their legal recognition, operational efficiency, and regulatory treatment. Similarities between traditional finance and its blockchain counterpart were clear, yet square-pegging regulations onto DAOs proved challenging due to distinct characteristics such as autonomous code, decentralized control, and non-hierarchical structures.[6] To limit these regulatory uncertainties, Initial Development Teams (IDTs) frequently adopted anonymity similar to Bitcoin's origins.[7] Nevertheless, secondary service providers, pivotal for investment and operations, were still subject to regulatory oversight. Consequently, completely anonymous stakeholders found themselves in a legal vacuum with exposed liability risks and restricted access to essential services.[8] While older DAOs like Bitcoin and Ethereum were unofficially given a grace period to reach sufficient decentralization and an autonomous nature, regulatory bodies worldwide have increasingly driven to establish comprehensive blockchain regulations. This has led IDTs to undertake the challenge of progressive decentralization, gradually transitioning the contribution framework and assets to the community until the point of sufficient decentralization. All this must be achieved while navigating nascent regulatory challenges *and* achieving product-market fit.

---

[3] *Nakamoto*, Bitcoin: A Peer-to-Peer Electronic Cash System, Transform. Gov. People, Process Policy, vol. 15, no. 4, pp. 580–596, 2009.

[4] *Schirrmacher/Jensen/Avital*, Token-Centric Work Practices in Fluid Organizations: The Cases of Yearn and MakerDAO, 42nd Int. Conf. Inf. Syst. ICIS 2021 Build. Sustain. Resil. With is A Call Action, no. December, 2021.

[5] *Hassan/De Filippi*, Decentralized autonomous organization, Internet Policy Rev., vol. 10, no. 2, pp. 1–10, 2021.

[6] *Peirce*, Token Safe Harbor Proposal 2, SEC, pp. 1–7, 2021. Available: https://www.sec.gov/news/public-statement/peirce-statement-token-safe-harbor-proposal-2.0. Accessed 29 August 2023.

[7] *Nakamoto* (fn. 3), pp. 580–596.

[8] *Axelsen/Jensen/Ross*, (fn. 2). pp. 51–75.

Due to policy makers assessing that sufficiently decentralized autonomous organizations will operate outside of the traditional regulatory framework, some argue that DAOs require direct legislative intervention.[9] [10] But legal ambiguities that progressively decentralized autonomous organization must navigate, including securities, corporate and tax laws, suggest otherwise.[11] Others suggest that the industry should be self-regulated, due to the unique properties of blockchain technology providing the ability for organizations to prove regulatory equivalence.[12] The article posits that ultimately the question is not *whether* DAOs should be regulated but *how* they should be regulated. Striking a balance that balances the nurturing of innovation while addressing DAOs' potential risks and protecting consumers and investors, is essential, and the absence of appropriate regulation could result in significant uncertainties for DAO participants and associated entities, impacting liability and operational optimization.[13]

This article explores the spectrum of decentralization (technical, economic and legal) with a focus on the role of progressive decentralization in shaping the regulatory approach towards DAOs. It delves into the current regulatory landscape highlighting the importance of clear securities laws, legal recognition, and addressing challenges when interfacing with traditional legal frameworks. By examining the benefits and risks associated with DAO regulation, we advocate for progressive regulatory measures that stimulate innovation while safeguarding participants' interests, concluding with recommendations for regulators, practitioners, and policymakers alike.

II. Background

1. Primer on the blockchain technology stack, DAOs and the dimensions of decentralization

Blockchain uses immutable cryptographic signatures to record transactions that ensure collusion resistance and eliminate the need for central intermediaries.[14] Blockchains are predominately public and permissionless, meaning there

[9] *European Parliament*, EU parliament report on MiCA, 2022.

[10] *W. Hinman*, Digital Asset Transactions : When Howey Met Gary (Plastic) Remarks at the Yahoo Finance All Markets Summit : Crypto, pp. 1–6, 2018.

[11] *European Parliament*, (fn. 9).

[12] *Axelsen/Jensen/Ross*, (fn. 2). pp. 51–75.

[13] *117th Congress*, Lummis-Gillibrand Responsible Financial Innovation Act, vol. 2022, pp. 1–69, 2022

[14] *Yaga/Mell/Roby/Scarfone*, Blockchain Technology Overview (2018) —National Institute of Standards and Technology Internal Report 8202. Gaithersburg, MD: National Institute of Standards and Technology. Available: https://doi.org/10.6028/NIST.IR.8202, Accessed 12 September 2023.

is no restriction for anyone to access, participate, leave, fork the technology.[15] With the blockchain technology stack, this is known as the settlement layer, a foundational layer responsible for managing the blockchain's state. Similar to how the Bitcoin protocol compensates miners with tokens for validating and securing the network, it also establishes incentives for validators and miners to maintain the integrity of the blockchain.[16]

On top of the settlement layer is the protocol layer. This layer is responsible for programming applications and governing specific activities or tasks. Effectively this is a set of principles and rules that all participants in a given industry have agreed to follow as a prerequisite to operating in the industry. DeFi protocols are interoperable, meaning they can be used by multiple entities at the same time to build a service or an app. The protocol layer provides Liquidity to the DeFi ecosystem. One example of a DeFi protocol is Uniswap, a decentralized exchange trading protocol on Ethereum used to exchange tokens in a peer-to-peer, permissionless manner.[17]

Protocols enable the creation of the token and the application layer. The token layer which encompasses a wide range of tokens, including both non-fungible and fungible variants like stablecoins and governance tokens. They can be separated into payment tokens (coins like Ether, Bitcoin, etc.), security tokens (virtual representation of traditional stocks, shares and assets) and utility tokens (like DAO governance tokens).[18]

Finally, the application layer interfaces with both the underlying network and the end-users for developers to build decentralized applications (dapps). Consumer applications providing interoperable and functional utility to users such as decentralized finance, social media applications, and games are some use cases.

Certain protocol layers such as Ethereum allow developers to compose "smart contracts," coded scripts integrated into the Ethereum blockchain that establish transaction-specific governance rules. With these developers can construct dapps that engage with these smart contracts.[19] As long as the settlement layer is active, a smart contract will self-execute business logic unconditionally, autonomously, and irreversibly. The smart contracts' code will not be modified once it is deployed onto the protocol, but they can be upgraded through the use

---

[15] *Abdulhakeem, S./Hu,* Q., Powered by Blockchain Technology, DeFi (Decentralized Finance) Strives to Increase Financial Inclusion of the Unbanked by Reshaping the World Financial System. Modern Economy, 12, 1-16, 2021.

[16] *Nakamoto,* (fn. 3), pp. 580–596.

[17] *DIDO Wiki,* Decentralized Finance (DeFi) Layers, SEC, pp. 1–7, 2021. Available: https://www.omgwiki.org/dido/doku.php?id=dido:public:ra:1.2_views:2_tech_views:defi layers, Accessed 11 August 2023.

[18] Ibid.

[19] *Ethereum Foundation,* Introduction to Smart Contracts. Available: https://ethereum.org/en/developers/docs/smart-contracts/. Accessed 23 August 2023.

of administrative keys. Similarly, changes to protocol rules typically require approval from protocol stakeholders—one party is unable to unilaterally change the rules of the protocol.

The group of individuals and entities governing and being governed by blockchain technology stack, constitute what is known as a Decentralized Autonomous Organization (DAO). The stakeholders utilize these properties to create rule-based organizations, in which they make decisions governed by smart contracts and governance tokens to enhance transparency, user ownership and immutability.[20] Built upon permissionless settlement layers like Bitcoin[21] and Ethereum[22] DAOs proliferate multiple blockchains, nearing an estimated count of 5,000 DAOs, 1.7m token holders, and 700, 000 active voting members as of 2022.[23] The genesis of these organizations can be traced back to 2014 when Vitalik Buterin envisioned DAOs as decentralized entities operating on the internet, capable of autonomous functions and occasionally delegating tasks to individuals.[24] Technology is at the center; humans on the edges. In this sense, it was intended that these organizations would coordinate sufficiently around on-chain components, such as blockchain protocols and smart contracts, solely create dapps and transacting online with token payments. This follows the concept "code is law", an idealistic view that the rules and business logic of an organization could be coordinated on-chain, by code alone.[25]

The DAO hack illustrated that the technology had not matured enough to allow operations to be executed effectively by governance mechanisms embedded solely based on the blockchain technology stack. It also emphasizes the importance of what is known as off-chain governance, a more fluid and informal process that relies on social and institutional mechanisms for coordination including interactions with the non-digital (or real) world activities such as paying taxes, managing funds or hiring individuals. Despite the presumed decentralized nature of DAO governance, power within these networks is not always uniformly distributed among stakeholders, resulting in varying degrees of influence.[26] Various stakeholder groups, including core contributors, delegates, service providers, investors, and influential figures, exert influence on each oth-

---

[20] *Beck/Müller-bloch*, Governance in the Blockchain Economy: A Framework and Research Agenda, J. Assoc. Inf. Syst., vol. 19, no. 10, 2018.

[21] *Nakamoto* (fn. 3), pp. 580–596.

[22] *Wood*, Ethereum: a secure decentralised generalised transaction ledger, Ethereum Proj. Yellow Paper., pp. 1–32, 2014.

[23] *DeepDAO*, Available: https://deepdao.io/organizations. Accessed 13 August 2023.

[24] *Ethereum Foundation*, DAOs, DACs, DAs and More: An Incomplete Terminology Guide. Available: https://blog.ethereum.org/2014/05/06/daos-dacs-das-and-more-an-incomplete-terminology-guide. Accessed 9 August 2023.

[25] *Filippi/McMullen*, Governance of Blockchain Systems: Governance of and by Distributed Infrastructure (2018) Blockchain Research Institute and COALA Research Report, Available at: https://hal.archives-ouvertes.fr/hal-02046787/document, Accessed 16 August 2023.

[26] *Filippi/McMullen,* (fn. 25).

er's decisions in the absence of third-party enforcement mechanisms.[27] Following, commentators have begun to distinguish between endogenous rules, which are developed by and for the blockchain community, and exogenous rules imposed by external entities. On-chain rules primarily fall under the endogenous category, typically created by the DAO's community but relying on market dynamics to incentivize participation. In contrast, off-chain governance encompasses both endogenous elements, such as social norms, and exogenous elements like regulatory frameworks, which indirectly influence the DAOs' governance and operations.[28]

It is in the intersection between these exogenous elements and DAOs' decentralized nature, that DAOs seem to have developed a state of 'alegality', operating beyond the direct jurisdiction of traditional legal systems.[29] This has led to some categorizing DAOs similar nation-states rather than conventional organizations. Other scholars have even advocated for recognizing DAOs as autonomous entities that limits the extent that they can legally accept liability, akin to the autonomy classification applied in land and maritime environments.[30] In understanding DAOs' intersection between their nature and legal categorization, it is crucial to recognize that their autonomous features are interrelated with decentralization. They work together to distribute power intrinsically and block extrinsic powers from taking control. For example, Bitcoin's widely decentralized network of geographically diverse and potentially anonymous miners and validators significantly complicates any attempts by single governments, intermediaries, or bad actors to exert extrinsic power, such as through bribery, fines or violence, to control the network. The autonomy and effectiveness of the DAO and its technology stack, is in part a function of its degree of decentralization.[31] Therefore, an assessment or quantifiable degree of decentralization becomes pivotal when understanding how DAOs exist within the current regulatory landscape. DAOs and their technology stack can be said to be decentralized on three dimensions:

Technical Decentralization	primarily relating to the security of DAO's technology stack. At a fundamental level, the technology stack can provide greater resilience and transparency for permissionless and public transactions.

---

[27] *Filippi/McMullen*, (fn. 25).

[28] *Filippi/McMullen*, (fn. 25).

[29] *De Filippi/Mannan/Reijers*, The legality of blockchain technology (2022) 41 Policy and Society 358.

[30] *Myhre/Hellandsvik/Petersen*, A responsibility-centered approach to defining levels of automation, Journal of Physics: Conference Series, vol. 1357, 2019., pp. 30

[31] *Shapiro*, Autonomy vs Decentralization, Available at: https://lex-node.medium.com/autonomy-vs-decentralization-ceb2645f9cd5, Accessed 16 August 2023.

Economic Decentralization	primarily relating to the economies of DAOs and their technology stack. DAOs can scale governance and operations by distributing economic resources including trade, services, and tokens.
Legal Decentralization	primarily relating to the legality of DAOs and their technology stack. As DAOs pursue sufficient decentralization, they must navigate complex and unclear legal issues from liability and fiduciary duties, taxation and intellectual property, and employment law and privacy.[32]

It is extremely challenging or even impractical for the majority of DAOs to automatically start as a fully decentralized on any of these dimensions. Instead, they exercise progressive decentralization, gradually shifting the decision-making power and control away from the IDT, toward broader and more distributed participation.[33] This transfer of control is achieved by distributing decision-making power, providing tokens to a wider user base, offering bounty opportunities, and by assigning the IP and revenues to the DAO rather than the initial entity. To achieve this goal compliantly DAOs increasingly establish associated operational entities that can hold assets, contract with employees, contractors, and service providers, and act as "legal wrappers" to protect DAO participants from unlimited liability. Although DAOs' legal wrappers are often misinterpreted as the DAOs themselves, they are best understood under the concept of Cybernetic Organization (CybOrg or 'BORG'), a traditional legal entity that uses blockchain technologies to augment the entity's governance and activities.[34] The goal is for a DAO to become legally decentralized. The BORG supports the DAO in achieving sufficient decentralization while offering a means of achieving regulatory compliance, tax optimization, and engagement in contractual "off-chain" transactions.[35]

In summary, designing a DAO is a complex undertaking. IDTs face the usual startup challenges, such as finding product-market fit while progressively decentralizing governance and operations to limit regulatory risks. At the same time, although policy makers have assessed "sufficient decentralization" as an important milestone to de-risk DAOs, there have been limited guidelines in quantifying or establishing its definition.

---

[32] *Jenkins*, Principles & Models of Web3 Decentralization. Available: https://a16z.com/wp-content/uploads/2022/04/principles-and-models-of-decentralization_miles-jennings_a16zcrypto.pdf, Accessed 26 September 2023.

[33] *Wright*, Measuring DAO Autonomy: Lessons From Other Autonomous Systems, IEEE Transactions on Technology and Society, vol. 2, no. 1, pp. 43–53, 2021.

[34] *Shapiro*, Assimilating the BORG: A New Framework for CryptoLaw Entities, Available at: https://delphilabs.medium.com/assimilating-the-borg-a-new-cryptolegal-framework-for-dao-adjacent-entities-569e54a43f83, Accessed 16 August 2023.

[35] *Brummer/Seira*, Legal Wrappers and DAOs, SSRN, pp. 1–31, 2022.

III. Legal and Regulatory Issues with Progressive Decentralizing Autonomous Organizations

The progressive decentralization of each of the aforementioned dimensions (technical, economic, and legal) is critical to the legitimacy and effectiveness of DAOs. In the following section, we provide an inexhaustive examination of the main legal and regulatory issues that affect DAOs during their decentralization process. It is expected that there will be overlaps with some legal and regulatory factors affecting the different dimensions but the framework will regardless shed light on pointers to improve the regulatory approach that should be applied to progressively decentralizing autonomous organizations.

1. Technical Decentralization

The disintermediation of the technology layer is a fundamental dimension to decentralizing a DAO. It reinforces the security of the network can be reinforced by removing the need for trusted intermediaries managing the smart contracts and rules relating to the DAO's blockchain technology stack.[36] From the IDT to governance token holders, and all in between, stakeholders within the DAO closely collaborate to propose modifications or enhancements to the technology layers. However, at the initial stages of the decentralization process, these processes are typically administered and managed by the IDT with restricted access to administration keys that could make significant changes to technology layer.[37] From the liability differences between operate and those who govern the blockchain technology layer(s); the differentiation of liabilities on technology layers depending on decentralization or autonomy; and how the technology can be used to improve regulatory equivalency; this section assesses the legal and regulatory facts that stakeholders must consider when decentralizing the technology dimension.

a) Delineating liability between governing and operating the technology layer(s)

There are billions in dollar value secured across the various technology layers that DAO members govern and operate.[38] Recent legal cases emphasize the importance of delineating these DAO members that govern and those operate. Governors use their tokens to engage in the high-level meta-governance of the DAO and technology stack, and our responsible for overseeing low-level oper-

---

[36] *Zarrin/Phang/Saheer et al.*, Blockchain for decentralization of internet: prospects, trends, and challenges. Cluster Comput 24, 2841–2866 (2021).

[37] *AMFE*, AMFE DeFi Whitepaper, Available at: https://www.afme.eu/Portals/0/DispatchFeaturedImages/AFME%20DeFi%20Whitepaper.pdf, Accessed 15 September 2023.

[38] *DeepDAO* (fn. 23).

ational governance of DAO and technology stack including software development and network growth. Sufficient decentralization equates to complete immutability where governors and operator lack unilateral authority to make changes to the technology stack. Consequently, the influence exerted by governors or operators is connected to whether the technology has reached a level of decentralization. In this discussion, we delve into the nuances of these roles and their implications for potential liability.

DAOs are legally categorized as unincorporated partnerships or associations, meaning joint and several liability for all the members involved. While the pseudonymous nature of individuals interacting with blockchains complicates this endeavor, certain jurisdictions have already begun to explore the potential ramifications of identifying and holding users accountable for their interactions within DAOs. This is seen in the recent in the Tornado Cash appeal [39] where, Judge Pitman emphasized that the Treasury Department had accurately identified an entity, encompassing the decentralized autonomous organization (DAO) that manages the service. He wrote,

> "The DAO functions as a distinct entity, with its voting members aligning towards a shared goal. The setup closely mirrors that of a corporate structure where not all shareholders may participate in voting, yet the organization's entity status remains unaffected."

The risk of joint and several liability was emphasized further in the Ooki DAO case, where judges classified the DAO as a for-profit *unincorporated association* consisting of token holders that "govern" the protocol with their tokens, holding all the DAO members personally liable for the debts of the association.[40]

This becomes especially pernicious considering that most tokenholders do not operate or interact directly with the settlement or protocol but use a front-end interface that makes calls on their behalf, and in cases where users may remain unaware that the possession of specific governance tokens creates these liability. As mentioned by the dissenting statement of the Ooki DAO case, the CFTC's Commissioner, Summer K. Mersinger, calling the decision to impose liability on bZx's co-IDTs "arbitrary" and "based on an unsupported legal theory amounting to regulation by enforcement while federal and state policy is developing." This poses significant risks, including hindrances to development in the blockchain industry.

Some nuances to this growing jurisprudence does exist, including a recent Dutch Appeal, where Prosecutor Martine Boerlage focused on the influence

---

[39] *FIOD*, Arrest of suspected developer of Tornado Cash, Available: https://werken.belastingdienst.nl/expertises/fiod, Accessed 20 September 2023.

[40] *CFTC*, Commodity Futures Trading Commission v. OOKI DAO, Civil Action No: 3:22-cv-5416.

that the co-developers Roman Semenov and Roman Storm had on the development process citing evidence taken from group chats on Pertsev's phone:

"The defendant sits along with Semenov and Storm in the driver's seat and determines what does or does not happen within Tornado Cash,"[41]

In this statement, she caveats the liability by creating a hierarchical framework between tokenholders governing the technology layers, the core team involved in the day-to-day development operations, or those who have more voting power (a similar assessment was made in the Ooki DAO case too).[42]

This being said, a few questions here are whether there was an assessment of the autonomous code and decentralized nature of the DAO; and whether this would create limited liability exposure for the developers.[43] Therefore, regulating through enforcement needs to be limited, especially for unsuspecting token holders of autonomous code to ensure that innocent tokenholders and users are not regulated unjustly.

b) Self-regulatiion through disclaimers of technical risks

An underlying principle of blockchain technology is to scale social consensus through deference of trust onto the technology layer. This is compounded by the different technology layers being open-source to improve their security over time, forkable so that they can be improved if social consensus is not found, and transparent so that the transactions can be audited. Unfortunately, during the progressive decentralization process, there are a number of DAOs that do not provide clarity on how decentralized their relevant layers, from legal, to economic and technology. This follows the concept, "decentralization theater", that defines "any system that produces not decentralization, but the appearance of decentralization". A skewed asymmetry between the operators and the governors is created which sharply contradicts the original promise of transparency and democracy that DAOs could usher, creating liability risks for developers and ultimately diminishing protections for both consumers and investors.[44]

To address potential liability issues faced by users of DAO technology stack, some regulators AMFE have proposed a level of self-regulation in the form of disclosure regimes.[45] This approach aims to offer transparent information regarding the level of decentralization within the DAOs technology stack includ-

[41] *FIOD*, (fn. 39).

[42] *FIOD*, (fn. 41).

[43] *Lexology*, UK High Court Rules on Liability of Bitcoin Software Developers, Available: https://www.lexology.com/library/detail.aspx?g=408b2242-bc4d-4b5e-86e9-b954a5b97560, Accessed 26 September 2023.

[44] *P2P Foundation*, Decentralization_Theater, https://wiki.p2pfoundation.net/Decentralization_Theater, Accessed 20 September 2023.

[45] *AMFE*, (fn. 37).

ing whether it is custodial or non-custodial and who are the operators of administrative keys. Certain initiatives have already taken steps in this direction by providing Transparency Reports that offer a clear understanding of the DAO's decentralization level and its underlying protocol.[46] When structured carefully and transparently, disclaimers can define the boundaries of contractual obligations, reducing the risk of participants imposing liability on DAOs. This is aligned with some of the disclosure regime that Commissioner Pierce suggested in her Safe Harbour Proposal to minimizes compliance burdens for early-stage projects while upholding investor protection.

There is a clear interplay between technology, economic and legal decentralizaiton here. Technical decentralization is clearly a precursor to legal decentralization. The DAO Model Law describes how functional and regulatory equivalence concepts can be applied to adapt existing corporate rules and regulations to accommodate blockchain-based DAOs.[47] The concept of functional equivalence refers to establishing an equivalence between an object or process that is already regulated by existing laws and another object or process that falls outside the scope of those regulations. By considering the function and objectives of regulations, it becomes possible to leverage blockchain technology to achieve similar outcomes without creating entirely new regulatory frameworks. The example used is that UNCITRAL Model Law for Electronic Commerce, which establishes functional equivalence between paper-based documents and electronic documents.[48] The Imperative of Regulatory Equivalence Blockchain to prove revenue flows, Blockchain to prove corporate existence, blockchain to licenses, blockchain. This approach can simplify the regulation of DAOs. Instead of creating entirely new corporate rules specifically for tokenized shares or blockchain-based assets, existing rules governing traditional corporate assets could be adapted to cover blockchain-based assets. For example, shares recorded on a blockchain-based system could be considered valid titles to a share, transferable via a blockchain-based registry.

c) Dilenation between Autonomous Code and Centralized Code

From the front-end on the application layer to the back-ends on the protocol layer and settlement layer, by implementing decentralized measures, there are a number of technology layers that a DAO can decentralize over time. When assessing the decentralization a technology layer is, it is important to note that

---

[46] *Arbitrum DAO*, Transparency report: Initial foundation setup. Available: https://docs.arbitrum.foundation/foundational-documents/transparency-report-initial-foundation-setup. Accessed 5 August 2023.

[47] *COALA*, DAO Model Law (2021), Available at https://coala.global/wpcontent/uploads/2021/06/DAO-Model-Law.pdf. Accessed 16 August 2023.

[48] *United Nations Commission on International Trade Law*, UNCITRAL Model Law on Electronic Commerce, Adopted in 1998. New York: United Nations, 1999.

decentralization is a spectrum. On one hand, a high level of decentralization can be identified where upgrades to the technology layer that can only be implemented through on-chain governance accompanied executable on-chain code, and on the extreme, there is no administrative ability to upgrade the layer at all. On the other hand, some technology layers are completely managed and administered by centralized intermediaries with no-connection to decentralized governance, through code or law.

Understanding the varying levels of technical decentralization make it difficult to assess the liability of developers that create the code, especially when there are potential financial regulatory frameworks that may cover the activities that a layer executes. This is showcased in the Risley case, where a private litigant accused Uniswap Labs, the developers of the Uniswap protocol, for facilitating "rampant fraud" on the Uniswap decentralized exchange. Through the court's explanation:

> "... it defies logic that a drafter of computer code underlying a particular software platform could be liable under Section 29(b) for a third-party's misuse of that platform. As discussed, smart contracts are self-executing, self-enforcing code..."

The ruling drew a distinction between the protocol layer, "Uniswap protocol" that anyone can access in a permissionless way and the application layer "Uniswap decentralized exchange" a front-end website interface, that serves as a user-friendly gateway to the underlying protocol. Ultimately, it was held Uniswap protocol cannot be held accountable for the losses of its users or the damage caused by third parties and effectively categorized the protocol layer as decntralized and autonomous technoloy.[49]

The ruling also set a precedent by asserting that developers shouldn't be held responsible for the misuse of their code by others. Although a ruling of such nature would have limited innovation in this nascent industry, this exact stance was taken in the Tornado Cash case. The developers created fully decentralized non-custodial protocol that could be used to anonymize crypto transactions and the code could only be amended through on-chain governance. Yet third-party individuals, including North Korea's Lazarus Group, misused the platform for money laundering purposes. Due to be being used as a primarily as a laundering tool for criminal organization groups, the Treasury Department's Office of Foreign Asset Control (OFAC) imposed sanctions on Tornado Cash, and a core developer, Pertsev, who contributed code to the crypto anonymizer, was imprisoned soon after.[50] In the appeal, Prosecutor Martine Boerlage focused on the influence that the co-developers Roman Semenov and Roman

---

[49] *Complaint*, Risley v. Universal Navigation Inc. et al., 1:22-cv-02780-KPF (S.D.N.Y.) ("Risley").

[50] *FIOD*, (fn. 39).

Storm had on the development process citing evidence taken from group chats on Pertsev's phone:

"The defendant sits along with Semenov and Storm in the driver's seat and determines what does or does not happen within Tornado Cash,"

In the Tornado Cash appeal, the judge also implies that smart contracts may have property rights. This recognition could provide a foundation for future cases where the ownership or rights to a smart contract are disputed.[51] In these future cases, prosecutors will have to refute the current jurisprudence that developers cannot be responsible for autonomous code. This not only brings into question how to asses the decentralization of the technology layer, especially as that the Tornoda Cash protocol could be accessed through multiple user interfaces, not just those supplied by the IDT.

These frictions are also seen in the recent EU's proposed Data Act which introduces provisions related to "safe termination and interruption," colloquially known as the "kill switch," for smart contracts. These provisions mandate the integration of internal functionalities within smart contracts, empowering them to either initiate a reset or issue directives to cease operations, thereby preempting nerfarious activities in the future.[52] These types of rules could not apply when the technology layers or DAO is sufficiently decentralized. Furthermore, even if they only deploy the smart contract without having any technical possibility to change it afterwards, by having access to the technical layer, deployers may qualify as crypto-asset service providers (CASPs) under the Market in Crypto-Assets law (MiCA). Otherwise enforcing centralization and mandated back-door code, could act against the benefits of the technology, as the ultimate state of the technology is to remove any intermediary with power to activate a kill switch. [53] [54]

Depending on the activity and nature of the transaction, there may be financial regulation compliance, especially on the application layer. Although for the protocol layer, it has been shown to be more autonomous, for the application layer where most of the users interact and it is harder to decentralize, many operators have began to implement compliance steps such having decentralized front-ends or as seen with Uniswap, removing non-compliant aspects from the website or DAOs geo-blocking US citizens from accessing some of it's services due to the unclear application of traditional laws to DeFi.[55] In case a smart con-

---

51 *FIOD*, (fn. 39).

52 *European Union*, Press Release, Available: https://ec.europa.eu/commission/presscorner/detail/en/ip_23_3491r, Accessed 22 September 2023.

53 *EUCI*, The Data Act Smart Contracts Position, https://eu.ci/the-data-act-smart-contracts-position-p/, Accessed 22 September 2023 https://eu.ci/the-data-act-smart-contracts-position-p/.

54 *EUCI*, (fn. 53).

55 *Cointelegraph*, Uniswap delists 100-tokens from interface including options and index-

tract or other relevant software used to provide crypto-asset services can be modified by individuals, one can assume that at least a part of the services is not sufficiently decentralized. Following this logic, if a technology layer is created to be autonomous, there should not be any liabilities to the developers involved, it is still a legal area that needs to be explored.

An a global level, the implications of sanctions including the fact that the Treasury Department's Office of Foreign Asset Control (OFAC) linked Tornado Cash to global malicious activities, such as those alleged with North Korea's Lazarus Group, underlines the international ramifications of cryptocurrency use and its potential misuse. The case showcases how the U.S. government may approach entities it believes are facilitating international criminal activities, even if those entities are decentralized. Dutch law makes it illegal to conceal or disguise the origin and movement of funds, and prosecutors said Tornado was used to place almost 75 % of all crime-related crypto on the Ethereum blockchain. The developing jurisprudence is that if the code is autonomous, if they are used for an illegal purpose, those that developed the code can still be prosecuted. Ultimately, depending on the decentralization stage of the DAO, there could be differing levels of legal and fiduciary duties. If so, future proceedings may do little to resolve more general questions of whether developers will be held responsible for the open-source software they develop.

2. *Economic Decentralization*

As DAOs attempt to decentralize their economic dimensions by distributing governance tokens to their network, they find themselves in a complex and ever-changing regulatory landscape, particularly concerning securities laws that lack a clear framework for classifying crypto assets. Consequently, the issuance, promotion, or secondary market trading of DAO governance tokens may raise compliance concerns in certain jurisdictions.[56] From the ICO launch of Ethereum Network in 2014, there has been a catalyst of regulatory debate, where the sale of 60 million pre-mined ether tokens, was sold to investors, an activity that may not have had the same treatment with regulators' current understanding of the law. Due to blockchain's global nature, the treatment of major jurisdictions holds significant implications for crypto asset trading and the regulatory paradigm crafted over the past eight decades.[57]

es, Available: https://cointelegraph.com/news/uniswap-delists-100-tokens-from-interface-including-options-and-indexes, Accessed 11 September 2023.

[56] *Gässl/Daniel/Weidinge/Julian*, Unlocking the Potential of DAOs: Legal Challenges, Regulatory Solutions, and Opportunities for a New Paradigm in Business (2023), 10.13140/RG.2.2.23934.77128.

[57] *Coindesk*, Sale of the Century: The Inside Story of Ethereum‘s 2014 Premine. Available at: https://www.coindesk.com/markets/2020/07/11/sale-of-the-century-the-inside-story-of-ethereums-2014-premine/, Accessed 28 August 2023.

a) No regulation by enforcement in securities law

In April 2019, the SEC published a "Framework for 'Investment Contract' Analysis of Digital Assets," in April 2019, employing the Howey Test from SEC v. W.J. Howey Co. to determine whether tokens or coins qualified as "investment contracts" subject to securities regulations. The Howey Test consists of three prongs:

"The investment of money"	This prong considers the acquisition of digital assets in exchange for value, whether in fiat currency, other digital assets, or alternative forms of consideration.
"Common enterprise"	Typically, the SEC found that digital assets met this prong as the fortunes of purchasers were intertwined with each other or the promoter's success.
"Reasonable expectation of profits from the efforts of others"	This prong considers the acquisition of digital assets in exchange for value, whether in fiat currency, other digital assets, or alternative forms of consideration.

At the same time, it was suggested that a security could become "sufficiently decentralized" over time so that it no longer is a security token under the so-called Howey test.[58] In the context of digital assets, the pivotal question has been whether the platform achieved decentralization. For instance, in 2018, under the Hinmann doctrine, the SEC clarified that Bitcoin and Ethereum were not considered securities because their underlying networks had attained sufficient decentralization, reducing reliance on any single third party. It was suggested that contractual and technical structuring of digital assets could allow them to function more like consumer items, or community enablers, and less as regulated securities. This legal reasoning was extended in the *Risley* case, where Judge Failla refused to "stretch the federal securities laws" to cover the issuance of a crypto asset, adding to the legal jurisprudence and case law that cites Bitcoin (BTC) and Ether (ETH) as "commodities".[59]

According to commenters, there are significant challenges with the SEC's current classification The SEC's "decentralize-and-morph" approach, established after the 2014 ether ICO created an unpredictable and intricate evaluative process for tokens[60]. The rush to decentralize to comply with SEC guidelines

58 *Hinman*, (fn. 10), pp. 1–6.

59 *Complaint*, Risley v. Universal Navigation Inc. et al., 1:22-cv-02780-KPF (S.D.N.Y.) ("Risley").

60 *Cohen/Strong/Gregory/Lewin/Freemann/Chen/Sara*, The Ineluctable Modality of Securities Law: Why Fungible Crypto Assets are Not Securities, Available at https://dlxlaw.

can hinder long-term project development and innovation. Furthermore, this approach has proven to be unwieldy and inconsistent in practice.[61] This is in stark contrast to other jurisdictions such as the EU where despite the European Securities and Markets Authority (ESMA) providing vague guidance, "... where the coins or tokens qualify as financial instruments it is likely that the firms involved in ICOs conduct regulated investment activities", refused to engage in regulation by enforcement. Following, this has allowed for the development of industry-wide collaborative effort to regulate activities related to crypto assets under the Markets in Crypto-Assets Regulation (MiCA).[62] It implored the other jurisdictions such as the US, take a similar approach and limit the negative impacts of regulating by enforcement, and instead work with stakeholders to provide better clarity on supporting DAOs to reach sufficient decentralization so their governance tokens will be considered commodities.

b) Creation of Self-Regulatory Organizations (SROs) to develop reliable self-regulatory standards for digital securities

According to commenters, there are significant challenges with the SEC's current classification approach with the primary criterion for classifying crypto assets as securities hinges on their degree of decentralization.[63] Investments reliant on third parties require necessary information disclosure about these parties to protect uninformed investors. The recent enforcement strategy of the SEC should be evaluated while recognizing that the SEC did not adequately emphasize the importance of self-regulation.

A rigid and rigorous strategy of enforcement may contradict the systematic promotion of self-regulatory initiatives. In contrast, the CFTC, through Commissioner Brian Quintenz, recently promoted self-regulatory initiatives with regard to cryptocurrencies. Self-regulation within the DAO ecosystem can play a pivotal role in alleviating the burden of securities laws. By establishing and adhering to robust internal governance frameworks, DAOs can demonstrate their commitment to responsible and transparent operations. In Switzerland, FINMA successfully created an efficient self-regulatory framework. Similar initiatives have occurred in Hong Kong, the United Kingdom, Japan, and the United States. These self-regulatory bodies contribute to the development of

com/wp-content/uploads/2022/11/The-Ineluctable-Modality-of-Securities-Law-%E2%80%93-DLx-Law-Discussion-Draft-Nov.-10-2022.pdf (discussion draft), Accessed 07 August 2023.

[61] SEC v. LBRY, No. 21-CV-260-PB, 2022 WL 16744741 (D.N.H. Nov. 7, 2022); SEC v. Ripple Labs, Inc. et al., No. 20-10832 (S.D.N.Y. filed Dec. 22, 2020).

[62] *ESMA*, ESMA alerts firms involved in Initial Coin Offerings (ICOs) to the need to meet relevant regulatory Requirements (Doc. No. ESMA50-157-828 European Securities and Markets Authority, Available, http://perma.cc/A4BP-9QS4. Accessed 30 August 2023.

[63] *Cohen/Strong/Gregory/Lewin/Freemann/Chen/Sara*, (fn. 60).

reliable self-regulatory standards, acknowledging the importance of self-regulation as a tool beneficial for the markets.[64] This proactive approach to self-regulation can help build trust with regulators and potentially influence the scope and extent of regulatory oversight.

The hallmark of Decentralized Autonomous Organizations (DAOs) lies in their heavy reliance on transparent on-chain financial records. Within the framework of DAOs, the blockchain itself serves as an auditing mechanism, effectively reducing or even eliminating the necessity for traditional auditing processes, such as those outlined in the Sarbanes-Oxley Act, as well as rendering auditors superfluous. Unlike traditional securities, DAOs function within an ecosystem where trust is expressly and transparently articulated, thus diminishing the imperative need for an identical level of regulatory scrutiny. Even when trust mechanisms like multi-signature schemes are integrated into DAO structures, the inherent transparency of blockchain technology ensures a lucid and all-encompassing comprehension of where trust is positioned. This unique characteristic substantiates the argument against subjecting DAOs to securities laws.

In summary, the interplay between transparency, self-regulation, and DAOs' reliance on transparent on-chain financial records challenges the traditional application of securities laws. Through self-regulation, DAOs can demonstrate their commitment to responsible governance, potentially influencing the regulatory landscape and reducing the need for stringent securities law enforcement within their operations.

c) Bespoke regulation through Safe Harbour regime

Despite industry calls for regulation, the SEC has yet to establish a bespoke regulatory treatment for crypto assets. In addition to self-regulatory approaches, certain regulatory approaches could support DAOs to achieve sufficient decentralization whilst issuing compliant governance tokens to their network. As noted by Hinman, tokens may initially bear resemblance to securities during the early stages of project development due to the active involvement of the Initial Development Team (as previously mentioned in this article). However, subjecting them to extensive registration, reporting, disclosure, and compliance requirements could stifle innovation, as not all early-stage projects can bear such burdensome costs. This aligns with Hinman's perspective that disclosures and investor protection remain crucial for both consumers and investors, and elements of securities law cannot be circumvented purely on technical grounds. Commissioner Pierce's proposal, therefore, introduces this Safe Harbor to facilitate compliance for DAOs seeking to launch tokens.

---

64 *ChainTech/France Digitale*, Toward a Regulatory Framework for Crypto-asset. Available at: http://www.francedigitale.org/actu-europe/europe-est-le-nouveau-icontinent-et-paris-est-place/, Accessed 07 August 2023.

Commissioner Pierce's proposal introduces a safe harbour to facilitate compliance for DAOs looking to launch tokens. She emphasizes the importance of secondary trading for tokens to reach users and provide developers and service providers on the network with a means to exchange tokens for fiat or other cryptocurrencies. This aligns with recent case law in Ripple, where the argument was made that secondary sales of tokens should not be classified as securities offerings. Given that the operation of DAOs initially resembles a security offering, Commissioner Pierce suggests a 3-year exemption period along with a simplified disclosure framework for tokens. This approach reduces compliance burdens for early-stage projects and ensures access to liquidity while maintaining investor protection. It also proposes strengthening protections for token purchasers by requiring semi-annual updates to the development plan, introducing a block explorer, and implementing an "exit report" to formally determine if "sufficient decentralization" has been achieved. Specific guidelines are outlined for the analysis conducted within the exit report to ascertain whether the network has genuinely achieved the desired level of decentralization.

Ultimately, the current SEC's approach limits both DAOs' business opportunities and ability to progressively decentralize, as their governance tokens being classified as a security would complicate investment deals and prohibit many centralized exchanges from listing the token without a specific license and registration process.[65] This is demonstrated by the increasing number of IDTs that decide to geo-block US citizens from their platform.[66] An innovative paper, titled "The Ineluctable Modality of Securities Law: Why Fungible Crypto Assets Are Not Securities," presents a more practical approach.[67] The proposed approach involves separating investment contracts from crypto assets, concluding that the crypto asset itself is not a security. Investment contracts arise when an IDT or DAO participant(s) sell crypto assets to fund project development, but the crypto asset remains distinct from the investment contract. The U.S. District Court of the Southern District of New York ruling re-affirms this view in that a token may not be seen as a security, but the sale of the tokens can be.[68] Applying this approach to the Ethereum ICO, the initial sale would be considered a securities transaction, subject to relevant registration and disclosure requirements, subsequent trading of Ethereum on crypto exchanges or among third parties would not be treated as security transactions.

---

65 *W. Hinman*, (fn. 10), pp. 1–6.

66 *Throuvalas*, ApeCoin Geo-Blocks North American Users From Staking, Available: https://cryptopotato.com/apecoin-geo-blocks-north-american-users-from-staking/, Accessed 23 August 2023.

67 *Cohen/Strong/Gregory/Lewin/Freemann/Chen/Sara*, (fn. 60).

68 *SEC*, Securities and Exchange Commission v. Ripple Labs Inc., 1:20-cv-10832, (S.D.N.Y. Jul 13, 2023) ECF No. 874.

This approach offers simplicity by eliminating complex legal theories, avoids the need for assets to shift their security status over time, and appropriately assigns regulatory responsibility to the SEC for capital-raising activities. It also calls for new legislation to regulate crypto markets, bridging existing regulatory gaps. As a policy recommendation, this novel framework should guide regulators globally and in the U.S. in shaping regulations for the crypto industry and furthermore offers courts a clearer path when dealing with high-stakes securities law cases involving crypto assets. It represents a more coherent alternative to the SEC's current approach, enhancing market participant protection and fostering innovation.

The interplay of economic and legal decentralization presents a challenge, resulting in a chicken-or-the-egg paradox. True economic decentralization may require legal decentralization (use of digital assets), and the use of digital assets necessitates economic and legal decentralization. This paradox underscores the value of a regulatory safe harbor under U.S. securities laws, even if it's applicable briefly during web3 system inception.[69] In the absence of a safe harbor, many web3 systems earnestly pursue progressive decentralization strategies. These typically involve precautions related to digital assets, such as limiting transferability, issuances, and U.S. listings. This approach becomes crucial for systems embracing open decentralization, which relies on fully operational decentralized economies, unlike DeFi protocols using full decentralization models that don't mandate economic decentralization.

Some IDTs are exploring options such as Regulation A[70] and Regulation D[71] exemptions, tokenizing shares, adhering to audited financials, and demonstrating sufficient decentralization through self-regulation and industry-wide standards, to align with regulatory expectations. However, available securities registration and exemption options are likely incompatible or impractical with the effective operation of the DAO itself. In the interim, courts and litigants dealing with crypto asset classification cases should consider this paper's approach. Judge Failla refused to "stretch the federal securities laws to cover the conduct alleged" in the complaint, referring to Bitcoin (BTC) and Ether (ETH) as "commodities," dismissing the plaintiff's Motion to Dismiss. It provides a clearer and more elegant solution without introducing convoluted theories, benefiting pending cases and preserving crypto asset markets and investor value.

[69] *Jennings*, (fn. 32).
[70] 17 C.F.R § 230.251 et seq.
[71] 17 C.F.R, (fn. 70).

3. Legal Decentralization

Compliantly achieving sufficient decentralization through legal decentralization is an important goal for DAOs. During this process, DAOs must overcome a variety of legal issues, including with respect to taxation, liability, employment law, intellectual property, privacy, and more. In the following section, provide an international focus to this process with a focus on EU and US laws to contextualize the global nature of decentralized networks working the technology.

a) Reconciling tax and IP laws with progressively and sufficiently decentralized autonomous organizations

As the DAO ecosystem continues to expand, it becomes increasingly evident that decentralization and anonymization do not provide complete immunity from taxation and legal obligations. DAOs, with their global and decentralized structure, challenge traditional legal principles when it comes to determining their entity status, equity holders, and tax responsibilities. Various factors, including the residency of company founders, jurisdiction of intellectual property (IP) and DeFi platform rights, on-chain operational activities, and employment arrangements, can all carry tax implications in both the U.S. and EU.

An often-underappreciated source of legal risk for DAOs, particularly those lacking decentralization and autonomy, arises from tax law. Some speculate that DAOs might be subject to taxation as pass-through entities, meaning that while the DAO itself remains untaxed, individual members would be liable to pay income taxes on their respective shares of the organization's profits. This raises questions about the legal status of DAOs within existing legal frameworks.

The ongoing debate regarding the definition and differentiation of DAOs from centralized entities underscores the urgent need for a clear tax-related definition. While the U.S. Federal Government has not directly addressed DAO taxation, the "Lummis-Gillibrand Responsible Financial Innovation Act" categorizes DAOs as taxable entities, necessitating registration as LLCs, corporations, or similar entities. States are also exploring legislative measures to clarify the legal status of DAOs. In response to regulatory queries, DAOs employ various legal structures, including legal wrappers and bespoke frameworks, with profound implications for taxation, securities law, and anti-money laundering requirements.[72] True DAOs, exemplified by Bitcoin and Ethereum, pose unique tax questions due to the absence of centralized contractual arrangements. For "true DAOs" like Bitcoin and Ethereum, the situation is more complex, as the

---

[72] *Schwartz,* Squaring the Circle: Smart Contracts and DAOs as Tax EntitiesAvailable at: https://www.friedfrank.com/uploads/siteFiles/Publications/Decentralized%20Autonomous%20Organizations%20_%20Decentralized%20Law.pdf, Accessed 23 September 2023.

absence of a clear contractual arrangement and profit-sharing mechanism challenges their classification as taxable entities under U.S. tax regulations. The classification of these entities as taxable for U.S. tax purposes becomes challenging when there is no clear mechanism for profit division, particularly when DAOs engage workers similarly to traditional businesses. In such cases, obligations such as VAT, social security contributions, tax withholding, tax reporting, and more may apply, creating complexities that DAOs did not initially account for. To mitigate tax risks, DAOs may turn to DAO-adjacent BORGs, provided these entities remain independent from DAOs.

One potential solution is the use of a "full DAO wrapper," which simplifies tax treatment for both wrapped DAOs and their governance token holders. To secure favorable tax treatment, DAOs can utilize DAO-adjacent BORGs, provided these entities are genuinely independent. Careful structuring is essential, as U.S. tax principles prioritize substance over form. Factors such as ownership of assets and management roles can influence the tax classification of DAOs and their members. However, this approach requires disclosure of members' identities and the issuance of annual tax forms limiting the decentralized nature of DAOs.[73]

Throughout a DAO's lifecycle, numerous taxable events can occur, from fundraising to token issuance. The ownership of intellectual property (IP) rights plays a critical role in tax implications, with jurisdiction and asset valuation being significant factors. During the progressive decentralization process IDTs transfer IP to an entity or foundation that functions and operates independently of any central authority as a DAO. Factors such as mission, operational activity and constituency determine the best legal response to the issues a DAO raises. Ownership considerations of the underlying IP platform or blockchain protocol are a key factor in determining whether the operations of the business or a transfer of IP rights will trigger tax implications. IP developed in a specific jurisdiction may trigger tax laws if commercialized or transferred outside the jurisdiction based on factors such as the fair market value or the revenues generated. Likewise, if there is a preference to have the IP held by the DAO or other offshore entity, valuation of the assets to be sold or transferred is part of the strategic planning to determine how best to migrate those assets.[74]

Taxation is not merely an administrative concern but a fundamental component of the legal framework within which DAOs operate. It presents an opportunity for DAOs to engage with regulators and influence the development of tax policies aligned with their decentralized nature. This approach fosters innovation, attracts investments, and establishes a solid foundation for a decentralized

---

[73] *Shapiro,* (fn. 23).

[74] *Ooi/Vincent*, Tax Events in the Life Cycle of Digital Tokens (March 8, 2023). Austaxpolicy.

future. While DAOs and BORGs provide frameworks to potentially avoid tax liabilities, further collaboration with policymakers and regulators is necessary to ensure clarity and compliance. It is proposed that due to this field being a compliant and ongoing area of research and should not be overly regulated until sufficient research is completed.

b) Facilitating Regulatory Equivalency through Self-Regulation

Excessive focus on shoehorning blockchain-based governance into traditional legal systems may risk mialign with the decentralized ethos of these technologies. Instead, self-regulating communities can establish rules and guidelines that align with existing legal frameworks in various jurisdictions. This helps decentralized systems comply with relevant laws and regulations.

Self-regulation often involves decentralized decision-making processes that are transparent and open to the public. This allows participants to collectively determine rules and policies that comply with legal requirements. Potential characteristics of this cryptonative legal system, could include integrate smart contracts and protocols that embed legal requirements on the technology layer. More specifically DAOs could create dispute resolution mechanisms that comply with legal standards, allowing participants to resolve disputes without resorting to traditional legal systems. Some protocols such as Q blockchain are pursuing this by allowing blockchain-based organizations to be connected to on-chain or off-chain dispute resolution.[75]

Self-regulating entities within decentralized systems can implement KYC and AML procedures to verify user identities and prevent illegal activities, in line with financial regulations. A potential trend towards alegal and on-chain enclaves that function as isolated economic entities mirror some of the thoughts in Network States. Within these enclaves, the opportunity arises to create alternative legal frameworks rooted in distinct philosophies of on-chain arbitration. One example highlighted is privacy pool associations, which enable anonymous free association and are conducive to flexible jurisdictional boundaries. These enclaves could give rise to KYC (Know Your Customer), grey, and black markets, each governed by its own set of fundamental legal rights. Grey markets, positioned between the extremes of "anything goes" black market cryptoanarchy and heavily regulated KYC markets, could potentially champion cryptonative rights. If these grey markets unite and gain substantial economic influence, they could exert pressure on KYC markets, advocating for the recognition of cryptonative legal principles and rights. In essence, these grey markets may function as a collective force akin to trade unions, all operating under a com-

[75] Q, Q Constitution. Available from: /https://q.org/files/Q_Constitution.pdf, Accessed 19 September 2023.

mon charter with the goal of safeguarding and advancing crypto native rights in the face of regulatory and jurisdictional challenges.

The industry has already began developing and promoting international standards that facilitate cross-border legal compliance that will eventually allow decentralized systems to operate in multiple jurisdictions. An example of this is seen with the DAO Model Law which seeks to achieve self-regulation through the principle of regulatory equivalent – providing DAOs with a legal framework that takes into consideration their alegal nature and provides legal recognition that aligns registration requirements for corporate entities. While deploying a smart contract on a blockchain might not mirror traditional corporate registration, it can still meet the objectives of transparency and certainty, as blockchain deployment is publicly verifiable. Furthermore, the DAO Model Law outlines specific requirements for DAOs, ensuring that they adhere to principles of transparency, governance, and legal compliance. The goal is of COALA's DAO Model Law is to create a model law that assists states in modernizing their company law frameworks, adapting substantive rules to better accomodate DAOs. This approach aims to depart from traditional corporate structures and consider the unique features of blockchain technology. The objective is to create an independent national legislative model rooted in self-regulation. Importantly, these rules would be adopted solely by the blockchain community, thereby establishing a distinct legal framework for DAOs.

Self-regulation in decentralized systems can help these systems align with legal requirements, protect user rights, and navigate complex legal landscapes while preserving decentralization principles. Even regulators such as the AFME acknowledges that some elements within the decentralized finance (DeFi) sphere may prefer a self-governing model to evade centralization and regulatory intervention. This approach provides a framework for balancing the advantages of decentralized technology with the need to comply with legal standards and regulations. That being said,, it's imperative to delve deeper into how DAOs interface with the regulated financial services sector, especially if they choose to maintain a self-governance approach.

c) DAO legal recognition and definition

In addition to creating a connection between the dapp and the DAO participants, distributing assets and operations, this risk underscores the need for IDTs to adopt bespoke international corporate governance structures. However, the anonymity and decentralized nature of DAOs often create difficulties in identifying which entities or individuals hold power and accountability or make the decisions – especially during the progressive decentralization process.

Although there are numerous DAO legal designs, for increased compliance, the structure executed includes the IDT as a software development company, and the DAO is provided with two legal wrappers, one to launch the token and another to engage with the , connect with the dapp and the DAO participants access to manage off-chain assets such as legal contracts, intellectual property, and operations through on-chain governance. This strategic choice encompasses structures such as those available in the Cayman Islands, the British Virgin Islands (BVI), and Panama.[76] [77]

Furthermore, selected jurisdictions are proactively crafting DAO-specific corporate entities, designed to furnish DAO participants with heightened flexibility and security as they navigate the progressive decentralization journey. This highlights an important difference between these DAO-wrappers and the DAO itself. The concept of exogenous rules creates friction with the apparent alegality of DAOs. The framework of BORGs helps to reconcile this friction. It provides the conceptual logic for DAOs to retain their decentralized and alegal status, while the legal-wrappers, despite raising unwarranted centralization risks, from a commercial and regulatory perspective, these legal-wrappers are a reasoned step towards the DAO actively achieving sufficient decentralization.

The previous section explored how legal analysis by Hinman and evolving case law suggest that achieving sufficient decentralization in DAOs could result in categorizing their governance tokens as non-securities or commodities. However, it remains a question whether attaining legal decentralization would also mitigate the joint and several liability risks faced by DAO participants. Despite these protective measures, the risk persists that the entire DAO entity structure may be construed as an unincorporated partnership. Regardless of whether those structures or legal wrapper are used, MiCA brings a new aspect into this discussion, whether or not the DAO structure is decentralization. Under the MiCA regulation, IDTs pursue sufficient decentralization to avoid arduous compliance costs under the MiCA Regulation. This might certainly be the case, but in many jurisdictions including Germany, DAOs may be considered legal entities if the token holders pursue a common purpose, even if the DAO is not registered with an authority. This issue was examined in the Ooki DAO case, which demonstrated that legal decentralization alone may not exempt DAOs from financial regulation compliance. While it might initially appear contradictory to legal commentary suggesting that legal decentralization should absolve DAOs from the obligation to comply with securities regulations, the applicability of this exemption hinges on the nature of the services offered and whether a traditional law or regulation is breached, effectively limiting the potential of a crypto-native jurisdiction. .

In situations where DAO participants breach legal boundaries or fail to fulfill their legal obligations, the concept of piercing the DAO's legal veil may come

[76] *Wyoming Senate*, Wyoming DAO Act, 2022.
[77] *MRI*, Non-Profit Entities Act. 2021.

into play, as illustrated by the Ooki DAO case. The CFTC based its decision on California legal precedents related to contract and tort law, which hold that individual members of a for-profit unincorporated association can be held personally liable for the association's debts. FTC Commissioner Summer K. Mersinger issued a dissenting statement, criticizing the decision to impose liability on bZx's co-IDTs as "arbitrary" and based on an unsupported legal theory that amounts to regulation through enforcement while federal and state policies are still evolving. As she pointed out, the CFTC can rely on three bases to charge a person with violations of the CEA and CFTC rules committed by another entity: (1) principal-agent liability, (2) aiding-and-abetting liability, and (3) control person liability.

This distinction is further emphasized by cases of DAOs dissolving their legal wrapper once they have reached sufficient decentralization.[78]

The need for global legal recognition and a clear definition for DAOs, along with the attainment of sufficient decentralization, is becoming increasingly evident. To address these challenges, a vital solution emerges: the establishment of a precise definition for DAOs. This definition serves as a fundamental cornerstone upon which regulatory consistency can be constructed.

DAOs, characterized by their decentralization and often the absence of conventional hierarchical structures, had previously operated in a legal gray area. One of the most noteworthy aspects of Judge Pitman's ruling is the recognition of a DAOs as an entity, likening it to the structure of a corporation. This landmark decision could have wide-ranging consequences, affecting how DAOs are treated across various legal contexts, including contracts and tax matters. AFME, for instance, seeks to confer legal status upon DAOs, recognizing that some entities in the DeFi space strive for the highest degree of decentralization and aim to operate without significant regulatory intervention, relying on a self-governing model. However, careful consideration must be given to how a DAO interfaces with the regulated financial services industry in such cases.

In the DAO Model Law's effort to provide DAOs with a legal framework, it contemplates the possibility of granting legal recognition to DAOs. This recognition would entail achieving regulatory equivalence between the registration requirements for traditional corporate entities and the deployment of a DAO's smart contracts on a Permissionless Blockchain. While deploying a smart contract on a blockchain may not be functionally identical to the traditional corporate registration process, it can still accomplish the policy objectives of transparency and certainty, as the deployment is verifiable by the public on the blockchain.

[78] *MakerDAO*, The Maker Foundation Focuses On Its Dissolution (2021), available at https://blog.makerdao.com/the-maker-foundation-focuses-on-its-dissolution/. Accessed 16 August 2023.

Additionally, the concept of "sufficient decentralization" emerges as a crucial factor capable of mitigating both legal liabilities and securities law risks. Upon reaching sufficient decentralization, the governance token will no longer be considered a security, and there would be a removal of the unlimited liability risks as seen with the DAO participants in Ethereum or Bitcoin.[79] Axelsen, Jensen, and Ross process the definition of "sufficient decentralization" as a verifiable state, where (1) the design of the DAO is collusion resistant and based on long-term equilibrium; (2) its governance processes have unrestricted and transparent access.[80] To make this concept effective, it becomes essential to establish a quantitative assessment for determining what qualifies as "sufficient decentralization." While case law has addressed the technical decentralization of DAO software, further exploration is needed, focusing on economic and legal decentralization. Recent work by a16z, Latham and Watkins,[81] and more recent contributions by Hansen and others offer valuable insights at both the legislative and jurisprudential levels.

Achieving a globally agreed-upon definition of sufficient decentralization is vital, but without a universally accepted recognition and definition of DAOs, this could lead to inconsistent treatment of these innovative governance structures, constraining their growth. Safe Harbour Guidelines are crucial to ensuring that DAOs can achieve genuine decentralization while complying with corporate, tax, securities, and other relevant laws. Simultaneously, it is imperative to hold non-compliant DAOs accountable to maintain the integrity of the regulatory framework. As we grapple with the regulatory complexities surrounding DAOs, it becomes clear that the way forward involves defining DAOs, quantifying decentralization, and establishing regulatory equivalences that transcend geographical boundaries. These efforts are instrumental in striking a harmonious balance between innovation and compliance within the rapidly evolving realm of DAOs.

IV. Recommendations for Addressing Legal and Regulatory Challenges

Navigating the complex legal and regulatory landscape surrounding pDAOs requires a multifaceted approach. As an answer to the initial question posed, it is suggested that global policy combines elements of no regulation, self-regulation, and bespoke regulatory frameworks to provide a comprehensive guide for

[79] *Hinman*, (fn. 10), pp. 1–6.

[80] *Axelsen/Jensen/Ross*, (fn. 2). pp. 51–75.

[81] *Latham & Watkins LLP/a16z Crypto*, Decentralization Factors for Token Smart Contract Protocols (2023), available at https://www.sites.lwcommunicate.com/38/14700/landing-pages/rsvp-form-(blank-generic).asp, Accessed 20 September 2023.

shaping the future regulatory environment for DAOs. The following paragraph showcases detailed recommendations.

1. No Regulation

No regulation is often better than bad regulation: While it is crucial to establish some regulatory measures to ensure the safety and security of participants in the cryptocurrency space, maintaining a degree of regulatory flexibility is equally important. Developing a DAO with a crypto-based business model based on smart contracts presents unique challenges. The IDT must strike a delicate balance between addressing traditional business challenges and ensuring that its operations adhere to decentralized principles to avoid regulatory complications. Embracing a "no regulation" stance for specific aspects of DAOs can foster innovation and prevent overly restrictive rules from stifling growth. This approach has been applied within the European Union, the initial draft of the Markets in Crypto Assets (MiCA) regulation included provisions for DAOs but were ultimately omitted from the final version.

Progressive Regulation requires a risk-based approach: The concept of technology-neutral regulation is challenged by blockchain technology and therefore regulatory practices around the decentralization of DAOs must adapt to the different technology layers and business models. As each layer and business model will have its own strengths and weaknesses regarding centralized attack vectors and regulatory importance, it is likely that regulators will assess some DAOs as having greater systemic risk than others. A risk-based approach to DAO supervision, where required, will therefore support a holistic view of decentralization dimensions. [82]

No regulation through enforcement: Due to the lack of clarity on how to regulate all the dimensions of decentralization and the pressing need exists for clear regulations governing the intersection between Decentralized Finance (DeFi) and traditional law, rather than relying on regulation through enforcement, recent cases underscore the need for unambiguous rules. The Risley ruling emphaizses this by asserting "the Court declines to stretch the federal securities laws to cover the conduct alleged, and concludes that Plaintiffs' concerns are better addressed to Congress than to this Court. Furthermore, the dissenting statement in Ooki, stressed that the CFTC seemingly acted outside the scope of its authority in acting in a manner not intended by Congress. It was noted that the CFTC engaging in regulation by enforcement will lead far-reaching policy implications.[83] Although there are still ambiguities in the litigation, it

[82] *Axelsen/Jensen/Ross*, (fn. 2). pp. 51–75.

[83] *Goodwin Law*, Regulation by Enforcement, available at https://www.goodwinlaw.com/en/insights/publications/2023/05/insights-otherindustries-dcb-regulation-by-enforcement, Accessed September 12 2023.

is better to allow the courts and legislators to create appropriate laws rather than relying on regulators that to not have the correctly defined powers.[84]

2. Self-Regulation

Development of industry standards: Formal regulation requiring authorisation to regulated financial activities is important but encouraging self-regulation within the DeFi community and involving industry associations, practice guidelines, any forms of collection action can help to promote industry-led accountability. These voluntary standards should primarily aim to protect market participants rather than serve simply as regulatory tools. From transparency reports, audits disclosures and on-chain dispute resolution, these activities will reduce the risks of decentralization theatre and foster trust among participants and the broader community.

Blockchain-based regulatory tools: Blockchain technology can transform how regulators supervise and enforce regulation. In the realm of regulatory compliance, blockchain innovations, such as zero-knowledge identity proofs, have the potential to streamline Know Your Customer (KYC) and Anti-Money Laundering (AML) checks while preserving user privacy. While on-chain governance offers enhanced participation and binding investor resolutions, it grapples with the imperative of legal compliance. Regulators have expressed openness to utilizing smart contracts to enforce behavioural remedies in competition cases. Leveraging smart contracts for achieving progressive decentralization could become an appealing option in this context.[85] Bridging the gap between technological innovation and regulatory adherence represents a crucial challenge that necessitates exploration.

Blockchain should be perceived as complementary to established legal frameworks rather than as outright replacements. This notion introduces the concept of 'code' as a complement or augmentation to existing legal structures. This paradigm shift has engendered a novel system of private law, characterized by the introduction of code-based regulations that may extend beyond the purview of conventional legal mandates. It is vital to underscore that this phenomenon does not diminish the essential role played by traditional legal systems. Ultimately, achieving a harmonious alignment between code-based regulations and legal frameworks stands as a critical imperative.[86]

---

[84] *Plaintiff*, Risley v. Universal Navigation Inc. et al., 1:22-cv-02780-KPF (S.D.N.Y.) ("Risley").

[85] *Evan Miller*, A Tale of Two Regulators: Antitrust Implications of Progressive Decentralization in Blockchain Platforms, 77 WASH. & LEE L. REV. ONLINE 387 (2021).

[86] *Buterin/Illum/Nadler/Schär/Soleimani,* Blockchain Privacy and Regulatory Compliance: Towards a Practical Equilibrium. (September 6, 2023). Available at SSRN: https://ssrn.com/abstract=4563364 or http://dx.doi.org/10.2139/ssrn.4563364, Accessed 20 September 2023.

3. Regulation

Industry collaboration and harmonization: Ensuring that there is limited fragmentation of laws and reduced forum shopping will be important to achieving a progressive regulatory approach with steps towards this seen in transnational crypto regulation such as the European Union's MiCA.[87] A key element of this process is building foundational taxonomy for DAOs and the different decentralization dimensions. The UK government's has attempted to achieve this through consultant processes with industry to understand digital property rights, the legal implications of smart contracts, and the integration of DAOs into jurisdictional frameworks demonstrate a commitment to reducing excessive legislation while learning from the industry and promoting innovation. However, in ISCSO's recent policy paper completed in collaboration with internation regulators, the industry was not involved in the consoltuion process.[88] Further research and global cooperation should be encouraged to determine the appropriate, proportionate, and comprehensive regulatory solutions for the unique challenges posed by DAO.

DAO-Specific Laws: It was not in this papers scope to exhaustively discuss all the relevant legal and regulatory issues that DAO face when decentralizing i. e. employment and data protection laws. It will be important to take these into consideration when developing comprehensive DAO-specific legislation that provides clarity on the operational framework of these entities. This includes the promotion of regulatory global uniformity by adopting industry-developed frameworks like the DAO Model Law. By striving for global recognition of DAOs through international agreements, similar to the Hague Trust Convention, an international framework for DAOs could be built to facilitate their recognition and address the joint and several liability issues that exist on a global scale.

A Grace period for DAO seeking sufficient decentralization: By support for a 'Level Playing Field' and working towards consistent regulation despite varying levels of centralisation. It is crucial to recognize the substantial difference between progressively and sufficiently decentralized organizations, as outlined in the Hinman case. This concept of sufficient decentralization is seen not only in the US but also in the EU where Recital 12a7 of the regulation treats decentralized activity similarly to the approach in the United States, allowing regulated activity for entities that are deemed "sufficiently decentralized." A quantitative approach that allows DAOs to be audited for their level of decen-

---

[87] https://www.esma.europa.eu/press-news/esma-news/esma-seeks-first-input-detailed-rules-crypto-markets

[88] *IOSCO*, Policy Recommendations for Decentralized Finance (DeFi) Consultation Report Available: https://www.iosco.org/library/pubdocs/pdf/IOSCOPD744.pdf, Accessed September 6 2023.

tralization would be vital and could be clarified through regulatory technical standards.

In the mean time, there would need to be regulation that supports DAOs who are moving in the process of progressive decentralization by introducing a grace period from a risk-based perspective. This would once again allowi the EU to align with proposed safe harbour proposals from the US which could require authorisation prior to conducting regulated financial activities; support DAOs developing correct legal and accountability frameworks and remove certain legal risks for IDTs.

V. Conclusion: Balancing Progressive Decentralization with Regulation for DAOs

With the increasing certainty on the regulation of crypto, the number of DAOs will likely continue to evolve, and the growth of the token economy and innovation of blockchain-based business models as well.[89]The trajectory of progressive decentralization for DAOs necessitates a nuanced regulatory approach that strikes a delicate balance between compliance and the preservation of foundational principles. As these autonomous entities redefine how we organize, collaborate, and govern in the digital era, it becomes imperative to adopt a regulatory framework that accommodates innovation while addressing legal complexities.

Progressive decentralization represents the evolutionary journey undertaken by DAOs, transitioning from centralized origins to enhanced decentralization over time. This distinction holds immense significance in the legal domain, determining the legal status, liability, and recognition of DAOs. Regulatory authorities worldwide diverge in their approaches to progressive decentralization, with some favouring permissive stances acknowledging the gradual nature of decentralization, while others exercise caution, imposing stringent criteria for legal recognition.[90] DAOs grapple with the complex issue of unincorporated risks, arising from the development of technology layers and operational businesses. These challenges, stemming from on-chain and off-chain elements, underscore the need for comprehensive regulatory frameworks. The paper frameworks three regulatory approaches: no regulation, self-regulation, and bespoke regulation.

Adapting to evolving regulations while preserving decentralization principles is crucial for the DAO community. DeFi's impact on regulations necessitates distinctions between regulated and non-regulated entities within the DAO

[89] *Axelsen/Jensen/Ross*, (fn. 2). pp. 51–75.
[90] *IOSCO*, (fn. 88).

sphere. This is further exacerbated by DAOs frequently operating across multiple jurisdictions with different views on decentralization, resulting in the matter becoming a topic of strategic importance as the uncertainty hinders investments, which impacts the competing growth and innovation objectives mentioned earlier. There is clearly scope for alignment with the EU Council's negotiation mandate, treating decentralized activity in a manner similar to the US: "This regulation applies to natural and legal persons and the activities and services performed, provided or controlled in any manner, directly or indirectly, by them, including when part of such activity or services is performed in a decentralized way."[91] Furthermore, to enable DAOs to flourish globally, an international framework akin to the Hague Trust Convention can address jurisdictional complexities. However, the question of the extent of decentralization required remains to be solved. As there is no definition of "sufficiently decentralized" proposed, nor is there, like in the US, any proposal of allowing a grace period for DAOs to mature to any given level of "sufficient decentralization",[92] such will likely have to evolve through regulatory technical standards set by the EU financial regulators.[93]

The future of DAOs lies at the intersection of innovation and regulation. Embracing elements of no regulation, self-regulation, and thoughtful legislation paves the way for a solid regulatory approach. In this ever-evolving landscape, DAOs have the potential to revolutionize interactions, transactions, and governance while contributing positively to the global economy. Balancing these elements will be crucial in ensuring the success and responsible growth of DAOs in the digital age.

---

[91] *Council of the European Union*, Proposal for a Regulation of the European Parliament and of the Council on Markets in Crypto-assets, and amending Directive (EU) 2019/1937, vol. 2021, no. November, pp. 1–405, 2021.

[92] *Peirce,* (fn. 6), pp. 1–7.

[93] *Alvesson/Sandberg*, Generating Research Questions through Problematization, Academy of Management Review, vol. 36, no. 2, 2013. A.

When is a DAO Decentralized?*

Henrik Axelsen, Johannes Rude Jensen, and Omri Ross

Abstract Decentralized autonomous organizations (DAO) have grown tremendously in recent years, spurred by the growth of decentralized financial (DeFi) applications. With the increasing importance of DeFi and distributed ledger technologies (DLT) in financial services, global regulators increasingly voice the intent to regulate these activities, resulting in a significant compliance burden for DAOs, unless they are deemed "sufficiently" decentralized. In this paper, we investigate dimensions of decentralization through thematic analysis, leveraging the extant literature and expert interviews. We propose a definition of "sufficient decentralization" and present a pragmatic assessment framework artifact to enable DAO communities, regulators, and other stakeholders to develop a view of whether a DAO is sufficiently decentralized. We propose five aggregate dimensions that we consider critical for assessing the decentralization of any DAO. Based on publicly available information, we evaluate the artifact by assessing the level of decentralization of a prominent DAO. We extrapolate our findings into five general propositions on the implications of the supervision of regulated financial activity in crypto. Our findings contribute new practical insights on the topic of compliance and decentralized organizations to the growing DLT discourse in information systems and management disciplines. Further, we contribute to the growing regulatory discourse in decentralized finance by proposing a methodology for regulatory compliance assessment.

I. Introduction

In financial markets, regulatory objectives traditionally focus on (1) proper functioning and integrity of markets, (2) financial stability, (3) protecting the collective interests of consumers and investor protection, while also (4) aiming to reduce criminal activity and (5) preserving monetary sovereignty.

---

* Originally published by the authors in Complex Systems Informatics and Modeling Quarterly no. 31, 2022, 51 f.

The authors wish to thank the anonymous reviewers as well as Danny Dehghani, Jon Isaksen, Michael Zargham, Griff Green, Angela Kreitenweis, Nina Siedler, Marina Markezic, Kris Paruch, and Matthew Barlin for their valuable insights and feedback

The crypto economy has experienced rapid growth in recent years, amounting to USD 3 Trillion in late 2021.[1] Due to its open-source nature, the sector is subject to high competition and enables decentralized finance (DeFi). DeFi replicates traditional financial services; hence the industry is becoming increasingly important to regulators.[2,3]

The crypto economy operates on permissionless blockchain technology. Regulators see this technology as imperative to innovation, growth, and global competitiveness. While crypto remains primarily unregulated, regulators across the globe are motivating and implementing crypto regulation to meet the challenge of ensuring consumer protection, innovation, and growth without stifling innovation.[4,5]

In recent years, scholars from a wide variety of disciplines have found a shared interest in examining the implications of the technical properties of blockchain technology in their fields. Concepts such as the self-enforcement and formalization of rules, automatization, decentralization of authority, transparent execution of business processes, and codification of trust appear to be conducive to wide-ranging theoretical and industrial innovation.

While there are multiple working definitions of the concept of decentralized autonomous organization (DAO) in industry, most take the form of fluid organizations or loosely organized communities, self-directed and governed through smart contracts without the presence of central authority or a managerial hierarchy.[6],[7]

DAO tends to operate through bottom-up interaction and coordination among a set of independent and distributed rational agents. This has increased interest in how DAOs can mitigate principal-agent problems and reduce misconduct by improving[8] through shifting power dynamics. Some observers compare DAOs to nation-states rather than traditional organizations.[9] In this analogy, the formal (on-chain) smart contracts are comparable to a "computational constitution." At the same time, cultures are nurtured through communication emerging around the design, development, and maintenance of the products governed by the DAO.

---

[1] Global Cryptocurrency Market Charts|CoinMarketCap. https://coinmarketcap.com/charts/. Accessed on Jul. 24, 2022.

[2] European Comission Digital Finance Strategy for the EU J. Chem. Inf. Model, 2020, 1689f.

[3] Financial Stability Board Statement on International Regulation and Supervision of Crypto-asset Activities, 2022.

[4] Lummis-Gillibrand Responsible Financial Innovation Act, 2022, 1f.

[5] European Parliament EU parliament report on MiCA, 2022.

[6] *Hassan/De Filippi* Internet Policy Rev., vol. 10, no. 2, 2021, 1f.

[7] *Schirrmacher/Jensen/Avital* 42nd Int. Conf. Inf. Syst. ICIS 2021

[8] *Kaal* 2020 https://wulfkaal.medium.com/daos-governance-legal-design-experimentation-25b2d0f58a29. Accessed on Jul. 24, 2022.

[9] *Voshmgir/Zargham*, Foundations of Cryptoeconomic Systems, 2020.

While Ethereum remains the dominating network, DAOs are now proliferating across blockchains, facilitated by innovation in the underlying infrastructure. There are currently some 5 000 individual DAOs, counting more than 1.7m token holders, and some 700 000 active voting members.[10]

Implementing regulatory objectives imposes a high compliance burden for industry participants[11] in traditional finance. For European actors, the total cost of compliance ranges between 2 and 25 % of total operating expenses, depending on the size and complexity of the institution.[12,13]

Being subjected to traditional financial institutions' comparatively strict compliance requirements may prove challenging, if not impossible, for DAOs as they are designed today. Regulatory compliance imposes capital and liquidity requirements, strong centralized controls and separation of functions, management hierarchies, and complicated reporting.

Hence, if existing regulation is applied without scrutiny, the novel and poorly defined concept of a DAO may give rise to both conventional and emerging regulatory risks. A key driver among these risks is the prevailing ideological assumption that for regulation to have an effect, a subject in the form of a legal or physical person is required to be held accountable for obligations arising from DAO activities, including those related to regulated financial activities.

Recently, global regulators indicated that the issuance of crypto assets, which may otherwise be subject to compliance requirements, may be exempt if distributed by an entity predominantly or exclusively operating as a 'decentralized entity.[14,15]

Yet, none of the proposals published to date offer a working definition of what might constitute 'sufficient decentralization.'

As follows, designing a decentralized crypto-based business model based on "smart contracts" is complicated: In addition to the usual challenges in finding product market fit, product leadership, sales, recruitment, development, and scaling, founders must seek to operate their projected business in a decentralized manner or risk negative regulatory implications.[16]

While founders may opt for the 'Nakamoto model'[17] and operate in full anonymity, secondary service providers required to fund and execute a project are

---

[10] DeepDAO. Available: https://deepdao.io/organizations. Accessed on Jul. 24, 2022.

[11] *Walden*, Progressive Decentralization : A Playbook for Building Crypto Applications, 2020, 1 f.

[12] European Commission, Study on the costs of compliance for the financial sector, 2019.

[13] EBA, Study of the Cost of Compliance with Supervisory Reporting Requirements. 2021.

[14] European Parliament, EU parliament report on MiCA, 2022.

[15] *Hinman*, Digital Asset Transactions : When Howey Met Gary (Plastic), 2018, 1f

[16] *Walden*, Progressive Decentralization : A Playbook for Building Crypto Applications, 2020, 1 f.

[17] *Nakamoto*, Transform. Gov. People, Process Policy, vol.15, no. 4, 2009, 580 f.

also subject to regulation. Consequently, fully anonymous (anon) stakeholders may find themselves operating in a vacuum, with limited access to ancillary services.

This article asks the following research question: '*When is a DAO (sufficiently) decentralized?*' We present an artifact designed to assess the level of decentralization in any given DAO across several dimensions. We seek to contribute new practical and actionable insights on the topic of decentralized organizations to the growing distributed ledger technology (DLT) discourse in the information systems and management disciplines. Further, we contribute to the growing regulatory discourse in crypto assets and decentralized finance by providing a pragmatic assessment tool for regulatory compliance assessment.

II. Background

1. Blockchain Technology and "Decentralized Autonomous Organizations"

Blockchain is a subset of DLT where transactions are recorded through immutable cryptographic signatures. A blockchain's primary function is maintaining an append-only ledger in a peer-to-peer network,[18] using a consensus mechanism to validate transactions. Permissionless blockchains are decentralized computer networks that maintain a single global version of a shared database and a shared account ledger that is visible to all stakeholders.[19] Permissionless blockchains are open, so anyone can join, leave, read, and write as they please. No central party authorizes access, and its cryptographic primitives ensure collusion resistance.[20] Bitcoin[21] and Ethereum[22] are important instances of permissionless blockchains.

DeFi apps are financial solutions built with "smart contracts" operating through permissionless blockchain technology.

Smart contracts are scripts that automatically carry out specific business logic. Financial services or products created as smart contracts work autonomously without the need for monitoring or intervention from the software developers who originally designed the application due to the deterministic characteristics of the underlying blockchain.

This means that, as long as the blockchain is active, a smart contract will execute business logic unconditionally and irreversibly.[23] Typically, a smart con-

[18] *Kolb/Abdelbaky/Katz/Culler*, ACM Comput. Surv., vol. 53, no. 1, 2020, 1f.

[19] *Jensen/von Wachter/Ross*, Complex Syst.Informatics Model. Q., no. 26, 2021, 46f.

[20] *Wüst/Gervais*, Crypto Valley Conference on Blockchain Technology (CVCBT), 2018, 45f.

[21] *Nakamoto*, Transform. Gov. People, Process Policy, vol.15, no. 4, 2009, 580f.

[22] *Wood*, Ethereum Proj. Yellow Paper, 2014, 1f.

[23] *Beck/Müller-Bloch*, J. Assoc. Inf. Syst., vol. 19, no. 10, 2018.

tract will carry out a set of instructions that allow participants to lend or swap an underlying base asset or other financial assets that have been 'tokenized'.[24] DAOs utilize these properties to create rules-based organizations, in which they make decisions instituted in code. A DAO will typically consist of multiple interacting smart contracts responsible for different parts of the DAO, including treasury management, the tallying of votes, and the token itself. All these smart contracts are deployed on the blockchain and maintained as stateful applications. Both users and smart contracts are represented by addresses and compute transactions in the database containing instructions on how to change the state. Transactions emitted to the network are then sequenced in blocks and circulated with the network, at which point a global state-change is enacted.

To illustrate the above, in Figure 1 we present a layered taxonomy in which the *protocol layer* represents the consensus model determining the logic by which blocks are generated and distributed; the *application layer* represents the virtual machine in which smart contracts are deployed, and the *interface* and *user* layers represent the web-based interface through which users can create and sign transactions.

When a user participates in DAO voting, this process is carried out through one or more transactions in which the user (1) maintains a balance of governance tokens on an address to which they control the private keys and (2) connects their wallet to sign a message or a transaction, enabling them to signal their approval or dismissal of a governance proposal.

While there are multiple ways to implement this logic, the leading solutions rely either on the collection of off-chain signatures through a voting interface (User A) or the direct collection of votes and implementation of pre-deployed code changes by the DAO contract (User B).

In response to voter apathy, DAOs may implement the option for vote-delegation. This is typically carried out directly in the token contract and implemented as a feature in which a token holder can assign the voting power associated with their balance to a third-party address without losing custody of the tokens.

[24] *Ross/Jensen/Asheim*, 40th Int. Conf. Inf. Syst. ICIS, 2019, 1 f.

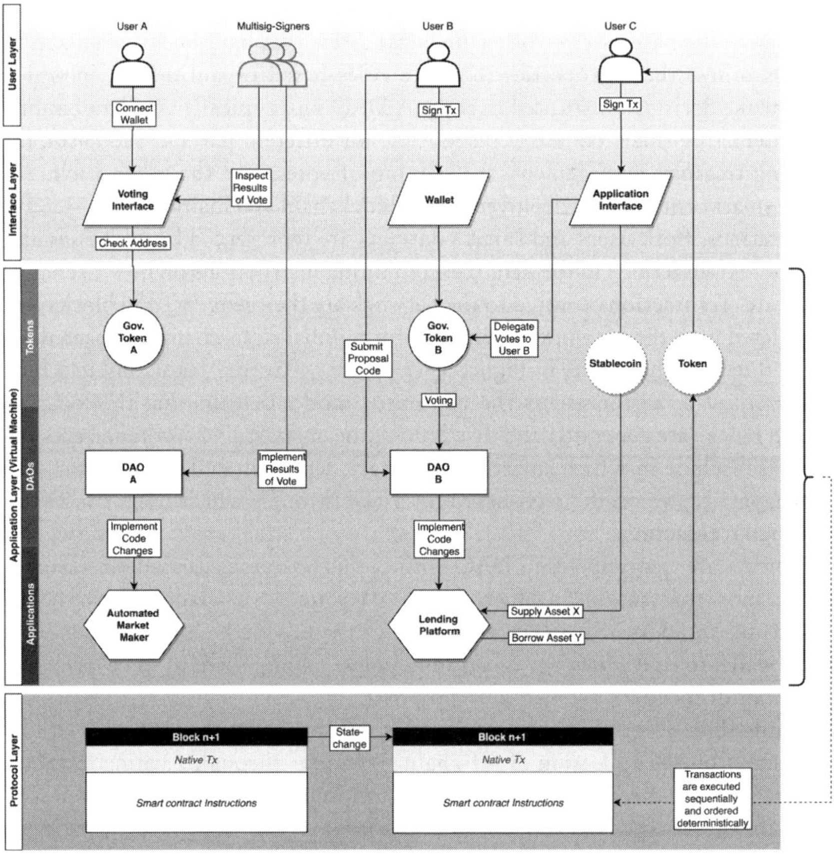

Figure 1. Blockchain, application layer, and users

2. *The Problem of Defining Decentralization within a Regulatory Context*

DAOs are mostly designed and instantiated by a small group of individuals who distribute power and control governance, with a promise to decentralize the governance process at some defined later stage.[25]

Without legal recognition, most jurisdictions today may simply treat unregistered DAOs as unincorporated general partnerships, resulting in community members having personal, joint, and several liability for debts or legal actions arising from operating the DAO.

Increasingly, therefore, DAOs establish themselves with 'legal wrappers' to protect DAO participants from unlimited liability, optimize tax treatment or

[25] *Wright,* IEEE Trans.Technol. Soc., vol. 2, no. 1, 2021, 43 f.

engage in contractual 'off-chain' transactions, even if not focused on regulatory compliance expectations and 'sufficient decentralization'.[26]

Because the common instantiation method is centralized from a design perspective, such a 'wrapper' constitutes incorporation. It relates only to the autonomy and legal capacity of the organization, which technically does not prevent the concept of decentralization. Yet, DAOs that operate using a governance token, issued with a 'reasonable expectation of profits to be derived from the entrepreneurial efforts of others,' are likely to be considered to undertake regulated financial activity.[27]

Some scholars propose that a DAO, like autonomy classification for land and maritime environments,[28] be considered autonomous to the extent that it can legally accept liability.[29] In practice, the level of autonomy and anonymity can vary, but a DAO is normally self-directed through voting on- and off-chain; it can be financial or non-financial in purpose, but the traditional legal system seems secondary to its existence and purpose.[30]

In 2018, a US Securities and Exchange Commission (SEC) representative suggested that contractual and technical ways exist to structure digital assets, so they function more like consumer items or community enablers and less as regulated securities. At the same time, it was suggested that a security could become 'sufficiently decentralized' over time so that it no longer is a security token under the so-called Howey test.[31] Since then, likely accelerated by the increasing success of DeFi, regulators across the globe have increasingly looked to regulate DeFi and DAOs, and uncertainty has prevailed.

Efforts to regulate DAOs as limited liability companies have emerged.[32,33] More recently, progressive senators in the US are working on regional regulation of DAOs, yet this is still early draft, subject to extensive negotiations of political views.[34]

As the first major region attempting to regulate crypto assets at the supranational level, the EU bloc emerged in 2020 with a digital finance package. The EU draft regulation included DAOs in the negotiation phase[35] with legal identity and limited liability for the community members. However, it was omitted in the final version of the regulation, called the Markets in Crypto Asset (MiCA) regulation, approved in principle on June 30, 2022.

---

[26] *Brummer/Seira*, Legal Wrappers and DAOs ! SSRN, 2022, 1 f.
[27] *Hinman*, Digital Asset Transactions : When Howey Met Gary (Plastic), 2018, 1 f.
[28] *Myhre/Hellandsvik/Petersen*, Journal of Physics: Conference Series, vol. 1357, 2019.
[29] *Wright*, IEEE Trans.Technol. Soc., vol. 2, no. 1, 2021, 43 f.
[30] *Myhre/Hellandsvik/Petersen*, Journal of Physics: Conference Series, vol. 1357, 2019.
[31] *Hinman*, Digital Asset Transactions : When Howey Met Gary (Plastic), 2018, 1 f.
[32] Wyoming Senate, Wyoming DAO Act, 2022.
[33] MRI, Non-Profit Entities Act, 2021.
[34] Lummis-Gillibrand Responsible Financial Innovation Act, vol. 2022, 1 f.
[35] European Parliament, EU parliament report on MiCA, 2022.

Much remains to clarify how DAOs will eventually become regulated, likely through a global policy setter, given the nature of DLT and the world-wide-web. At the time of writing, the final MiCA text is not published. Still, based on the EU Council's negotiation mandate, the regulation appears to treat decentralized activity in a manner similar to the US: 'This regulation applies to natural and legal persons and the activities and services performed, provided or controlled in any manner, directly or indirectly, by them, including when part of such activity or services is performed in a decentralized way...Where crypto assets have no offer or and are not traded in a trading platform which is considered to be operated by a service provider, the provisions of (this regulation, ed.) do not apply.'[36] (recital 12a).

This EU regulation appears to align with the global trend that certain crypto assets may become exempt from specific compliance requirements, even if constituting an activity that might otherwise be a regulated financial activity. But the question of the extent of decentralization required remains to be solved. As there is no definition of 'sufficiently decentralized' proposed, nor is there, like in the US, any proposal of allowing a grace period for DAOs to mature to any given level of 'sufficient decentralization',[37] such will likely have to evolve through regulatory technical standards set by the EU financial regulators. Combined, the typology suggests overlapping assumptions open for problematization.[38]

This is further exacerbated by DAOs frequently operating across multiple jurisdictions with different views on decentralization, resulting in the matter becoming a topic of strategic importance as the uncertainty blocks investments, which impacts the competing growth and innovation objectives mentioned earlier.

3. Arriving at a Working Definition for Decentralization

The notion of 'decentralization' has its origins in political science and, in the present time, generally refers to the dispersion or distribution of functions and powers. Without an understanding of the powers of different stakeholders, where and how they exercise their powers, and to whom and how they are accountable, it is difficult to understand whether decentralization is taking place.[39]

The concept of decentralization has been applied mainly within the government of nation-states and political science,[40] administration,[41] fiscal area,[42] and

[36] Council of the European Union, Proposal for a Regulation of the European Parliament and of the Council on Markets in Crypto-assets, and amending Directive (EU) 2019/1937, vol. 2021, no. November, 1 f.

[37] *Peirce,* Token Safe Harbor Proposal 2, SEC, 2021, 1 f.

[38] *Alvesson/Sandberg*, Academy of Management Review, vol. 36, no. 2, 2013.

[39] *Agrawal/Ribot*, J. Dev. Areas, vol. 33, no. 4, 1999, 473 f.

[40] *Treisman*, The Architecture of Government, 2007.

[41] *Hutchcroft*, Governance, vol. 14, no. 1, 2001, 23 f.

[42] *Blackorby/Brett*, J. Econ. Theory, vol. 92, no. 2, 2000, 300 f.

environment,[43] but also across a diverse range of disciplines, such as complex systems engineering,[44] space safety engineering,[45] cybernetics,[46] management science,[47] economics around principal agent theory,[48] finance,[49] law and technology,[50] crypto-economic systems[51] and more.

Within the nascent literature on crypto, the most applied definition of decentralization was proposed by Ethereum co-founder Vitalik Buterin with the introduction of the term 'DAO' in 2013.[52]

Here, decentralization is presented as a response to the latent issues of centralized systems, to which decentralized systems can introduce fault tolerance and deter attacks or collusion. In a later publication,[53] Buterin suggested that decentralization be viewed across several dimensions: (1) An architectural dimension as in how many computers the system is made up of; (2) a political dimension as in how many controls those computers; and (3) a logical dimension as in how the interface and data structures add up.

Some scholars and practitioners suggest that decentralization is a misleading term, as it has a slightly negative connotation, and no large-scale social, economic, or political institution can be fully decentralized and automated without human intervention. Decentralization is then considered more specific to an activity, not to an organization design dimension; instead, we might consider using collaborative models.[54]

It follows that measuring decentralization is complicated; 'A true assessment of the degree of decentralization in (a country) can be made only if a comprehensive approach is adopted, and rather than trying to simplify the syndrome of characteristics into the single dimension of autonomy, interrelationships of various dimensions of decentralization are taken into account.'[55,56]

We propose that "sufficient decentralization" is defined as a verifiable state, where (1) the design of the DAO is collusion-resistant and based on long-term equilibrium; (2) its governance processes have unrestricted and transparent access.

---

[43] *Larson/Ribot*, Eur. J. Dev. Res., vol. 16, no. 1, 2004.
[44] *Siljak*, Decentralized control of complex systems. Vol. 1, 1991.
[45] *Levenson*, Engineering a Safer World, 2012.
[46] *Zargham/Nabben*, Aligning 'Decentralized Autonomous Organization' to Precedents in Cybernetics, SSRN, 2022.
[47] *Richardson/Vandenberg/Blum/Roman*, Journal of Management, vol. 28, no. 2, 2002, 217f.
[48] *Bergman/Lane*, Journal of Theoretical Politics, vol. 2, no. 3, 1990.
[49] *Nakamoto*, Transform. Gov. People, Process Policy, vol. 15, no. 4, 2009, 580f.
[50] *Wright/De Filippi*, Decentralized Blockchain Technology and the Rise of Lex Cryptographia, SSRN, 2015.
[51] *Voshmgir/Zargham*, Foundations of Cryptoeconomic Systems, 2020.
[52] *Buterin*, Ethereum Found. Blog, 2014, 1f.
[53] *Buterin*, The Meaning of Decentralization 2017.
[54] *Voshmgir*, 'Decentralisation' is a misleading term, Pre-print, 2022, 4f.
[55] *Sharma*, The Indian Journal of Political Science, vol. 67, no. 1, 2006, 49f.
[56] OECD/Korea Institute of Public Finance, OECD Fiscal Federalism Studies, 2013.

III. Methodology

This article follows an inductive approach to framework development.[57] We chose thematic analysis as a method to reflect and unravel the surface of the 'reality' of DAO decentralization[58] through interviews and literature review. We analyzed the data in six phases: (1) familiarize yourself with the data, (2) generate initial codes, (3) search for themes, (4) review themes, (5) define and name themes, and (6) produce the report.

We chose an explorative, qualitative research approach to identify the relevant dimensions of decentralization in a DAO. We conducted semi-structured, open-ended expert interviews to identify possible themes to supplement literature review findings.

Potential interviewees were approached through contacts from ongoing token engineering projects. We conducted eight interviews with experienced DAO experts and stakeholders (Table 1), each lasting 45–60 minutes.

At the beginning of each interview, we ensured proper consent and confidentiality. We used an interview guide[59] with 10 open questions probing the interviewees' perspectives on aspects of the structural elements of a DAO (decentralized, autonomous, organization) and additional dimensions for assessing decentralization specifically. Interviews were recorded and transcribed, amounting to 82 pages of transcripts and notes.

DAO Expert	*Expert role*	*DAO experience*
E1	Complex Systems Architect and Designer	6 years
E2	Cryptoeconomist, token engineer, ecosystem designer	4 years
E3	Engineer, Data Scientist, DAO advisor	5 years
E4	Founder, DAO ecosystem tooling	4 years
E5	Serial entrepreneur, Co-founder misc DAOs	8 years
E6	Lawyer, Specialist in DLT/Blockchain projects	5 years
E7	Lawyer, Crypto Asset Specialist/DeFi legal expert	5 years
E8	Lawyer, DeFi specialist, National regulatory body	5 years

Table 1. Overview of Interviewees

Although mainly conducted through one-to-one interviews in search of the 'decentralization surface' of DAOs and with unclear requirements from the outset,

[57] *Nickerson/Varshney/Muntermann*, European Journal of Information Systems, vol. 22, no. 3, 2013, 336f.
[58] *Braun/Clarke*, Qualitative Research in Psychology, vol. 3, no. 2, 2006, 77f.
[59] *Iyamu*, Educ. Inf.Technol., vol. 23, no. 5, 2018, 2249f.

our search process matches elements of a design science research (DSR) method,[60] where the artifact design process informed an iterative process with stakeholders, leading to the final result. Our approach is summarized in Figure 2:

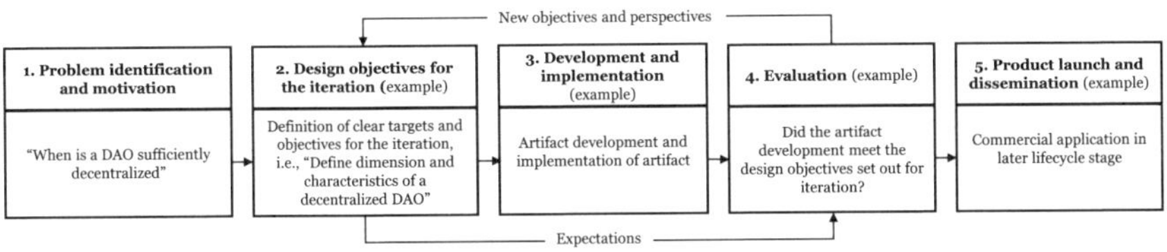

Figure 2. Our search process outline

After (1) reviewing transcripts and notes from interviews, we (2) extracted dimensions of decentralization and aligned them to the literature on DAOs and DeFi manually. The unit of analysis was the practices conducted by DAO communities, the subsystems used to perform these, and the technical infrastructure supporting them. All three authors were involved in the data analysis. As two authors were involved in the data collection, the third author maintained distance and acted as a devil's advocate to ensure the analysis remained objective and independent of our preconceptions and the interviewees' views.[61]

As each expert had their own practical experience from working with DAOs, we first conducted a within-case analysis to gain familiarity with the data and generate a preliminary theory; then, we examined the data for cross-case patterns.[62] The coding procedure comprised several rounds of analysis and refinements of the codes. The topic of decentralization is multi-dimensional and complicated, having to determine the primary angle of analysis either by business subsystem, policy, or technical architectural dimension. During this procedure, we gradually moved from an inductive to an abductive approach,[63] using labels to categorize the interviewee-specific language and grouping similar ones.

Our data sampling strategy remained open to new theoretical insights on what constitutes decentralization.[64] In (3) the search for themes, we clustered initial 52 first-order concepts across 7 DAO subsystems, 4 policy dimensions, and 4 technical architectural layers, further (4)(5) synthesizing these into 15 second-order themes across 5 aggregate dimensions. As we analyzed the data and generated theoretical concepts, we cross-referenced our findings with the extant literature in an iterative process to align our findings.

---

60 *Gregor/Hevner*, MISQ, vol. 37, no. 2, 2013, 337 f.
61 *Gioia/Corley/Hamilton*, Organ. Res. Methods, vol. 16, no. 1, 2013, 15 f.
62 *Eisenhardt*, Acad. Manag. Rev., vol. 14, no. 4, 1989, 532 f.
63 *Gioia/Corley/Hamilton*, Organ. Res. Methods, vol. 16, no. 1, 2013, 15 f.
64 *Urquhart/Lehmann/Myers*, Inf. Syst. J., vol. 20, no. 4, 2010, 357 f.

Our literature review followed a 'light approach'[65] where we developed the research protocol, defined – and refined – the research question, and added criteria for DAO research while focusing mainly on decentralization and acknowledging related characteristics to autonomy and organization. The DAO subsystems were identified using a DAO reference model.[66] Still, as the framework should satisfy regulatory and supervisory expectations of a risk-based approach, we also investigated a technical reference model proposed by regulators.[67]

Once we had derived the first-order concepts, second-order themes, and aggregate dimensions, we built the data structure as appears in Figures 3a and 3b below.

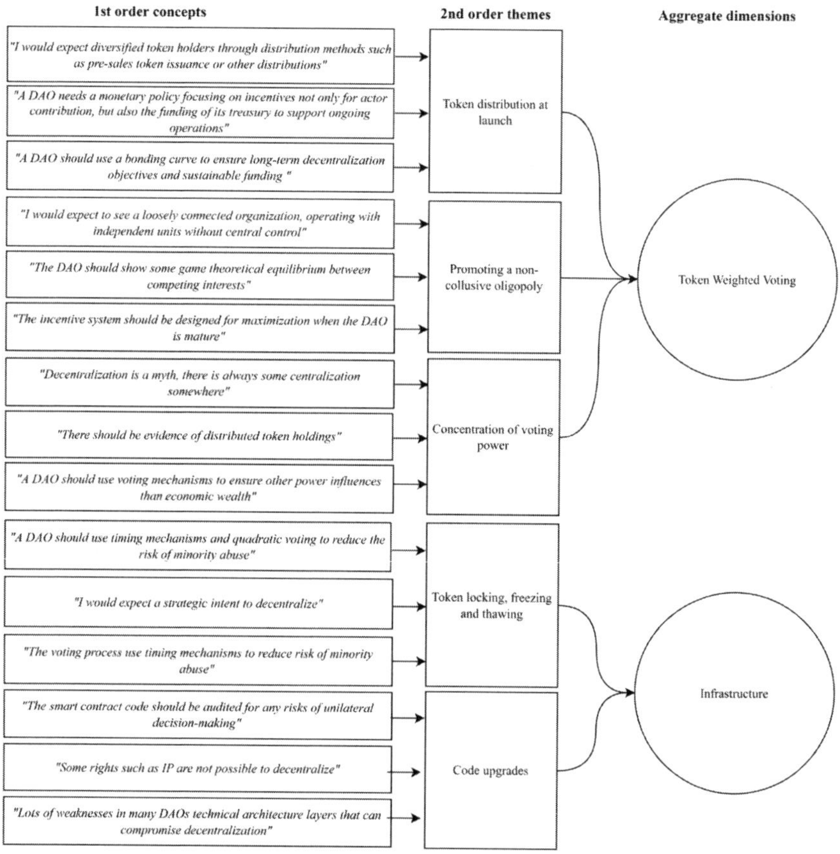

Figure 3a. Coding of data to themes (1 of 2)

[65] *Iyamu*, Educ. Inf. Technol., vol. 23, no. 5, 2018, 2249f.

[66] *Wang/Ding/Li/Yuan/Ouyang/Wang*, IEEE Trans. Comput. Soc. Syst., vol. 6, no. 5, 2019, 870f.

[67] *Schär*, Fed. Reserve Bank St. Louis Rev., vol. 103, no. 2, 2021, 153f.

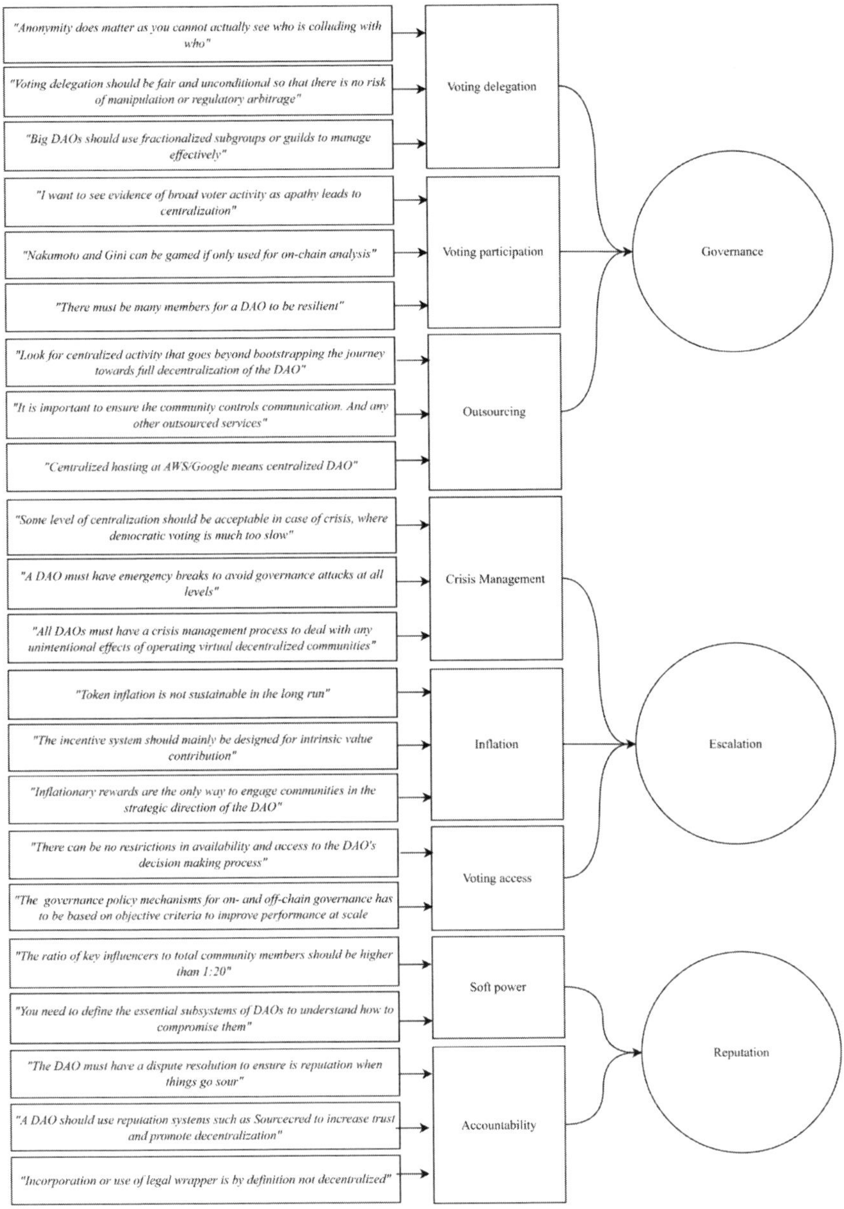

Figure 3b. Coding of data to themes (2 of 2)

The artifact was evaluated ex-ante by a representative from a regulator to ensure a level of alignment to regulatory expectations of the framework artifact.

IV. Introducing "TIGER" Assessment Framework

The proposed artifact comprises a generalized DAO score-card evaluation framework. The framework facilitates a directional analysis of critical DAO components from a systems perspective, where compromising one subsystem may compromise the entire system.[68,69]

In the output component, we leverage traditional supervisory methods[70] and aim to score and consolidate each characteristic to generate an assessment score for each critical dimension that may affect the entire DAO level of decentralization if compromised. The central assessment approach is to which extent, on each dimension and its characteristics, we observe evidence of independent groups of agents operating under mandates without any centralized element of control.

The assessment is designed for point-in-time. Thus, no 'safe harbor' assessment component is included, which could be relevant depending on the specifics of the DAO in question. We have, however, aimed to integrate strategic intent to allow a 'grace period' to impact the scores. The actual application of scores requires some calibration and further consultations across DAOs and jurisdictions to evolve into a regulatory technical standard.

1. A Taxonomy of Agents in a DAO

Permissionless blockchains are essentially a vast network of databases maintaining a shared space. Transactions are batched and circulated with the network in the form of blocks which, once accepted by the network, amend the database with the most recent balance assigned to the known addresses. Maintaining a distributed database of transactions in this fashion introduces a high level of integrity. Still, it necessitates the encryption of user identities, as anyone with access to the database would otherwise be able to view the accounts balances of the individuals using the network.

Permissionless blockchains solve this issue with *private-key infrastructure* (PKI), in which a private/public key pair is used to generate any number of addresses. Traditional PKI is pseudonymous, as the user's identity is encrypted, but still predisposed to simple heuristic address clustering of transaction patterns.[71] As such, blockchain technology presents a fascinating paradox: Pseudonymous identities are essential in protecting user privacy but, at the same

[68] *Voshmgir/Zargham*, Foundations of Cryptoeconomic Systems, 2020.
[69] *Voshmgir*, 'Decentralisation' is a misleading term, Pre-print, 2022, 4f.
[70] EBA, Guidelines on Common Procedures and Methodologies for Srep and Supervisory Stress Testing, 2018.
[71] *Wang/Ding/Li/Yuan/Ouyang/Wang*, IEEE Trans. Comput. Soc. Syst., vol. 6, no. 5, 2019, 870f.

time, offer a design challenge for DAOs. Yet, the replicated nature of the database means that pseudonymous transaction data is available perpetually, enabling stakeholders to access the full transaction history for an address. Different agent definitions are shown in Table 2.

Agent type	Description	Sample of Evidence
Verifiably Independent Agent (VIA)	A publicly identifiable token holder (maybe with a sizeable reputational interest in maintaining the integrity of their address) with a long and repeated history of participation in governance and a public presence in the associated communities.	Proof of (real or pseudonymous) identification measures across multiple governance discussions and social media sites, a discernible asset trail, and/or identification standard tokens (Ethereum naming service)
Presumably Independent Agent (PIA)	A token holder with a presumed vested interest in a sound governance process and	An address with a transaction history indicating repeated and non-automated use on a near daily basis, coupled with interactions in other DAOs and a discernible transaction pattern.
Unidentifiable Agent (UIA)	All addresses not operated by a PIA or a VIA.	Addresses with indications of automation and repetitive transaction patterns or clusters.

Table 2. Agent definitions

2. *The TIGER Assessment Questionnaire*

After several iterations and pattern analysis, the conceptual artifact was optimized and consolidated to contain 15 characteristics with suggested questions and quantifiers for assessment as shown in Table 3. We summarize the requirements[72] in five general categories of DAO subsystems (items with grey background in column 1 of Table 3) based on expert input and literature:[73] Token Weighted Voting; Infrastructure; Governance, Escalation, and Reputation ("TIGER").

---

[72] *Baskerville/Pries-Heje*, Bus. Inf. Syst. Eng., vol. 2, no. 5, 2010, 271 f.
[73] *Wang/Ding/Li/Yuan/Ouyang/Wang*, IEEE Trans. Comput. Soc. Syst., vol. 6, no. 5, 2019, 870 f.

Topical Analysis		*Variables*
Category	Question	Quantifier
Token Weighted Voting and Incentives		
Token distribution at launch	Did the team conduct a "fair" token launch designed to balance incentives for further decentralization with requirements for long-term funding and investor returns?	Percentage of units allocated to addresses associated with insiders, including core-team members, advisors, investors, early collaborators, and service providers.
Promoting a non-collusive oligopoly	Does the DAO algorithmically incentivize multilateral participation by rewarding non-colluding groups of agents for strategic participation?	Percentage of units allocated to clearly differentiated stakeholder groups indicated by a misalignment in assumed preferences
Concentration of voting power	How distributed are governance tokens amongst active/passive stakeholders?	Number of VIAs required to mount >51 % of voting power in majority voting schemes?
Infrastructure		
Token locking, freezing and thawing	Does the token contract code include the ability for any set of stakeholders to lock, move, freeze, and thaw token balances on some or all addresses?	Number of VIAs required to freeze token balances in all or some addresses.
Code upgrades	Is there evidence of the possibility of enforcing unilateral decision-making in the code that may compromise decentralization? While most code upgrades will preserve address, state, and balance, any ability to change smart contract code will impose significant security risks to the DAO and its stakeholders.	The number of agents of any type required to effectively implement a proposal or other non-specified changes to the smart contract code. Code changes or upgrades may be implemented either following official voting sessions or unilaterally.
Access	To what extent is access to decision-making through voting or other means accessible to external parties or contributors in a meaningful and unrestricted way?	Mixed assessment relating to quorum and timing: (1) How many verifiably independent agents does it take to produce a positive voting outcome for a "general" Improvement Proposal (Nakamoto coefficient for governance), and (2) Does the voting process allow proper time and access for token holders to vote on any topic?

Topical Analysis		*Variables*
Category	Question	Quantifier
Governance		
Voting delegation	Is any voting delegation fair and unconditional so there is no risk of manipulating reported delegation?	How many VIAs with clearly distinctive preference profiles are presently available for delegation
Voting participation	Is there evidence of broad voter activity?	Percentage of token float with active participation in governance
Bootstrapping	Is there any centralized activity that goes beyond bootstrapping the journey toward full decentralization of the DAO?	*Qualitative assessment*: Is there evidence of centralized control measures that are not required for the long-term health of a decentralized DAO?
Escalation		
Crisis management	Does the constitution or policies include crisis management and dispute resolution mechanisms?	Percentage of tokens required to enact crisis management decision-making
Inflation	What is the distribution between token inflation accruing to user A. External (oligopolistic) incentives for non-colluding VIAs (LPs, open-source developers, etc.) and user B. Insider VIAs such as investors, founders, early stakeholders, etc.?	The percentage split user A/ user B.
Voting access	Are there any restrictions on availability and access to the DAO's decision-making process?	Mixed assessment relating to quorum and timing: (1) How many VIAs do it take to produce a positive voting outcome for a "general" Improvement Proposal, and (2) if the voting process allows proper time and access for token holders to vote on any topic.
Reputation		
Soft power	Is there evidence of co-optation or informal manipulation?	*Qualitative assessment*: Past evidence or forward-looking assessment of how many known high-profile agents can theoretically swing a vote

Topical Analysis		*Variables*
Category	Question	Quantifier
Responsibility alignment	Does the DAO code or applicable norms introduce the notion of accountability for decision-makers in a fashion that appears symmetrical to the power and responsibility vested in decision-makers?	*Qualitative assessment*: No evidence of asymmetry between responsibility and accountability, for instance, unjust overruling or veto.
Accountability	Are measures for conflict and reputation management implemented?	*Qualitative assessment*: Evidence of dispute resolution measures to mitigate centralized attack vectors around reputation

Table 3. TIGER Assessment Questionnaire

a) Token-weighted Voting and Incentives

The assessment of this dimension includes:

Analysis of whether the tokens are fairly distributed among the community, founders, and collaborators while also locking token liquidity for the future funding of the DAO's activities. Fair launch considerations include considerations over the pricing of the token across the issuance period(s). Essentially the assessment is a determination of whether the DAO's monetary policy is fair and whether anyone, including the core team, is benefiting unfairly compared to the DAO community long term.

When assessing whether the DAO incentivizes multilateral participation by allocating tokens to clearly differentiated stakeholder groups, it is important to notice that some collaboration and common focus are to be expected. In addition to quantifying units allocated to independent groups, the assessor could also look for signals: Is there any tangible evidence of cartels? Is it reasonable to assume that token holders are colluding unfairly? Are big investors talking to the founders and asking them what to vote for, or the other way around?

The concentration of voting power would include a Nakamoto-coefficient analysis of on-chain and off-chain voting history. The Nakamoto coefficient is a simple, quantitative measure of a system's decentralization.[74,75] The coefficient is based on the Gini coefficient and calculated based on the number of critical subsystems in a system and how many entities one would need to compromise to control each subsystem.

[74] *Srinivasan*, News. Earn. Com, 2017, 1 f.

[75] *Jensen/Von Wachter/Ross*, How Decentralized is the Governance of Blockchain-based Finance? Empirical Evidence from four Governance Token Distributions, 2020.

b) Infrastructure

The assessment includes:

Analysis of how the DAO limits large token holders (so-called whales) from having outsized influence. Some DAOs introduce the notion of time-locked voting. This allows token holders to increase the weight of their vote by locking their shares for a certain amount of time after voting has ended, trading the opportunity cost for increased voting power. Freeze and thaw measures may also be applied to the benefit of late-joiners and/or to reduce whale influence.

Analysis of centralization of control that is not automated in a sufficiently decentralized manner, which includes an assessment of the degree of autonomy in software vs. human centrality but also a view of any single point(s) of failure or single point(s) of control concerns.

Access is assessed both to quorum and timing, assessing how many VIAs it takes to produce a positive voting outcome for a "general" Improvement Proposal, which we could label as the Nakamoto co-efficient for governance, and second, whether the voting process allows proper time and access for token holders to vote on any topic or if (unfair) restrictions apply.

c) Governance

Assessment of governance processes is critical to determine whether there are possible centralized attack vectors in a DAO:

Voting delegation, sometimes referred to as liquid democracy, shares the core principles of political democracy. In this case, a DAO assigns specialists to participate in an electorate with the power to make decisions on behalf of DAO members. This increases centralization, on the other hand, it may improve the quality of decision-making as in the traditional world's representative democracies. In some cases, voting delegation may constitute manipulative and/or regulatory arbitrage through conditional delegation, so the assessment should review delegation mandates to ensure the delegated mandate is not an attempt to arbitrage. The analysis can range from a simple count of the number of individual components in the DAO network and the relative size of these to more advanced network analysis and statistical tests, where a DAO uses more advanced voting delegation.

From a narrow perspective, the assessment of voting participation analyses voter turnout participation in collective decision-making, which is a dynamic metric that may affect the security of any plutocratic governance system. Simple token-weighted voting may risk the undue influence of 'whales' (large token holders). Balanced techniques adopted by DAOs include sociocracy, where decisions are made by consent, not by consensus. Quadratic voting and other alternative voting mechanisms, such as holographic consensus or multi-signature wallet (multi-Sig), are also gaining traction across DAOs. The assessment may also include a fairness assessment of the voting process, where DAOs sometimes use timing mechanisms to reduce the risk of minority abuse. This process tackles the risk of majority voters gaining an advantage over minority voters; the downside is that the voting process becomes exceptionally long. Another method to ensure a fair voting process is "conviction voting," which is based on the community's aggregated preference and uses time as a utility to strengthen "conviction" to one's vote. A third example includes express voting that may encapsulate intensity or broader community support and thereby reduce the costs of democratic coordination.

Sometimes, DAOs establish a foundation to own rights that cannot easily be decentralized. Although this implies a centrally controlled activity, it should be viewed in context and be considered acceptable if the purpose of the centralized effort is only to bootstrap the journey towards decentralization. Outsourcing also includes software deployment strategy and hosting policy, where, according to statista.com[76] more than 64 % of the world's cloud market is currently controlled by three dominant vendors (AWS, Google, and MSFT), who therefore likely host most of the blockchain/Web3 infrastructure that exists, including full nodes, validator nodes, and middleware. This is potentially a significant attack vector for censorship and centralized control.

d) Escalation

Consideration of the following issues helps in assessing escalation:

A DAO is only as decentralized as its crisis mode allows. Hence, the assessment should investigate how control measures can be centralized in any crisis. A crisis should be defined through stress testing of the DAO business system and financial and technical resilience. Crisis mitigation and contingency measures should preferably be specified in the DAO constitution or policies for events that can impact the long-term sustainability of the DAO. Some centralization is expected to deal effectively with crisis containment, where fluid democracy may not always be the most efficient. Still, the assessment should determine the extent to which such centralization is subject to democratic control.

An inflationary token model adds new tokens to the market over time, often through a schedule or as mining rewards or for specific contributions. For the determination of decentralization, the critical assessment point is that any value associated with inflation or deflation benefits all token holders fairly, not for the benefit of non-collaborative agents for any strategic or other participation.

[76] Global cloud infrastructure market share 2021 | Statista. Available: https://www.statista.com/statistics/967365/worldwide-cloud-infrastructure-services-market-share-vendor/. Accessed on Jul. 24, 2022.

Availability and access should be equal to all, so any restrictions in access to the DAO, including its decision-making process, may suggest a level of centralized control. The assessment would include a Nakamoto coefficient analysis for both on- and off-chain activities around voter activity and token holdings and a review of voting policies.

e) Reputation

For assessment of reputation, the following considerations are suggested:

Soft power through co-optation or informal manipulation is an everyday phenomenon in politics. In DAO communities that allows actors to engage pseudo- or anonymously, it is critical to assess that these features are not used manipulatively. Again, the analysis may potentially involve sophisticated network and statistical analysis.

DAOs cannot act outside their rules, but because their smart contracts may contain errors or unforeseen events may occur, rule change mechanisms are necessary for resilience purposes. On the other hand, fully decentralized DAOs must also acknowledge their delegated mandates, with accountability following delegated responsibility.

Increasingly, DAOs implement dispute resolution mechanisms or use dispute resolution services from emerging online third-party decentralized dispute resolution service providers. Other measures, such as implementing tools like Sourcecred[77] to create trust in the community, or slashing to penalize unwanted behavior or dishonest validation, are similar mechanisms of democratic control designed to incentivize network participation.

V. Evaluation

The artifact evaluation was conducted two-fold; First, we field-tested the general concept with a DeFi expert from an EU-based supervisory authority. Second, we applied the TIGER framework to a prominent DAO using publicly available sources.

The field-test evaluation emphasized a pragmatic approach favoring comprehensive coverage of topics of regulatory concern rather than the collection of quantitative data. The introduction of partial compromisation having a full impact on the overall assessment result was deemed justifiable but raised several questions, including (1) how to deal with the lack of a grace period in the current implementation of the recently released MiCA package and (2) how to create a level-playing field for 'institutional DeFi' (where traditional, currently regulat-

[77] SourceCred|SourceCred. Available: https://sourcecred.io/. Accessed on Jul. 24, 2022.

ed financial institutions offer decentralized financial products operated by DAOs).

In the remainder of this section, we present a sample evaluation of a DAO as a reference guide to how regulators or industry participants may approach the discretionary application of the TIGER framework.

We use the Compound protocol and its associated governance processes for the sample evaluation. It is important to note that the sample application provided here serves only as a reference guide due to the lack of access and transparency for internal data. While DAO governance primarily happens in public fora, a regulatory authority would arguably have access to a wealth of quantitative and qualitative data provided and collected by the counterparty and its partners.

While this level of access is not attainable in the academic context due to privacy regulations, the level of public governance data available is sufficient in providing a cursory reference application of the framework. Further, if a DAO is already decentralized before enforceable regulation is agreed upon, a regulator/supervisor will need to rely on the same publicly available information we access here. The Compound protocol offers an interesting entry point to the evaluation of the TIGER framework, as the protocol team was amongst the first to issue a governance token (COMP) and the adjacent infrastructure, which led to the present generation of DAO governance.

While stablecoin issuer MakerDAO had already issued their governance token (MKR) years prior, the Compound team was amongst the first to explicitly link the issuance of the token with the usage of the protocol in a bid to incentivize liquidity provisioning. This sparked a period of rapid escalation, commonly referred to by industry observers as 'DeFi Summer,' in the 3rd Quarter of 2020 as the major decentralized exchange Uniswap (UNI) immediately followed suit in a bid to defend market share against aggressive attempts at siphoning liquidity by the rapidly emerging competitor 'SushiSwap' (SUSHI). The ensuing period saw waves of governance tokens enter the market, mimicking the previous ICO frenzy.[78]

1. *Introducing the Compound DAO*

Compound[79] is an on-chain market for peer-to-peer lending, enabling users to collateralize and borrow against a selection of 18 assets. At the time of writing, the protocol manages ~€3.7bn in collateral assets deposited by ~300 000 depositors, of which ~9000 users have taken out an aggregate of ~€895m in outstanding debt against their deposits.

[78] *Fenu/Marchesi/Marchesi/Tonelli*, International Workshop on Blockchain Oriented Software Engineering (IWBOSE), 2018, 26f.

[79] Compound. Available: https://compound.finance/ Accessed on Jul. 24, 2022.

Protocol decision-making is governed by token-holders utilizing the token (COMP) within the governance contract. The Compound Governance process involves submitting pre-deployed code changes to risk management and asset modules above, which stakeholders can then inspect and vote for or against implementing in binary voting sessions. Proposals are generally used to implement system parameter modifications, but proposals for adding new markets or entirely new features are occasionally implemented as well.

Further in this section, we present a cursory application of the TIGER framework, utilizing a score-card methodology in which we assign a score between 1–5 for each dimension. While there are clearly identifiable areas of improvement, we assess that the Compound DAO is *sufficiently* decentralized when we factor in the protocol age. Over time, we expect a gradually increasing decentralization as the protocol matures and increasingly larger private and institutional stakeholders join the DAO.

The overall score of our assessment is 3.8 on a scale of 5, split on each aggregate dimension as appears in Figure 5, with no critical dimension failing. A detailed assessment follows below.

Figure 4. Compound decentralization radar

2. COMP Token Weighted Voting Distribution

The COMP token has a max supply of 10m units, of which 7.15m is in circulation at the time of writing. The COMP supply has a daily inflation rate, currently set at 1139 COMP daily, distributed across market participants (Table 4), alongside a 4-year vesting period for insider shareholders ending in June 2024.

Stakeholder Groups	COMP Allocation	Percentage of Total Supply
Shareholders of Compound Labs, Inc.	2 396 307	23.96 %
Founders & team	2 226 037	22.26 %
Future team members	372 707	3.73 %
Users	4 229 949	42.30 %
Community Allocation	775 000	7.75 %

Table 4. COMP allocation to stakeholder groups[80]

As evident, the COMP tokens allocated to shareholders in Compound Labs, Inc. Founders, and team members (present and future team members) comprise a narrow minority share of 49.95 % of the total token supply, assuming that the recipients retain all tokens after vesting.

While the narrow minority does not technically produce a concentration of voting power in the hands of stakeholders with presumed shared interests, it should be noted that in the theoretical event of a highly contentious issue between insiders and (external) community members, challengers would need to mount 50.05 % of the token float to push through a decision, which is deemed unlikely.

Yet, the distribution of tokens amongst smart contracts and agent types[81] is such that, at present, only a few VIAs retain an adequate amount to mount a hostile proposal process. On this basis, we assign a passing score of 3 out of 5, informed by the relative concentration of votes.

3. COMP Infrastructure Assessment

The Compound team has implemented a well-reasoned and simple user interface for the governance process, enabling non-technical users to participate in the governance process.

[80] https://messari.io/asset/compound/profile/supply-schedule. Accessed on Jul. 24, 2022.

[81] Compound Token Contract and Distribution Chart. Available: https://etherscan.io/token/tokenholderchart/0xc00e94cb662c3520282e6f5717214004a7f26888. Accessed on Jul. 24, 2022.

The Compound Governor and Timelock methods require the deployment of code with the proposal submission. From proposal submission through voting and the mandatory two-day delay following a successful vote, the governance process implements a full week period for any decision made by DAO stakeholders.

In contrast to the frequently used option of using the popular tool Snapshot[82] to collect votes through signatures, this methodology mitigates the need for a single or multi-signer solution which can be required to implement the results of the vote when using Snapshot. Instead, approved proposals are immediately implemented by the contract once they pass. While this methodology has previously imposed costs on voters due to the high execution fees on the Ethereum blockchain, the team has implemented the casting and delegation of votes by offline signatures,[83] mitigating voter apathy and improving accessibility of governance participation. Delegation functionality is implemented in the COMP token contract and delegates the voting power for the tokens from one address to another. Users interested in delegating voting power to multiple delegates can split tokens over multiple accounts and delegate to multiple delegates. The COMP token smart contract does not allow freezing addresses, manipulating balances, or upgrading the contract code through upgradeable "proxy contracts."

On this basis, we assess that the Compound governance model and the associated smart contract infrastructure are sufficiently decentralized, yielding a 5/5 score.

4. COMP Governance Dynamics

The Compound governance model utilizes delegation strategies, through which token holders can delegate voting power to active participants. To create a proposal, an address must hold in excess of 25000 COMP (€1.5m) or lock 100 COMP (€6000) to create an 'autonomous proposal,' which can become ratified if delegated an excess of 25000 COMP.

Governance proposals are time locked in review for three days, after which voting is initiated for an ensuing three-day period. Proposals gathering a majority of votes with a lower threshold of 400000 COMP votes are queued for implementation for two days.

The governance of Compound is primarily in the custody of the delegate VIAs, retaining an aggregate of 92.6 % of voting power with 2377404 COMP tokens in delegation. Of the top 60 delegates, accounting for 99.9 % of the total

---

[82] Snapshot. Available: https://snapshot.org/#/. Accessed on Jul. 24, 2022.

[83] Compound | Docs – Governance. Available: https://compound.finance/docs/governance#delegate-bysignature. Accessed on Jul. 24, 2022.

voting weight, there is no additional delegation, so it is fair to assume the said VIAs also control these tokens.

The VIA delegates yield decisive authority over the Compound protocol, for which approximately 70 % of the 36 proposals decided upon in 2022 (including failed and canceled votes) were decided by less than ten delegates wielding a clear majority. So far, in 2022, on average, ~600 000 COMP was active in each proposal, again mainly controlled by VIAs.

Through the lifetime of the DAO, 113 proposals have been voted upon, averaging 2.3 per month. The average voter turnout has increased slightly over time to 66 participating addresses per proposal in 2022, up from 56 addresses per proposal in 2020, the first year of operation.[84]

Based on this assessment, it appears evident that while Compound governance is managed by a relatively small subset of VIAs with, in most cases, presumed identical preferences, said stakeholders would be unlikely to mount a hostile proposal against users, given the token distribution.

On this basis, we assign a passing score of 3 out of 5, informed by the relative concentration of votes.

5. COMP Escalation and Crisis Management

The Compound governance system uses timelock to introduce sufficient time for careful review of the proposal code before implementation. The community implemented an automated 'Proposal Threshold Alert' as an early indicator of potential governance attacks. The alert informs the community if a wallet has accrued sufficient COMP to meet governance thresholds. Further, the Compound Comptroller contract includes elements of a crisis management mechanism with a pause guardian. Compound Labs previously controlled this, but since 2021 transferred it to a community multi-Sig wallet created by community members, where a small group of 4–6 stakeholders, chosen by the community, can pause Mint, Borrow, Transfer, and Liquidate functions. In our understanding, this does not constitute a complete 'emergency shutdown' mechanism, so we assess that the multi-Sig does not provide full crisis management capability.

The lack of any special escalatory privileges awarded to early stakeholders became evident early in the life of the protocol when a bug in a proposal placed 280 000 COMP tokens at risk of emission to liquidity providers. While the Compound team removed the ability for users to claim these tokens through the interface, this did not stop users from simply interacting directly with the smart contracts.

[84] Compound|Governance. Available: https://compound.finance/governance. Accessed on Jul. 24, 2022.

In what appears to be a somewhat misguided attempt to return the tokens to the protocol, the founder of Compound Labs, Robert Leshner, threatened to collect information on non-cooperative stakeholders to inform the US tax authorities.[85] While these attempts were ridiculed by the community members, the case resembles the user B situation in Figure 1 above. It provides an example of how all stakeholders, regardless of their seniority in the community, cannot influence decisions governed through smart contracts.

Based on the lack of discriminatory privileges awarded to key stakeholders, outside of the ability to amend the contract web interface, we assess that the Compound DAO is sufficiently decentralized on this dimension, yielding a score of 5/5.

6. COMP Reputation and the Impact of Soft Power on Decision-Making Processes

Compound governance primarily occurs in designated online fora, where governance participants pitch and discuss proposals before developing and deploying a proposal code. Discussions are generally cross posted on social media[86] with parallel discussions occasionally led on chat servers.[87] On average, new posts are submitted daily to bi-weekly, indicating a moderate to high activity level.

By cross-referencing with data from LinkedIn[88] we note that the official organization appears to employ 19 employees with titles indicating a commercial relationship with Compound Labs Inc. We did not find evidence of any inordinate influence in proposal submissions by these employees. However, the picture is different when we assess the influence of large vs. small token holders in what we presume is the primary governance forum[89] for pre-proposal discussions: Out of a total of 113 proposals to date, 97 are included in the pre-proposal discussion. Of these, at least 53 posts have been authored by individuals in founding roles or with clear connections to the founding team or major token holders. Of these 53 posts, 32 were authored by the service provider Gauntlet,[90] a firm specializing in financial modeling, which previously completed a market

---

85 *Leshner.* Available: https://twitter.com/rleshner/status/1443730726751506432. Accessed on Jul. 24, 2022.

86 Compound Labs (@compoundfinance)/Twitter. https://twitter.com/compoundfinance. Accessed on Jul. 24, 2022.

87 Compound Discord. Available: https://discord.com/channels/402910780124561410/585968001661009920. Accessed on Jul. 24, 2022.

88 Compound Labs: Overview|LinkedIn. Available: https://www.linkedin.com/company/compound-labs/. Accessed on Jul. 24, 2022.

89 Latest Proposals topics – Compound Community Forum. Available: https://www.comp.xyz/c/proposals/6. Accessed on Jul. 24, 2022.

90 Gauntlet. Available: https://gauntlet.network/. Accessed on Jul. 24, 2022.

risk assessment report on Compound.[91] Gauntlet is identified as the controller of the fourth biggest delegate address, yielding 118,494 COMP at the time of writing this article. While Gauntlet is a frequent and active participant in Compound governance, the primary emphasis is on topics clearly related to risk management or the addition of new assets to the platform and does not appear manipulative.

There appears to be no dispute resolution mechanism. In the Compound chat forum on Discord; this has been debated, with some community members objecting to any dispute resolution mechanism and others firmly in support. The topic has not been subject to a formal vote. On this basis, we assign a score of 3 out of 5 on this dimension.

VI. Discussion

In this article, we propose an information system (IS) focused conceptual artifact based on a review of the literature, combined with expert insights from a group of industry stakeholders and experts. The artifact demonstrates the feasibility of structured assessment methods of the level of DAO decentralization both on-chain and off-chain, mapped to generalized, critical processes of DAOs. We address the research question: 'When is a DAO (sufficiently) decentralized?'

In analyzing whether a DAO is sufficiently decentralized, we might expect some quantified evidence of chaos, swarm, and/or a self-organized, distributed, decentralized community, as opposed to an ordered, strong organization with centralized command and control that characterizes the traditional organization.

Hence, the critical focus of analysis is whether the DAO stakeholders or 'actors' are empowered with delegated authority and whether they operate sufficiently independently of each other and in their own self-interest in an uncoordinated and voluntary manner.

We propose that "sufficient decentralization" is defined as a verifiable state, where the design of the DAO (1) is collusion resistant and based on long-term equilibrium, and (2) its governance processes have unrestricted and transparent access.

From a regulatory perspective, an alternative approach could simply be to analyze (1) if the DAO is conducting a regulated activity, and if so, (2) if there is an accountable legal or physical person upon whom regulation can be enforced; if not, then the DAO being sufficiently decentralized has to be acknowledged.

---

[91] Gauntlet Compound report. Available: https://gauntlet.network/reports/compound. Accessed on Jul. 24, 2022.

In our view, such an approach is too simplistic and does not accept the fundamental premise that DLT/Blockchain is a transformative technology that will foster innovation and growth.

In terms of conciseness and robustness attributes of the assessment framework, the challenge lies in the complexity of decentralization as a concept. We avoid an extensive classification scheme that could lead to cognitive overload when assessing a given level of decentralization point in time while also defining enough dimensions and characteristics to clearly differentiate the objects of interest.[92]

From a practical and theoretical perspective, it seems evident that no DAO can start decentralized, as any project must be initiated by a small core team, bootstrapping development until the project matures and attracts open-source contributors. However, as discussed, the European regulators did not play any particular emphasis on this critical point when agreeing on the final text of the MiCA regulation. Some US regulatory proposals suggest a safe harbor rule,[93] proposing a grace period to allow a DAO to become sufficiently decentralized, thus introducing the concept of 'gradual decentralization.' In our proposed assessment framework, we acknowledge this by suggesting that the assessment includes a perspective on the mature DAO design, not just the point-in-time view.

We extrapolate our contributions into the following generalized propositions:

P1: The concept of technology-neutral regulation is challenged by DLT/Blockchain. DAOs exist and realize benefits through increasing degrees of decentralization. DAO legal design should therefore support the internal decentralization accomplished by the DAO so that a balance is achieved between external and internal decentralization,[94] not the other way around. When regulators in the coming years design technical requirements for the supervision of DAOs, they need to acknowledge this underlying premise and embrace that DLT/blockchain is a transformative technology that requires unique regulatory approaches.

P2: Regulators need to embrace the concept of a 'grace period' for a DAO to achieve sufficient decentralization. The MiCA regulation did not include this, but it seems challenging to embrace DeFi and the concept of sufficient decentralization without it. We suggest an assessment approach where not only the point-in-time assessment is material to the decision of decentralization but also the design intent, thereby introducing a grace period from a risk-based perspective, allowing the EU to practically align crypto regulatory compliance to the safe harbor proposals from the US and common sense.

---

[92] EBA, Guidelines on Common Procedures and Methodologies for Srep and Supervisory Stress Testing, 2018.

[93] *Peirce*, Token Safe Harbor Proposal 2, SEC, 2021, 1 f. pp. 1–7, 2021.

[94] European Commission, Study on the costs of compliance for the financial sector, 2019.

P3: In the short term, for 'Institutional DeFi,' a level playing field needs to be developed by financial regulators and supervisors, including a 'cut-off' strategy, with clear boundaries for acceptable centralized activity, to allow DLT/Blockchain-based businesses to develop properly, respecting the new technological feature regime. From a regulatory perspective, and in the words of MiCA, complete decentralization seems to require full automation. Still, when elements of human governance are introduced, it is difficult to think of complete decentralization as outlined in MiCA. Some automated features also become centralized through the front-end website hosting or other elements. Regulators must accept that a new playing field for DAOs will develop over the coming years.

P4: Regulatory practices around DAO decentralization will evolve across blockchains and business models, each with its own strengths and weaknesses regarding centralized attack vectors and regulatory importance. A risk-based approach to DAO supervision, where required, will therefore need to be developed with a holistic view of decentralization across political, technological, social, and economic dimensions, as well as across underlying technology infrastructures that behave very differently from a risk perspective. We foresee regulators will designate some blockchains to have more systemic risk than others.

P5: DLT/Blockchain will transform how regulators supervise and enforce the regulation. The number of DAOs grew by a factor of 8x in the past year.[95] With the increasing certainty on the regulation of crypto, the number of DAOs will likely continue to evolve, and the growth of the token economy and innovation of blockchain-based business models as well. Some sample DAO business models[96,97] are listed in Appendix 1.

These developments pressure regulators to keep pace with developments in two dimensions: (1) Supervisors with a traditional finance focus will be challenged as their supervisory toolkits and skillsets become disconnected and obsolete. Regulators and supervisors must embrace the available and emerging investigative techniques to analyze DAO structures and processes in real-time, on- and off-chain; (2) A focus on automated and embedded supervision should be prioritized.[98]

Our work contributes to practice by identifying criteria for DAOs, regulators, and supervisors to consider when assessing whether a DAO is 'sufficiently decentralized,' complementing the understanding beyond technical difficulties by taking a holistic view of DAOs as complex socio-technical systems.

---

[95] Emre on Twitter. https://twitter.com/n4motto/status/1534642569220706304. Accessed on Jul. 24, 2022.

[96] DAOs List – Messari. Available: https://messari.io/governor/daos. Accessed on Jul. 24, 2022.

[97] Full-Time DAOs – Coopahtroopa. Available: https://coopahtroopa.mirror.xyz/5vTIKBRzMpVAiNyc7CnABXjh3ToJrjQOnOdkwqvb3l8. Accessed on Jul. 24, 2022.

[98] *Auer,* Fed. Reserve Bank Dallas, Glob. Inst. Work. Pap., no. 371, 2019.

Our findings contribute actionable insights to the information system literature by emphasizing how DLT and blockchain technologies may be assessed from a socio-technical perspective. We contribute to DAO communities and regulators with a pragmatic tool to understand to what extent an otherwise regulated activity may be considered sufficiently decentralized and thereby avoid significant and costly compliance requirements.

VII. Conclusion

We investigate the topic of decentralization as it relates to DAOs, using a thematic analysis method to identify relevant patterns to assess whether sufficient decentralization is presented. Through the framework's design, we demonstrate the feasibility of implementing a structured method for the assessment.

We propose a definition of 'sufficient decentralization' and incorporate the notion of a representative democracy via delegated mandate in the assessment framework. Still, it remains to be concluded what level of delegation and decentralization is acceptable under different regulatory regimes. Some regulators seem to suggest complete decentralization as the only acceptable level. However, complete decentralization in DAOs is challenging to grasp, as they are socio-technical constructs.

We design a generalized assessment framework with suggested quantifiers. Still, the application of all characteristics and levels of quantified assessment will likely vary, depending on the need for regulatory monitoring by jurisdiction. Hence, the framework design is flexible to accommodate change as regulatory practices evolve and regulatory technical standards become defined. We demonstrate the practical application of the framework artifact by assessing the level of decentralization of Compound, an algorithmic money market DAO operating on the Ethereum blockchain.

Our findings suggest that decentralization in DAOs is not a myth. Still, due to the technical features of blockchains, it can be complicated to investigate and assess the true level of DAO decentralization. Our contribution is a pragmatic framework that can guide aspiring DAOs, regulators, and supervisors to advance the decentralization agenda as the crypto and traditional economies increasingly overlap and integrate. We extrapolate the findings into five general propositions on the implications of decentralization on the supervision of regulated financial activity in crypto.

Appendix 1: Sample DAO Business Models

Category[99]	Description
Media DAO	Media DAOs such as Mirror (https://mirror.xyz/) empower writers and make it possible to work alone or collaboratively to publish, crowdfund, and create auctions and editions of media projects or digital artwork through tokens.
DAO Operating system	DAO operating systems or "platforms" such as Aragon (https://aragon.org/) or DAOstack (https://daostack-1.gitbook.io/v1/) provide a complete software stack and infrastructure for building and running a DAO, including various apps for token management, voting, and finance.
Social DAO	The Social or Community DAO category covers a broad range of DAOs that focus more on social capital than financial capital; they include communities that evolve from group chats to co-working DAOs or just a meeting place. An example is Filmmaker DAO (https://www.filmmakerdao.com/), which coordinates filmmakers' efforts to enable more IP ownership.
Protocol DAO	Protocol DAOs were initially intended to transition power from a founder team into a broader community, finding new ways for projects to issue fungible tokens into the market. These DAOs now constitute the bulk of decentralized finance (DeFi) protocols, such as Aave (https://aave.com/), Uniswap (https://uniswap.org/), or MakerDAO (https://makerdao.com/) and typically with a transaction focus aiming to compete with traditional finance.
Collector DAO	Collector DAOs are the home of NFT art-focused DAOs, such as PleasrDAO (https://pleasr.org/) enable their community to share the cost of expensive assets and co-own digital art, in the case of PleasrDAO specializing in what the members determine are culturally significant art pieces, that are further fractionalized for trading on DeFi protocols such as Uniswap v3 NFT.
Investment DAO	Investment DAOs such as Seed Club DAO (https://www.seedclub.xyz/) enable their community to co-invest, build and accelerate digital communities, land, or other assets deemed relevant for an investment focus.
Impact DAO	Impact DAOs, such as Climate DAO (https://climatedao.xyz/), focus on sustainability and conservation agendas. They are frequently driven by activist communities collaborating with research institutions or having educational activities.

[99] Sources: DAOs List – Messari. https://messari.io/governor/daos (accessed Jul. 24, 2022) and Full-Time DAOs – Coopahtroopa. https://coopahtroopa.mirror.xyz/5vTIKBRzMpVAiNyc7CnABXjh3ToJrjQOnOdkwqvb3l8 (Accessed on Jul. 24, 2022).

Category[99]	Description
Service DAO	Service DAOs, such as BrightID (https://www.brightid.org/) support DAOs with all required infrastructure and operational services, for instance, token, governance, or operational services, including voting, recruitment, legal, risk management, community management, technology, treasury, or, in the case of BrightID, a decentralized digital identity DAO.
Grants DAO	Grant DAOs such as Gitcoin (https://gitcoin.co/) enable their communities to donate funds and vote through governance proposal rounds on how the distributed funding capital is allocated to various projects, typically focusing on digital common goods aligned with Ostrom principles and not for profit.

Legal personality of Decentralized Autonomous Organizations (DAOs): Privilege or Necessity?

Florian Möslein and Daniel Ostrovski

Abstract The legal classification of DAOs has sparked extensive debate in legal literature. Regarding their legal personality, there is widespread agreement that non-wrapped DAOs are recognized as partnerships and endowed with legal personality in most jurisdictions. Thus, even without formal registration with competent authorities, DAOs can serve as the nexus for contractual relationships. This paper delves into the question of whether DAOs can also serve as the nexus for licensing and other prudential requirements in financial regulation. Considering that DAOs lie at the core of DeFi as its governance mechanism, the legal structure and personality of a DAO can significantly impact DeFi regulation. To explore this, we first present the abstract concept of legal personality as a nexus for contractual and regulatory law. Subsequently, we assess DAO governance and classify both non-wrapped and wrapped DAOs as entities with legal personality. We then scrutinize the role that DAOs play in DeFi and investigate the legal challenges that arise from utilizing DAOs as the nexus for contractual and regulatory matters. We recognize that while both non-wrapped and wrapped DAOs' legal personality may be a sufficient nexus for contractual law, their governance structure and the legal design of their legal personality are not very well suited for the purposes of regulatory law. Therefore, we conclude that if DAOs are to be regarded as the foundation for the regulation of DeFi, the design of their legal personality requires *lege ferenda* adjustments.

I. Introduction

Decentralized Autonomous Organizations (DAOs) are increasingly disrupting our economy.[1] In particular, these code-driven, community-governed entities are transforming our financial system by driving a shift towards more decentralized structures: By providing financial services, DAOs form the backbone of Decentralized Finance (DeFi), an emerging model for organising and

[1] More extensively on their origins and economic relevance, for instance, World Economic Forum, in collaboration with the Wharton Blockchain and Digital Asset Project, White Paper, p. 7 et seq., available at https://www.weforum.org/whitepapers/decentralized-autonomous-organizations-beyond-the-hype/ (7.08.2023).

enabling cryptocurrency-based transactions, exchanges and financial services.[2] DAOs are designed to be decentralized and autonomous: they are not controlled by a single entity or individual but operate on the basis of smart contracts that automatically execute certain actions based on pre-defined rules.[3] As all decisions are recorded on distributed ledgers, DAOs promise to operate in a highly transparent manner. However, they also face challenges of governance and regulatory uncertainty. A variety of current court cases reflect this uncertainty and illustrate the different legal issues raised by DAOs.[4] At the heart of these cases is the question of whether – and to what extent – DAOs have legal personality. This contribution therefore first explains the legal concept of legal personality (see below, at II.), then examines the legal status of DAOs (see below, at III.) and finally looks at the specific challenges in the field of DeFi (see below, at IV.). The analysis shows that legal personality is neither a privilege nor a necessity, but a fact. It also highlights the limitations of legal personality for DAOs, in particular with regard to limited liability and access to financial markets. The conclusion is that the legal personality of DAOs, although existing de *lege lata*, may require a different design de *lege ferenda*.

II. Personality as a legal concept

1. Legal Persons between Legal Fiction and Social Fact

In ancient Latin, the word "persona" describes the masks that were used in Greek drama in order to enable actors to assume their roles and define their identities.[5] In contrast, modern psychology defines personality as "the enduring characteristics and behaviour that comprise a person's unique adjustment to life, including major traits, interests, drives, values, self-concept, abilities, and emotional patterns".[6] While both understandings agree that personality contributes

---

[2] In detail *Möslein/Kaulartz/Rennig*, RDi 2021, 517; see also *Auer/Haslhofer/Kitzler/Saggese/Victor*, BIS Working Paper No. 166, https://www.bis.org/publ/work1066.htm (07.08.2023); *Harvey/Ramachandran/Santoro*, DeFi and the Future of Finance, 2021, p. 27.

[3] In a similar sense *Verstappen*, Legal Agreements on Smart Contract Platforms in European Systems of Private Law, 2023, p. 92.

[4] See, for instance, True Return Systems, LLC v. MakerDAO, 22-CV-8478 (VSB) (S.D.N.Y. Jun. 21, 2023); Christian Sarcuni, et al., v. bZx DAO, et al., 22-CV-618 LAB-DEB (S.D. Cal. Mar. 27, 2023); Commodity Futures Trading Comm'n v. Ooki Dao, 3:22-cv-05416-WHO (N.D. Cal. Dec. 20, 2022); Cox v. CoinMarketCap OpCo LLC, et al., CV-21-08197-PCT-SMB (D. Ariz. Dec. 14, 2021).

[5] *Brozek*, in: Kurki/Pietrzykowski (eds.), Legal Personhood: Animals, Artificial Intelligence and the Unborn, 2017, p. 3 (4 et seq.); cf. also *Gindis*, Journal of Institutional Economics 12 (2016), 499.

[6] Definition of the American Psychological Association, see https://www.apa.org/topics/personality (7.08.2023).

to determining behaviour, the psychological concept refers to very genuine and authentic individual features whereas the original understanding relates to a deliberate attribution that confers actors a different and artificial character. As a legal concept, personality is often understood close to this original meaning.[7] While natural persons acquire legal personality simply by being born (or even before that), legal persons are conferred personality by some orchestrated legal process, for instance by registration with some administrative or judicial agency or immediately by legislation. Legal personality therefore resembles a mask-like fiction, and legal persons are accordingly qualified as fictious or artificial persons:[8] The corporation, for instance, is perceived as "an artificial being, invisible, intangible, and existing only in contemplation of law".[9]

As a consequence of this artificialness, which has been particularly advocated by proponents of the so-called fiction theory,[10] and opposed to the unambiguous legal personality of natural persons, the question whether and which entities are granted legal personality is highly discretionary: Whether or not organizations, trees, rivers or other elements of nature, or technological devices like artificial intelligence are vested with legal personality is by no means pre-defined. As Friedrich Carl von Savigny has put it, a legal person is "a person which is assumed to be so for purely juristic purposes".[11] Even advocates of the so-called real entity theory who, in the tradition of Otto von Gierke,[12] assume that legal personality represents a social fact, agree that legal personality requires legal intervention.[13] They just interpret that chartering differently, i.e. as the recognition of a pre-legal reality.[14] Ultimately, legal personality therefore needs to be triggered by the lawmaker. The debate on new legal entities for autonomous systems (so-called e-persons) illustrates that the recognition of new types of legal entities is a very political issue.[15]

---

[7] See, for example, *Gaakeer*, Law & Literature 28 (2016), 287 (287 et seq).

[8] For a brief and early overview, also of the German debate *Radin*, Columbia Law Review 32 (1932), 643.

[9] Trustees of Dartmouth College v. Woodward (17 US) 4 Wheat 518, at 636 per Mashall CJ.

[10] While this theory is strongly connected to the German jurist Friedrich Carl von Savigny, it has greatly influenced common law scholars, cf. *Nékam*, The Personality Conception of the Legal Entity, 1938, p. 64 et seq.; *Machen*, Harvard Law Review 24 (1911), 253 (255).

[11] *Savigny*, System des heutigen römischen Rechts, 1840, § 85, p. 236 (transl. by Rattigan as Savigny, Jural Relations, 1884, p. 176).

[12] For an extensive account see *Micheler*, Company Law: A Real Entity Theory, 2021.

[13] In the same sense *Schillig*, Some Reflections on the Nature of Decentralized (Autonomous) Organizations, available at SSRN: https://ssrn.com/abstract=3915843, at p. 11: "Although committed to the principle of freedom of association, the theory did not deny that a legal person can exist only through the law's legitimizing force" (7.08.2023).

[14] Cf., for instance, *Claassen*, Philosophy Compass 18 (2023), 1 (5).

[15] In particular European Parliament resolution 2015/2103/INL of 16 February 2017 with recommendations to the Commission on Civil Law Rules on Robotics (2015), para 49; see also *Wagner*, Fordham Law Review 88 (2019), 591; *Teubner*, Ancilla Juris 2018, 35; *Riehm*, RDi 2020, 42.

2. Nexus for Contracts

The recognition of legal personality is based, however, on fundamental considerations that vary remarkably across different areas of law and their specific perspectives. In company law, legal personality is widely seen as a device that establishes a single contracting party that is "distinct from the various individuals who own or manage the firm" and can therefore serve as a "counterparty in numerous contracts with suppliers, employees, and customers, coordinating the actions of these multiple persons through exercise of its contractual rights".[16]

While economic theory often analyses the firm as a "nexus of contracts",[17] its legal conception can therefore be more accurately qualified as a "nexus for contracts":[18] Legal personality enables entities to engage in contractual relationships with private counterparties. The most important implication of this capacity is the separation between the assets of the corporation and its shareholders. Asset partitioning enables companies not only to own a pool of assets that is distinct from other property owned by their shareholders, but also to shield that pool from the creditors of the companies' directors and shareholders.[19] This so-called entity shielding is in fact believed to be the "*sine qua non* of the legal entity".[20]

A related, but less widely discussed implication of legal personality concerns the representation of companies and ultimately their governance structure: In order to operate as a nexus for contractual relationships with private counterparties, legal persons need to rely on natural persons which have the authority to represent them as their statutory organ (or, more precisely, as members of that organ).[21] Unlike natural persons, legal persons simply do not have the capacity to act themselves. As a consequence, the law cannot restrict itself to recognize their legal personhood, but it also needs to assign the competence to represent these legal persons in a legally effective manner vis-à-vis private counterparties: "It is therefore a necessary part of corporate personality that there should be rules by which acts are attributed to the company".[22] Otherwise, legal

---

[16] *Armour/Hansmann/Kraakman/Pargendler*, in: Kraakman et al. (eds), The Anatomy of Corporate Law, 2017, p. 1 (5).

[17] *Fama*, Journal of Political Economy 88 (1980), 288 (293); for the conceptual basis cf. *Jensen/Meckling*, Journal of Financial Economics 3 (1976), 305; see also *Alchian/Demsetz*, The American Economic Review 62 (1972), 777 (778), describing the firm as "the centralized contractual agent in a team productive process".

[18] *Armour/Hansmann/Kraakman/Pargendler* (fn. 16), p. 5.

[19] See generally *Hansmann/Kraakman*, The Yale Law Journal 110 (2000), 387 (394, 434–435).

[20] *Hansmann/Kraakman/Squire*, Harvard Law Review 119 (2006), 1335 (1338).

[21] In more detail, for instance, *Gerner-Beuerle/Schillig*, Comparative Company Law, 2019, p. 195 et seq.

[22] Meridian Funds Management Asia Ltd v. Securities Commission [1995] 2 AC 500, 506 (Lord Hoffmann).

persons were unable not only to enter into contracts, but also to provide for their performance and, if necessary, to enforce them in a court of law.[23]

Conversely, the creditors of companies are limited to making claims against assets held by the companies. They have therefore typically no claims against the assets of the companies' shareholders. Exceptionally, however, corporate laws provide for a piercing of the corporate veil. The concept of limited liability is not a necessary corollary of separate legal personhood, but it typically complements the concept of legal personality: "Owner shielding" achieved by limited liability is the counterpart of the "entity shielding" based on legal personality.[24] By protecting shareholders from the companies' creditors' claims limited liability lowers their risk and enables them to diversify their investments.[25]

Whether and how these different considerations can be applied to DAOs requires further discussion, but already their understanding as "a nexus of contracts, built entirely in software"[26] or, respectively, as a "nexus of smart contracts"[27] points to striking parallels with these profound lines of corporate law debate: "The nexus of smart contracts on the blockchain represents a fundamental challenge to business association law".[28]

3. Nexus for Regulation

Legal personality does not only play a role in that horizontal dimension of contractual relationships between the entity and private partners. It also has a vertical dimension that concerns its relationship with state bodies: "Beyond its fundamental role as a nexus for contractual relationships with private counterparties, the corporation also operates as a distinct nexus for the imputation of legal rights and duties vis-à-vis the state".[29] Due to the regulatory power of the state, this second relationship is characterized by subordination rather than by a balanced, contractual coordination.[30] In a recent article, Mariana Pargendler has convincingly demonstrated that in this respect as well, the legal spheres of the corporation and its shareholders are typically separated. Similar to asset

---

23 Similar *Gerner-Beuerle/Schillig* (fn. 21), p. 195 (referring to "the making and accepting of offers, the terminating of contracts, the accepting or rejecting of the delivery of goods, the making of payments through company accounts, etc").

24 *Armour/Hansmann/Kraakman/Pargendler* (fn. 16), p. 9 (also arguing owner shielding to be less fundamental than entity shielding as it can be achieved „by contract, without statutory fiat").

25 Cf. *Manne*, Virginia Law Review 53 (1967), 259 (262).

26 *Werbach*, The Blockchain and the New Architecture of Trust, 2018, p. 110.

27 *Möslein*, in: Festschrift for Christine Windbichler, 2020, p. 889.

28 *Rodrigues*, Iowa Law Review 104 (2019), 679 (728); in a similar vein *Schillig* (fn. 13).

29 *Pargendler*, University of Pennsylvania Law Review 169 (2021), 717 (720).

30 The distinction between the equilibrium relationship of private law and the subordinate relationship of public law is deeply rooted in German legal scholarship, cf. for instance *Leipold*, BGB Allgemeiner Teil I, 2008, § 1 para. 9 et seq.

partitioning, regulatory partitioning is not absolute. Sometimes, the law peeks behind the corporate veil and imputes certain legal rights or duties of shareholders to the corporation (veil peeking).[31] In addition, again similar to the considerations regarding the nexus of contracts, the law needs to assign competences of representation to natural persons in order to enable entities to operate effectively as a nexus for regulation. Otherwise, they could neither apply for licenses nor object to wrongful administrative acts. Regulatory law even shapes parts of the governance structure of subjected entities in order to achieve goals of the common good such as financial stability or environmental protection.[32]

The concept of the legal person as a nexus for regulation gains particular importance for entities operating in financial markets. Actors on such markets are subject to intensive supervision and to numerous public law duties. Market entry already requires a license. In order to be granted such license, entities need to fulfil certain conditions, some of which relate to their size, capital, legal form and also their legal personality. Other criteria do not relate to the entity itself, but to its members or directors. For instance, Art. 13 of the CRD IV Directive[33] provides that an authorisation to commence the activity of a credit institution shall only be granted where at least two persons effectively direct the business of the applicant credit institution. Moreover, these persons need to fulfil the reputation, knowledge, skills and experience requirements set out in Art. 91 para. 1 of the Directive.[34] The MiFID II Directive incorporates these and other key governance requirements of CRD IV into the legal regime for investment firms.[35] While all these requirements of regulatory law have been tailored to traditional forms of companies, the increase of DAO activities on financial markets raises the question of whether DAOs can or should qualify as a nexus for regulation as well. After all, this issue relates to the more fundamental question of their legal personality. Moreover, even with regard to DAOs operating in financial markets, it reaches far beyond financial markets law and concerns, for example, also money laundering law: Who has respective obligations and who can be the addressee of supervisory measures if DeFi projects of DAOs have money laundering implications?[36]

---

[31] For various examples in different areas of law, see *Pargendler* (fn. 29), p. 757–780.

[32] Extensively *Rast*, Unternehmerische Organisationsfreiheit und Gemeinwohlbelange, 2022.

[33] Directive 2013/36/EU of the European Parliament and of the Council of 26 June 2013 on access to the activity of credit institutions and the prudential supervision of credit institutions and investment firms, amending Directive 2002/87/EC and repealing Directives 2006/48/EC and 2006/49/EC, OJ L 176, 27 June 2013, p. 338–435.

[34] In more detail on these (and other) requirements to be met by the management body: *Busch*, Corporate Governance of Financial Institutions According to CRD IV & MiFID II: Preliminary Draft, available at SSRN: https://ssrn.com/abstract=3061735 (7.08.2023).

[35] *Wundenberg*, in: Veil (ed.), European Capital Markets Law, 2022, p. 623, 625.

[36] In more detail *Klaas*, BKR 2023, 162.

III. Legal status of DAOs

While the precise legal qualification of a DAO depends on the applicable jurisdiction, there are large parallelism between most jurisdictions regarding the applicable legal forms and the related questions of their application to DAOs.[37] All around the world, corporate laws address similar basic agency problems, and they therefore show a common anatomy.[38] More particularly, most jurisdictions provide legal forms that are created by registering a company with the competent authorities but also offer other legal forms that emerge simply from agreements between shareholders or from actual acts taken by several persons that pursue a common purpose. Typically, the former alternative of company creation applies to corporations whereas the latter applies to partnerships. This divide between two different options of creating companies corresponds to the distinction between "wrapped" and "non-wrapped" DAOs. While non-wrapped DAOs emerge without any explicit choice of a specific legal form by the founders or participants of the DAO, "wrapped" DAOs are registered with competent authorities and their legal form is therefore chosen and established on purpose.[39] In order to analyze the differences between wrapped and non-wrapped DAOs in more detail, some brief considerations on the operation of DAOs and their governance are necessary.

1. DAO Governance

In contemporary corporate law debate, the term "governance" or "corporate governance" describes the factual and legal framework that determines the management and supervision of a company.[40] In other words, governance describes the structures and processes that the management of companies is based on. Generally, governance aims at balancing the interests of different stakeholders like investors, shareholders, customers, authorities and management.[41] The idea of corporate governance follows from the various principal-agency relationships within companies, in particular from the agency problems that arise

[37] *Mienert*, Dezentrale Autonome Organisationen (DAOs) und Gesellschaftsrecht, 2021, p. 81.

[38] *Armour/Hansmann/Kraakmann*, in: Kraakman et al. (eds.), The Anatomy of Corporate Law (3rd ed. 2017), p. 2.

[39] *Moore*, Australian National University Journal of Law and Technology 2 (2021), 109 (113).

[40] In a broad perspective, for instance Hopt et al. (eds.), Corporate Governance in Context, 2005; cf. also Grundmann/Möslein/Riesenhuber (eds.), Contract Governance – Dimensions in Law and Interdisciplinary Research, 2015.

[41] *Roberts*, in: Möslein/Omlor (eds.), FinTech-Hdb., 2021, § 4.1.

from the relationship between the management and the shareholders, where both actors can have divergent or even opposite interests in specific situations.[42]

As an alternative to conventional companies, DAOs aim at solving this principal-agent-problem in a more efficient, technology-based way.[43] Similar to companies, they are established as a tool for decentralized decision making, and they therefore provide a governance framework designed to serve the purposes of the specific DAO. As in other, corporate or contractual institutions, their governance framework pre-structures the decision-making process. In order to analyse the legal implications of DAOs on corporate law, procedural law and financial supervision law, their governance processes are a prerequisite that needs to be understood. In order to serve this purpose, we first provide a short overview on DAO governance before we then (see section IV.1) explain what it entails and what role it plays within the DeFi ecosystem.

In its core, DAO governance consists of a voting mechanism where DAO members can decide about specific proposals related to the structure of the DAO or to its business operation by either a "yes" or a "no" vote.[44] The DAO members are the holders of so-called governance tokens. Governance tokens are a specific form of crypto asset that are issued by the DAO protocol. Much like shares, they can be directly transferred to investors but can also be traded on (secondary) crypto markets. Governance tokens transfer their respective holders the right to vote within the DAO. In most cases, they also entail some form of pecuniary or financial participation in the DAO and the growth of the protocol.[45]

The tailoring of voting mechanisms differs from DAO to DAO. Voting rights, voting quorums, roles within the governance etc. depend on the specific design of the governance tokens of the individual DAO. By way of example, we describe the design of one of the most established DAOs, the MakerDAO which

---

[42] *Jensen/Meckling* (fn 17), p. 360; *Tse*, Victoria University of Wellington Law Review 51 (2020), 313.

[43] Cf. *Jentzsch*, Decentralized Autonomous Organization to Automate Governance, https://lawofthelevel.lexblogplatformthree.com/wp-content/uploads/sites/187/2017/07/WhitePaper-1.pdf (7.08.2023).

[44] *Mienert* (fn. 37), p. 152.

[45] Cf. *Nadler/Schär*, Decentralized Finance, Centralized Ownership? An Iterative Mapping Process to Measure Protocol Token Distribution, https://doi.org/10.48550/arXiv.2012.09306 (7.08.2023); INATBA, Regulating for the Future, Policy Notes on Decentralized Autonomous Organisations, Part 2 of 4, https://inatba.org/reports/inatba-publishes-policy-notes-on-decentralised-autonomous-organisations-part-2-of-4/ (7.08.2023); World Economic Forum, Decentralized Finance (DeFi) Policy-Maker Toolkit, Whitepaper, https://www.weforum.org/whitepapers/decentralized-finance-defi-policy-maker-toolkit/ (7.08.2023); *Rikken* et al., The Ins and Outs of Decentralized Autonomous Organizations (Daos), Unraveling definitions, characteristics and emerging developments of DAOs, https://dx.doi.org/10.2139/ssrn.3989559 (7.08.2023).

governs the DeFi-protocol Maker[46]. Maker DAO is one of the prototypical examples for a DeFi DAO due to its well-advanced decentralization process.[47]

Like most DAOs the Maker DAO governance consists of both off-chain[48] and on-chain[49] governance elements. Off-chain governance is facilitated through the Maker forum[50] and entails free discussions, informal polls about Maker-specific topics and so called "Signal Requests".[51] Signal Requests are a form of more formal poll that, other than discussions and informal polls, can have immediate impact on the proposal. The exact impact however depends on the specific request as signal requests are governed by the specific framework that allows them.[52] However, formal decisions that can even change the protocol are made through on-chain governance. On-chain governance is performed in a weekly and a monthly cycle depending on the specific change that is proposed. While weekly governance votes are aimed at recurring operational decisions that require quicker action (e.g. rates and debt ceilings),[53] the monthly governance cycle facilitates more fundamental, structural decisions like the edition of a new Core Unit.[54]

For a vote to be successful it needs to reach the ratification requirements. The yes-votes need to outweigh the no-votes and the yes-votes need to be represented by at least 10.000 MKR (the governance token of the MakerDAO).[55] Once a vote is successful the change to the protocol, framework or any other subject of the vote will be implemented.

---

[46] The Maker protocol is a DeFi protocol that issues the USD pegged stablecoin "Dai".

[47] Maker is even in the process of dissolving its foundation, that promoted the development of the Maker protocol until recently, *cf. Christensen*, MakerDAO Has Come Full Circle, https://blog.makerdao.com/makerdao-has-come-full-circle/ (7.08.2023).

[48] Off-chain governance refers to processes that are not facilitated on a blockchain but rather on a forum or other means of communication outside the respective blockchain.

[49] On-chain governance refers to processes that are facilitated directly on the blockchain, e.g., a vote that is made by sending a specific token to a designated smart-contract address.

[50] See https://start.makerdao.com/ (7.08.2023).

[51] Cf. Maker Operational Manual, https://manual.makerdao.com/governance/off-chain/off-chain-governance (7.08.2023).

[52] See Maker Operational Manual (fn. 51); an example for a Signal Request possibility is the initiation of an emergency response procedure, cf. Maker Forum, https://mips.makerdao.com/mips/details/MIP24#specification-proposal-details (7.08.2023).

[53] Maker Forum, https://mips.makerdao.com/mips/details/MIP16#sentence-summary (7.08.2023).

[54] Core Units are units consisting of several persons that are established and voted on by the governance token holders to work on and achieve specific projects and goals. A proposal that sets up a Core Unit provides for a budget, a mandate that sets the objectives and directions as well as a "Facilitator", an individual that is the person in charge and the point of contact for the respective Core Unit, cf. Maker Operational Manual, https://manual.makerdao.com/makerdao/structure/core-units (7.08.2023).

[55] Maker Operational Manual, https://mips.makerdao.com/mips/details/MIP51#MIP51c2 (7.08.2023).

This process shows that the governance of a DAO like the MakerDAO is fully member-driven. As opposed to traditional companies, no centralized authority has the ability to make a decision without a member-vote. Therefore, DAOs try to solve the fundamental principal-agency-problem by eliminating the agent and, more generally, any form of centralized management. In this respect, they are fundamentally different to (at least most) conventional corporate forms that are given legal personality in most jurisdictions. In DAOs, the management is typically conducted by the members themselves. Governance tokens transfer them the decision-making authority not only with regard to fundamental, structural issues but also with respect to the operation of the day-to-day business, thereby reducing the traditional division between shareholder and management.[56]

2. *Wrapped vs. Non-Wrapped DAOs*

The term "wrapped" refers to a "wrapper" as something that a DAO is "wrapped" in. The term is used in the context of the classification of a DAO as a company in the legal sense.[57] Generally, corporations as well as partnerships are understood as "organizational forms that allow a number of people to join together to pursue a common (commercial) purpose".[58] They are based on (some form of) a contractual agreement between their founders. In that sense, at least, they can be qualified as a nexus of contracts also from a legal perspective.[59]

A DAO can be qualified as an association of persons who pursue a common purpose by participating in this DAO. In the DeFi market, for instance, this purpose may consist in the governance of the DeFi protocol. This goal should constitute a common (commercial) purpose in the above-mentioned sense, so that the DAO can be qualified as either a partnership or a corporation. Most business laws, however, follow a "*numerus clausus* principle" which limits the available legal forms to those recognized by the competent jurisdiction.[60] In order to be legally recognized and therefore have legal personality, a DAO needs to be classified as a company form recognized by the competent jurisdiction. Depending on this classification, DAOs may already be able to have legal personality *de lege lata*. In that case, the question whether DAOs should have legal personality *de lege ferenda* would not even arise: Legal personality would then neither be a necessity nor a privilege, but simply a legal fact.

---

[56] *Tse* (fn. 42), p. 323; *Park/Chun/Kim*, Understanding Decentralized Autonomous Organizations (DAOs) as a Reaction to Corporate Governance Problems, Digital Strategy Review 2022.

[57] *Mienert* (fn. 37), p. 224; see also *Kaal*, Annals of Corporate Governance 5 (2021), 237.

[58] *Cahn/Donald*, Comparative Corporate Law, 2010, p. 105; with regard to German law cf., for instance, *Schäfer*, MüKoBGB, 2020, Vor. *§ 705*.1.

[59] Cf., however, *Koutsias*, Business Law Review 38 (2017), 136.

[60] *Reul*, DNotZ 2007, 184 (188).

a) Non-Wrapped DAOs

A DAO is created merely by programming smart contracts on a blockchain; there is no registration or any other form of formal legal act which is necessarily implied: The code just has to go "live". In lieu of any legal register, the only register where such DAO is included is a distributed ledger. According to the concept of real entity theory, its existence is just a social – or rather technological – fact. Bearing the "*numerus clausus* principle" in mind, one might at first sight suppose that due to the lack of any (legal) registration anywhere, such DAO lacks legal personality.

DAOs that are not registered with any competent authority are often referred to as "non-wrapped DAOs" as they lack the wrapping of a legally recognized corporate form. That wording is somewhat misleading, though. Not being "wrapped" does not necessarily mean that the DAO is not recognized at all by the applicable jurisdiction. Most business laws know legal forms that do not require any registration but might nonetheless imply legal personality. For example, US business law knows general partnerships and German business law recognizes the "Gesellschaft bürgerlichen Rechts" (GbR, cf. Sections 705 et seq. German Civil Code) as the legal form for civil law partnerships, and the "offene Handelsgesellschaft (oHG, cf. Sections 105 et seq. German Commercial Code) for commercial partnerships.[61] These legal forms do not need any registration (even though the applicable company law might provide for a legal registry even for private partnerships, such as German partnership law since its recent reform).[62] Their establishment requires, in principle, nothing more than compliance with the above-mentioned definition.[63] It implies nothing more than working together within a DAO for a common purpose, namely the governance of a DeFi protocol. In most cases a contractual agreement can be constructed at least on the basis of the participation in the governance process.[64] Participation

---

[61] Cf. *Mienert*, How can a decentralized autonomous organization (DAO) be legally structured?, Legal Revolutionary Journal LRZ (2021), http://dx.doi.org/10.2139/ssrn.3992329 (7.08.2023).

[62] With the entry into force of the Act on the Modernisation of Company Law (so-called MoPeG) on 01.01.2024, a new register is being created for GbRs. The registration of the GbR is in principle voluntary (and, in particular, not a pre-condition of legal personality, cf. Sec 705 para. 2 German Civil Code in the version applicable as of 1.1.2024). Many legal transactions, however, require the GbR to be registered. For instance, it cannot acquire real property without being registered (cf. Sec. 47 para. 2 German Land Registry Code). In more detail, for instance, *John*, NZG 2023, 243; *Wertenbruch*, ZPG 2023, 1.

[63] Cf. *Mienert* (fn. 61).

[64] *Schillig*, Decentralized Autonomous Organizations (DAOs) under English Law, Law and Financial Markets Review 2023, https://doi.org/10.1080/17521440.2023.2174814 (7.08.2023); *see in detail* (for German law) *Mann,* NZG 2017, 1014 (1016); *Filippi/Wright*, Blockchain and the Law: The Rule of Code, 2018, p. 142.

in the decentralized governance makes most DAOs legal entities.[65] If their purpose is of a commercial nature, they will be treated as commercial partnerships, otherwise as private partnerships. The qualification as a partnership comes with all advantages and disadvantages of legal recognition, including the ability to own assets, but also to enter legal commitments and bear liabilities.[66] What it does not necessarily imply, however, is limited liability so that the participating token-holders may well run into personal liability. Even without any registration with a competent authority, a DAO can therefore have the ability to bear rights and obligations, just by being created on a distributed ledger and used as a governance tool. In that sense, legal personality is therefore the default for a DAO, at least in the DeFi market, but this does not necessarily imply limited liability. Insofar as partnerships are equipped with legal personality under the applicable law even without registration, the question is therefore not whether DAOs need legal personality or not. The question is rather whether that specific legal form fits to the inherent principles and ideas of DAOs.

b) Wrapped DAOs

A "wrapped" DAO is a DAO that is not only registered on a distributed ledger but is in addition legally structured in a way that enables it to get legally registered. As has been shown, DAOs may acquire legal personality even without such a wrapper. But the wrapper can mitigate the disadvantages that arise from the classification of a DAO as a partnership. Most commonly it is argued that the wrapper has the main purpose of shielding governance token holders from personal liability as a partner in the partnership. In that perspective, the wrapper serves as a limited liability device. The typically chosen company forms are in fact legal forms with limited liability, in particular LLCs and foundations. All chosen wrappers have in common that there is asset partitioning between shareholders and the company. This separation is a necessary condition of limited liability and the exclusion of personal liability of the shareholders. Other forms, like partnerships, do not limit the liability of the partners (i.e. the "shareholders" of the partnership). Other legal forms of incorporation are no options for DAOs due to their legal requirements regarding the structure and the registration act.[67]

---

[65] Even though English law provides a narrower definition of partnerships DAOs should qualify as partnerships under English law too, cf. *Schillig* (fn. 64); INATBA (fn. 45).

[66] *Schillig* (fn. 64); *Mienert*, (fn. 61); *Mienert* (fn. 37), p. 192.

[67] *Hahn*, NZG 2022, 684 (686); in detail *Mienert* (fn. 37), p. 101; *Langheld/Haagen*, NZG 2021, 724 (725).

aa) Foundations

A traditional corporate form that is often used for the incorporation of DAOs is the foundation.[68] Most jurisdictions offer this legal form albeit with many differences. Foundations are organizations that are set up for a specific purpose and that have or can acquire assets to fulfil this specific purpose.[69] They are created by one or more founders that determine the purpose of the foundation. However, these founders do not become "shareholders" of the foundation. A foundation does not have any shareholders, but it may well have beneficiaries.

Core principles of foundations make them attractive as a legal wrapper for a DAO. After a foundation is created the underlying founder's will cannot be changed – even by the founders themselves ("solidification principle"). This feature correlates well with the "immutability" principle which is intrinsic to the idea of blockchain technology and therefore also applies to DAOs.[70] Accordingly, a foundation is autonomous in its actions as it is only bound by the rules underlying the foundation and the founder's initial will. This autonomy corresponds well with the core definition of a DAO since DAOs are created to make them autonomous from the developers once they start to operate.[71]

However, foundations do differ in their legal requirements and consequences between jurisdictions, especially regarding flexibility and taxation.[72] Some jurisdictions offer foundations that are better suited for DAOs than the offers of other jurisdictions. In fact, many projects choose jurisdictions like Switzerland and the Cayman Islands.[73]

bb) Limited Liability Company (LLC)

Another way of "wrapping" a DAO is the creation of a Limited Liability Company ("LLC") or a similar corporation. While LLCs offered by some jurisdictions are less viable options for DAO incorporation, other jurisdictions' LLCs have many benefits for DAO incorporation. In fact, some legislators have recently adopted their LLC statutes in order to offer a suitable framework specifically for DAOs. Namely the BBLLC ("Blockchain-Based Limited Liability Company) in the US State of Vermont as well as the DAO LLC in the State of

---

[68] For example, the developers of the Maker Protocol created a foundation under Swiss law – however, the Maker DAO itself could still be an unincorporated entity as the Maker Foundation is clearly separated from the Maker DAO, cf. Maker Foundation, The Maker Protocol: Maker DAO's Multi-Collateral DAI (MCD) System, https://makerdao.com/en/whitepaper/ (7.08.2023); *see also Schillig* (fn. 64).

[69] Cf. *Jakob/Uhl*, BeckOGK BGB, 1 July 2022, § 80.126 et seq.

[70] *Mienert* (fn. 61).

[71] Cf. *Mienert* (fn. 61).

[72] Cf. *Jakob/Uhl* (fn. 69), § 80.840.

[73] Cf. *Mienert* (fn. 61).

Wyoming are LLCs that were designed by the legislator to fit for the purposes of a wrapped DAO.

Under Vermont Law a BBLLC may provide for its governance in whole or in part through blockchain technology, 11 V.S.A. § 4173. This means that any decisions by the members of the BBLLC can be made through DAO governance processes, either on-chain or off-chain. Thus, governance structures in their technology-based form are recognized by the law and thereby made legally secure. Also, the BBLLC provides for limited liability of its members while also being equipped with legal personality.[74] However, the Vermont Law still requires the BBLLC to appoint a representative (agent) for the BBLLC. It also needs to designate an office for notification purposes (cf. 11 V.S.A. § 4007 in conjunction with § 4176). These requirements contrast with the decentralization idea that characterized the origins of DAOs. Instead, the law forces DAOs to establish a certain degree of centralization.

The appointment of an agent within the state is also a requirement of the Wyoming DAO LLC, Wyo. Stat § 17-31-105 (b). However, this agent does not need to be a "manager" of the DAO; the Wyoming DAO Supplement act states *expressis verbis* that the management shall be vested in the DAOs members or the members as well as a smart contract, cf. Wyo. Stat § 17-31-109. Also, the registration of the DAO can be made by any person by delivering an original (and a copy) of the articles of organization of the DAO, Wyo. Stat § 17-31-105 (a). The delivering person does not need to be a member of the DAO. With these rules, Wyoming enabled the core of typical DAO governance to be legally compliant while also providing for legal personality and limited liability.

c) *Summary*

Under most jurisdictions, DAOs acquire legal personality without having to register with state authorities. As partnerships they are generally not bound to specific corporate structures. However, this default qualification puts DAOs in an ambiguous situation: They do have legal personality but without limited liability. Moreover, the precise rules that are applicable to the respective DAO are often unclear. It therefore does not come as a surprise that more and more DAO projects opt into other legal forms and get "wrapped". Yet there is also scepticism about such incorporation. Based on their mantra "code is law" crypto-enthusiasts often oppose the idea of incorporation. They argue that incorporation could require centralization and thereby undermine the idea of a decentralized, non-hierarchal organization. Moreover, regulation and incorporation could hinder the development and innovation in the DeFi sector due to compliance and regulatory hurdles that apply.

---

[74] Cf. *Mienert* (fn. 61).

IV. DAOs in Decentralized Finance (DeFi)

1. Economic and Organizational Functions

DAOs play their most prominent role in financial markets. In fact, they are the basis of decentralized finance. In that so-called Decentralized Finance (DeFi) sector, two levels of governance overlap. In addition to internal governance structures of DAOs that have been discussed above, DAOs themselves govern the DeFi protocol. More precisely, the whole purpose of the DAO consists in governing the underlying DeFi protocol. DAO governance is no purpose in itself.[75] We therefore observe two different layers of governance: The first layer concerns governance in the sense commonly used by software engineers, meaning the development and modification of the software of the distributed ledger protocol respectively. The second layer is conceptually closer to the common definition of "corporate governance". Governance in this sense means taking advantage of DAOs for decision making with regard to the underlying business.[76] Both governance perceptions follow the procedure explained above. However, the second aspect is more accessible and interesting for legal analysis.[77]

Analyzing the decisions that can be made through governance in this second sense shows the organizational and economic functions that DAOs fulfil in the DeFi market. Understanding these functions is a prerequisite for determining a suitable legal framework and for deciding whether DAOs need legal personality in order to comply with those legal standards. Therefore, it is necessary to analyse the rights and obligations embedded in the DAO governance and its participants.

By way of example, we refer to the Maker Protocol and its DAO. The assigned voting rights to the governance token holders are listed in the Maker Protocol Whitepaper and the frameworks that were created by the DAO's governance in the last couple of years. The whitepaper lists specific rights and obligations of DAO governance:[78] Governance token holders can vote on the addition of new collateral asset types and their risk parameters as collateral for the lending of DAI, they can change existing risk parameters or add new risk pa-

[75] Cf. INATBA (fn. 45).

[76] *Hemmelmayr,* RDi 2023, 71 (75).

[77] It should be noted however, that the first meaning can be of significant legal interest as shown in the Wyoming Decentralized Autonomous Organization Supplement, cf. Wyo. Stat § 17-31-109 that requires that all smart contracts utilized by a DAO LLC shall be capable of being updated, modified or otherwise upgraded.

[78] It should be noted that the MakerDAO Whitepaper is outdated, and Maker governance got more complex and sophisticated in the past years with big changes ahead. However, the basic logic remains the same and for the purposes of this paper the simplified governance mechanics as they were described in the Maker Whitepaper are sufficient; see for more details on the changes to Maker governance *Christensen,* The 5 Phases of Endgame, https://forum.makerdao.com/t/the-5-phases-of-endgame/20830 (27.11.2023).

rameters to existing collateral asset types, they can modify the DAI Savings Rate, choose the set of oracle feeds, choose the set of emergency oracles, trigger emergency shutdowns, allocate funds of the Protocol to different needs and ultimately upgrade the protocol in general.[79] It is noteworthy that these rights are named as "responsibilities" of the governance token holders in the Whitepaper. This correlates with the idea that governance is understood in a "corporate governance" sense so that the governance token holders fulfil the function of the management of the Maker Protocol.

A closer look at these responsibilities and a comparison with regulatory requirements in the traditional financial market underscores the core position of the DAO governance. The DAO governance authorizes the governance token holders to vote on the allocation of funds in the DAO treasury and the transfer of resources in general.[80] In traditional financial regulation the management of funds and resources is a core task of the management of a financial service provider. Compliance with minimum own funds obligations, for example, is seen as one of the most important pillars for secure banking, as shown by the mere existence of the Basel Framework.[81] In accordance, the recently adopted MiCAR[82] also provides regulatory requirements to the funds of crypto service providers and crypto asset issuers. Addressees are obliged to hold minimum own funds (cf. Art. 35 MiCAR for issuers of asset-referenced token and Art. 67 para. 1 in conjunction with para. 4 a) MiCAR for crypto service providers) and a reserve of assets (Art. 36 MiCAR for issuers of asset-referenced token). While it is unclear whether DAOs are addressees of the MiCAR at all, it is obvious that if this is the case, it will be the governance token holders that are ultimately competent to decide whether and how to comply with these requirements.

The picture gets even clearer when looking at the rights of the governance token holders to change product specifics like the DAI savings rate and the approval of collateral assets in exchange for the issuance of the DAI stablecoin. While the savings rate seems to be just one product specific at first glance, a closer look shows that the savings rate is a major governance tool within the Maker Protocol (as well as other stablecoin protocols). By decreasing or increasing the savings rate MKR token holders can influence the price of DAI and therefore govern the stability of the stablecoin.[83] The stabilization of the price

[79] Maker Foundation (fn. 68).

[80] Cf. *Axelsen* et al., Complex Systems Informatics and Modeling Quarterly 31 (2022), 51; *Wright*, Stanford Journal of Blockchain Law & Policy 6 (2021), 1; *Rikken* et al. (fn. 45).

[81] See the Basel Framework at https://www.bis.org/basel_framework/index.htm?m=2697 (7.08.2023).

[82] Regulation (EU) 2023/1114 of the European Parliament and of the Council on markets in crypto-assets, and amending Regulations (EU) No 1093/2010 and (EU) No 1095/2010 and Directives 2013/36/EU and (EU) 2019/1937.

[83] MakerDAO Blog, The DAI Savings Rate, https://blog.makerdao.com/dai-savings-rate/ (7.08.2023).

of a stablecoin, like the DAI, is one of the essential tasks of a stablecoin issuer. This relevance is clearly expressed in the regulation of stablecoins. For example, Art. 34 para. 5 MiCAR obliges issuers of asset-referenced tokens to create policies describing the stabilization mechanisms of their issued token. Another example is the New York bill draft 10985-04-3 which proposes a specific regulatory regime for digital assets. The proposed amendment to the general business law of New York prohibits the use of the term "stablecoin" unless a stablecoin ratio equal to 1.0 or greater is maintained at all times, G.B.L. Art. 23-C § 359-o para. 10.

These examples show that DAO governance entails decisions to processes and compliance regimes that are crucial to regulatory oversight and therefore for consumer protection, market functioning, and market stability. In DAOs, these decisions are not made by a board of directors like in most conventional incorporated companies, but they are typically made by the owners themselves, i. e. by the governance token holders. DAO governance therefore replaces traditional management and needs to be viewed in all legal aspects as exactly that: the managerial authority of the respective DeFi protocol.

2. *Legal Challenges*

In the core application of DAOs in financial markets, there are striking parallels with the corporate law debate and its conceptualization of the corporation as both a nexus for contracts and a nexus for regulation.

a) DAOs as a Nexus for Contracts

More specifically, to return to the terminology of this debate, the question arises as to whether DAOs can be not only a nexus of (smart) contracts but also a nexus for contracts.[84] It has been shown that legal personality as such is not in question, since DAOs have this quality at least by virtue of their qualification as partnerships. Legal personality enables DAOs to enter into contractual relationships with private counterparties, and it also implies a separation between the assets of the DAO and its token holders.[85] The real question, however, is whether this entity shielding based on the legal personality of DAOs has as its counterpart an owner shielding achieved through limited liability: The limitation of liability plays a key role in current debates about DAOs,[86] and increasingly also in lawsuits. In the field of DeFi, these lawsuits are particularly large

[84] See above, II.1.

[85] Cf. *Chiu*, Regulating the Crypto Economy: Business Transformations and Financialisation, 2021, p. 111, 114 et seq.; *Tendon/Ganado*, Revue Trimestrielle de Droit Financier 1 (2018), 1 (4).

[86] Illustratively, for instance, *Fenwick/Vermeulen*, in: Compagnucci/Fenwick/Wrbka (eds.), Smart Contracts: Technological, Business and Legal Perspectives, 2021, p. 161, 172–176.

in financial terms and therefore have a pioneering character. In a recent ruling, for instance, a federal judge in California denied motions attempting to excuse token holders of the bZx DAO (also known as the "Ooki DAO", a DeFi lending protocol) from liability in a novel class action lawsuit filed against that decentralized autonomous organization.[87] The court ruled that the suit's plaintiffs are allowed to proceed in suing not only bZx's leadership but also the many token-holding members of the bZx DAO.[88] The token holders, the court argued, "elected to forgo registering the DAO as an LLC or other legal entity with limited liability".[89] It found that the plaintiffs „have stated facts sufficient to allege that a general partnership existed among the BZRX token holders".[90] As a consequence, owning a token and participating in governance votes could create legal liability for its holders: A DeFi app with a DAO structure could therefore, at least in certain circumstances, extend legal liability to anyone who simply holds the governance token.

b) DAOs as a Nexus for Regulation

While the lack of limited liability in the contractual relationships of DAOs is widely discussed, their economic and organizational relevance in DeFi markets shows that the question of whether (and to what extent) DAOs have legal personality goes far beyond contract law. To return to the terminology of the corporate law debate again, DAOs are not only relevant as a nexus for contracts, but also, and maybe foremost, as a nexus for regulation. In the field of DeFi, the core question is whether DAOs can be the reference point of prudential duties and related measures of supervisory authorities.

Even market access requires such nexus for regulation. European financial law is based on a requirement of authorisation, the so-called licensing principle, for instance according to Art. 8 CRD IV with regard to credit institutions: Persons or entities wishing to carry out the regulated financial activities must obtain a license from the competent authorities.[91] The activities in question are subject to specific rules (regulation) that must be complied with from the outset and on an ongoing basis (supervision). Due to the licensing principle, DAOs can

---

[87] At their core, these proceedings relate to a flash attack where funds had been diverted in order to purchase a levered short position. The plaintiffs were victims of that hack that drained bZx for $55 million. In more detail *Harvey/Ramachandran/Santoro* (fn. 2), p. 133.

[88] Christian Sarcuni, et al., v. bZx DAO, et al., 22-CV-618 LAB-DEB (S.D. Cal. Mar. 27, 2023).

[89] Christian Sarcuni, et al., v. bZx DAO, et al., 22-CV-618 LAB-DEB (S.D. Cal. Mar. 27, 2023), para. 17.

[90] Christian Sarcuni, et al., v. bZx DAO, et al., 22-CV-618 LAB-DEB (S.D. Cal. Mar. 27, 2023), para. 18.

[91] For an extensive overview on the licensing principle and its implications for FinTech cf. the contributions in Vicente/Duarte/Granadeiro (eds), Fintech Regulation and the Licensing Principle, 2023.

only operate legally in DeFi markets if they are able to obtain such a license. Despite their legal personality, this is by no means a matter of course. With regard to the German implementation of the European licensing principle in Section 32 para. 1 of the German Banking Act (KWG), for example, the prevailing view in both legal literature and supervisory practice is that (commercial) partnerships as such cannot obtain a license, even though they may conclude legal transactions in their own name and may also be holders of rights.[92] Although commercial partnerships can be a nexus for contracts because of their legal personality, they cannot be a nexus for regulation. On the contrary, the personally liable partners – all of them! – must have the necessary license. These conditions may well be different in other jurisdictions, and indeed they are different for European licensing requirements for other financial services. For example, according to its Art. 2 para. 1 the MiCA regulation applies not only to natural and legal persons, but also to "certain other undertakings" so that DAOs are presumably included in its regulatory regime, at least unless the respective crypto-asset services "are provided in a fully decentralised manner without any intermediary".[93]

Nevertheless, the example of the German Banking Act illustrates that legal personality may well be limited to the contractual sphere, and that therefore a nexus for contracts does not necessarily provide a nexus for regulation. As a result, the licensing principle may effectively exclude DAOs from access to (certain) financial markets. Given their diversity and number, it is virtually impossible for every single token holder to have the necessary license. In contrast, a somewhat different approach has been taken by the US Commodity Futures Trading Commission (CFTC) when it took enforcement action against Ooki DAO for offering illegal digital asset trading and lending services: The CFTC opted to sue the DAO directly (rather than all of its token holders), defining it as an entity comprised of all those individuals who hold the Ooki DAO tokens and use them to cast votes over the organization's governance.[94] Even if DAOs are able to obtain a license in order to operate legally in DeFi markets, however, they face the difficulty that many supervisory regulations are tailored to centralized management structures, and they do not fit well with decentralized

---

[92] Cf. *Fischer/Krolop*, in: Fischer/Schulte-Mattler (eds.) KWG, CRR, 2023, KWG § 32.37 et seq., with further references.

[93] Recital 22 MiCAR. Another example is Art. 2 para. 1 lit. d of the Regulation on European crowdfunding service providers for business (ECSP Regulation). It refers to legal persons (who provide crowdfunding services), but many argue that this includes commercial partnerships, even in German literature (even though commercial partnerships do not qualify as "juristische Personen" under German law), see for instance *Engelmann-Pilger*, BKR 2022, 144 (145); *Izzo-Wagner/Otto*, BKR 2022, 155 (156); *Oppenheim/Taesler*, BKR 2023, 96 (97).

[94] In more detail *Field*, The law is coming for DAOs, https://coingeek.com/the-law-is-coming-for-daos/ (7.08.2023); see also Commodity Futures Trading Comm'n v. Ooki Dao, 3:22-cv-05416-WHO (N.D. Cal. Dec. 20, 2022).

DAO governance. In order to provide for an operational nexus for regulation in DeFi markets, DAOs and regulatory requirements need to be substantively aligned.

V. Conclusions

Legal personality for DAOs is neither a necessity nor a privilege. With respect to private law relationships in which entities act as a nexus for contracts, DAOs acquire legal personality as (commercial) partnerships in most jurisdictions, notably the US and Germany. To qualify as a partnership, there is no requirement to register with state authorities or to have a specific governance structure. It typically implies no more than cooperation within a DAO for a common purpose such as the governance of a DeFi protocol. A contractual agreement can be construed on the basis of participation in the governance process. However, the qualification as a partnership is a mixed blessing for DAOs: They acquire legal personality, but not limited liability. All token holders can therefore be held liable, without the possibility of diversifying their investments. In addition, the rules that apply to partnerships are often not well suited to DAOs, particularly to their unique governance structure.

As DAOs play their most prominent role in financial markets and form the basis of Decentralised Finance (DeFi), their legal status has implications that go far beyond private law: In the DeFi sector, DAOs are relevant not only as a nexus for contracts, but above all as a nexus for regulation. However, legal personality does not necessarily imply this ability. Even the necessary licenses cannot necessarily be obtained through commercial partnerships. Instead, some jurisdictions require, at least for certain financial services, that each personally liable partner holds the necessary license. Where legal personality is restricted in this way, the licensing principle effectively excludes DAOs from access to the relevant financial markets. Even where DAOs have market access, their market operation is hampered by the fact that many prudential rules are tailored to centralised management structures. Because of these limitations, DAOs are effectively unable to act as a nexus for regulation on DeFi markets. Their legal personality – although existing *de lege lata* – therefore requires a different design *de lege ferenda* if their access to such markets is desired in terms of legal policy.

Limited Liability as Applied to DAOs

Biyan Mienert

Abstract This paper examines the legal implications of Decentralized Autonomous Organizations (DAOs), which operate under different circumstances than traditional legal entities. DAOs seek to span the globe, bringing together thousands of members regardless of their physical location or cultural or financial background. However, their decentralized structure raises complex questions about the determination of applicable law, corporate status, and external actions that cannot be adequately answered using classical theories. The paper discusses whether legal recognition and regulation of DAOs should provide for limited liability, and the legal and practical challenges associated with such recognition. The paper concludes by discussing the need for a legally secure framework for consumer protection, tackling the often-unknown liability risk associated with DAOs.

I. Introduction

Although cryptocurrency regulation rapidly evolves across various sectors, leading to increased legal clarity, particularly in Europe, many Decentralized Autonomous Organizations (DAOs) continue grappling with significant legal uncertainty. This ambiguity still hinders growth and widespread adoption. Consequently, establishing a DAO necessitates more than just technical prowess; it also demands astute legal engineering to ensure seamless real-world operations and safeguard the interests of developers and contributors. This also comes with vast complexity, as the types of DAOs, and the term DAO has become so widely applied to so many disparate phenomena that, in practice, it is hard to define a clear and distinct meaning.

Nevertheless, it can be stated that most DAOs operate under different circumstances than many of today's traditional legal entities and other business associations. DAOs will not be run by boards or managers but will be governed by democratic or highly participatory processes or algorithms.[1] Rather than operating in one or a few countries, DAOs seek to span the globe and bring together thousands of members regardless of their physical location or cultural or

[1] *Wright,* The Rise of Decentralized Autonomous Organizations: Opportunities and Challenges, Stanford Journal of Blockchain Law & Policy. 2021 June 30; https://stanford-jblp.pubpub.org/pub/rise-of-days (10.09.2023).

financial background. DAOs often seek to avoid written agreements or other formalities, with members primarily agreeing to manage their affairs through software and the rules of the code.[2] A definitive description of a DAO remains elusive. Despite the original conception of DAOs, the term "DAO" has been broadly applied to various dissimilar phenomena. As a result, summarizing these diverse concepts within a single definition proves challenging.[3] By aiming for an inclusive characterization, DAOs could be described as a new form of scalable, open, self-organized networks that are coordinated by crypto-economic incentives, as well as self-executing code on the blockchain to achieve common goals.[4]

The original idea of a DAOs promises to extend the basic benefits of organizational structures, such as access to markets and cost efficiency, and to set new milestones by enabling groups to automatically control and coordinate certain actions and behaviors through the use of smart contracts, thereby operating more efficiently and transparently. In this respect, DAOs also radically challenge key issues and definitions of a company, such as the hierarchical organizational structure, the separation of company members from market participants, the cultural or technical homogeneity of members, and many other natural definitions of a company.[5]

Naturally, a DAO's decentralized structure and automated operations raise complex questions about the determination of applicable law, corporate status, and external actions that cannot be adequately answered using classical theories. According to the current legal situation, one of the most significant risks is the nearby classification of DAOs in most jurisdictions as some general partnership due to their structure, with the associated personal liability of all participants. The liability of the participants would be unlimited and personal. Since many consumers participate in such DAOs, a legally secure framework should be created for consumer protection, which tackles this often-unknown liability risk. This leads to the central question of this paper on whether legal recognition and regulation of DAOs should provide for limited liability and the legal and practical challenges associated therewith.

---

[2] See *Mienert*, Blockchain-based decentralized autonomous organizations, and corporate law, Ph.D. Marburg 2022, 44.

[3] See for different concept trends *Delphi Labs*, Assimilating the BORG: A New Framework for Crypto LawEntities, Medium 20.04.23.

[4] See *Mienert*, Blockchain-based decentralized autonomous organizations, and corporate law, Ph.D. Marburg 2022, 44.

[5] *Kaal*, Blockchain-Based Corporate Governance, University of St. Thomas (Minnesota) Legal Studies Research Paper No. 19-10, 2019, 10.

II. Limited Liability in Traditional Business Entities

The concept of limited liability for shareholders has evolved in three distinct periods: no limited liability (1600-1800), hybrid liability regimes (1800-1930), and broad owner shielding in the twentieth century. Limited liability became a uniform attribute of the modern corporation due to the growth of large, complex corporations with dispersed shareholding structures, where it became untenable for individual shareholders to have culpability for the actions of corporations. This allowed risk-averse persons to take business risks they may have otherwise avoided. Shareholders that enjoy limited liability only stand to lose what they have invested in the event of insolvency. Consequently, they can also invest in multiple corporations without having to monitor any of them closely.

Recognizing the constant interplay between law and economics, it becomes evident that the evolution of corporate legal frameworks has been driven by the need to reconcile public policy aspirations with the realities of the social and economic landscapes. Indeed, the push-pull dynamics between these two spheres have often resulted in significant shifts in legal structures.

As we enter the era of DAOs, we are beginning to see familiar patterns of friction between the current legal structures and emerging blockchain-based entities. This incompatibility and the resulting pressure for innovation echo the dynamics of corporate evolution observed in the past. Notably, in Germany, the Limited Company (GmbH) creates a precedent for how legal frameworks can adapt to incorporate new forms of associations. This artificial creation by the legislator illustrates how the law has, in the past, responded to the exhaustion of available corporate structures, paving the way for the development of hybrid entities that combine elements from existing corporate forms. The reason for this was that the legal forms of stock corporations and partnerships alone were insufficient to meet practical needs and that a company with the advantage of limited liability had to be created between these forms of association. The same considerations could also now lead to the conclusion, regarding the development of new technologies – especially in the area of blockchain and artificial intelligence – that corporate law must open up to new decentralized structures in which leading decisions under corporate law are also made by algorithms.

III. Limited Liability for DAOs: Potential Advantages

The apprehension over potential liability for DAO members has been notably amplified due to recent enforcement actions against DAOs, particularly in the United States. Notably, the cases of OokiDAO, where the DAO was classified as a general partnership by the CFTC, and the subpoena by the SEC against

SushiSwapDAO underpin the hostile regulatory environment for DAOs within the US.[6] As a consequence also a drop in DAO- participation is notable.

Despite these concerns, the prospect of personal and unlimited liability for DAO developers and governance token holders regarding the organization's debts seems, at first look, relatively limited. This can be attributed to the formidable evidentiary hurdles a claimant might need to overcome. These challenges span the identification of a legal partnership, establishing the relevant jurisdiction, and the potentially even more complex task of demonstrating the defendant's partnership status at the time the DAO debt was accrued. Given the high volatility and mobility of governance token holders and, to a lesser extent, developers, this could indeed pose a complex legal endeavor.

Still, DAO members have a dual role as shareholders and governing bodies, which leads to a two-track member liability. Firstly, there is a potential personal liability as shareholders for company debts. Secondly, there is the liability of members based on their governance role.

However, the effectiveness of both liability systems can be called into question in a decentralized organization. In a decentralized organization, management responsibility is distributed among a hardly manageable group of members, which leads to an extensive devaluation of liability as an effective means of traffic and creditor protection and behavior control. This calls into question the effectiveness of personal liability for company debts as personal security and challenges the institute of behavioral liability of the directors.

The rise of new technologies, such as blockchain and artificial intelligence, has brought about unprecedented challenges for corporate law and the traditional forms of business entities. As we navigate this uncharted territory, we must adapt our legal perspectives to address the evolving needs of these novel organizational forms. Particularly for DAOs, unique issues related to member liability and self-governance require careful consideration to ensure long-term sustainability and success. Recognizing these concerns underscores the urgency for legislative action.

Drawing from the lessons of corporate law evolution, we then focus on the concept of limited liability, a doctrine that has facilitated the growth and dynamism of traditional corporations. In the context of DAOs, limited liability could play an equally, if not more, crucial role. By protecting DAO participants' personal assets, limited liability promotes an environment conducive to innovation and risk-taking within the decentralized economy. This protective layer mitigates potential financial repercussions, thereby fostering a more open and daring exploration of new ideas and strategies.

---

[6] *Nikhilesh/Knight*, Sushi DAO, Key Contributor Served With SEC Subpoena, Coindesk, March 21, 2023, available at: https://www.coindesk.com/policy/2023/03/21/sushi-dao-key-contributor-served-with-sec-subpoena/ (10.09.2023).

Limited liability also helps minimize perceived risks, attracting more investors and contributors to DAOs. With reduced concerns about personal financial liability, these organizations can more easily secure the necessary capital and talent to expand and scale their operations, further driving growth and success.

Lastly, introducing limited liability for DAOs facilitates their integration into existing legal frameworks. By clarifying the rights and responsibilities of those involved, this measure ensures appropriate regulation and fosters collaboration between DAOs and traditional businesses. Consequently, this alignment helps create a more stable and supportive environment for the development and growth of DAOs in the long run.

IV. Legal and Practical Challenges in Applying Limited Liability to DAOs

1. Approaches

In the last few years, we have observed a proliferation of potential methods to create limited liability for DAOs. Legal solutions typically fall into three categories: Full Entity 'Wrappers,' Partial Entity Wrappers,' and Adjacent Entities, each with unique attributes and examples.[7]

Moreover, unincorporated DAOs may adopt "Constitutions" or participation agreements for structure and risk mitigation, such as SAFE DAO or COW DAO.[8] Some jurisdictions, like Wyoming and Vermont, have enacted "DAO laws" to grant limited liability to DAO members under specific conditions, like forming "DAO Limited Liability Companies". However, these can potentially conflict with the autonomous nature of DAOs and may have other drawbacks, as these DAO laws often introduce specific rules for DAOs which can lead to unintended outcomes, given the possible confusion and unpredicted implications caused by its sometimes arbitrary modifications to standard LLC rules.

Regulation of DAOs, in the form of a specific DAO law, should provide uniformity and legal certainty while offering flexibility for further innovation by not imposing formal registration requirements.

First, it is essential that the DAO is recognized as a company with legal capacity so that it has rights and legal obligations and can therefore take legal action.

Secondly, a precise tax classification is required that creates clear structures for companies and tax authorities, especially given digital assets. [9]

---

[7] For an overview, see: Mienert, Biyan, How Can a Decentralized Autonomous Organization (DAO) Be Legally Structured? (December 1, 2021). Legal Revolutionary Journal LRZ 2021, available at SSRN: https://ssrn.com/abstract=3992329 (10.09.2023).

[8] See https://forum.safe.global/t/sep-1-safedao-participation-agreement/110; (10.09.2023).

[9] *Oren*, ICO's, DAO's, and the SEC: A Partnership Solution, Columbus Law Review Vol. 2018 No. 2, 617, 653.

Third, the consistent limitation of the personal liability of token holders is necessary for a low-friction secondary market. In order to comply with consumer and investor protection, a limitation of liability prevents secondary market buyers of tokens from assuming unknown or undesirable legal liability – especially in light of the fact that a reference to the personal liability of the parties involved, as in the dxDAO whitepaper, is the absolute exception.[10]

Fourth, the possibility explained above should be opened to represent digital company shares of the DAO in the form of actual equity tokens. Consequently, the complete dematerialization of company shares would be necessary for a genuine equity token *de lege lata*.

Fifth, decision-making within the DAO company should be enabled by a single body in assembly decision-making and/or an algorithm.

Finally, DAO companies should be enabled to store and digitally transmit all necessary documents or accounting Blockchain-based. Such digital decentralized self-governance by the totality of DAO members would be a novelty in the law of corporations; it is more in line with the principle of self-governance that characterizes personal corporations.

It remains to be seen whether it would be easier and quicker to adapt existing company law structures to the requirements of a DAO than to create a completely new one.

The DAO model Laws mostly try to fulfill the noted points. The COALA model law is the most prominent, which has been the root of most DAO laws.[11]

The Model Law for, published in 2021, has inspired various legislators, including those from Wyoming, the Marshall Islands, and Utah. This law has spearheaded strong use cases based on the flexible LLC model, demonstrating its potential in these settings.

However, a point of contention exists around Article 5(3) of the model law, which places unlimited liability on members who vote against the enforcement of a court order. This provision seems to contradict the well-established principle of limited liability. It is argued that there are different ways to achieve on-chain enforcement without risking the current idea of limited liability.

Another point of disagreement lies within Article 4(k). It imposes a dispute resolution mechanism as a formation requirement for Decentralized Autonomous Organizations (DAOs). Although this may appear excessive, DAOs present a unique use case that could benefit from blockchain-based Online Dispute Resolution (ODR). Especially larger DAOs are likely to encounter various internal disputes that could be resolved effectively through such a mechanism.

---

[10] "As DAOs do not (yet) enjoy legal personality in various jurisdictions, Reputation Holders may potentially be considered jointly and severally liable for the dxDAO's actions and obligations." See. dxDAO Whitepaper, 2019, 18.

[11] Coalition of automated legal applications (COALA), Model Law for Decentralized Autonomous Organizations (DAOs), 2021.

The model law also proposes that DAOs should be considered pass-through entities for taxation purposes (Article 20). However, this issue could be problematic and potentially be outside the scope of such a model law. Furthermore, it could raise concerns among token holders who might not want to bear responsibility for the DAO's tax liabilities.

In principle, the law does not impose implicit fiduciary duties on developers, members, or representatives toward each other or third parties, which is considered a reasonable approach.

The model law does not represent a fully elaborated rule set poised for direct implementation. Instead, it serves as a compendium of guiding principles designed to aid legislators in formulating DAO laws. Bearing in mind the aforementioned points and the critiques associated with the model law, legislators should adopt a minimalist approach when crafting a law concerning DAOs. This would allow the law to evolve in tandem with the adoption and adaptation of DAO structures in the market. Instead of initiating an overly regulated framework – a mistake made in the past – legislators should resist the urge to constrain DAOs within preexisting structures. Such an approach encourages flexibility, growth, and innovation in the DAO landscape while mitigating the risk of stifling these burgeoning entities with overly rigid legislation.

2. Consequence

Due to adding limited liability, creditor protection mechanisms for DAOs, like registration, accounting, and financial reporting obligations, become significant factors. The liability issue in DAOs is multi-faceted, necessitating an in-depth analysis of liability, creditor protection, and behavioral control.

A notable proposal involves establishing an independent liability fund for DAOs through mandatory insurance, similar to the liability structure of a German GmbH (limited liability company) or the German partially limited liability partnership (PartG mbB). This idea suggests that private insurance companies, with their industry knowledge and software protocol expertise, could assess the risks associated with a DAO and determine premiums accordingly.

This approach provides creditors with a central, easily identifiable, solvent debtor and significantly reduces the risk of liability claims for DAO members. It could potentially offer a balanced liability structure that addresses the lack of behavioral control inherent in DAOs, underscoring the importance of tailoring solutions to the unique challenges and opportunities presented by these innovative structures.

The legislative challenge lies in the effective design of this mandatory insurance, considering the cross-border activities of blockchain organizations. The issue of adapting minimum insurance amounts to company size and field of activity arises. However, these amounts can be significantly higher than the amounts that could be raised by members of decentralized organizations if mandatory minimum capital requirements were established. Private insurance companies can assess the risk associated with establishing a decentralized organization based on industry knowledge and expert review of the software protocols used and can consider this when determining premiums. This provides creditors of the decentralized organization with a central, easily identifiable, and solvent debtor for their liability claims. At the same time, the risk of liability claims for members of the decentralized organization would be significantly reduced. Overall, this approach could develop a balanced liability structure for decentralized (autonomous) organizations that also responds to the lack of behavioral control through the personal liability of individual human responsible parties.

3. An alternative new approach, the BORG Model[12]

Delphi Labs recently proposed the BORG (Blockchain Organized and Governed) model as a novel approach to the legal structuring of Decentralized Autonomous Organizations (DAOs). The model aims to blend the advantages of legal entity setups, such as enforceability and compliance, with the immediate trust and resilience inherent in DAOs. It seeks to enforce smart contract use through entity governing documents, establishing a system of on-chain checks and balances with the DAO to reduce various costs, including transaction, monitoring, agency, and potential legal fees.

The BORG model advocates for a stricter application of the term "DAO" in line with criteria set by pioneers like Stan Larimer, Dan Larimer, and Vitalik Buterin. The model introduces a new category for tech entities, preserving the original definition and purpose of DAOs. Many organizations currently presenting themselves as DAOs, such as LLC-wrapped or CoOp-wrapped entities, would be better classified as BORGs. This allows them to operate openly as innovative intersections of technology, law, and social experimentation, without the pressures of maintaining the pretense of decentralization and autonomy.

The BORG model offers a complementary solution to truly decentralized organizations through DAO-adjacent BORGs, utilizing existing entity types to support the DAO while still ensuring decentralization. This decentralizes government-related risks and encourages competition among legal models, avoiding pitfalls tied to specific "DAO laws" or "DAO entities."

---

[12] See *Delphi Labs*, Assimilating the BORG: A New Framework for Crypto Law Entities, Medium, https://delphilabs.medium.com/assimilating-the-borg-a-new-cryptolegal-framework-for-dao-adjacent-entities-569e54a43f83, 20.04.23; (10.09.2023).

The model introduces specialized BORGs such as Security BORGs, Protocol-Beneficial Value (PBV) BORGs, Grant BORGs, and IP BORGs. Security BORGs encapsulate emergency multi-sigs within legally accountable entities. PBV BORGs address legal issues arising from DAOs managing Protocol-Controlled Value (PCV), mitigating concerns about property rights, tax obligations, and regulations. Grant BORGs oversee the distribution of grants to projects in line with DAO objectives but may face tax complexities due to their service provider role. IP BORGs are tasked with managing and protecting a DAO's intellectual property assets.

While the BORG concept is not fundamentally new in its legal structuring—many DAOs have used more centralized entities for similar purposes—the rebranding might provide a fresh perspective and enable safer legal structures, especially in legally hostile environments like the US. Future exploration and refinement will be necessary to address the legal and operational challenges these BORGs will likely face.

V. Case Studies and Precedents

Within the ever-evolving realm of Decentralized Autonomous Organizations (DAOs), the adoption of limited liability structures is gaining momentum, signaling a trend towards increased legitimacy and regulatory compliance. As mentioned above notable case shedding light on this topic is the recent legal dispute involving Ooki DAO, which faced a lawsuit from the Commodity Futures Trading Commission (CFTC) as an unincorporated association. The CFTC argued that Ooki DAO fell under the classification of an unincorporated association according to state law, thus subjecting it to litigation as such. This lawsuit raised concerns about potential personal liability for Ooki DAO's voting participants and marked a significant milestone for Ooki DAO and the wider DAO community.

This case presented several crucial insights. Firstly, the CFTC's defense of classifying Ooki DAO as an unincorporated association serves as a critical point of consideration for future DAOs. Secondly, the CFTC affirmed the legal protection provided by "wrapping" DAOs, a process that shields DAO participants from liability. This validation offers a degree of legal certainty and provides an argument for incorporating a DAO. Additionally, the CFTC's perspective on the defining characteristics of an association, particularly in relation to voting, is likely to drive advancements in DAO governance processes, potentially leading to innovations such as anonymous voting or other novel mechanisms.

However, it is crucial to acknowledge that merely "wrapping" a DAO does not grant immunity from all legal violations. Individuals who engage in, aid, or abet illegal activities can be held liable under various statutes and theories of contributory liability, even if their actions are carried out through a business entity. This was evident in the case against OOki DAO/bZx developers, who faced allegations of violating the Commodities Exchange Act.

Considering this context, the most effective means of protection for DAO participants may involve two key components. First, diligent adherence to legal regulations, which is complex, given the dynamic and fragmented regulatory landscape. Second, potential participation in a DAO through a recognized business entity. These factors, along with the insights gained from recent legal developments like the Ooki DAO case, are key considerations for the future regulation and growth of DAOs.

VI. Conclusion

In concluding this exploration of the application of limited liability to DAOs, we are poised to witness a period of profound change and evolution in the decentralized economy. The application of limited liability to DAOs promises to foster growth and innovation and effectively address pertinent legal challenges. However, it simultaneously raises significant questions concerning jurisdiction, governance, and the delicate equilibrium between anonymity and transparency.

It is crucial to recognize the necessity of careful consideration of the legal and regulatory implications associated with DAOs, particularly in light of recent regulatory issues.

Developing a comprehensive and effective legal framework for DAOs necessitates ongoing dialogue and collaboration among all relevant stakeholders, including regulators, DAO creators, investors, and other parties with vested interests. This open communication is paramount to addressing, understand, and overcome the complexities and challenges inherent to the field.

There is currently no definitive "one size fits all" solution for DAOs. Until an inclusive legal framework is established which acknowledges DAOs' ability to operate fully decentralized with limited liability legal recognition and straightforward taxation, each DAO will have to navigate its unique legal landscape. This assertion is particularly pertinent when a DAO Token is involved, as it can potentially complicate the legal setup, given that Tokens are often classified as securities. This classification carries with it additional legal obligations, such as the need for prospectuses or registration with the relevant legal authorities.

Considering the current legal climate, each DAO should seek individual legal counsel to ascertain the best course of action tailored to its specific needs and circumstances. As we continue to grapple with these legal conundrums, we remain optimistic about the potential of DAOs to transform the landscape of our digital economy, provided we maintain a vigilant eye on the evolution of their regulatory frameworks.

Organizational Structure and the Regulation of DAOs*

Christopher Wray

Abstract This paper argues that organizations are generally social structures, and DAOs are too to the extent that they have non-trivial aims or control off-chain assets. Regulation is typically applied and enforced by way of the structural affordances of organizations. Analysis of a hypothetical case illustrates that a common DAO structure is sufficiently similar to that of a conventional employer organization for certain elements of employment regulation to be applied and potentially enforced. However, smart contracts make it possible for a DAO to secure by technical means certain protections or policy aims that would otherwise motivate the enforcement of conventional regulatory requirements. Thus there is scope for regulatory objectives to be achieved in part by way of a principle of functional equivalence of the novel technological arrangements of DAOs to certain existing regulatory requirements.

I. DAOs as organizations

What is an organization? In the sense of a set of persons collaborating to achieve some common purpose, an organization is the structure of relationships between the collaborators and the processes, in accordance with that structure, by which those collaborators coordinate their understanding, intentions and actions, and by which the structure itself is maintained or adapted[1]. An organization is a structure. This is both etymological (distinguishing "organs", i. e. functional units, and their relations to one another) and a conceptual necessity where the work of the organization involves collaboration across domains of knowledge or expertise, or across contexts, geographical, temporal or otherwise – i. e.

* This contribution is the revised version of a presentation at the International Conference on DAO Regulation, held at the Faculty of Law, University of Lisbon, on 20 April 2023. The author wishes to disclose his interest as a member of the Coalition of Automated Legal Applications (COALA), which produced the DAO Model Law cited in this paper; and as a co-founder and shareholder of Legal Graph Company Limited (Legra), which develops software for organizations, including smart contract-based budgeting tools for distributed financial control and dispute resolution.

[1] *Wray*, Systems of co-operation: organizational hierarchy and the practice of management, http://christopherwray.eu/CW-management_philosophy-20200531.pdf (31.05.2020); *Checkland/Scholes*, Soft systems methodology in action, 1999; *Beer*, Brain of the Firm, 1995.

where the work of the organization involves distinct functions, which must therefore be coordinated.

Structureless or "flat" organizations are a special case and do not generalize. An organization may truly lack structure because its purpose is so simple: it has a sole objective function to which every collaborator independently aligns themselves without further coordination, which implies that there be no requirement for domain knowledge or expertise such as to exclude any potential collaborator, nor any relevant local context or situational awareness to which a potential collaborator would have to orient themselves. The objective function is truly objective: interpretable by all and context-free. Most aims in life are not this simple.

Alternatively, an organization may be called structureless or flat because it lacks a formal hierarchy, especially the relatively fixed structure of power relations that an organizational chart purports to represent. It is usually acknowledged in such cases that there is nonetheless some social structure to the organization. This structure may be called "emergent" to reflect its dynamic nature or its basis in relationships other than a hierarchy of top-down power relations. The risk in such cases is that the informality of the structure entails its lack of transparency, which makes it harder for every collaborator to understand and participate in the processes which coordinate their actions and which maintain and adapt the structure itself – reintroducing the rigidity of a top-down power hierarchy.

Whatever else a decentralized autonomous organization (a DAO) may or may not be, it is an organization. To claim that a DAO just is the set of smart contracts which determine how its members are able to participate in changing the state of the underlying blockchain is either to claim that there are no other relevant relationships between the members (in particular, no social relationships, no off-chain communication which might influence on-chain behaviour – not a credible position to take) or to admit that there is such off-chain structure but that it is informal, emergent or otherwise not subject to the same transparency and clarity of process as the on-chain structure and processes, unless the DAO falls under the above special case of having an exceptionally simple purpose. This paper will focus on the general case in which the purpose of the DAO is more complex and thus the issue of the DAO's off-chain structure is central.

How, in this general case, should a DAO's other key attributes – its decentralization and its autonomy – be understood? It may be argued that they refer only to the technical attributes inherent in the DAO's smart contracts and the (public, permissionless) blockchain on which they are deployed: the potential decentralization of inputs to those smart contracts (i.e. voting power), where those inputs have been tokenized and distributed across a potentially large and diverse set of persons who control the private keys corresponding to those tokens (or not, of course – and where the ultimate control is in fact centralized, this potential decentralization will not be realized); and the potentially autonomous operation of these smart contracts – independent of the wider social environment – where there is sufficient distribution of the power to update the state of the blockchain by appending new blocks strictly in accordance with the inputs and algorithms of the smart contracts deployed upon it, such that even powerful actors in this wider environment (e.g. governments, regulators, legal institutions, persons having highly concentrated voting power in respect of a given DAO, the developers of a given smart contract or blockchain) are unable to intervene in the processes encoded in those smart contracts (and, similarly, where such block-producing or mining power is not sufficiently distributed, this potential autonomy will not be realized).

These concepts of decentralization and autonomy may be seen as reciprocal and multi-scale. The decentralization of voting power, i.e. its distribution across a diverse set of tokenholders, comprises the autonomy of the DAO as from its members, i.e. the independence of its decision-making from a subset of members having concentrated voting power; the decentralization of voting power among diverse tokenholders depends upon the autonomy of each tokenholder such that they cannot as a group be influenced or coerced in their voting. The decentralization of block-producing power comprises the autonomy of the operation of the DAO's smart contracts in its wider social environment, i.e. their independence from intervention by any subset of block producers having concentrated block-producing power or any powerful social actor such as a government or court that might coerce them, and thus the dependence of the outputs of the smart contracts solely upon the logic encoded in them and the inputs to them received from tokenholders. The autonomy of DAOs within the wider social environment grounds the credibility of decentralization of social power.

Note that even under this minimally technical interpretation of a DAO's decentralization and autonomy, the consequences at the larger, social scale cannot be isolated from the non-technical, lower-level reality: if individual tokenholders lack autonomy, i.e. they can be influenced or coerced in their voting, then voting power is not ultimately decentralized; if voting power is not decentralized, then the DAO is not autonomous; if DAOs are not autonomous, then they do not in themselves credibly support greater decentralization of power at a societal level. This amounts to *reductio ad absurdum* of the above minimally technical interpretation of the key attributes of a DAO. Whether an organization is decentralized and autonomous depends upon the relative autonomy of its individual members and the relative decentralization of the structure of relationships between them – where any such relationships, if they have any causal force whatsoever, will begin to affect the autonomy of individual members' decisions in relation to the organization. In the general case where a DAO's purpose is complex, for the reasons set out above the organization will necessarily be structured and that structure will usually include off-chain communications and social relationships between individual members of the DAO. Therefore lack of transparency of this off-chain structure and clarity as to the processes that maintain and adapt this structure will call into question the decentralization and autonomy of the organization, i.e. whether the DAO is a DAO at all.

II. Regulating DAOs as organizations

The purpose of regulating organizations is to support or enforce some policy at a societal level. Regulators can only engage with an organization to the extent that it offers some affordance for them to do so. Those affordances are determined by the structure of the organization. An organization that is incorporated so as to be recognized as having legal personhood, such as an English private company limited by shares, will be subject to regulation of its process of incorporation e.g. in England, the minimal formalities of registering with Companies House[2] and subsequently filing annual accounts etc. The purpose of this relatively minimal regulation of the registration and reporting requirements is to establish key aspects of its organizational structure. This provides a basis for other, specific regulation, e.g. corporate taxation, workers' rights or enforcement of contracts. Identifying the members (shareholders) supports the tax authority in enforcing their tax obligations; identifying the board of directors, in whom accountability for control of the organization is ultimately centralized, supports the company court in enforcing the governance obligations set out in company law, or the employment tribunal in enforcing workers' rights, or the commercial court in enforcing contractual obligations with respect to a counterparty, or a financial regulator in enforcing financial services and markets regulations.

A common feature of organizations in most jurisdictions is the centralization of accountability for the actions of the organization in a subset of the persons involved in the collaboration to achieve the organization's purpose, typically a board of directors or trustees. This provides a simple affordance for exerting regulatory pressure: ultimately, if directors fail to respond to requests from regulators or courts, they may face personal civil or criminal liability, or a court may substitute directors with its own appointees, who can then exercise the powers concentrated in the board. Similarly, centralization of control of financial assets, in particular credit balances held by banks, provides a simple affordance for exerting regulatory pressure: the specific officers named on the bank mandate, and ultimately the board of directors or trustees which creates or updates that bank mandate, may be held accountable for their instructions to the bank to transfer funds on behalf of the organization; and the bank itself may be

2 Parliament, U.K. Public General Acts, 2006 c. 46, Part 2.

subject to a court order (in England, a third party debt order) to transfer funds directly where the organization has failed to settle a judgment debt.

Perhaps the key technological feature of a DAO is the potential truly to decentralize control of on-chain assets among tokenholders. This decentralization of financial control ranges from the simplicity of a diverse DAO membership without any particular concentration of voting power voting their tokens on each and every proposal to transfer on-chain financial assets such as crypto-currencies or other tokens, fungible or non-fungible, having some market value; through more complex structures for decision-making such as (potentially recursive) delegation of power over on-chain assets to sub-sets of the membership ("sub-DAOs") or more complex decision-making processes such as authorizing a sub-DAO or even a third-party treasury manager to make decisions over on-chain assets within certain parameters, such parameters being set by the DAO; to the illusory case of votes of DAO members that do not technically effect the transfer of funds, the real power to do so remaining in the hands of a few e.g. founders who control a multi-signature wallet that holds funds on behalf of the DAO.

To the extent that a DAO purports to control (i.e. control in a decentralized manner) any asset, that asset must be a crypto asset, i.e. a digital asset that exists purely on-chain as the state of a blockchain. With respect to any other kind of asset, e.g. funds in a bank account, intellectual property rights, movable property or real estate, there will usually be individuals capable of being identified by a court as having possession (of chattel property) or having the power to direct the disposal of the asset on behalf of the organization. For instance, where intellectual property rights were purportedly assigned to the organization by contract, either those who purported to sign the contract on behalf of the organization had actual or ostensible power to act in that capacity, in which case they could do so again subsequently to dispose of those rights; or they did not, in which case there was no contract and the rights were never assigned. Once control is legally centralized in individuals in this way – whether as a creditor e.g. a bank, as an officer of the organization e.g. a signatory on a bank account, as a partner, or as a trustee e.g. one of up to a maximum of four legal owners of real property in England, or trustee for members comprising an unincorporated association – regulatory pressure may be brought to bear on those individuals: ultimately, court orders and personal civil or criminal liability.

There would not seem to be any principled basis for seeking (and little reason to expect that governments and regulators will in practice adopt) an alternative regulatory approach for organizations whose assets are controlled in a centralized manner by individuals, since this centralization provides the usual affordance for the application of regulatory pressure and raises the familiar motivations for placing special obligations (fiduciary or statutory duties) on those individuals: the potential conflict between principal (the organization as a whole, or the members) and agent (the individual or individuals with control over assets belonging to the organization or membership); the protection of minority interests in the organization from abuse by the majority (e.g. in an English company, unfair prejudice[3]); and the protection of wider social interests, whether as consumers or more generally in addressing the negative externalities of an organization's operation e.g. in respect of the natural environment.

This raises the possibility of hybrid organizations that are truly DAOs, having decentralized control of crypto assets, and yet legally own (subject to recognition of their legal personhood, which will be discussed in the following section) other kinds of asset. Such organizations would likely find themselves subject both to existing regulation or litigation as it is able to address points of centralized control, and to any novel regulation that has been adopted in order to address the unique affordances of decentralized financial control of crypto assets among a potentially very large DAO membership.

There are therefore two scenarios in which a DAO might find itself subject to existing regulation designed for centralized organizations. The first, as set out in the previous section, is where the structure of the organization is not flat but in fact a more complex set of relationships and processes, some of which are not represented and carried out on-chain, which structure tends naturally to result in the respective centralization of certain elements of decision-making in certain parts of that structure. The second is where the organization owns assets other than crypto assets. Each scenario gives rise to the potential for centralization of decision-making or control such as to provide an affordance for regulatory intervention. Furthermore, under these scenarios, unless the DAO provides transparency in representing to all members its full structure, both on-chain (i.e. technical control of crypto assets) and off-chain, as an organization it will suffer the disadvantages of an opaque power structure in respect of decisions generally and/or lack of clarity specifically regarding the control of its off-chain assets. The off-chain structure will reflect the social depth we expect in any complex organization: formal and informal relationships and information flows; not only roles but also behavioural norms and the values by which actions are assessed; goals and intentions that vary widely in scope across a range of temporal scales, and the network of dependency relations between them[4].

---

[3] Parliament (fn. 3), Part 30.
[4] *Checkland/Scholes* (fn. 2).

III. Regulating DAOs as DAOs

This section will consider the case of a hypothetical DAO that holds only crypto assets so that the focus may be its organizational structure and the implications for its regulation. It is also assumed for the purpose of this analysis that the legal personhood of the DAO is recognized on the basis set out in the COALA DAO Model Law[5] (as more or less faithfully adopted in 2023 in the State of Utah[6]).

Under the Model Law, a DAO is defined[7] as "smart contracts deployed on a public, permissionless blockchain, which implements specific decision-making or governance rules enabling a multiplicity of actors to coordinate themselves in a decentralized fashion. These governance rules must be technically, although not necessarily operationally, decentralized." The commentary to this article elaborates "technically decentralized" as providing "at least the potential of decentralized governance". Article 3(18) defines a member as "any person or DAO who has governance rights in a DAO". As a matter of interpretation, these governance rights determining membership must relate to the governance rules implemented on-chain, i. e. they must be rights exercised by way of technical control of the inputs to the DAO's smart contracts. If members' exercise of their governance rights were instead to depend on some action by some agent(s) who might or might not act in accordance with the members' choices, then there would not be the potential for decentralized governance as those agents would comprise a technically centralized means for effecting the rights of members (even if in fact they tended to do so faithfully and thus governance decisions were usually decentralized operationally).

One of the simplest organizational processes that such a DAO could follow is to allocate the crypto assets of the DAO to proposals voted upon by the members, using on-chain voting as the final step to effect the transfer of those crypto assets. Even in this simplest case, there are likely various off-chain social structures and processes that provide for, e. g. discussion of proposals and initial non-binding votes to assess the level of support before proceeding to a final vote. This is in practice a common organizational form for DAOs (though there are also many instances of DAOs following this form that do not have decentralized control of their crypto assets but instead centralized control by e. g. a group of founders, who tend to respect the off-chain votes of members and thereby implement operational decentralization despite the lack of technical decentralization; these instances would not qualify as a DAO under the Model Law).

[5] Accessed at https://www.lextechinstitute.ch/wp-content/uploads/2021/06/DAO-Model-Law.pdf (19.04.2022).

[6] Laws of Utah, 2023, c. 85.

[7] COALA (fn. 6), Art. 3(7).

Even in this simplest case, at the point of transfer of crypto assets to the blockchain address specified in a proposal, control is centralized once again in the hands of those who control the address that received the crypto assets, which in the case of a larger proposing group would typically be the leader or leaders of that group. Even where a proposal relates to resources for a team or teams for a longer period e.g. a quarterly budget for some aspect of a DAO's operations, the granting of crypto assets by the DAO can mark the end of decentralized financial control and the beginning of re-centralized control of those assets from the perspective of those collaborators who have an interest in receiving a share of them. Of course, the DAO could insist that all such grants of assets are made to groups structured as a DAO (a sub-DAO), so that decentralized financial control applies recursively as assets are granted to proposals, until some sub-sub-[...]DAO grants resources directly to an individual for work for which that individual is solely responsible. This is effectively to insist that all DAO purposes, however complex, be decomposed top-down into tasks small enough to assign to an individual. This may apply to certain kinds of work but does not generalize to e.g. most knowledge work or complex services.

In the analysis of *Coase*[8] of the organization (firm) and the market, the reason why organizations exist at all rather than all work being subdivided as necessary and contracted out at the best price available in the market is because of market transaction costs – including the specification of the work in such detail that compensation for failure to perform the work could be enforced contractually, as well as market search costs and dispute resolution costs. One of the potential benefits of a DAO as an organization, rather than merely a technological platform for market transactions, is to enable the kinds of collaboration that can only take place inside organizations, including more complex or cross-disciplinary collaboration that cannot be fully specified in advance and tends to evolve substantially as work progresses.

Returning to the grant of assets in respect of a proposal, assume that all of the collaborators who, at the time the proposal was made and approved and the assets were granted, expected to receive some remuneration or resource out of those granted assets are also members of the DAO. The question then arises: where to draw the organizational boundary? Were some or all of those collaborators not members of the DAO, the situation might appear on its face closer to a market transaction in which the proposed work was contracted out (even if there were some overlap in membership of the DAO and those involved in the work of the contractor). But where all the collaborators are also members of the DAO, the situation appears on its face as the internal affair of an organization, albeit one with more participatory budgetary decision-making than a conventional enterprise. Is the activity of those collaborators the work of the DAO, or

[8] *Coase*, Economica 4 (1937), 386 ff.

not? Are they workers or employees of the DAO, or are they independent contractors or the employees of an independent contracting party?

Assume that one of the collaborators has a social falling out with one of the group's leaders and is subsequently excluded from the collaboration and denied any share of the granted crypto assets. Imagine that this excluded individual resides in England and brings a claim in employment tribunal for unfair dismissal[9] (and that key tests for such a claim are otherwise met, e.g. they have been working as part of this group for at least the qualifying period for bringing such a claim). Here, then, is a substantive regulatory issue applied to a DAO. It would not be surprising for a tribunal to find on some such facts that there was indeed an employer, whether the group's leader or leaders as sole trader or partners under contract to the DAO, or the DAO itself given that it has legal personhood and the collaboration involved (by assumption) only the members of the DAO; and perhaps to uphold the excluded individual's claim against that employer.

This scenario was designed to reflect one of the simplest cases of a DAO operating as a DAO: controlling only crypto assets and having minimal structure in respect of that control, i.e. votes on specific work proposals by all members by way of smart contracts that directly effect the transfer of those assets in accordance with those votes; and building on the specific regulatory framework for legal personhood of the DAO and limited liability of the members under the Model Law, which substitutes for conventional corporate registration and reporting requirements the technical affordances inherent in such a DAO that are intended as their functional equivalents or otherwise to address the same policy concerns. Nonetheless, this hypothetical DAO still provides regulatory affordances in the domain of employment law, and those affordances are to be found in the off-chain structure of the DAO. The unfairness of a dismissal might turn on whether the excluded individual was offered a fair process by which to challenge the decision to exclude them, or who within the organization heard that appeal and re-affirmed the decision to exclude them. An alternative claim for unlawful deduction of wages[10] might depend on the (off-chain) communications that may have given rise to an expectation of remuneration on behalf of the individual that bound the DAO as employer. In the details of this scenario, the on-chain structure of the DAO and the processes implemented by its smart contracts do not determine these issues, and a tribunal would look to the relevant, social structure and processes that exist off-chain.

---

9 Parliament, U.K. Public General Acts, 1996, c. 18, Part X.

10 Parliament (fn. 10), Part II.

IV. DAO-specific regulation of DAO workers

Could DAO-specific regulation be drafted such as to address the above hypothetical scenario? What could be some elements of a hypothetical DAO Worker Model Law? Assuming that a continuing core feature of DAO decision-making will be voting by the whole DAO membership on high-level proposals for work to be undertaken or in setting parameters for other decision-making that involves only sub-sets of members or third parties, one question is whether decentralized financial control can be extended, even if only partially, to financial decision-making in respect of collaboration at a more fine-grained level that will inevitably be carried out by subsets of DAO members in their own local contexts or domains of knowledge (and across domains in the case of cross-disciplinary work) – and all without requiring top-down decomposition of tasks, i. e. sub-DAOs all the way down, which again does not generalize to more complex, cross-disciplinary collaboration?

The concept of the DAO membership as a whole setting parameters for decision-making by others can be extended to the reversion of decisions to the whole DAO in exceptional circumstances. The structure of decision-making by subsets of members or individual members of the DAO, at least as regards the transfer of the crypto assets that comprise remuneration for work, could reflect a process for the resolution of disputes that is encoded into smart contracts, the transparency of which achieves functional equivalence with e.g. a fair appeal process following a decision to dismiss. Such a process could be relatively complex as compared with conventional dismissal procedures, e.g. it could provide for multiple escalations of a dispute by a dissatisfied party to ever larger subsets of the membership until the whole DAO votes finally to resolve the dispute. Yet such a process, despite its complexity, could nonetheless be practical to implement because it is fully encoded in the smart contracts which handle the crypto assets in dispute, allowing the technology to play to its strengths. A potentially fair process in resolving a dispute between a worker and whoever controls their remuneration (perhaps by controlling their continued employment) is not exactly the same as a right to bring a claim for unfair deductions from wages or unfair or wrongful dismissal, but then the nature of piece-work or zero-hours contracts even under existing employment law are such that the original policy aims are arguably not always achievable.

This author has proposed (see the disclosure of interest in fn. 1) just such a model for smart-contract based distributed financial control of (crypto) remuneration and resources across dynamic networks of collaborative relationships (of members relying on other members for agreed roles or responsibilities, and responsibilities depending on other responsibilities so as to give a potentially deep dependency graph), the financial elements of which are encoded in smart contracts to reflect a complete or partial budget initially approved by the DAO membership as a whole, following which control over the release of budgeted assets is distributed to local decision-makers, but with the potential for progressive escalation, if appealed, to involve larger parts of the local graph and ultimately up to the whole DAO membership. The merits and weaknesses of such an approach will not be discussed further here other than to suggest that from a policy perspective, a technical guarantee of transparency and increasingly broad participation in resolution of workplace disputes and of automatic implementation of the outcome in terms of what is at stake financially for the workers involved offers compelling advantages over the practical reality of bringing this kind of claim in an English employment tribunal, at least in this author's experience representing such claimants.

This is by no means a comprehensive review of employment law policy aims and measures. The invitation is to consider further which elements of the full, social structure of DAOs as organizations are relevant to employment legislation or other regulatory regimes and amenable to on-chain representation such that technical guarantees of certain decision-making procedures may achieve functional equivalence with regulatory requirements that would otherwise have to be enforced judicially. Even given a comprehensive set of such specific regulations, and a DAO that is fully compliant with them, it seems unlikely that even the simplest cases would stay entirely within their scope. Thus the suggestion is not that DAOs could or should avoid all requirements in any or all regulatory domains, but rather that specific regulation could substitute for some part of those regulatory requirements a functionally equivalent set of technical requirements that a DAO could meet in order to fall under this partial alternative regime. Perhaps this could be reframed simply as "reg tech": the automation of straightforward regulatory requirements using appropriate technology, with the public benefit that regulators' limited resources can be focused on the more complex or serious cases, and more importantly that participants in collaborative endeavours benefit from greater transparency of the organizational structures in which they participate and in some cases automated implementation of procedures that achieve regulatory policy aims such as protection from unfair treatment.

V. Conclusion

The central argument of this paper is that if a DAO can be addressed judicially, whether in virtue of its independent legal personality – as an incorporated entity or, under a legislative framework such as the COALA DAO Model Law, without incorporation – or else as an unincorporated association or partnership, then it will be regulated as an organization first and as a novel technological arrangement second. The functional equivalence of technical aspects of a

DAO to certain regulatory requirements or otherwise in addressing policy aims can support specific regulation, such as the Model Law, that takes advantage of the inherent transparency or protections of process and structure that has been encoded in smart contracts and in the state of public, permissionless blockchains. However, regulators and courts will look to the whole structure of a DAO, some of which will subsist off-chain even in the simplest DAO (outside the special case of a simple aim reducible to an objective function relating only to the state of a blockchain, alignment to which arguably does not amount to organization as such). When considering further specific regulation for DAOs, the questions to ask are: what is the whole structure, on-chain and off-chain; and how might elements of that structure be represented on-chain in order to secure by technical means the protections or policy aims that would otherwise motivate the enforcement of conventional regulatory requirements?

Decentralized Autonomous Organizations (DAOs) Before State Courts

How can private international law keep up with global digital entities?

Florence Guillaume[*]

Abstract This paper examines civil and commercial disputes involving Decentralized Autonomous Organizations (DAOs) and the complex questions of private international law that arise. The legal capacity of a DAO to be a plaintiff or defendant in court varies across jurisdictions, highlighting the need to determine the applicable law to a DAO. A distinction must be made between different types of DAOs. There are currently a few jurisdictions, notably in the United States, that have enacted DAO legislation defining a legal status for such entities. Those regulated DAOs are governed by both computer code and company law. In other jurisdictions, existing company structures can be used to offer a legal wrapper to DAOs. However, the vast majority of DAOs currently in existence are constituted and solely governed by code, posing challenges in bringing them before a state court.

I. Introduction

A Decentralized Autonomous Organization (DAO) is a social organization structure that allows several people to pool resources in order to achieve a common goal, with the characteristics of being an internet-native organization. While a precise definition of a DAO may prove elusive due to its adaptable nature for founders' requirements, it is still feasible to outline several distinguishing features. As of today, all DAOs have in common that they are blockchain-based organizations with governance rules inscribed on smart contracts.[1]

[*] The author extends sincere gratitude to Mr. Sven Riva for his meticulous review of this paper and his highly relevant and greatly appreciated comments.

[1] According to Vitalik Buterin, DAOs are the logical extension of smart contracts as they are nothing else than "long-term smart contracts that contain the assets and encode the bylaws of an entire organization." *Buterin*, Ethereum White Paper – A Next Generation Smart Contract & Decentralized Application Platform (Blockchain Lab, November 2013) https://blockchainlab.com/pdf/Ethereum_white_paper-a_next_generation_smart_contract_and_decentralized_application_platform-vitalik-buterin.pdf accessed 1 June 2023. For an over-

In addition to being created and operated by technology, a DAO is collectively owned and managed by its members who are part of a community whose access is given by holding DAO's tokens. A DAO has a treasury that is only accessible with the approval of the DAO members and does not, in principle, have a hierarchical structure.[2]

That being said, it is not possible to draw up an exhaustive list of the different types of DAOs. Those digital entities exist on a wide spectrum, from social DAOs – that are a collection of people organized around a particular interest – to investment DAOs – that are a group of people who pool capital and invest in projects.[3] For example, the first widely known DAO was a form of venture capital fund called "The DAO" which was launched in 2016 on the Ethereum blockchain; participants could submit projects to be funded and the decision-making process was distributed between the approximatively 10,000 token holders of The DAO.[4] Some DAOs are utilized in decentralized finance (DeFi) to operate protocols and applications on the blockchain network, facilitating the trading of digital assets for users. But DAOs can also be operating systems that enable more complex forms of DAOs to use their infrastructure to operate.[5]

view of the DAO's genesis, see *Riva*, Decentralized Autonomous Organizations (DAOs) in the Swiss Legal Order (2019/2020) 21 Yearbook of Private International Law, 2021, 601, 607-610; *Hassan/De Filippi*, Decentralized Autonomous Organization, 10(2) Internet Policy Review, 2021, 6, available at https://policyreview.info/pdf/policyreview-2021-2-1556.pdf accessed 1 June 2023.

[2] *Riva* (fn. 1), 612-616, defined a DAO as "the entity created by the deployment of an autonomous and self-executing software running on a distributed system that allows a network of participants to interact and manage resources on a transparent basis and in accordance with the rules defined by the software code". *Hassan/De Filippi* (fn. 1), adopted the following definition: "A DAO is a blockchain-based system that enables people to coordinate and govern themselves mediated by a set of self-executing rules deployed on a public blockchain, and whose governance is decentralised (i. e., independent from central control)".

[3] See e. g., The UK Law Commission, Decentralized Autonomous Organisations (DAOs) – Call for evidence (November 2022), 9-22, available at https://www.lawcom.gov.uk/project/decentralised-autonomous-organisations-daos accessed 1 June 2023. The UK Law Commission stated that "it is important to recognise the inherent breadth and flexibility of the DAO organisational form", and defined a DAO as "a novel type of technology-mediated social structure or organisation of participants comprised of a variety of composite elements". Ibid., 9. For a taxonomy of DAOs, see also *Gogel/Kremer/Slavin/Werbach*, Decentralized Autonomous Organizations: Beyond the Hype, World Economic Forum, 2022, 13-15, available at https://www3.weforum.org/docs/WEF_Decentralized_Autonomous_Organizations_Beyond_the_Hype_2022.pdf accessed 1 June 2023. The definition of a DAO adopted in this report is: "A decentralized autonomous organization (DAO) is a general term for a group that uses blockchains and related technologies to coordinate its activities. Ibid., 6. See also *Wright*, The Rise of Decentralized Autonomous Organizations: Opportunities and Challenges, Stanford Journal of Blockchain Law and Policy, 2021, available at https://stanford-jblp.pubpub.org/pub/rise-of-daos/release/1 accessed 1 June 2023.

[4] See *Jentzsch*, Decentralized Autonomous Organization to Automate Governance, 2016, https://archive.org/stream/DecentralizedAutonomousOrganizations/WhitePaper_djvu. txt accessed 1 June 2023.

[5] For example, Aragon and DAOstack are DAO platforms offering templates of DAOs

It has been observed that the goals of a DAO may undergo changes during its lifetime. However, DAOs that run operational protocols, such as DeFi DAOs, maintain a direct connection to the objectives of their respective protocols.[6] It is also worth mentioning that founding members can retain control over the DAO, or accept that their influence on governance will be diluted as new members acquire governance tokens. This shows that DAOs provide considerable flexibility when it comes to devising governance structures. In the concept that is adopted for this paper, DAOs are digital entities that are organizations constituted to pursue any purpose that could be reached by means of the various classical forms of companies.[7]

To this day, DAOs have garnered limited legal attention, with only a handful of jurisdictions taking steps to clarify their legal status through specific legislation. In the states where such legislation has been enacted, its scope is constrained, failing to encompass all forms of DAOs. Moreover, the existing legislation fails to consider the fundamental aspect that DAOs are inherently international entities, necessitating an initial analysis through the prism of private international law. Since DAOs play – and will keep playing – a key role in DeFi, providing them with a defined legal status would most likely promote the development of this alternative to traditional finance.[8] But the legal status of DAOs remains highly uncertain, as demonstrated by the question of whether a DAO can be a party to proceedings in a state court.

DAOs are subject to disputes in the same way as any form of company or, more generally, any form of organization of persons regardless of its legal form. This paper will focus on civil or commercial disputes involving a DAO. Such disputes may arise among the members of a DAO, between the DAO and its

---

that are preconfigured to undertake different types of projects. In this paper, the Blockchain network as such is not included in the term "DAO". On this topic, *Riva* (fn. 1), 616, introduced a useful distinction between two forms of DAOs: "top layer DAOs" and "ground layer DAOs". The first form of DAOs corresponds to the notion, adopted in this paper, of a digital company. The second form of DAOs does not claim to function in a way similar to companies, their purpose being rather to serve as a payment mechanism by "issuing" a cryptocurrency or to enable other DAOs to use their infrastructure to operate. Bitcoin and Ethereum, for example, can be described as "ground layer DAOs" in this respect. As noted by *Hassan/Filippi* (fn. 1), 3, "the term [DAO] is today understood as referring not to a blockchain network in and of itself, but rather to organisations deployed as smart contracts on top of an existing blockchain network".

[6] *Gogel/Kremer/Slavin/Werbach* (fn. 3), 13.

[7] See *Guillaume*, L'effet disruptif des smart contracts et des DAOs sur le droit international privé, in: Richa/Canapa (ed.), Droit et économie numérique, 2021, 35-59, 46-47.

[8] In a report on DAOs published by the World Economic Forum, the contributors acknowledge that "[p]erhaps the greatest threat to DAOs today is uncertainty. Without clear legal status, DAOs cannot take advantage of the same protections as corporations, such as legal personhood, limited liability and simplified tax arrangements" (*Gogel/Kremer/Slavin/Werbach*, fn. 3, 8).

members, and with third parties.[9] In theory, there are two different ways to resolve a dispute involving a DAO. The litigation can be submitted to a state court, on the one hand, or to a private dispute resolution mechanism such as arbitration or mediation, on the other hand. Each of these options has its advantages and disadvantages, which must be balanced when choosing a dispute resolution method. Among the criteria of choice, one must take into consideration, first of all, the capacity of a DAO to sue and to be sued before a state court. This capacity depends on the type of DAO and the jurisdiction where the lawsuit is filed.

Because of the uncertain legal status of DAOs, the same DAO may have capacity to act and defend in one state but not in another (II.). The choice of the forum will thus depend on the capacity of the concerned DAO to be a plaintiff or defendant in court. Furthermore, the jurisdiction of state courts raises delicate questions of private international law. It is indeed not a small task to determine where to file the claim (III.). However, before bringing a case before a state court, one must ensure that the decision on the merits will have the expected effect. It is therefore necessary to verify that the decision can be enforced in the event that the losing party does not comply with it spontaneously. This key issue can prove delicate in practice, particularly when enforcement is to take place on-chain (IV.). When the resolution of a dispute involving a DAO is entrusted to a state court, the plaintiff will face several practical difficulties, such as the service of judicial documents on the defendant. This is the consequence of the pseudonymous environment of blockchain platforms, which frequently poses challenges in identifying the defendant (V.). Entrusting the resolution of a dispute involving a DAO to a private dispute resolution mechanism makes it possible to bypass the difficulties associated with proceedings before a state court. But the choice of the method of dispute resolution – state court versus private dispute resolution mechanism – depends mainly on the type of dispute and the parties involved (VI.).

II. The capacity of a DAO to be a party to a state court proceeding

Before filing a lawsuit in a state court, it is necessary to ascertain the capacity of the parties to sue and to be sued. When the dispute involves a DAO that is likely to be a plaintiff or defendant in the proceedings, a distinction must be made according to the type of DAO.

[9] See *Guillaume/Riva*, Blockchain Dispute Resolution for Decentralized Autonomous Organizations: The Rise of Decentralized Autonomous Justice, Chapter 10, in: Bonomi/Lehmann/Lalani (ed.), Blockchain and Private International Law, 2023, 549-641.

1. Appearance of regulated DAOs before state courts

Some DAOs exist in a hybrid form, by which is meant that the DAO is governed not only by the computer code, but also by the company law of the state in which it is incorporated. There are currently a few jurisdictions, notably in the United States, that have enacted DAO legislation defining a legal status for such entities. The so-called "American model", adopted by Vermont[10], Wyoming[11], Tennessee[12] and more recently Utah[13], consists in authorizing the incorporation of DAOs in the form of a Limited Liability Company (LLC). A DAO based in Vermont is known as a blockchain-based LLC (BBLLC), Wyoming and Tennessee DAOs are referred to as DAO LLCs, and a DAO in Utah is identified as a Limited Liability DAO (LLD). In this case, the DAO and the LLC are "merged" as one, and the DAO just becomes a way for the company to organize itself using blockchain technology and to act in the Web 3 space.[14] This type of DAO whose code is consistent with the law of a state can be referred to as a "regulated DAO".

DAO legislation was also introduced in other jurisdictions, namely Malta[15] and the Marshall Islands[16]. Malta was a pioneer in this field by adopting the first DAO law, but this legislation did not prove to be adapted to the needs of DAO users. The Marshall Islands offer an off-shore LLC-based model that allowed the creation of non-profit DAOs before introducing a new law to also allow for-profit DAOs to be incorporated.

Furthermore, in some jurisdictions, existing company structures can be used to create a link between a DAO and the physical world.[17] This is the case, for example, in Switzerland, where DAOs are being attached to legal entities, main-

[10] Vermont Act No 205 (S.269), An act relating to blockchain business development https://legislature.vermont.gov/Documents/2018/Docs/ACTS/ACT205/ACT205%20As%20Enacted.pdf accessed 1 June 2023.

[11] Wyoming Act No 73 (SF0038), Wyoming Decentralized Autonomous Organization Supplement https://legiscan.com/WY/text/SF0038/id/2359146 accessed 1 June 2023.

[12] Tenn. Code. Ann 48-250-101 et seq.; HB 2645, https://www.tba.org/docDownload/1943411 accessed 1 June 2023.

[13] Utah Decentralized Autonomous Organizations Act; HB 357, https://le.utah.gov/~2023/bills/static/HB0357.html accessed 1 June 2023. This DAO law is not yet in force at the time of writing.

[14] See *Guillaume/Riva* (fn. 9), chapter 2.3.2, 563-569.

[15] Chapter 592, Innovative Technology Arrangements and Services Act https://legislation.mt/eli/cap/592/eng/pdf accessed 1 June 2023.

[16] Decentralized Autonomous Organization Act 2022, https://rmicourts.org/wp-content/uploads/2022/12/PL-2022-50-Decentralized-Autonomous.pdf accessed 1 June 2023.

[17] For an overview of the currently most commonly used legal wrappers, see *Brummer/Seira*, Legal Wrappers and DAOs, 30 May 2022, 6-19, available at https://papers.ssrn.com/sol3/papers.cfm?abstract_id=4123737 accessed 1 June 2023. See also *Wright* (fn. 3), and *Mienert*, How can a Decentralized Autonomous Organization be legally structured?, Legal Revolutionary Journal, 2021, available at https://papers.ssrn.com/sol3/papers.cfm?abstract_id=3992329 accessed 1 June 2023.

ly associations or foundations.[18] This type of arrangement is typically chosen to enable the DAO to outsource administrative tasks to a legal entity or delegate the management of the DAO's treasury to it. The DAO is thereby "materialized" and can, for example, enter into valid contracts with third parties, utilizing the association or the foundation as its representative in the physical world. Depending on its needs, a single DAO may use several legal entities, in different jurisdictions, for example to hold specific goods (e.g., IP rights, property rights on a real estate), to carry out specific activities (e.g., fundraising), and to obtain certain services (e.g., holding a bank account). However, the concept can also be approached from another perspective, wherein an organization of persons (regardless of its legal structure) is attached to a DAO, using it as a management tool or as a means to access the Web 3 space. In this context, the question arises as to whether it remains a DAO or if it becomes an organization of persons that structures its governance through a DAO, as is seen in the above-mentioned regulated DAOs.

These examples show that practice has developed several ways for allowing a DAO to carry out functions it would otherwise not be able to (e.g., hiring employees, contracting with commercial partners, owning property), and thus making up for the lack of legislation. From a procedural perspective, when a DAO is attached to a legal wrapper, the latter in principle has the capacity to sue and be sued in court and therefore the DAO can be a party to litigation "through" the legal wrapper. However, even if the various legal wrappers offer practical solutions to DAO users, they entail a significant amount of legal uncertainty. In particular, the exact scope of the legal relationship between the DAO and the legal entity is unclear.[19] Moreover, attaching the DAO to a legal wrapper brings an element of centralization in the sense that the legal entity anchors the DAO in the territory of a particular state. This entails significant practical consequences when it comes to linking the DAO to a state using the rules of private international law.

These models established by practice must be distinguished from the DAOs which have a legal status granted by the law of a state. Today, the predominant focus lies on American limited liability companies (LLCs), namely the BBLLCs, DAO LLCs, and LLDs. True regulated DAOs are constituted and governed by the computer code *and* the company law of the state in which they are incorpo-

[18] Similar legal structures are also available in other countries, notably the UK. See UK Law Commission (fn. 3), 37-44.

[19] Some authors have noted in this regard that there is a risk in some jurisdictions that a court may pierce the corporate veil of the legal wrapper to directly reach the DAO members. A court may pierce the veil if the legal entity is found to be operating as a mere extension or *alter ego* of its members. The separation between the legal entity and its members is thereby disregarded and individual members are held personally liable. This means that DAO members may still face potential personal liability despite the existence of a legal wrapper. See *Brummer/Seira* (fn. 17), 4.

rated. When such a DAO has a legal personality granted by the law of its state of incorporation, there is no particular problem when it appears before the courts of that state. A DAO with legal personality can sue and be sued in its own name, as well as carry out business activities, have its own treasury, and enter into contractual relationships. For example, a Vermont BBLLC may appear in court in the same capacity as a standard LLC before Vermont courts. But its ability to sue and be sued in other jurisdictions depends on the scope of its recognition as a foreign legal entity in the forum state.[20]

This paper will not elaborate further on the resolution of disputes involving a regulated DAO. The focus will be on issues that arise in the context of resolving a dispute involving a DAO with no legal wrapper.

2. *Appearance of maverick DAOs before state courts*

The vast majority of DAOs currently in existence are constituted and governed only by computer code and are not formally linked to a legal entity. Such DAOs are not established under the law of a state and derive their existence solely from their code. Those DAOs – which "operate without any formal legal recognition, eschewing dependence on governmental authority for their existence"[21] – can be referred to as "maverick DAOs"[22]. When a dispute involves a maverick DAO, the question arises as to how to bring the defendant-DAO before a state court. Identifying the appropriate party to sue is indeed one of the primary challenges encountered while pursuing a DAO. In order to determine whether it is possible to sue the DAO itself, the plaintiff has to qualify the DAO in the legal order of the forum. The qualification process will establish the capacity or lack thereof to defend.

a) When the DAO qualifies as a company

Qualification is the process of classifying a fact into a category of law from which will derive a legal regime. The qualification of a DAO, in order to determine its legal status, is a complex operation when the legal order of reference (in principle, the legal order of the forum) does not know the DAO, because there is no proper category. In this case, qualification involves determining the legal institution of domestic law that has the most in common with the DAO being examined. Since DAOs exist as inherently international entities, the qualification must first be made at the level of private international law. This will allow the identification of the conflict of law rule determining the law applicable to

---

[20] See *Guillaume/ Riva* (fn. 9), chapter 2.3.2, 563-569, and chapter 3.2.2, 575-579.

[21] *Brummer/Seira* (fn. 17), 3.

[22] This terminology is borrowed from *Riva* (fn. 1), 619.

the DAO. The operation thus consists in classifying the DAO being examined into one of the categories of private international law.

For example, in Swiss private international law[23], two different qualifications are likely to apply: the qualification as a company and as a contract. A DAO may be qualified as a company if it falls within the notion of "organized association of persons" or "organized unit of assets" in the sense of Article 150 para. 1 of the Swiss PILA.[24] This notion includes "all social combinations that have a social organization or that are at least organized as a whole".[25] The entity must have an organized internal structure that is recognizable by third parties.[26] Whether a DAO qualifies as a company under Swiss private international law therefore depends on its level of internal organization. If a DAO is sufficiently organized, it will be governed by the law designated by the conflict of law rules applicable to companies.[27]

Switzerland adheres to the criterion of organization in matters of company law (Article 154 para. 1 of the Swiss PILA).[28] This principle dictates that an entity, once it meets the requirements to be qualified as a company (i. e., when it is sufficiently organized), is typically governed by the law of the state under which it is organized. Where the company has not been validly constituted under the law of the state under which it is organized, it shall be governed by the law of the state in which it is administered (Article 154 para. 2 of the Swiss PILA). The criterion of administration is consequently employed in a subsidiary manner within Swiss private international law when the primary connection to the state of organization cannot be used.[29] A company that has been validly constituted under foreign law, whether it be the law of its organization or the law of its administration, is automatically recognized in Switzerland.[30] When these rules are applied to a regulated DAO, like a Vermont BBLLC, it is probable for the DAO to be qualified as a company and subject to the laws of the state under which it is organized, namely Vermont law.[31] Applying Swiss private international law, a BBLLC validly constituted under Vermont law would be automatically recognized as a company in Switzerland. As a result, the DAO would enjoy an equiv-

---

[23] Swiss private international law is codified in the Federal Act on Private International Law of 18 December 1987 (SR 291; the "Swiss PILA").

[24] *Guillaume*, Art. 150, in: Bucher (ed.), Commentaire romand: Loi sur le droit international privé – Convention de Lugano, 2011, n. 4-8.

[25] Swiss Federal Council, Message concernant une loi fédérale sur le droit international privé (loi de DIP), 10 November 1982, FF 1983 425.

[26] *Guillaume* (fn. 24), n. 3.

[27] See *Riva* (fn. 1), 622; *Guillaume/Riva* (fn. 9), chapter 2.3.1, 557-563.

[28] *Guillaume*, Art. 154, in: Bucher (ed.), Commentaire romand: Loi sur le droit international privé – Convention de Lugano, 2011, n. 14. The criterion of organization corresponds to the criterion of incorporation. Ibid.

[29] *Guillaume* (fn. 28), n. 16.

[30] *Guillaume* (fn. 28), n. 40-44.

[31] *Riva* (fn. 1), 625-627.

alent legal status in Switzerland as it does in the state of Vermont, granting it, for instance, the ability to appear before Swiss courts.

The legal analysis becomes more intricate when dealing with a maverick DAO. The determination of whether such an entity qualifies as a company relies on the level of organization, necessitating a case-by-case examination. In general, a DAO has a social organization determined by the network of smart contracts that constitute its protocol. Even if the internal structure can be more or less organized, the code of a DAO necessarily defines the way the entity is governed. Furthermore, the governance is recognizable by third parties since the code is open source on the blockchain, at least on a public blockchain[32] (e.g., Ethereum). In the author's opinion, the mere absence of a hierarchical structure (such as a board of directors or general assembly) in the organization of a DAO, instead utilizing a decentralized governance system, does not inherently exclude its qualification as a company. Furthermore, the fact that a DAO is administered solely on the blockchain on which it is operated and, possibly, on the internet insofar as the votes relating to the governance of the DAO are made online (e.g., discussed on GitHub and executed on Snapshot) does not preclude a qualification as a company either. In the author's point of view, if the level of internal organization is sufficient, a maverick DAO can be qualified as a company under Swiss private international law.[33] But, as already indicated, this analysis must be carried out on a case-by-case basis, depending on the organizational characteristics of the DAO under review.

When the DAO being examined can be qualified as a company, this leads to an additional difficulty in determining the governing law. Under Swiss private international law, the law applicable to a DAO would in principle be the law of the state under which it is organized (Article 154 para. 1 of the Swiss PILA), subsidiarily the law of the state in which it is administered (Article 154 para. 2 of the Swiss PILA). With these criteria in mind, how can one determine the law applicable to a maverick DAO? A maverick DAO is, by definition, not linked to a legal order and is therefore not organized under the law of a state. The administration of the DAO is normally carried out online and is therefore not located within a state, at least when the governance is truly decentralized. Anchoring this type of DAO within the confines of a specific state would, therefore, be entirely artificial.[34] These two connecting factors (organization and administration) cannot therefore be applied to maverick DAOs. These criteria alone do not

---

[32] A public (permissionless) blockchain is freely accessible to all without authorization; Bitcoin and Ethereum, for example, are public blockchains. This term is opposed to private (permissioned) blockchains which are not open networks and for which access is subject to authorization; these blockchains are managed by a central authority, for example a bank or a state authority.

[33] Same opinion: *Riva* (fn. 1), 625-627.

[34] *Guillaume* (fn. 7), 53-55.

provide a means to ascertain the governing law for such DAOs, which in itself is not a surprising conclusion insofar as they are not legal entities. It should therefore be concluded that maverick DAOs cannot be recognized in Switzerland as foreign companies[35], cannot have legal personality in Switzerland and cannot appear before Swiss courts.

It is possible, however, to consider some exceptions where the place of administration test could apply to a maverick DAO, for example where participation in the DAO is restricted to persons residing in a particular state, thus providing for *de facto* administration in that state.[36] If participation in a maverick DAO is restricted, for example, to Swiss residents, the application to the DAO of the law of the state in which it is administered (i.e., Swiss law) will lead to examine whether the DAO can be qualified as a company under Swiss substantive law.[37] In the author's opinion, this qualification is appropriate in view of the fact that a DAO meets the four core elements of the concept of a company in domestic law: a contractual basis, a group of persons, a common goal, and a collaboration resulting in a union of efforts or resources.[38] It will then be necessary to identify the Swiss company form that bears the closest resemblances to the DAO under examination. This analysis may result in the application of legal rules associated with forms such as a simple partnership[39] or a limited liability company[40]. Ultimately, if it can be confirmed that the maverick DAO being examined has been validly constituted in accordance with the rules governing the

[35] The legal existence of maverick DAOs in Switzerland could only be recognized by adapting the system of determining the law applicable to companies to the particularities of DAOs. This would imply admitting that a company could legally exist without having been constituted under state law. Such a solution would make it possible to recognize the legal existence of a maverick DAO validly constituted under its code. See *Riva* (fn. 1), 631-637. In this respect, note that Swiss law is flexible enough to recognize the legal existence of a foreign company that was not validly constituted under the law of its incorporation if it was validly constituted under the law of the state where it is administered (Article 154 para. 2 of the Swiss PILA). See *Guillaume* (fn. 28), n. 17. By expanding this rule somewhat, it would be possible to consider that the law of the state of administration equals to the code of the DAO inscribed on the blockchain.

[36] In this particular case, the connection to the state of administration provided for in Article 154 para. 2 of the Swiss PILA leads to a real outcome. See *Guillaume/Riva* (fn. 9), 562.

[37] The qualification under Swiss substantive law must be made, in principle, in accordance with the Swiss Code of Obligations (Federal Act on the Amendment of the Swiss Civil Code – Part 5: The Code of Obligations; SR 220; the "Swiss CO").

[38] The four core elements of the concept of a company can be deduced from Article 530 para. 1 of the Swiss CO, which states that a company "is a contractual relationship in which two or more persons agree to combine their efforts or resources in order to achieve a common goal." See *Guillaume* (fn. 24), n. 10.

[39] See Article 530 para. 1 of the Swiss CO (fn. 38).

[40] Article 772 para. 1 of the Swiss CO states that "[a] limited liability company is a company with separate legal personality in which one or more persons or commercial enterprises participate. Its nominal capital is specified in the articles of association. It is liable for its obligations to the extent of the company assets".

Swiss company form that closely aligns with it (such as a Swiss simple partnership or a Swiss limited liability company), its legal existence can be recognized in Switzerland. The DAO's legal status, and in particular the existence of a legal personality and the ability to appear before Swiss courts, would depend on the legal status of the Swiss company into which it is transposed.

b) When the DAO qualifies as a contract

In the event that a maverick DAO does not fall under the notion of an "organized association of persons" or an "organized unit of assets" under Article 150 para. 1 of the Swiss PILA, it cannot be qualified as a company under Swiss private international law.[41] When the DAO being examined is not sufficiently organized to be qualified as a company, it must be qualified as a contract. This rule follows from Article 150 para. 2 of the Swiss PILA which states that "[s]imple partnerships that have not provided themselves with an organization are governed by the provisions [...] relating to the law applicable to contracts".[42] Consequently, the DAO would not be qualified as a distinct legal entity; instead, it would be subject to contract law. In other words, the conflict of law rules applicable to companies cannot be applied to determine the law governing the DAO. Additionally, such a DAO cannot be recognized as a company in Switzerland.

The qualification of the DAO as a contract (and not as a company) means that the connecting factors applicable to companies (organization and administration) are not relevant as such. It is therefore no longer the DAO as a separate entity that is taken into consideration in determining the applicable law, but the legal relationship among the DAO members. This arises from the understanding that the DAO is no longer perceived – in applying the private international law rules – as a separate social entity distinct from its constituent members. The legal relationship among the DAO members is governed by contract law (Article 150 para. 2 of the Swiss PILA). The contract between the DAO members is usually governed by the law chosen by the parties (Article 116 para. 1 of the Swiss PILA). A choice of law may be made in the smart contract code.[43] The

[41] See chapter II.2.a).

[42] The term "simple partnership" is to be understood, in this context, as any form of association of persons (regardless of its legal form) that does not have a sufficient organization to qualify as a company within the meaning of Article 154 para. 1 of the Swiss PILA. *Guillaume* (fn. 24), n. 10.

[43] In the author's opinion, a choice of law can be made either in the smart contract itself or in the blockchain on which the smart contract is recorded. See *Guillaume* (fn. 7), 56. It should be noted in this regard that the HCCH Principles on Choice of Law in International Commercial Contracts of 19 March 2015 (the "Choice of Law Principles") apply irrespective of the means through which the contract was concluded. They are thus applicable to contracts concluded by electronic means (see Commentary to the Choice of Law Principles n. 1.9). In the author's opinion, the Choice of Law Principles should be also applicable to smart contracts and to DAOs, as long as the parties are acting in the exercise of their trade or profession.

chosen law must be carefully selected to ensure that it produces the desired legal effects on the relationships among DAO members. Within the legal effects that DAO members may seek, a few noteworthy ones include the recognition of the DAO's legal existence, the mitigation of personal liability for its members, and the capacity of the DAO to initiate legal actions. In addition to the choice of law, it is also possible to make a choice of court so as to ensure that a dispute between the DAO members is dealt with by the courts of a state that agrees to offer the protection of its judicial system for this type of legal relationship.[44]

In the absence of a valid choice of law, Swiss private international law stipulates that contracts are governed by the law of the state with which they have the closest connection (Article 117 para. 1 of the Swiss PILA). However, establishing such a connection becomes challenging when considering the contractual relationship among the members of a DAO, as this contract could potentially be qualified in various manners. In particular, one could argue that the members of a DAO are bound by a simple partnership agreement. It would then be appropriate to apply the law of the state in which the simple partnership carries out its principal activity or the law of the state where it is *de facto* administered.[45] These criteria could designate the state of residence of the founding members of the DAO if they still exercise a certain amount of control over the administration of the DAO, or the state of residence of the DAO members who manage it. In the author's opinion, if it is possible to identify such a state, this connection could lead to the application of the law of that state to the contract between the members of the DAO. However, in practice, if a maverick DAO is truly decentralized[46], establishing a connection with a specific state based on the criterion

[44] See *Guillaume/Riva* (fn. 9), chapter 5.4, 609-612. In the author's opinion, a choice of court can be made either in the smart contract itself or in the blockchain on which the smart contract is recorded. The HCCH Convention on Choice of Court Agreements of 30 June 2005 ("Choice of Court Convention") applies to contracts concluded "by any [...] means of communication which renders information accessible so as to be usable for subsequent reference" (Article 3(c)(2)). This formulation implies contracts concluded by electronic means. This international instrument should therefore be applicable to smart contracts and DAOs. The courts of the contracting states of the Choice of Court Convention may therefore refer to this instrument to determine their jurisdiction on the basis of an exclusive choice of court included in a smart contract. Note that an exclusive choice of court could, of course, remove the jurisdiction of Swiss courts and render all reasoning under Swiss private international law useless.

[45] Swiss Supreme Court, ATF 142 III 466, No 6.1.4.

[46] Decentralization is a difficult concept to grasp in the context of a DAO. The term can refer to both the governance and the architecture of the DAO, which may lead to considering the level of decentralization of the blockchain system on which the DAO is deployed. It is also difficult to distinguish decentralization from the operational autonomy of the DAO. See *Hassan/De Filippi* (fn. 1). See also *Garcia/Leung*, Data Points to Measure Blockchain Network Centralization, 2020, available at https://ketsal.com/wp-content/uploads/2020/10/Ketsal-Open-Standards-Measures-of-Blockchain-Network-Centralization-Oct-21-2020.pdf accessed 1 June 2023; *Shapiro*, Defining Decentralization for Law, 2020, available at https://lex-node.medium.com/defining-decentralization-for-law-58ca54e18b2a accessed 1 June 2023.

of the principal activity location or the *de facto* administration location becomes unfeasible.

If it is possible to identify a state with which the DAO has the closest connection and this state is Switzerland, the maverick DAO being examined would be governed by Swiss law. It would then be necessary to qualify the DAO in Swiss substantive law.[47] The qualification as a simple partnership may be the most appropriate in this context.[48] The relationships among the members of the DAO would then be governed by the rules applicable to the Swiss simple partnership.[49]

A simple partnership under Swiss law has no legal personality and has no capacity to act or defend in court. If a lawsuit was initiated for matters involving the DAO, proceedings could be initiated against each individual partner as the simple partnership does not offer a corporate shield. Under this legal regime, each partner is jointly and severally liable for the debts contracted within the framework of the partnership. In other words, if a DAO is a Swiss simple partnership, the plaintiff can pursue any one member of the DAO for the entirety of their loss. The application of the rules on simple partnership therefore presents a significant risk for DAO members. However, in the author's opinion, the rules governing a Swiss simple partnership are not fit for DAOs.[50] Demanding that every member in a maverick DAO assumes responsibility beyond their initial contribution is unjust, particularly in the case of having governance tokens that solely grant voting privileges in the DAO's decision-making process. This is especially true when the DAO comprises thousands of pseudonymous members. In addition, there are instances where individuals may not even be aware of their membership in a DAO, particularly when they received governance tokens through an airdrop. Furthermore, the pseudonymity of DAO members contradicts the personal structure of the simple partnership, which requires the partners to be faithful and loyal to each other.

For simplicity's sake, in this paper, the term "truly decentralized DAO" refers to a DAO whose governance is truly decentralized. In this sense, MakerDAO would be a good example of a "truly decentralized DAO".

[47] The application of Swiss law leads to a new qualification in Swiss substantive law, potentially distinct from the qualification previously made in private international law.

[48] *Guillaume/Riva* (fn. 9), 557-559.

[49] Articles 530ff. of the Swiss CO. See *Müller*, Blockchain und Gesellschaftsrecht: ein Streifzug durch Möglichkeiten und Hürden: unter besonderer Berücksichtigung der Decentralized Autonomous Organization, Expert Focus: Schweizerische Zeitschrift für Wirtschaftsprüfung, Steuern, Rechnungswesen und Wirtschaftsberatung, 2019, 485; *Hess/Spielmann*, Cryptocurrencies, Blockchain, Handelsplätze & Co. – Digitalisierte Werte unter Schweizer Recht, in: Reutter/Werlen (ed.), Kapitalmarkt – Recht und Transaktionen XII, 2017, 145; *Wagner/Weber*, Corporate Governance auf der Blockchain, Schweizerische Zeitschrift für Wirtschafts- und Finanzmarktrecht, 2017, 59, 67.

[50] Same opinion: *Guillaume/Riva* (fn. 9), 559; *Hess/Spielmann* (fn. 49), 191-192.

The foregoing analysis shows that it is a legally challenging undertaking to determine the legal nature of maverick DAOs. Furthermore, the solution could differ from one DAO to another, and from one jurisdiction to another.[51] In Switzerland, the key consideration revolves around determining whether a maverick DAO possesses adequate organization to be qualified as a company. If so, the relationships among the DAO members would be governed by company law. However, if a DAO is not sufficiently organized to be qualified as a company, the relationships among its members would be contractual in nature. Depending on the qualification, the DAO would be recognized in Switzerland as a company and be able to appear before the Swiss courts in its own name. Nevertheless, the qualification of the DAO may vary across jurisdictions, potentially leading to a scenario where the same DAO can have the legal authority to initiate and defend lawsuits in one jurisdiction while lacking it in another. The choice of the forum will thus depend in particular on this issue.

III. Determining jurisdiction for a dispute involving a DAO

A dispute involving a DAO is, in most cases, international in nature. It is therefore the rules of private international law of each state that will determine in which cases their courts have jurisdiction to rule on a civil or commercial case involving a DAO. There are no conflict of jurisdiction rules adopted at the supra-national level with a worldwide scope determining the jurisdiction of state courts in civil or commercial matters.[52] The lack of coordination between states in this respect means that proceedings may well be brought before the courts of several states. Thus, it will be the responsibility of the plaintiff to select the forum that offers the most favorable outcome by carefully evaluating the benefits and drawbacks of the different available options. Given the uncertainty of a DAO's ability to appear before state courts, the choice of forum will depend primarily on the DAO's ability to sue or be sued in its own name.

In some cases, the plaintiff will prefer to take action against the DAO itself, while in other cases, action against the members of the DAO (or some of them) will prove to be a better solution. It may well happen that the liability of the DAO members is preferred to that of the DAO itself. These elements (and others) will have to be weighed against the circumstances of the case and the law that will apply on the merits. When the plaintiff is the DAO, it will also face difficulties to bring a claim before a state court. In particular when it does not have the capacity to sue in its own name, it may be very complicated to determine who should file the lawsuit in the DAO's name, especially when the DAO

---

[51] For an analysis of the legal situation in the UK, see UK Law Commission (fn. 3), 23-36.

[52] In case where the parties agreed on a choice of court, the Choice of Court Convention (fn. 44) may apply. This convention is in force in 33 states.

is truly decentralized and brings together a vast network of pseudonymous members located across the globe.

The challenges that a plaintiff will encounter in the process of bringing a defendant-DAO before a state court will be illustrated in this paper by considering three types of disputes: disputes pertaining to DAO governance, contractual disputes, and tort-related disputes. Private international law rules must be used to determine which courts have jurisdiction over a dispute related to the governance of a DAO, as well as a dispute in contract or tort-related matters involving a DAO. For the sake of convenience, it will be assumed that the jurisdiction issue arises before the Swiss courts. Even if the conflict of jurisdiction rules are not unified at the supra-national level, they are sufficiently similar in the various countries for the reader to be able to apply the reasoning in their legal system of reference.

1. Disputes related to the governance

A dispute related to the governance of a DAO could be, for example, a dispute over the compliance of a proposal with the DAO's constitution. In order to determine the forum for such an action, the first question to be resolved is qualification. As was seen above[53], under Swiss private international law, a maverick DAO may be qualified as a company if it demonstrates sufficient organization; alternatively, if its internal organization is deemed insufficient, it is qualified as a contract.

a) When the DAO qualifies as a company

When a maverick DAO qualifies as a company[54], a dispute over the governance of the DAO can be characterised as a company law matter and shall be settled in accordance with the law governing the DAO. As was seen above, it is quite difficult to determine in practice the law applicable to a DAO.[55] The same difficulties are encountered in determining the jurisdiction.

Under Article 151 para. 1 of the Swiss PILA, actions against the company, its shareholders or members, or persons liable under company law are subject to the jurisdiction of the Swiss courts at the seat of the company. A dispute over the governance of the DAO is therefore prone to falling under the jurisdiction of the Swiss courts at the seat of the DAO. The Swiss courts also have to apply Article 22 para. 2 of the Lugano Convention[56], which establishes an exclusive juris-

[53] See chapter II.2.
[54] See chapter II.2.a).
[55] See chapter II.2.a).
[56] Convention on jurisdiction and the recognition and enforcement of judgements in civil and commercial matters of 30 October 2007 (OJ 2007 L 339/3; the "Lugano Convention").

diction before the courts of the state in which the company has its seat in proceedings which have as their object the validity of the decisions of the organs of a company.[57] The question will therefore arise as to whether a DAO could be qualified as a company within the meaning of the Lugano Convention, which would lead to the application of this conflict of jurisdiction rule. The notion of company in the sense of the Lugano Convention must be interpreted autonomously. In the author's opinion, it should be the same as the one used in Swiss law when determining the jurisdiction of the Swiss courts.[58] In Switzerland, the seat of a company is deemed to be located at the place designated in the articles of incorporation (i. e., the statutory seat or registered office) or, in the absence of such a designation, the seat is located at the place where the company is administered in fact (i. e., the administrative seat).[59]

Applying these rules to locate in Switzerland a dispute related to the governance of a DAO leads to great difficulties. It is usually impossible to determine where the seat of a maverick DAO is located.[60] There is no place of incorporation, which means that the criterion of the statutory seat or registered office fails to link a maverick DAO to a state. Even if the code of a DAO could be considered as a company's articles of incorporation, it is very unlikely that a maverick DAO would designate a seat in its protocol. Furthermore, there is no place of administration that could point to a state. The criterion of the administrative seat fails to create any link with a state because a maverick DAO is a community of pseudonymous members spread around the world who jointly manage the operations of the entity through online platforms. Thus, the criterion of the administrative seat can only point to the internet or the blockchain itself. It is therefore unlikely that the plaintiff will be able to establish a sufficient link between a maverick DAO and the jurisdiction of Swiss courts.

Therefore, if disputes related to the governance of a DAO are matters of company law, connecting factors of Swiss private international law fail to link those disputes to Switzerland. The same conclusion can be reached for other jurisdictions. Even though the connecting factors used in other states for determining the jurisdiction of their courts are not necessarily identical to those in Switzerland, they are very similar. It is therefore likely that it will not be possible to establish a sufficient link between a maverick DAO and the jurisdiction of a state court. This situation leads to a negative conflict of jurisdiction, meaning

---

[57] The same rule can be found in Article 24 para. 2 of the EU Regulation No 1215/2012 of the European Parliament and of the Council of 12 December 2012 on jurisdiction and the recognition and enforcement of judgements in civil and commercial matters (OJ 2012 L 351/1; the "Brussels Ibis Regulation"), which applies in Member States of the European Union.

[58] *Guillaume*, Art. 22 CL, in: Bucher (ed.), Commentaire romand: Loi sur le droit international privé – Convention de Lugano, 2011, n. 40.

[59] Article 21 para. 2 of the Swiss PILA. This rule also applies when the jurisdiction of the Swiss courts is to be determined on the basis of Article 22 para. 2 of the Lugano Convention.

[60] See chapter II.2.a).

that no state has jurisdiction over issues pertaining to the governance of a maverick DAO. This could lead state courts to admit jurisdiction on the basis of weak or artificial links between the DAO and their jurisdiction.[61]

However, there are some exceptions worth mentioning in this context where it could be possible to recognize the existence of an administrative seat. As an illustration, if the members of a maverick DAO all reside in one state, the place of administration of the DAO may be anchored in that state. For example, the members of NEDAO[62] must be residents of the Canton of Neuchâtel in Switzerland. In case of a dispute pertaining to the governance of NEDAO, Swiss courts – and more precisely the courts of the Canton of Neuchâtel – could have jurisdiction over the case based on the criterion of the administrative seat. Another similar situation arises when the DAO is attached to a legal entity, such as a Swiss association, to outsource administrative tasks to that entity. If it can be established that the legal entity is responsible for the administration of the DAO, it is plausible that Swiss courts located at the seat of that entity would have jurisdiction over any disputes pertaining to the governance of the DAO.

b) When the DAO qualifies as a contract

When a maverick DAO does not qualify as a company, then it must be qualified as a contract under Swiss private international law.[63] In this case, disputes related to the governance of a DAO are matters of contract law.

The jurisdiction of Swiss courts is determined by the conflict of jurisdiction rules applicable to contractual matters. These rules provide for action before the Swiss courts of the defendant's domicile or those of the place of the performance of the contract. They will be detailed below with respect to a contractual dispute involving a DAO.[64] At this point, it suffices to say that locating a forum in Switzerland for the purpose of bringing an action relating to the governance of a DAO will be complicated in practice when the DAO is not perceived as a social entity distinct from its members. In this scenario, the conflict of jurisdictions rule focuses on the legal relationship between DAO members and presents challenges in application, particularly when it is not possible to anchor these legal interactions within a state's boundaries. It is of course possible to remedy this legal uncertainty by agreeing on a choice of court. For example, a choice of

---

61 When no state can provide an effective forum, there is no alternative but to consider that state courts should exercise universal jurisdiction. See *Guillaume/Riva* (fn. 9), chapter 3.4, 585-588.

62 NEDAO is a DAO being developed as a community project for the people of the Canton of Neuchâtel in Switzerland. To join NEDAO, members must have their public key certified with the residents' office to prove that they reside in the Canton of Neuchâtel. However, their pseudonymity is safeguarded as their public key is not linked to their identity.

63 See chapter II.2.b).

64 See chapter III.2.

court clause could be inserted in the protocol of the DAO.[65] Such a choice of court should in principle be binding on the DAO members. They would then have to submit all disputes relating to the governance of the DAO to the state courts designated in the choice of court clause.

When Swiss courts have jurisdiction, the dispute shall be settled in accordance with the law chosen by the parties if there is a valid choice of law (Article 116 para. 1 of the Swiss PILA) or, failing that, under the law of the state with which the contract between the DAO members has the closest connection (Article 117 para. 1 of the Swiss PILA). As was mentioned above[66], this connection is difficult to apply to the contract between the members of a maverick DAO which is truly decentralized. But, in some cases, it could be possible to establish a close connection with a specific jurisdiction on the basis of the criterion of the place of the principal activity or the place of the *de facto* administration. When a connection can be established with Switzerland, allowing for the application of Swiss law to the relationships among the DAO members, it is likely that the regulations governing simple partnerships will become applicable.[67]

2. *Disputes of a contractual nature*

A dispute of a contractual nature involving a DAO could be, for example, a dispute with a contractual partner caused by the non-execution or improper execution of a smart contract. Mistakes in the process of converting the terms of the legal contract[68] into the code of the smart contract, errors in the code or bugs, as well as unforeseen circumstances that were not programmed in the smart contract may lead to unwanted outcomes in the execution of the smart contract. A conflict can also emerge due to disparities in the interpretation of the smart contract's code, such as when an external source (referred to as an "oracle") misinterprets a factual element, leading to the execution of the smart contract in an unintended manner. For example, it may happen that the oracle relies on a non-updated exchange rate of a cryptocurrency and executes the transaction at an outdated rate.[69] A party to a smart contract can also feel ag-

[65] See chapter II.2.b).

[66] See chapter II.2.b).

[67] See chapter II.2.b).

[68] Legal contracts are contracts that are legally binding upon the parties. In this paper, the term "legal contract" refers to an underlying traditional contract to which the smart contract is linked. In this situation, the smart contract may serve to perform one or more contractual provisions on-chain; the smart contract may also be a simple reproduction of the legal contract which is legally binding upon the parties. Smart contracts are not necessary linked to an underlying traditional contract and can exist by themselves. In this case, the smart contract may be the legal contract itself.

[69] See e.g., the allegations from investors who suffered heavy losses on the MakerDAO platform on 12 March 2020. United States District Court, Northern District of California, order of 22 February 2023 in the *Peter Johnson v. Maker Ecosystem Growth Holdings Inc. et*

grieved when the smart contract executes as planned, but the result contravenes principles of fairness and justice. All those situations may be qualified as contractual matters in the legal orders that recognize a contractual scope to a smart contract.[70]

Assuming that a relationship between a DAO and a third party defined by a smart contract can be qualified as a contractual relationship in the legal sense, it is possible to use connecting criteria provided for by the rules of private international law to connect the contractual relationship to a jurisdiction. A dispute shall be settled before Swiss courts in accordance with the law chosen by the parties if there is a valid choice of law (Article 116 para. 1 of the Swiss PILA) or, failing that, under the law of the state with which the contract has the closest connection (Article 117 para. 1 of the Swiss PILA). With regard to jurisdiction in contractual matters, the connecting criteria used in Switzerland refer either to the location of the parties or to the location of the contractual relationship itself.

In contractual matters, the first rule of jurisdiction to be considered is the forum of the domicile of the defendant. For example, Swiss courts have jurisdiction to hear disputes arising from a contract primarily when the defendant has its domicile in Switzerland (Article 112 para. 1 of the Swiss PILA and Article 2 para. 1 of the Lugano Convention[71]). Generally speaking, the seat of a company is deemed to be the domicile.[72] Failing any statutory seat or registered office, the seat is in principle deemed to be at the place where the company is administered in fact.[73] But, as was mentioned above[74], it is in principle not possible to establish

---

al. litigation (Case Number 20-cv-02569-MMC), available at https://law.justia.com/cases/federal/district-courts/california/candce/3:2020cv02569/358097/82/ accessed 1 June 2023. This class-action lawsuit filed against entities associated with MakerDAO, in which the plaintiffs alleged that the platform misrepresented the risks of holding collateral debt positions, has been dismissed.

[70] See *Guillaume* (fn. 7), 43-46. On the legal scope of smart contracts in Switzerland, see e.g., *Hari/Dupasquier*, Blockchain And Distributed Ledger Technology (DLT): Academic Overview Of The Technical And Legal Framework And Challenges For Lawyers, International Business Law Journal, 2018, 423, 443-444; *Carron/Botteron*, Le droit des obligations face aux 'contrats intelligents', in: Carron/Müller (ed.), 3e Journée des droits de la consommation et de la distribution, Blockchain et Smart Contracts – Défis juridiques, 2018, 1.

[71] The same rule can be found in Article 4 para. 1 of the Brussels Ibis Regulation, which applies in Member States of the European Union.

[72] See e.g., Article 21 para. 1 of the Swiss PILA: "For companies [...], the seat is deemed to be the domicile". Under Article 60 para. 1 of the Lugano Convention, "a company [...] is domiciled at the place where it has its: (a) statutory seat; or (b) central administration; or (c) principal place of business". The same rule can be found in Article 63 para. 1 of the Brussels Ibis Regulation, which applies in Member States of the European Union.

[73] See e.g., Article 21 para. 2 of the Swiss PILA: "The seat of a company is deemed to be located at the place designated in the articles of incorporation or in the articles of association. In the absence of such a designation, the seat is located at the place where the company is administered in fact".

[74] See chapter III.1.a).

the location of the administrative seat of a maverick defendant-DAO for the purpose of determining a forum. These conflict of jurisdiction rules, based on the location of the DAO, do not therefore make it possible to establish the jurisdiction of Swiss courts.

If a DAO bound under a smart contract suffers economical damage due to the non-execution or improper execution of the smart contract, locating the other party could open a forum at the domicile of the defendant, potentially giving jurisdiction to the courts of that state. The main challenge when a DAO seeks to file a claim against a third party lies in the identification of said party, enabling the DAO to initiate legal proceedings in a state court. As on-chain actors primarily act pseudonymously in the blockchain environment, it may be impossible to identify the person behind a wallet address and locate their domicile or their seat.[75] In the blockchain environment, the pseudonymity of the parties is an impediment to filing a lawsuit. It is indeed, in most jurisdictions, not possible to sue a person whose identity is not known in civil or commercial matters. That being said, it is becoming more and more easy to determine the identity of a person who uses the blockchain.[76] But since identifying a user is still complicated and expensive, the financial claim must be of substantial monetary value to justify the costs related to the identification. If this is not the case, the pseudonymity of the parties is a significant problem for access to justice. And, of course, the issue of the capacity of a DAO to sue in its own name remains.

There are alternative forums for resolving contractual disputes that are based on the location of the contractual relationship itself, such as the forum at the place of performance of the contract.[77] However, locating the performance of a smart contract in a state jurisdiction is virtually impossible as the execution of a smart contract occurs exclusively on-chain.[78] This challenge can be exemplified by a transaction conducted through the Uniswap protocol. Uniswap is a decentralized exchange (DEX) operating on the Ethereum blockchain, where users retain direct control over their funds. It enables users to trade ERC-20 tokens

---

[75] See *Kaal/Calcaterra*, Crypto Transaction Dispute Resolution, The Business Lawyer, 2017-2018, 109, 133, who are of the opinion that it is impossible to locate the parties to a smart contract transaction.

[76] See e.g., *Juhász/Stéger/Kondor/Vattay*, A Bayesian approach to identify Bitcoin users, PLoS ONE 13(12), 2018:e0207000, available at https://journals.plos.org/plosone/article?id=10.1371/journal.pone.0207000 accessed 1 June 2023. See also *Vos*, Are Bitcoin transactions anonymous and traceable? (Cointelegraph, 3 September 2022), https://cointelegraph.com/explained/are-bitcoin-transactions-anonymous-and-traceable accessed 1 June 2023.

[77] See e.g., Article 113 of the Swiss PILA: "If the characteristic obligation of the contract is to be performed in Switzerland, the action may also be brought before the Swiss court at the place of performance". Article 5 para. 1 of the Lugano Convention provides also for a forum in the courts of "the place of performance of the obligation in question", as well as Article 7 para. 1 of the Brussels Ibis Regulation, which applies in Member States of the European Union.

[78] See *Guillaume/Riva* (fn. 9), 585-586.

without the need for a third-party custodian. When a user intends to exchange one token for another, they can simply send their token to the Uniswap smart contract and receive a corresponding amount of the other token. The smart contract automatically calculates this amount based on the prevailing market price. The protocol Uniswap is owned and governed by the token holders of Uniswap DAO which is a truly decentralized maverick DAO. In the event that an individual manages to manipulate the market to their advantage when trading ERC-20 tokens, it may give rise to concerns regarding the proper execution of the smart contract. In such a scenario, how could the jurisdiction for a claim by an aggrieved party be determined by locating the performance of the smart contract within the borders of a specific state?

The foregoing observations are also valid, *mutatis mutandis*, for a dispute between a DAO and a contractual partner caused by the non-execution or improper execution of a legal contract. In addition, in this case, there is a significant risk, as the law stands, that a state court would consider that a maverick DAO does not have the power to enter into a contractual relationship and be entitled to rights and obligations of any kind in its own name. The rights and obligations of the DAO could be transferred to the DAO members assuming that at least one of them would be identifiable, and each identified member could be personally liable for the obligations of the DAO. Moreover, in cases where the DAO is attached to a legal entity (e.g., a Swiss association), for instance to delegate administrative tasks to that entity, the issue of the legal relationship between the DAO and the legal entity remains.[79] It will indeed be necessary to determine between the DAO and the legal wrapper, which one is engaged in the contractual relationship with the third party. The resolution of this question hinges upon the presence of a valid legal relationship between the DAO and the attached legal entity.

3. Disputes of a tortious nature

In matters relating to tort, the domicile of the defendant[80] and the place where the tort occurred are typically the decisive connecting factors for determining jurisdiction. The place of the tort can usually be located at the place of commission of the wrongful act and at the place where the damage occurs.[81] Again, it is

[79] See chapter II.1.

[80] See e.g., Article 129 of the Swiss PILA: "The Swiss courts at the domicile [...] of the defendant have jurisdiction to hear actions in tort" and Article 2 para. 1 of the Lugano Convention; Article 4 para. 1 of the Brussels Ibis Regulation for Member States of the European Union.

[81] See e.g., Article 129 of the Swiss PILA: "The Swiss courts at the place where the act or the result occurred [...] have jurisdiction" to hear actions in tort. The same rule can be found in Article 5 para. 3 of the Lugano Convention, under which "the courts of the place where the harmful event occurred" have jurisdiction in matters relating to torts; exactly the same rule is

difficult to identify these locations when the act is committed on-chain due to the ubiquitous nature of the tort. In this matter, the determination of the forum based on the location of the tort cannot be identified in general terms, as it will depend on the specific type of tort involved.

A dispute of a tortious nature involving a DAO could be, for example, a dispute related to the alleged negligence of the DAO in its handling of the security of the protocol. A California court had to consider such an action in the bZx DAO case where the plaintiffs held the defendants liable for their losses following a hack of the protocol that was managed by the DAO.[82] In this proceeding, the plaintiffs argued that bZx DAO – which was a maverick DAO – was to be qualified as a general partnership under California law. This qualification is indicative of the fact that legal scholars usually try to apply by analogy existing company law rules of their own jurisdiction to define the legal regime of maverick DAOs. The plaintiffs thus had to demonstrate the existence of a general partnership and argued that all the holders of the governance tokens of bZx DAO were members of the general partnership. They were able, on this basis, to bring the action for damages against some of the DAO "partners" and argued that the defendants were jointly and severally liable for their losses as members of a general partnership.

In a preliminary ruling[83], the California court addressed the issue of its jurisdiction and pointed out that when the action is brought against the partners of a general partnership, personal jurisdiction must be verified for each partner. The court had to verify its jurisdiction over one of the founders of bZx DAO who did not reside in California, as California's long-arm statute allows the exercise of personal jurisdiction over a non-resident defendant only if they have certain minimum contacts with California[84]: "California court[s] ha[ve] jurisdiction over only those individual partners who personally established the requisite minimum contacts with California".[85] Hence, the exercise of personal

also found in Article 7 para. 2 of the Brussels Ibis Regulation, which applies in Member States of the European Union.

[82] See Complaint document filed by *Christian Sarcuni et al. v. bZx DAO et al.* (2 May 2022) before the United States District Court, Southern District of California (Case Number 22-cv-618-LAB-DEB), available at https://www.classaction.org/media/sarcuni-et-al-v-bzx-dao-et-al.pdf accessed 1 June 2023. See also *Guillaume/Riva*, How to Resolve a Dispute Involving a DAO, The FinReg Blog, 21 July 2022, available at https://sites.duke.edu/thefinreg blog/2022/07/21/how-to-resolve-a-dispute-involving-a-dao/ accessed 1 June 2023.

[83] United States District Court, Southern District of California, order of 27 March 2023 in the ongoing *Christian Sacuni et al. v. bZx DAO et al.* litigation (Case Number 22-cv-618-LAB-DEB), available at https://casetext.com/case/sarcuni-v-bzx-dao accessed 1 June 2023.

[84] For the minimum contact test, see *International Shoe v. State of Washington*, 326 U.S. 310 (1945): "due process requires only that, in order to subject a defendant to a judgment *in personam*, if he be not present within the territory of the forum, he have certain minimum contacts with it such that the maintenance of the suit does not offend traditional notions of fair play and substantial justice."

[85] *Christian Sacuni et al. v. bZx DAO et al.* (fn. 83), 23.

jurisdiction over a non-resident defendant is permitted only if they have certain minimum contacts "such that the maintenance of the suit does not offend traditional notions of fair play and substantial justice" in accordance with the requirement of due process under the U.S. Constitution.[86] The California court also recalled that it may exercise either general or specific jurisdiction over a non-disputed defendant.[87] The former is possible when the defendant has substantial or continuous and systematic contacts with the forum state, while the latter can be exercised if several conditions are met, among which the defendant must have purposefully directed their actions at the forum state in matters relating to tort.[88] In the preliminary ruling, the California Court held that the plaintiffs failed to demonstrate that the defendant had sufficient contacts with California for the court to exercise jurisdiction over him.

This ruling shows how difficult it is to establish jurisdiction not on the location of the parties (*e.g.*, the domicile of the defendant) but on the location of the tort. Although it is undeniable that the place where the tort occurred helps to anchor the dispute in the jurisdiction of the court, determining this place is extremely difficult when the wrongful act is committed on-chain. A tort resulting from any activity carried out on the internet is characterized by its ubiquitous nature, which leads to considerable legal uncertainty. The result is a multiplication of international forums, since online data is universally distributed and can be consulted instantaneously by an indefinite number of internet users anywhere in the world. For this reason, jurisdiction is typically not limited solely to online service accessibility, but instead necessitates a specific connection with the forum (i.e., "minimum contacts" in American terminology). In the U.S., when the defendant was not present in the state in which the online unlawful act was committed, they must have acted intentionally or, at the very least, must have purposefully directed their actions at the forum state. It can be assumed that "[t]he defendants in such cases have potentially established purposeful contacts with the forum state so that they could have reasonably anticipated being sued there."[89]

It is worth noting that, in the bZx DAO case, even though the plaintiffs argue that bZx DAO is a general partnership, they are only holding responsible core members who have or had a great amount of control over the DAO's protocol and who, according to the plaintiffs, "owed [them] a duty to maintain the security of the funds deposited using the bZx protocol". In the author's opinion, it

---

[86] *Christian Sacuni et al. v. bZx DAO et al.* (fn. 83), 22.

[87] *Christian Sacuni et al. v. bZx DAO et al.* (fn. 83), 22. For the general and specific jurisdiction, see *Helicopteros Nacionales de Columbia v. Hall*, 466 U.S. 408 (1984).

[88] *Christian Sacuni et al. v. bZx DAO et al.* (fn. 83), 22. For the specific jurisdiction in tort matters, see *World-Wide Volkswagen Corp. v. Woodson*, 444 U.S. 286 (1980); *Picot et al. v. Weston*, 780 F.3d 1206 (9th Cir. 2015). For the purposeful contacts test, see *Burger King Corp. v. Rudzewicz*, 471 U.S. 462 (1985).

[89] *Felix/Whitten*, American Conflicts Law, 6th ed. 2011, n. 22, 71.

would be much harder to argue that participants who had small amounts of voting rights in bZx DAO are also liable for the damage, even if they had some decision power within the organization. As a result, it appears that different categories of members could bear different levels of responsibilities, putting identifiable core developers and core members of a DAO at greater risk of liability in case of a damage.

This liability scheme would resemble that of a limited partnership under Swiss law, where general partners who oversee and run the business have unlimited liability, while limited partners have limited liability up to the amount of their investment.[90] This U.S. decision could be of interest if Swiss law were to apply to the tort liability of members of a DAO. It raises the question of the most appropriate qualification under Swiss law for a maverick DAO: should it be classified as a limited partnership, a limited liability company, or a simple partnership? On the one hand, this issue pertains to the internal relationship among the DAO members who would bear liability for any wrongful act. It determines, among other things, whether each member is jointly and severally liable for the debts incurred by the DAO and their right to seek recourse against a co-debtor. On the other hand, it plays a crucial role in determining whether the plaintiff can pursue any individual member of the DAO for the full extent of their losses.

As for the law governing tort liability as such, a Swiss court would in principle apply the law of the state in which the tort was committed or, in some circumstances, the law of the state where the result occurred, in the absence of a choice of law.[91]

IV. Enforcement of a decision rendered by a state court

Challenges to seeking justice in case of a dispute involving a maverick DAO do not end with finding a court with jurisdiction over the dispute. Even if a state court has jurisdiction and renders a decision on the merits, the aggrieved party may find it impossible to seek the enforcement of the decision when the losing party does not comply spontaneously.[92]

The immutability that characterizes blockchain technology does not allow any authority to modify the state of the blockchain ledger, at least when the blockchain is public[93] (e.g., Bitcoin, Ethereum). Hence, state authorities have no enforcement power over crypto-assets: crypto-assets cannot be frozen, seized, or confiscated without control over the holder's private key. This can present a

90 *Guillaume/Riva* (fn. 82). See Article 594 of the Swiss CO.
91 See Article 133 of the Swiss PILA.
92 See *Guillaume/Riva* (fn. 9), chapter 3.5, 588-590.
93 In this paper, the term "blockchain" refers to a public blockchain. See fn. 32.

significant practical challenge as crypto-assets can be transferred swiftly and with ease. If smart contracts have been improperly executed, state authorities cannot exercise their enforcement power to adapt the execution of smart contracts, to stop them from executing altogether, or to restore the initial situation. They cannot enforce court decisions related to the governance of a DAO either, because the governance rules of a DAO are inscribed on immutable smart contracts and can only be changed by the DAO's members according to the governance rules themselves.[94]

The inability of states to exercise their enforcement power on the blockchain means that the enforcement of court decisions on crypto-assets relies exclusively on the willingness of the losing party. But one DAO member does not have the power to dispose of the DAO's crypto-assets if the protocol does not allow for it. Only the community of members acting within the parameters of the code can trigger an action from the DAO. However, obtaining a decision from a large number of pseudonymous members scattered across the globe presents a challenge for the DAO when it comes to transferring crypto-assets in compliance with a court order. Since DAOs are censorship resistant entities that are created and exist autonomously from any central authority, state authorities cannot force an action upon the DAO. This leads to a significant risk of non-compliance with a court order because people know that coercive enforcement is not a realistic possibility.[95]

Since a state has no power to enforce a judgment rendered by its courts on the blockchain, the efficiency of justice cannot be guaranteed. However, it is true that a state court could order a compensation (such as the payment of damages) to circumvent the impossibility of enforcement on the blockchain. As long as the DAO members (or, at least, some of them) are individuals who can be identified, it is also possible to exert pressure on them to get voluntary enforcement of a court order. For instance, when an individual declines to disclose the private key required to access the wallet containing the disputed crypto-asset, the court can issue an order compelling them to enable access to the crypto-asset, accompanied by the potential consequence of being held in contempt of court. Such an order can also be directed towards the custodian in cases where the disputed

[94] See e.g., *Wright* (fn. 3): "Current DAOs that rely on participatory voting also often require a formal vote to determine if and when funds are deployed for a particular purpose. No single DAO member or other individual has the unilateral ability to transfer funds or defraud the organization of collected assets, unless they are the sole member participating in the decision-making process."

[95] See *Perritt*, Towards a Hybrid Regulatory Scheme for the Internet, University of Chicago Legal Forum, 2001, 215, 258; *Clément*, Smart Contracts and the Courts, in: DiMatteo/Cannarsa/Poncibò (ed.), The Cambridge Handbook of Smart Contracts, Blockchain Technology and Digital Platforms, 2020, 285-286; *Rabinovich-Einy/Katsh*, Blockchain and the Inevitability of Disputes: The Role for Online Dispute Resolution, Journal of Dispute Resolution, 2019, 47, 73.

crypto-asset is held by a custodian. In addition, in the particular case where the DAO is attached to a legal entity through which it acts in the physical world, the authorities will of course be able to obtain enforcement of the court decision directly against the legal wrapper. But the enforceability of the court ruling on the DAO's crypto-assets hinges upon the nature of the relationship between the DAO and its legal wrapper. Furthermore, mechanisms can be put in place to ensure the execution of the court order, for example by means of an escrow agreement. Such mechanisms can also be used on the blockchain to hold in escrow crypto-assets, such as tokens or NFTs. With the exception of these cases, only a court order concerning physical assets – and not crypto-assets – can be enforced by force if a DAO does not spontaneously comply with the order issued against it.

V. Service of process to a DAO

The bZx DAO case[96] is a good illustration of the troubles encountered when bringing a DAO before a state court. However, a plaintiff initiating legal proceedings against a DAO will face additional problems, particularly regarding the service of court documents. In this regard, DAOs present an opportunity to explore novel and innovative methods of serving procedural documents.

In the U.S., the Commodity Futures Trading Commission (CFTC) served Ooki DAO – which is the successor of bZx DAO – by posting summons documents on Ooki DAO's online discussion forum and by submitting them via Ooki DAO's help chat box available on its website. The CFTC argued that it had served the procedural documents to Ooki DAO via the only avenue that the DAO itself made available for the public to contact it, and that this means did in fact provide notice to Ooki DAO. In this administrative proceeding, Ooki DAO is qualified by the CFTC as an unincorporated association because it "function[s] under a common name under circumstances where fairness requires the group be recognized as a legal entity".[97] Under California law, an unincorporated association is considered a separate legal entity from its members. It has the capacity to be sued, which allowed plaintiffs to list Ooki DAO as a defendant.

In a recent decision, a California Court[98] ruled that the qualification of Ooki DAO as an unincorporated association in the CFTC proceedings was appropri-

---

[96] See chapter III.3.

[97] *CFTC v. Ooki DAO* (fn. 98), 12-13.

[98] United States District Court, Northern District of California, order of 20 December 2022 in the ongoing *CFTC v. Ooki DAO* litigation (Case Number 3:22-cv-05416-WHO), available at https://casetext.com/case/commodity-futures-trading-commn-v-ooki-dao-1 accessed 1 June 2023.

ate. It also ruled that Ooki DAO was properly served in that capacity, because service via its online discussion forum and its chat box gave "actual notice to the party being served" in accordance with constitutional due process requirements.[99] This is a new way of using electronic means for the service of the litigation documents to the addressee. Service by electronic means is authorized by law in California but was, until now, usually meant for the service by email. This is a practical solution to the logistical impediment of serving on all the DAO token holders individually. But the manner in which the court documents are served "to the DAO" depends on the way in which the DAO operates, because a service can only be valid if the defendant has been served in a manner and at a time that make it reasonably possible for them to arrange for their defense.[100]

In an English case, the High Court of England and Wales granted an order permitting the service of court documents via a non-fungible token (NFT) on the blockchain.[101] Like the California court in the Ooki DAO case, the English court granted the plaintiff the right to alternative service because of the unique circumstances of the case and the impracticability of serving through conventional means. In this proceeding, the plaintiff alleged theft of cryptocurrency that he deposited within two wallets of third parties. The service was achieved by air-dropping the NFT representing the court documents into the two wallets where the plaintiff alleged to have suffered the fraud. Service via a wallet address is an innovative approach that utilizes blockchain technology to serve litigation documents[102] to unidentified individuals and initiate legal proceedings.

---

[99] *CFTC v. Ooki DAO* (fn. 98), 16.

[100] Otherwise, the decision on the merits would not be recognizable or enforceable abroad, notably in the country in which service took place. See e.g., Article 7 para. 1 of the HCCH Convention on the Recognition and Enforcement of Foreign Judgments in Civil or Commercial Matters of 2 July 2019 (the "Judgments Convention"): "Recognition or enforcement may be refused if (a) the document which instituted the proceedings or an equivalent document, including a statement of the essential elements of the claim – (i) was not notified to the defendant in sufficient time and in such a way as to enable them to arrange for their defence, unless the defendant entered an appearance and presented their case without contesting notification in the court of origin, provided that the law of the State of origin permitted notification to be contested; or (ii) was notified to the defendant in the requested State in a manner that is incompatible with fundamental principles of the requested State concerning service of documents". An equivalent provision can be found in Article 34 para. 2 of the Lugano Convention.

[101] High Court of England and Whales, *D'Aloia v. Persons Unknown, Binance Holding Ltd and others* (24 June 2022).

[102] The use of blockchain technology for the service of documents that must be served abroad would be a major improvement in the operation of the HCCH Convention on the Service Abroad of Judicial and Extrajudicial Documents in Civil or Commercial Matters of 15 November 1965 (the "Service Convention"). See *Guillaume/Riva*, Launching the HCCH Service Convention into the Crypto Space, in: Hague Conference on Private International Law (HCCH) (ed.), The HCCH Service Convention in the Era of Electronic and Information Technology, 2019, 47.

In common law states, service is of particular importance because personal jurisdiction depends on the ability to service the claim form.[103] While the legal scope of this procedural step varies across jurisdictions, it remains crucial for initiating legal proceedings in all jurisdictions. The manner in which court documents are served on the parties depends on the procedural rules of the forum. Courts are grappling with the growing challenge of serving process on defendants who can only be traced to an email address, a social networking site, a website, an online discussion forum, or a wallet address. This issue becomes especially prominent when dealing with unidentified defendants and makes it necessary to find alternative means of service by electronic means.

However, an additional practical difficulty arises when service of judicial documents must take place in another state. International service of documents in civil or commercial matters is subject to specific requirements.[104] In general, international service by electronic means is permissible only if the law of the addressed state does not prohibit such service.[105] Due to the fact that electronic service is only permitted in certain jurisdictions[106], there may be instances where serving court documents on the defendant becomes impractical or unattainable. If an alternative electronic means of service is used internationally, which is not recognized as valid in the defendant's country, the notice will be deemed invalid. The issue of service of court documents can therefore be a real challenge when the defendant is a DAO or a pseudonymous blockchain user.

---

[103] In UK, see e.g., *Hartley*, International Commercial Litigation, 3rd ed. 2020, 133-165. In the U.S., see e.g., *Felix/Whitten* (fn. 89), n. 16, 42-48; *Burnham v. Superior Court of California*, 495 U.S. 604 (1990).

[104] See Service Convention (fn. 102), which is in force in 81 states. It should be noted, however, that this convention only applies when the document is to be transmitted to an addressee abroad (Article 1 para. 1), and does not apply when the address of the person to be served with the document is unknown (Article 1 para. 2). Where the defendant's address is unknown, it is not possible to determine whether the document is to be sent abroad, and the convention is therefore not applicable.

[105] See Article 5 para. 1 of the Service Convention (fn. 102): the document must be served in the addressed state "a) by a method prescribed by its internal law for the service of documents in domestic actions upon persons who are within its territory, or b) by a particular method requested by the applicant, unless such a method is incompatible with the law of the state addressed".

[106] See e.g., Article 19 of the EU Regulation No 2020/1784 of the European Parliament and of the Council of 25.11.2020 on the service in the Member States of judicial and extrajudicial documents in civil or commercial matters (OJ 2020 L 405/40), which applies between Member States of the European Union. In Switzerland, electronic service of judicial documents (e.g., by email) is not permitted. However, the parties may use a specific platform for submitting legal documents; in the case of electronic submission, the submission and its enclosures must bear a qualified electronic signature (Article 130 of the Swiss Civil Procedure Code of 19 December 2008; SR 272).

VI. In search of alternatives to state justice

Considering the challenges involved in a judicial procedure, opting for a private justice system to resolve the dispute might offer a simpler and more efficient alternative to resorting to a state court. Among the Alternative Dispute Resolution (ADR) mechanisms offered by private justice, arbitration has long been the preferred option in cross-border business relationships. However, new modes of private justice that use technology to resolve the dispute have emerged, some of which take advantage of blockchain technology.

1. Arbitration

Arbitration is in principle linked to a state by the seat of arbitration. This way of resolving a civil or commercial dispute has the main advantage of issuing decisions that are binding on the parties and have a scope equivalent to that of a court decision when the procedure followed by the arbitrators is established or recognized by the states. Arbitral awards have thus in principle a *res judicata* effect and are considered as such equal to judgments rendered by state courts. Such decisions not only have effect in the state of the seat of arbitration but may also have legal effect in other states. In a contracting state of the Convention on the Recognition and Enforcement of Foreign Arbitral Awards of 10 June 1958 (the "New York Convention"), recognition and enforcement of an arbitral award will be relatively easy to achieve. In other states, the conditions for recognition and enforcement provided for in the rules of private international law of the state where enforcement is requested must be fulfilled, just like the recognition and enforcement of foreign court decisions.

Arbitration may be a good alternative to state justice to resolve disputes involving DAOs. An arbitration clause can be incorporated into the code of a smart contract, just like a choice of court clause.[107] Arbitration offers several advantages over state court proceedings, including the ability to assign dispute resolution to experts possessing specialized knowledge in the field of blockchain. Additionally, arbitration procedures are typically faster and, in certain instances, less costly than state court proceedings. Moreover, parties often enjoy greater flexibility in determining the rules that will govern their dispute before an arbitral tribunal.

Nonetheless, the same issues listed for state courts regarding the enforcement of the decision persist.[108] In order for an arbitration award to be effectively enforced, the parties must mutually agree to voluntarily execute the award, and the losing party must willingly comply with the award once it is rendered, as

[107] See chapter II.2.b).
[108] See chapter IV.

there is no external authority with enforcement powers over a DAO. Besides, the arbitration procedure may prove, in many cases, too cumbersome and costly for disputes arising from blockchain transactions.

2. *Other modes of private justice*

ADRs give access to a wide variety of opt-in private justice mechanisms that can be voluntarily chosen by the parties (e.g., mediation, conciliation, neutral evaluation). These modes of private dispute resolution are increasingly present online, as part of mechanisms for resolving disputes that take advantage of technology. Recently, new types of ODRs have been implemented on the blockchain to use this technology for resolving disputes of blockchain users.

a) Online dispute resolution

The advent of e-commerce has led to the development of online dispute resolution (ODR) mechanisms, which are simpler, faster and cheaper dispute resolution models than state justice and arbitration.[109] However, while decisions made in the context of ODR proceedings may be legally binding in the same way as a contract, they usually do not have the effect of an enforceable court decision. They are not enforceable by state authorities in the same manner as decisions rendered by state courts, nor do they fall within the scope of the New York Convention. The execution of the outcome of ODR depends entirely on the willingness of the losing party. In the jurisdictions where non-execution of the outcome of ODR would equate to the non-execution of a contractual obligation, the party seeking execution will have to obtain a court decision which orders the other party to execute the performance due. However, it may be too costly to obtain such a court decision. When parties entrust the resolution of their dispute to an ODR mechanism, there is thus a significant risk that the decision is not spontaneously executed by the losing party who is well aware of the difficulties related to the execution of the outcome of ODR with the assistance of state authorities.[110]

It is worth mentioning that some e-commerce platforms enjoy a privileged position allowing them to have control over payments. This is the case, for instance, of eBay which has teamed up with payment service providers to keep control over the payments.[111] When a buyer wishes to be refunded, the seller is encouraged to negotiate a solution, whether privately on eBay's platform or

[109] See *Guillaume/Riva* (fn. 9), chapter 4.2.1, 596-599.

[110] See *Guillaume/Riva* (fn. 9), chapter 4.1.2, 594-595.

[111] See e.g., *Koulu*, Law, Technology and Dispute Resolution – Privatisation of Coercion, 2019, 76-78; *Loebl*, Designing Online Courts – The Future of Justice Is Open to All, 2019, 4-7; *Schultz*, eBay: un système juridique en formation?, Revue du droit des technologies et de l'information 22 (2005), 27.

with the help of an external provider of negotiation services. In the event that negotiations prove fruitless and the payment was made using specific methods such as PayPal, the buyer can utilize eBay's internal ODR mechanism. Upon assessing the buyer's claim, eBay may decide to issue a refund and has the authority to enforce its decision using credit card chargebacks, occasionally without even consulting the seller. The combination of control over the payment method and the ODR mechanism produces an effective private enforcement mechanism. By enabling the self-enforcement of ODR decisions[112], eBay has successfully established a private justice system that serves as a genuine alternative to state justice.[113] Nonetheless, eBay's ODR mechanism relies on the assistance of an intermediary (such as PayPal) to enforce its decisions, indicating a lack of self-sufficiency. Furthermore, the ODR process is conducted exclusively by eBay itself, lacking the involvement of an independent third party with no vested financial interests. This could lead to a lack of impartiality in the dispute resolution.

b) Blockchain-based dispute resolution

Blockchain-based dispute resolution (BDR) mechanisms are conducted entirely on the blockchain and are configured in such a way that they can be performed using smart contracts.[114] This allows BDR mechanisms to avoid the main drawback of most ODR systems, which is the lack of coercive and independent means of enforcement. A BDR mechanism can indeed implement a direct and automatic decision enforcement mechanism by using a smart contract. Thanks to the use of this technology, the effectiveness of the dispute resolution process does not rely on the willingness of the parties to comply with the decision. It is therefore not surprising that BDRs are particularly interesting for the resolution of disputes involving a DAO.

As of today, there is one BDR that is operational for resolving disputes on the blockchain and is accessible to DAOs: Kleros.[115] This BDR mechanism – launched on the Ethereum blockchain in July 2018 – has the particularity of

---

112 About the notion of self-enforcement in the meaning of enforcement by private authorities, see *Schultz*, Online Arbitration: Binding or Non-Binding?, ADROnline Monthly, November 2002, 4. See also *Ortolani*, Self-Enforcing Online Dispute Resolution: Lessons from Bitcoin, Oxford Journal of Legal Studies 36 (2016), 595.

113 *Guillaume/Riva* (fn. 9), 601-602. Same opinion: *Loebl* (fn. 111), 36-37 and 66; *Cortés*, Online Dispute Resolution for Consumers – Online Dispute Resolution Methods for Settling Business to Consumer Conflicts, in: Wahab/ Katsh/Rainey (ed.), Online Dispute Resolution: Theory and Practice, 2012, 150.

114 See *Guillaume/Riva* (fn. 9), chapter 5, 602-612.

115 See *Guillaume/Riva* (fn. 9), chapter 6.1, 613-616. Disputes related to the governance of a DAO may be resolved by Kleros. Aragon Court was not as successful as expected and no longer seems to be operational.

relying on crowdsourcing in its dispute resolution process.[116] The characteristic feature of crowdsourcing is that the dispute is resolved by a jury composed of people who are not necessarily legally qualified, but who can take a stand on a dispute based on personal experience and technical qualifications.[117] The decision is therefore not based on a defined framework of rules or precedent. Jurors vote *ex aequo et bono*, considering the arguments and evidence presented by each party, in favor of one of the options proposed by the parties for resolving the case. But in reaching their decision, each juror endeavors to anticipate the choices of the other jurors in order to align their vote accordingly. The main characteristic of the decision-making process is indeed that it is designed so that jurors have an economic incentive to make a decision by consensus.[118] Consequently, jurors receive remuneration solely if their vote aligns with the majority decision. Parties can appeal an indefinite number of times, each new appeal instance having twice the previous number of jurors plus one. When there are no more appeals, the decision is final and is directly and automatically enforced through a smart contract.

Entrusting the resolution of a dispute with a DAO to a BDR seems to be a good solution today, mainly because it avoids the difficulties associated with a procedure before a state court. For the time being, state courts cannot guarantee access to justice in a reliable manner for disputes involving DAOs. Connecting factors have a difficult time locating matters of company law that concern the governance of DAOs and other civil or commercial relationships to which DAOs are parties (e.g., in contractual or tortious matters); it is hard (if not impossible) to identify the defendant when the parties involved benefit from pseudonymity in the blockchain environment; and the vast majority of DAOs do

---

[116] See *Lesaege/George/Ast*, Kleros Yellow paper, March 2020, available at https://kleros.io/yellowpaper.pdf accessed 1 June 2023.

[117] See *Van den Herik/Dimov*, Towards Crowdsourced Online Dispute Resolution, in: Kierkegaard/Kierkegaard (ed.), Law Across Nations: Governance, Policy and Statutes, International Association of IT Lawyers, 2011, 244-257, available at https://papers.ssrn.com/sol3/papers.cfm?abstract_id=1933392 accessed 1 June 2023. These authors call an ODR mechanism using crowdsourcing as a part of the dispute resolution process "Crowdsourced Online Dispute Resolution (CODR)". Other authors use the term "mob justice": *Schmitz/Rule*, Online Dispute Resolution for Smart Contracts, Journal of Dispute Resolution, 2019, 103, 117; or "peer-to-peer arbitration": *Abramowicz*, Cryptocurrency-Based Law, Arizona Law Review 58 (2016), 359, 405.

[118] The main economic mechanism used is the Schelling Point (or focal point). The Schelling Point is, in game theory, a solution to which the participants in a game who cannot communicate with each other will tend to adopt because they think that this solution presents a characteristic which will make the other participants choose it too. *Schelling*, The Strategy of Conflict, 2nd ed. 1980, 57. See *Aouidef/Ast/Deffains*, Decentralized Justice: A Comparative Analysis of Blockchain Online Dispute Resolution Projects, Frontiers in Blockchain, 2021, 4, https://www.frontiersin.org/articles/10.3389/fbloc.2021.564551/full accessed 1 June 2023; *Spagnuolo*, Crypto-economics considerations, *GitHub*, 21 November 2019, https://github.com/aragon/aragon-court/tree/v1.0.0/docs/3-cryptoeconomic-considerations accessed 1 June 2023.

not have the capacity to be a party to state court proceedings. Furthermore, even if a dispute involving a DAO can be brought before a state court, enforcement of the court decision on the blockchain is challenging when the losing party does not voluntarily comply. State enforcement authorities do not have the power to force a smart contract to execute in a certain way, nor can they freeze or seize crypto-assets from a DAO or an on-chain actor. BDRs allow litigants to circumvent these procedural difficulties by allowing direct and automatic enforcement of the decision as soon as it is final.

In comparison with state justice systems, the main drawback of BDRs is that they do not provide predictability as to the outcome of a dispute, especially when they do not refer to a defined framework of rules or principles to make a decision and when the dispute resolution system is not based on precedent either. The same situation can thus be solved differently depending on internal fairness considerations of each juror.[119] At the current stage of development, BDRs do not offer the same level of certainty as state courts, which adhere to legal rules and principles. Moreover, the decisions that can be obtained today through a BDR mechanism are, at best, binding in a similar manner to a contract. Like decisions rendered by other ODR mechanisms, they lack enforceability by state authorities to the same extent as decisions issued by state courts. They do not fall either within the scope of the New York Convention.[120] Due to the inability to enforce their decisions through off-chain mechanisms, BDRs are not ideally suited for resolving disputes involving physical property. For the time being, BDRs are predominantly effective in resolving disputes related to cryptocurrencies and other crypto-assets, as their decisions can be enforced directly on-chain through smart contracts.

Nevertheless, BDRs have the merit of guaranteeing access to justice for DAOs that do not have legal personality. In any scenario where enforcement of the decision needs to occur on-chain, this alternative dispute resolution method proves to be a suitable approach. By taking advantage of the self-enforcement mechanism provided by smart contracts, BDRs offer a resolution of the dispute that can be executed directly and automatically, making it an effective means of dispute resolution. But it is also inevitable that some proceedings involving DAOs will end up in state courts, especially (but not only) in the context of proceedings involving state authorities. In this case, the members of a DAO without legal personality will be directly involved in the legal proceedings and may incur personal liability. This risk could be avoided if DAOs had a defined legal status.

---

[119] *Buchwald*, Smart contract dispute resolution: The inescapable flaws of blockchain-based arbitration, University of Pennsylvania Law Review 168 (2020), 1369, 1407.

[120] See *Guillaume/Riva* (fn. 9), chapter 7.3.1, 633-638.

Granting DAOs – maverick DAOs included – legal status would provide some legal certainty in the Web 3 environment, not only for the members of DAOs but also for third parties who enter into legal relationships with them. Due to the fact that DAOs are at the core of Web 3, it is crucial to provide a dispute resolution mechanism tailored to the characteristics of DAOs. This would help reduce the risk associated with engaging with a DAO and enhance trust in DeFi. The lack of effective access to state justice for DAOs undoubtedly hinders the development of Web 3, particularly in the realm of DeFi.

DAOs and Civil Liability

Some Policy Considerations

Peder Østbye[*]

Abstract The rise of cryptocurrency and blockchain technologies has revived the attention to decentralized autonomous organizations (DAOs) for social cooperation enabled by algorithms and the internet. Novel DAOs must co-exist with long-established civil liability. DAOs might pose a challenge to the enforcement of civil liability, and civil liability might pose a challenge for DAO-organized activities. This paper explores the DAO and civil liability nexus and whether the existing practice of civil liability is adequate in promoting the high-level purposes of civil liability in their meeting with DAOs. It is explored whether policies are necessary to maintain responsibility for DAO-organized activities and for aligning such activities with public policy. Some policy recommendations are provided.

I. Introduction

The rise of cryptocurrency and blockchain technologies has revived the attention to decentralized autonomous organizations (DAOs) for social cooperation enabled by algorithms and the internet. Novel DAOs must co-exist with long-established civil liability. DAOs might pose a challenge to the enforcement of civil liability, and civil liability might pose a challenge for DAO-organized activities. This paper explores the DAO and civil liability nexus and whether the existing practice of civil liability is adequate in promoting the high-level purposes of civil liability in their meeting with DAOs. It is explored whether policies are necessary to maintain responsibility for DAO-organized activities and for aligning such activities with public policy.

This paper builds on the emerging literature addressing DAOs in the context of cryptocurrency and blockchain systems[1] and well as the broader literature on cryptocurrency and blockchain governance.

---

[*] Paper prepared for the International Conference on DAO Regulation – 20th April 2023, Lisbon Portugal. This paper should not be reported as representing the views of Norges Bank. The views expressed are those of the author and do not necessarily reflect those of Norges Bank. This paper is written in a private capacity. For correspondence, please use p.e.oest@gmail.com.

[1] See *S Hassan/PD Filippi*, Decentralized autonomous organization. Internet Policy

A branch of legal research intersecting with legal philosophy and techno-liberalism questions the role of law wholesale in the governance of DAOs. Following the analysis framework of Lawrence Lessig,[2] it is argued for governance by architecture and code instead.[3] Less disruptive than DAOs being entirely outside the realm of law, but in the same direction, is the question of whether DAOs are separate legal entities with separate legal duties (possibly subject to limited liability), which at the same time shields the participants in these organizations from personal liability, much like limited liability corporations today.[4]

Much legal research has justified the role of law in the governance of DAOs.[5] A growing body of legal research is devoted to the legal responsibilities of the participants operating DAOs.[6] Central topics are the responsibilities of protocol developers and coders.[7] Legal research has also studied the liability for at-

Rev. 10 (2) 2021, *Chiu, Iris HY*, Regulating the crypto economy: business transformations and financialisation, 2021, and *Allen, Darcy WE/Berg, Chris/Lane, Aaron M*, Trust and governance in collective blockchain treasuries, 2021 for an introduction to this literature.

[2] *See Lessig, Lawrence*, Code: Version 2.0, [2. ed.]. New York, NY, 2006.

[3] The Bitcoin white paper itself, *Satoshi Nakamoto*, Bitcoin: A peer-to-peer electronic cash system 2008, can be considered research into governance by architecture and code by analyzing decentralized validation of transactions without reliance on trusted third parties and, hence, the legal duties of such trusted third parties. Research has provided ever more sophisticated systems for decentralized validation of transactions; many implemented in new cryptocurrency systems. The interdisciplinary literature on blockchain governance is flourishing. *Liu, Yue/Lu, Qinghua/Zhu, Liming/Paik, Hye-Young/Staples, Mark*, A systematic literature review on blockchain governance, Journal of Systems and Software, 2023 provide a systematic literature review on blockchain governance, while *Kiayias, Aggelos/Lazos, Philip*, SoK: blockchain governance, arXiv preprint arXiv:2201.07188, 2022 provide a SoK on blockchain governance.

[4] See *Allen, JG*, Bodies without organs: law, economics, and decentralised governance, Stan. J. Blockchain L. & Pol'y 2020, 53 and *Wright, Aaron*, The Rise of Decentralized Autonomous Organizations: Opportunities and Challenges, Stan. J. Blockchain L. & Pol'y, 2020, 1. *Østbye, Peder*, Exploring DAO Members' Individual Liability, Available at SSRN 4045799, 2022 provides a critical approach.

[5] See, for instance *Hacker, Philipp*, Corporate governance for complex cryptocurrencies? A framework for stability and decision making in blockchain-based organizations, 2019 *Allen, Darcy WE/Berg, Chris/Lane, Aaron M*, Trust and governance in collective blockchain treasuries, Available at SSRN 3891976, 2021. There are also book volumes, such as *Chiu*, Regulating the crypto economy, 2021.

[6] See, for instance, *Zetzsche, Dirk A/Buckley, Ross P/Arner, Douglas W*, The distributed liability of distributed ledgers: Legal risks of blockchain, U. Ill. L. Rev., 2018, 1361 for a general assessment focusing on cryptocurrencies.

[7] See *Walch, Angela*, In code (rs) we trust, Software developers as fiduciaries in public blockchains, 2019 for a discussion of fiduciary duties and *Rodrigo Seira*, Blockchain Protocol Developers are not Fiduciaries, An Analysis of the Cryptoeconomics of Open Source Networks and the Role of Protocol Developers in Public Blockchain Network Governance 2018) and *Haque, Raina S/Seira, Rodrigo/Plummer, Brent/Rosario, Nelson*, Blockchain development and fiduciary duty, Stan. J. Blockchain L. & Pol'y, 2019, 1–16 for a response. See also *Østbye, Peder*, Who is Liable for Collusion in Cryptocurrency Protocol Development? Available at SSRN 3354868, 2019 *Østbye, Peder*, Who is Liable if a Cryptocurrency Protocol Fails?, Available at SSRN 3423681, 2019.

tacks on cryptocurrency systems,[8] and liability of validators and users for non-compliant transactions.[9] The growing body of literature on liability for autonomous algorithms and multi-agent systems powered by artificial intelligence is also highly relevant to this paper.[10]

This paper adds to the literature by analyzing how civil liability for DAO-organized activities can be aligned with high-level goals of civil liability, including instrumental public policy goals of civil liability. Much efforts has been put into to analyzing how civil liability should accommodate the "needs" of DAOs, and in this sense, this paper provides another perspective. Section II discusses what creatures DAOs are and, in particular, what kind of legal creatures they are. Section III explores the DAO and civil liability nexus. Section IV asks if DAOs necessitate specialized civil liability rules. Sections V and VI discusses two reasons why such a specialized liability regime might be necessary: to maintain responsibility for DAO-organized activities (in an efficient manner) and to align DAO-organized activity with public policy. Section VII briefly discusses whether "code is law" is a good policy. Section VIII provides concluding remarks.

II. What kind of (legal) creature is a DAO?

Decentralized autonomous organizations are not phenomena that emerged with cryptocurrencies and blockchain.[11] Philosophy and most sciences entail subdisciplines studying decentralized activities and their attributes, such as the study of competitive markets and their welfare properties in economics. The study of autonomous agents attracts a wide range of disciplines, including philosophy, law, social sciences, and computer science.

In the 90s, the term decentralized autonomous organizations was used to describe multi-agent systems enabled by algorithms and the internet. These systems are autonomous in the sense that they more or less make their own deci-

---

8 See *Østbye, Peder*, Who is Liable for an Attack on Cryptocurrency Consensus? Available at SSRN 3442597, 2019.

9 See *Østbye, Peder*, Who is Liable for Non-Compliant Cryptocurrency Transactions: Should Transaction Validators be Held Liable? Available at SSRN 3825893, 2021. See also *Sutherland*, Proof of Stake Alliance Research Report 2021 for a critique of proposed regulations in the US on the reporting duties of users.

10 See, for instance, *Abbot, R/Borges, G/Dacoronia, E/Devillier, N/Jankowska-Augustyn, M/Karner, E* u.a., Liability for Artificial Intelligence and other emerging digital technologies. Report from the Expert Group on Liability and New Technologies–New Technologies Formation, European Union, 2019 and *Beckers, Anna/Teubner, Gunther*, Three liability regimes for artificial intelligence: algorithmic actants, hybrids, crowds, 2021.

11 See *S Hassan/PD Filippi*, Decentralized autonomous organization. Internet Policy Rev. 10 (2), 2021.

sions in a self-governed manner and decentralized in the meaning that they are designed not to rely on trusted third parties.

With the advent of cryptocurrency and blockchain systems, decentralized autonomous organizations have become almost synonymous with decentralized organizations enabled by such systems. With this development, the abbreviation DAO has reached a mainstream audience. DAOs are understood in this narrow sense for the purpose of this paper. However, much of the analysis is applicable to multi-agent systems enabled by algorithms and the internet more generally.

There is a variety of DAOs in the cryptocurrency and blockchain space. The fundamental infrastructures in this space – cryptocurrency systems – have certain DAO properties and are often referred to as DAOs. In simplified layman's terms, cryptocurrencies are account units in a digital register replicated among many participants to be maintained without reliance on any trusted party. In more technical terms, cryptocurrency systems can be seen as decentrally designed computing systems where a native token—the cryptocurrency —is central to the incentive mechanisms to achieve consensus on the computations. This native token can be intended to function as money, as a price to utilize the distributed computing system, or both. Ethereum is an example, providing a complete programming language on the platform, which can be used for so-called smart contracts (automated execution of computations).[12]

The systems are designed to be maintained and operated in a permissionless decentralized manner in the sense that users need no approval from a centralized authority to develop the systems (as they are governed in by consented protocols implemented in open-source software),[13] use the system (initiating transactions),[14] participate in the peer-to-peer communication network,[15] and appending transactions (often in batches referred to as blocks) to the consented ledger according to a consensus mechanism.[16] The consensus mechanisms are

[12] This is not to be confused with the legal meaning of contracts.

[13] The protocol development process is well described elsewhere (see, for instance, *Narayanan, Arvind/Bonneau, Joseph/Felten, Edward/Miller, Andrew/Goldfeder, Steven*, Bitcoin and cryptocurrency technologies: a comprehensive introduction, 2016, *Antonopoulos, Andreas M*, Mastering Bitcoin: Programming the open blockchain, 2017, *Antonopoulos, Andreas M/Wood, Gavin*, Mastering ethereum: building smart contracts and dapps, 2018, and *Rodrigo Seira*, Blockchain Protocol Developers are not Fiduciaries: An Analysis of the Cryptoeconomics of Open Source Networks and the Role of Protocol Developers in Public Blockchain Network Governance, 2018)

[14] This is enabled by public-key cryptography and peer-to-peer technology.

[15] Full nodes provide the core of the peer-to-peer communication network. Full nodes are clients that have installed the software implementing the cryptocurrency protocol and keeping an updated version of the cryptocurrency ledger. A full node can initiate a transaction or propagate other users' transactions to other full nodes in the network according to peer-to-peer technology utilizing the general internet infrastructure.

[16] A full node can gather transactions and propose that these are appended to the ledger according to the consensus mechanism of the cryptocurrency. There is a large variety of con-

supposed to meet certain functionalities or specifications. Usually, we want the consensus mechanism to satisfy consistency (safety), availability (liveness), and fault-tolerance (including both crash failure and byzantine failure) requirements. There might also be other desirable functionalities, such as low energy usage and a high level of privacy. Various designs can more or less meet these specifications subject to certain limitations.[17]

DAOs also entail the organization and governance of applications (smart contracts) built on cryptocurrency systems. One category of applications is decentralized finance (DeFi), enabling automated financial services and products operated in a more or less decentralized manner.[18] Various DAO-operated applications pursuing different objectives are developing rapidly. DAOs may, for instance, operate social networks, virtual/augmented reality environments (metaverse), and dispute resolution. DAOs are sometimes framed as the organizational form native to Web3.[19] Another recent application is so-called "DeSci" for funding science projects.

For many DAO applications, it is necessary to feed real-world data into the applications. For instance, in a DeFi application, the oil price may be needed for certain financial products. This can be achieved by oracles performing such a function. Oracles may also serve more advanced functions. For instance, in online dispute regulation, oracles may serve as juries as to whether certain conduct is "unreasonable." Oracles may be organized as DAOs themselves.[20] One purpose is to prevent central parties to manipulate outcomes by feeding wrongful information, another is to benefit from the law of large numbers in obtaining the accurate information.

---

sensus mechanisms, and there is an ever-increasing number of proposals for new consensus mechanisms. *Wang, Wenbo/Hoang, Dinh Thai/Hu, Peizhao/Xiong, Zehui/Niyato, Dusit/ Wang, Ping* u.a., A survey on consensus mechanisms and mining strategy management in blockchain networks, Ieee Access, 2019, 22328–22370, and *Ferdous, Md Sadek/Chowdhury, Mohammad Jabed Morshed/Hoque, Mohammad A/Colman, Alan*, Blockchain consensus algorithms, A survey, arXiv preprint arXiv:2001.07091, 2020 for surveys of consensus mechanisms.

[17] The so-called CAP theorem (Consistency, Availability, and Partition-tolerance) and the FLP theorem (Fisher, Lynch, and Paterson) state some logical limitations on obtaining consistency, availability, and partition tolerance/fault tolerance simultaneously. For a brief description, see http://ug93tad.github.io/flpcap/ (accessed March 2023). For an accessible critique of the CAP theorem, see jvns.ca/blog/2016/11/19/a-critique-of-the-cap-theorem/ (accessed March 2023).

[18] See *Carter, N/Linda, J*, DeFi protocol risks: The paradox of DeFi – Regtech, Suptech and beyond: Innovation and technology in financial services, RiskBooks. https://doi. org/ 10.2139/ssrn, 2021 and *Aramonte, Sirio/Huang, Wenqian/Schrimpf, Andreas*, DeFi risks and the decentralisation illusion, 2021.

[19] Web3 is used as a term for a more decentralized internet enabled by cryptocurrency and blockchain technology.

[20] One example is Chainlink, see https://chain.link/ (accessed March 2023).

A central element of DAOs is governance tokens. Such tokens may be the native cryptocurrency of a cryptocurrency system. For instance, for cryptocurrency systems using proof-of-stake (PoS) consensus mechanisms, the governance function of the native cryptocurrency is obvious, as these are staked by validators to foster integrity. More generally, DAO protocols often entail "constitutions" and other advanced governance structures for protocol development. Specific governance "tokens" are used for participation in governance, such as voting over decisions on changing system parameters, protocol upgrades, and the use of "treasuries" to finance development. Such tokens allow for "on-chain" governance substituting and complementing "off-chain" governance. The tokens may have a more or less exclusive role in governance. Certain DAOs may hard-code a governance role (for instance, by granting control over admin keys) for certain participants[21] to perform certain functions.[22]

Although DAOs are based on decentralized design, such designs do not provide any guarantee against centralization.[23] Centralization may occur at the protocol level and network level.[24] Particular attention has been given to the centralization risks of consensus mechanisms in cryptocurrency systems with the consequence that validations are performed by a few entities and possibly coming under the control of one entity.[25] Holders of a large number of governance tokens may also be a source of centralization. This is obvious in systems based on PoS validation.[26]

---

[21] Often granted founding members.

[22] Such a function can be to trigger kill-switches in case of an attack or unforeseen event.

[23] See *Walch, Angela*, Deconstructing'decentralization': Exploring the core claim of crypto systems, 2019.

[24] See *Sai, Ashish Rajendra/Buckley, Jim/Fitzgerald, Brian/Le Gear, Andrew*, Taxonomy of centralization in public blockchain systems: A systematic literature review, Information Processing & Management, 2021, 102584 for various centralization metrics in cryptocurrencies.

[25] Much has been written on the centralization risk associated with Bitcoin PoW validation (See, for instance, *Joseph Bonneau/Andrew Miller/Jeremy Clark/Arvind Narayanan/Joshua A Kroll/Edward W Felten*, Sok: Research perspectives and challenges for bitcoin and cryptocurrencies 2015, *Narayanan/Bonneau/Felten/Miller/Goldfeder*, Bitcoin and cryptocurrency technologies 2016 Chapter 5, and *Sami Ben Mariem/Pedro Casas/Matteo Romiti/Benoit Donnet/Rainer Stütz/Bernhard Haslhofer*, All that glitters is not bitcoin–unveiling the centralized nature of the btc (ip) network, 2020). The specialized hardware necessary to remain competitive may create economies of scale. Besides, validation is organized in "mining pools," which exacerbates the centralization problem. Centralization risk may also come from other sources. Monopoly power (or government power) on validation inputs or complementary services can give a de facto monopoly power over a cryptocurrency (See *Østbye, Peder*, Who is Liable for Collusion in Cryptocurrency Protocol Development?, Available at SSRN 3354868, 2019 and *Sai, Ashish Rajendra/Buckley, Jim/Fitzgerald, Brian/Le Gear, Andrew*, Taxonomy of centralization in public blockchain systems: A systematic literature review, Information Processing & Management, 2021, 102584).

[26] However, such holdings may also give power in PoW systems, such as the power to launch certain attacks.

This techno-economical introduction serves as a backdrop to what we are interested in this section: what kind of creature a DAO is from a legal perspective. What a DAO is from a legal perspective is highly relevant for legal liability, naturally, as one of the main purposes of legal organization is to manage legal liability risks. Given the crucial implications of the legal organization of DAOs for liability, it is not surprising that the industry has been concerned with the legal-organizational mapping of DAOs.

There is an emerging literature exploring the legal status of DAOs, including jurisdictional-dependent black-letter law assessments.[27] It will be beyond the purpose of this paper to go into such details. What is essential for this paper is the policy implications of their legal status. One simple way of looking at DAOs is to consider them as an instrument for the DAO members. The DAO then inherits the properties of the persons controlling this instrument. If the DAO (contrary to being decentralized in the name) is controlled by a single person, the legal status of this person determines the legal status of the DAO. The DAO can be controlled by a single physical person, a partnership of physical persons, potentially jointly liable, or by some sort legal entitity such as a limited liability company or a trust. If the DAO is controlled by some legal entity absorbing the liability, this is sometimes referred to as a legal wrapper meant to shield other participants from liability. A theory explored both in theory and legal practice[28] is whether DAO can be considered a joint liability partnership among the participants.[29] It is also argued that some sort of nucleus of central agents may be identified among the participants for liability purposes.[30] This might, for instance, be certain influential protocol developers, validators, or holders of large amounts of governance tokens.[31]

However, DAOs could be given a legal status more distant from the persons behind or operating the DAO. Several jurisdictions are considering DAOs as a new form of legal person granted legal personhood. This requires that the DAO possesses autonomy to represent itself, comply with legal sanctions, and dispose over capital that can be used to pay damages and fines. Many DAOs do not

---

[27] See, for instance, *Law Commission*, Decentralised autonomous organisations (DAOs) Call for evidence. 2022

[28] See, for instance, the US CFTC enforcement action against Okki DAO, https://www.cftc.gov/PressRoom/PressReleases/8590-22 (accessed March 2023).

[29] See *Garcia Rolo, Antonio*, Challenges in the Legal Qualification of Decentralised Autonomous Organisations (DAOs): The Rise of the Crypto-Partnership?, 2019 and *Law Commission*, Decentralised autonomous organisations (DAOs) Call for evidence, 2022.

[30] See *Schrepel, Thibault*, The theory of granularity: A path for antitrust in blockchain ecosystems, Available at SSRN 3519032 2020. See also *Østbye, Peder*, Who is Causally Responsible for a Cryptocurrency?, Available at SSRN 3339537, 2019.

[31] See *Østbye, Peder*, Different Activity, Different Risk, Different Rules? Exploring Cryptocurrency System Service Providers' Duties and Responsibilities, 2021. See also *Østbye, Peder*, Exploring The Role of Law in The Governance of Cryptocurrency Systems and Why Limited Liability DAOs might be a Bad Idea, Available at SSRN 4007547, 2022.

satisfy these criteria, such as most cryptocurrencies. They cannot represent themselves (for instance, you cannot serve Bitcoin or Ethereum), and they don't have their own pockets to pay damages or fines.

Regulations granting legal personhood to DAOs aim at satisfying these criteria while preserving decentralization. This is a difficult task, and the efforts don't seem very successful so far. Regulatory granting of legal personhood to DAOs falls into a broader discussion on granting legal personhood to algorithms. While the DAO discussion is mainly concerned with the "decentralized" part of DAOs, there is a literature on the "autonomous" part, which is mostly explored in the context of artificial intelligence algorithms. This literature often has a philosophical character and is concerned with whether algorithms can possess the same qualities as physical persons and should be granted personhood for this reason. In this context, it is explored how liability can be enforced, for instance, requiring that they should have some insurance and capital backing in case of liability. They may also be subject to more punishment-like sanctions like being shut off in case of misconduct. One particular takeaway from this latter literature is that personhood is not necessarily a dichotomy meaning that either they have it or not.[32] Rather, DAOs could be subject to limited personhood and be able to act as agents[33] but not granted full personhood. In this respect, DAOs could be considered as agents for which the members and other participants are potentially unlimited responsible as principals. Principles of agency law can then serve as a starting point for holding the member-principals liable, which is also suggested as a principle for holding users and operators of autonomous algorithms liable more generally.

III. The DAO and civil liability nexus

Civil liability may emerge from torts, contracts, and violations of civil laws. Civil liability serves various purposes. On a fundamental level, civil and criminal liability protect physical integrity, private property, and personal autonomy. They maintain the social order by, for instance, providing legal certainty for contractual parties. Furthermore, liability is an instrument to induce behavior that corresponds with public policy. For example, legal duties and responsibilities are often grounded on the need for customer protection, market integrity, financial stability, and environmental protection, among others. Often economics is used to inform public policies, such as market failures preventing markets from producing efficient outcomes.

---

[32] See *Kurki, Visa AJ*, A theory of legal personhood, 2019.

[33] See *Beckers, Anna/Teubner, Gunther*, Three liability regimes for artificial intelligence: algorithmic actants, hybrids, crowds, 2021 for a discussion on liability of algorithms as agents.

Compensation is often argued as the main purpose of civil liability, contrary to the retribution and deterrence purpose of criminal liability. However, many civil laws serve instrumental purposes by providing incentives to comply with laws that promote public policies. For instance, regulatory agencies are often mandated to issue fines to persons that do not comply with regulations. Civil liability is relevant for misconduct towards fellow participants in a DAO and for misconduct performed by DAOs detrimental to third parties, potentially other DAOs.

Regarding liability between participants within DAOs, some participants may exploit other participants with various types of selfish behavior and attacks. Protocol developers might be negligent in leaving bugs or backdoors into the software clients. Although open-source development allows for public scrutiny, this provides no guarantee against misconduct and negligence. Protocol developers, holders of governance tokens, and other influential stakeholders may also pursue self-interests or the interests of certain stakeholders able to influence the protocol development detrimental to other users and society more generally. Such influence might mirror rent-seeking and interest group influence studied in the political economics literature.

DAOs are exposed to a variety of attacks at the operational level, such as the process of reaching a consensus on transactions. This involves both attack strategies involving replacing the consensus in a DAO with another consensus and manipulating the outcome of the consensus by misconduct, such as exploiting weaknesses in the incentive mechanisms or code vulnerabilities.[34]

Such attacks and other forms of misconduct raise civil liability issues between participants in a DAO. For instance, negligence or misconduct by protocol developers may constitute fraud or a violation of fiduciary duties. An attack can be a tort or a fraud.

When it comes to liability vis-a-vis third parties, the operation of a DAO may produce harm to third parties, for instance, by being involved in fraud, pollution, anticompetitive conduct, or financial harm through contagion during stress. DAOs may also violate civil laws that protect public policies, such as KYC rules, to prevent crimes.[35]

[34] Attacks on cryptocurrency systems are well explored in the literature. Several surveys and SoK papers are available (see, for instance, *Joseph Bonneau/Andrew Miller/Jeremy Clark/Arvind Narayanan/Joshua A Kroll/Edward W Felten*, Sok: Research perspectives and challenges for bitcoin and cryptocurrencies, 2015, *Conti, Mauro/Kumar, E Sandeep/Lal, Chhagan/Ruj, Sushmita*, A survey on security and privacy issues of bitcoin, IEEE communications surveys & tutorials, 2018, 3416–3452, and *Zhang, Rui/Xue, Rui/Liu, Ling*, Security and privacy on blockchain, ACM Computing Surveys (CSUR), 2019, 1–34). There is a wide range of attacks against particular DAOs, especially DeFi, see *Liyi Zhou/Xihan Xiong/Jens Ernstberger/Stefanos Chaliasos/Zhipeng Wang/Ye Wang/Kaihua Qin/Roger Wattenhofer/Dawn Song/Arthur Gervais*, Sok: Decentralized finance (defi) attacks, 2023.

[35] Enforced by regulatory agencies (possibly alongside criminal enforcement).

IV. Is a specialized DAO civil liability regime required?

As argued in Section II, civil liability plays a role in the governance of DAOs. However, this does not mean that a specialized civil liability regime for DAOs is needed. Frank Easterbrook[36] defended general law to address legal issues emerging with cyberspace and technology more generally. There is no need for a "law of the horse." Basic legal institutions, such as criminal law, tort law, contract law, and fiduciary law, have proven robust in addressing legal issues emerging with new technologies. Many of these legal frameworks have built-in standards to trade-off benefits and risks, such as the risk-utility approach to tort law. In regulatory circles, the "same activity, same risk, same rules" principle is a variant of this approach. Brownsword[37] calls this a coherentist approach, in the meaning that the legal issues raised by technology are forced to fit into a coherent body of general law, and argues that such an approach might subvert a more instrumental approach taking into account technological idiosyncrasies to cater to public policies. This characterization appears somewhat unfair since the general legal frameworks entail standards to accommodate idiosyncratic risks. Many regulatory frameworks promoting public policies, such as antitrust law, consumer protection law, and environmental law, are robust and allow for idiosyncrasies.

Still, there might be several reasons why general legal frameworks may have shortcomings in the governance of technologies. They might be overinclusive and underinclusive from a policy perspective and might not implement an efficient risk allocation or efficient enforcement. Specialized regulatory frameworks might instrumentally target public policy objectives most efficiently.[38] The cost, however, might be a lack of coherence and a lack of robustness. Coherence in law is more than just an outdated legal paradigm. Coherence is crucial for rational policies.[39] Consequently, specialized legal frameworks should be coherent in their instrumental implementation to promote the rationality of law and rational allocation of resources implied by law. Furthermore, specialized frameworks may lack robustness to slight changes in facts. A few changes in unforeseen factual circumstances may send the litigants back to fundamental

---

[36] *Easterbrook, Frank H*, Cyberspace and the Law of the Horse, U. Chi. Legal F. 1996, 207.

[37] *Brownsword, Roger*, Law 3.0: Rules, Regulation, and Technology, 2020.

[38] Regulators may benefit from modeling and simulation, and other technocratic scientific tools to shape precise rules fit for the purpose in the most instrumental way. For instance, economic modeling has a crucial role in informing antitrust law, economic regulation, and financial regulation.

[39] This can best be described by a simple example from probability theory. If your probability assessment for an event A to occur is 0.5, and your probability for not A to occur is 0.4, you are incoherent, and you can be exploited by arbitrage (in, for instance, betting). An example of lack of coherence often pointed out in law is the implicit value of human life in various legal frameworks.

law principles. The best way to proceed might be to achieve the benefits of both coherence and precise instrumentalism. This can best be achieved by taking a high-level view to preserve coherence at a policy level. Specialized civil liability can be justified to the extent that it generates coherence with the high-level goals of civil liability.

Achieving coherence in law is a challenging task. Analogical reasoning is prominent as the primary tool for coherence in legal analysis[40] and regulation. Analogical reasoning crucial when using precedence in interpreting law and is the point of departure when regulators speak of "same risk, same activity, same rules". For instance, is a decentralized finance operation sufficiently similar to a financial platform subject to registration and regulatory supervision, or are the relationships between protocol developers and other participants sufficiently similar to other relations where fiduciary duties exist? While analogical reasoning is economical (no need to reinvent the wheel), useful to discover hyptheses, often reliable, and an accepted method of inference,[41] there is also a risk of inferential fallacies.[42] Analogies are based on similarities, while dissimilarities may be understated. The similarities that are used as a basis for the analogy may not reflect the purpose of the legal rule the analogy is derived from. At the same time, those who argue against the liability theory will point at dissimilarities. Those dissimilarities may not reflect the rationale of the rule either. Hence, the use of analogies is dangerous without connecting these to the similarities and dissimilarities relevant to the rationale of the rule. While this seems obvious, this is a repeated fallacy. Differences in technology might not induce the same behavior as the rule an analogy is based on. As often with new technologies, they may require entirely new trade-offs not reflecting the trade-offs implied by the original rule. The risk-utility trade-offs might differ, which might warrant a more or less precautionary approach than an analogy accounts for. The efficient allocation of risk may be different. For instance, certain attacks on consensus might have similarities with fraud, but their availability might be central to the security mechanism of DAOs. Duties might be much more costly to perform, or the cost of not fulfilling duties might be much higher. Finally, the distributional effects implied by the rules might be different regarding new technologies. For instance, a presumably "strong" party (a supplier) may be a weaker party regarding new technologies and vice versa. Consequently, a rule based

[40] For an analysis of the role of analogy in legal reasoning, *Lamond, Grant*, Precedent and Analogy in Legal Reasoning, in: Zalta (ed.): The Stanford Encyclopedia of Philosophy, Spring 2016.

[41] For a general discussion of analogy and analogical reasoning, see *Bartha, Paul*, Analogy and Analogical Reasoning, in: Zalta (ed.): The Stanford Encyclopedia of Philosophy, Summer 2022.

[42] Analogies are not only subject to inferential fallacies but may also result in a path-dependencies and lock-in to inferior rules. If the original rule an analogy is based on is unsound, rules based on this analogy are also likely to be unsound.

on a improper use of analogy may not induce correct behavior, reflect the original trade-off, and give other distributional effects than those implied by the liability rule the analogy is based upon.

In the sections below, we will look into two areas where a specialized liability regime may potentially be necessary to promote high-level objectives of civil liability. The first area we will look into is if specialized liability rules are necessary to maintain responsibility for DAO-organized activities. The second area we will look into is whether it is necessary to have specialized civil liability rules to align DAO-organized activity with the public policies implied by civil liability.

V. Maintaining responsibility for DAO-organized activities (in an efficient manner)

Liability can be understood as being "responsible in law." Responsibility is indispensable for civil liability, both in providing rightsholders remedies for civil wrongs committed (ex-post justice), but also in providing incentives for compliance to those that influence risks and outcomes of activities (ex-ante justice). For these reasons, it is crucial to have the ability to hold persons involved in DAO-organized activities responsible. While legal responsibility has many elements such as causal influence, blameworthiness (such as negligence and intent), and foreseeability, we will focus on causal responsibility here as it might pose particular challenges in its meeting with decentralized activities.

A DAO-decision is often a group decision due to the decentralized design. But not always. If a system is de facto centralized by a single entity (for instance, by a member controlling most of the governance tokens), this entity will face difficulties by hiding behind the decentralized design characteristics as such to evade liability. Also, if a new consensus is established by some sort of attack, the attacker is likely to be a centralized participant to hold responsible. In the latter situation, protocol developers and validators may also be liability candidates, for instance, if they were negligent in not preventing the attack.

Things get more complicated when a DAO is decentralized, and the members can claim that their action alone has no causal influence on the system, making it difficult to single out one wrongdoer to hold responsible. There are two ways to hold a single participant responsible. One option is to frame a liability theory where a single participant is causally responsible for violating a duty. The other is to consider the group responsible and hold the participant directly or indirectly responsible for the group as a collective. Individual causal responsibility will be discussed first.

A question is if causal responsibility, as it is usually understood in law, will produce sound civil liability rules for DAO-organized activities. The default causality requirement in law is the counterfactual "but-for" test, which means that an action must be necessary to harm the interest protected. The "but-for" test might, in some cases, be inadequate as a causal requirement. The legal literature contains various examples stressing this test's shortcomings.[43] In the operation of DAOs, the shortcoming of this test is evident as, at least according to the design characteristics, in the absence of a network participant performing some function, the same function with a similar outcome would be performed by another participant.

The law, in actual applications, has dealt with this situation by using a more pragmatic approach that allows for a more holistic assessment. The question is whether an action is a substantial factor contributing to the harm.[44] Although the "substantial factor" concept might remedy some of the problems associated with a "but-for" requirement of causality in holding decentralized participants liable for harm from a DAO, in many cases, it would be a stretch to consider a participant's action substantial for the result. Such a test is likely to counter the moral intuition that those who perform functions entailing violating a norm should be held responsible for it. Also such an understanding may be counter to economic reasoning as lack of causal responsibility, in this case, would reduce incentives to mitigate risks by those who most efficiently can do so.

Other causality concepts could be beneficial to make the decentralized participants causally responsible, both for aligning responsibility with moral understanding and for economic reasons. Causal reasoning and inference is an interdisciplinary topic subject to lively research and development that might be useful in causal assessments and certain causal concepts that may be particularly useful for this situation, such as information passing and mechanistic concepts of causation. For instance, a decentralized participant may be considered causally responsible for passing information on to the system or being part of the mechanism resulting in the outcome.[45] Exploring such concepts could contribute to risk mitigation incentives and, hence, bring causal responsibility in line with economic principles providing contributors to DAOs to mitigate risk. Instead of counterfactual analysis and substantial contribution to a particular outcome, contribution to the mechanism as a whole can be relevant in this respect. For instance, the higher number of governance tokens held, the higher the

[43] For this particular case, the NESS condition, which accepts an action as a cause if it is a necessary element of a sufficient set of conditions, may be useful (see *Moore, Michael*, Causation in the Law, in: Zalta (ed.): The Stanford Encyclopedia of Philosophy, Winter 2019). *Halpern, Joseph Y*, Actual causality, 2016 provides a comprehensive analysis using models for finding under what counterfactual assumptions an action can be considered a cause. See also *Illari, Phyllis/Russo, Federica*, Causality: Philosophical theory meets scientific practice, 2014.

[44] See *Hylton, Keith N*, Tort law: A modern perspective, 2016, Chapter 12.

[45] See *Østbye, Peder*, Who is Causally Responsible for a Cryptocurrency? Available at SSRN 3339537, 2019. See also *Illari, Phyllis/Russo, Federica*, Causality: Philosophical theory meets scientific practice, 2014 for an elaboration on causal concepts.

contribution to the mechanism. In DAOs run by proof of work, hash-power can be considered a proxy of the contribution to the mechanism. Measurable efforts of certain protocol developers, sponsors, and other influencers may also be a proxy of contribution. More generally, network analysis can be utilized in causal assessments.

As an alternative or supplement to individual causal responsibility, liability theories based on group duties are an option to hold participants taking part in consensus liable. DAOs are characterized by being a group of interconnected participants where it is necessary for the participants to more or less coordinate upon activity to reach certain group outcomes. Instead of forcing causal responsibility on the individual, questions arise as to whether either the group as such should be subject to duties and responsibilities or if the participants should have membership duties and responsibilities.[46] As explored in Section II, several DAOs can either be considered to be a group of jointly liable members by their organization as such (such as a joint liability partnership) or be constructed as a group according to law.[47] Under such an approach, members of a DAO could be held jointly liable or liable pro rata. While joint liability may be suitable where members work for joint benefit, pro rata may be more suitable where there is a competitive element in the relationship between the members. This is coherent with traditional approaches in tort law. In tort law, producers of certain defective products may be liable according to their market share where

[46] A brief sidestep into philosophy may be enlightening in understanding group duties and responsibilities. See *Collins, Stephanie*, Group duties: Their existence and their implications for individuals, 2019. In moral philosophy, a topic is whether groups can have moral duties and responsibilities and the implications of such duties and responsibilities for the duties and responsibilities of the members. For this purpose, three types of groups can be identified: combinations, coalitions, and collectives. Combinations consist of members who share some features while not necessarily pursuing some common or shared goal. For instance, such a group could be all persons who own or have owned bitcoin. Collectives are the "strongest" form of group and consist of agents that have formed a group to pursue some goal and have established decision procedures to pursue this goal. Typical examples are countries and companies. Some DAOs might be considered collectives because the protocol sets up decision procedures for the system as a whole. Coalitions fall between combinations and collectives in the sense that the group members pursue a common goal. Still, there are no decision procedures for the group to act as an autonomous agent. Some systems can also be characterized as coalitions since their output can be considered an equilibrium generated by individually incentivized members. It has been argued in the philosophical literature that collectives can have duties, but not combinations and coalitions, which, of course, does not exclude that members of combinations and coalitions can have duties related to their role in the group. Besides the usefulness of such philosophical investigations into group duties and responsibilities for legal purposes, it is also useful to assess if it is valid from a moral philosophy perspective to point a moral finger at a DAO as such and say it should do more, for instance, to protect the environment and promote inclusion. While this is possible in some cases, in many cases, the moral finger can only be pointed at the members, for instance, for failing to coordinate and take action.

[47] However, the latter's purpose is often to shield members from liability rather than establish responsibility.

there is insufficient evidence of which producer caused harm to an injured person. An example is a person harmed by a drug produced by several companies where there is no evidence as to which producer served the injured person. Such an approach may also be useful regarding the liability of participants in DAOs. In some cases, there might be a lack of evidence on who performed a certain action due to the pseudo-anonymous nature of many DAOs. Pro-rata liability could be used to mitigate the liability vacuum created by such a situation.

Group liability is a way to maintain responsibility for DAOs and provide victims a remedy for civil wrongs. From a policy perspective, a crucial question is whether group liability can effectively foster incentives for efficient risk mitigation. While joint liability can provide incentives to mitigate risk, it might also encourage risk-taking as costs are externalized to other participants who are more suitable litigation targets. Risk-utility trade-offs and the least-cost avoider can guide liability allocation and whether a joint liability or a pro-rata principle is adequate.

While the allocation of responsibility should follow moral intuitions to achieve legitimacy, enforcement efficiency should also be taken into account. Considerations of administrative efficiency and enforcement costs may render some participants more adequate targets for liability. The least cost avoider principle states that risk should be borne by the party who can reduce the risk at the lowest cost. According to the least-cost avoider principle, liability is assigned to the least-cost avoider to promote efficient risk mitigation.[48] Efficient risk allocation can guide the liability allocation between various participants, such as protocol developers, validators, and holders of governance tokens in liability.

If DAOs are granted limited liability combined with immunity for the members, the members are not necessarily fully shielded from liability. In corporate law, the corporate veil is sometimes pierced in the sense that directors and owners of a limited liability company can be held personally liable in certain circumstances. Such veil-piercing is equally important to maintain responsibility for DAO-organized activities. The law provides numerous factors to consider in assessing whether the conditions for veil-piercing are present. Such factors will not be discussed in detail here. However, many factors are related to abusing the limited liability corporate form to escape personal liability. For instance, the veil may be pierced if a person merely uses a limited liability company as a vehicle for personal dealings. This may be the case if the assets of a limited liability company and a person are intermingled and misrepresented.[49] It is not

---

[48] See *Carbonara, Emanuela/Guerra, Alice/Parisi, Francesco*, Sharing residual liability: the cheapest cost avoider revisited, The Journal of Legal Studies, 2016, 173–201 for an analysis of the least cost avoider principle.

[49] See *Bainbridge, Stephen M/Henderson, M Todd*, Limited liability: a legal and economic analysis, 2016 for a comprehensive analysis of limited liability.

hard to imagine cases where DAOs are used as more or less scams or facades for the personal benefit of certain members. For instance, certain founders or investors may claim that a DAO is decentralized. At the same time, they have retained governance tokens or admin keys, which can be used to protect their personal interests (instead of the DAO).

VI. Aligning DAO-organized activities with public policies

As discussed in Section III, DAO-organized activities interfere with many public policies. It is beyond the scope of this paper to discuss all these policies. Instead a high-level perspective will be taken by aggregating interference with public policies as risks to society.

From a high-level perspective, based on economic principles, risks to society from DAOs should be rationally managed, and the law should contribute to such management. Based on decision theory, the law (including civil liability) may be considered an instrument to implement a cost-benefit analysis by minimizing the expected cost of errors.[50] Error may occur due to imposition of legal duties and responsibilities that deter beneficial behavior (type 1 error) or due to failure to prevent or mitigate harmful behavior (type 2 error). However, the error-cost approach to regulation may be difficult to apply directly in cases of deep uncertainty, where probabilities and possible impacts are challenging to quantify. Deep uncertainty often characterizes the effects of new technologies, such as DAOs.[51] Various decision rules have been developed to guide policies under deep uncertainty.[52] One way of looking at principles for policies under deep uncertainty is to place them on a spectrum between being precautionary to proactionary.[53] While precautionary policies are concerned with avoiding the worst outcomes, proactionary policies are more concerned with avoiding missing benefits. Some principles for decision-making under deep uncertainty seek to find some balance or at least offer a methodological framework to deal with this balance analytically. For instance, the info-gap theory provides a framework for balancing downside risks and possible windfalls (gains). High potential windfalls may justify a proactionary approach.

A question is if proactiaonary or precautionary policies should guide policies regarding civil liability for DAOs. Proponents of cryptocurrency and block-

[50] See *Østbye, Peder*, Rational Antitrust Analysis. An inquiry into antitrust assessment principles and procedures, 2013

[51] For instance, the benefits of the internet would be hard to predict in its early days. The same applies to the potential harms from the market power of social media tech giants enabled by the internet.

[52] See *Marchau, Vincent AWJ/Walker, Warren E/Bloemen, Pieter JTM/Popper, Steven W*, Decision making under deep uncertainty: from theory to practice, 2019.

[53] See *Crootof, Rebecca/Ard, BJ*, Structuring techlaw, Harv. JL & Tech. 2020, 347.

chain technologies, in arguing for proactionary principle, are not modest in the potential windfalls that could be lost by too harsh liabilities imposed on participants. The windfalls are usually related to access to a decentralized internet, censorship resistance, financial inclusion, and enabling a better, more fair financial system. In the US, the senators Kirsten Gillibrand and Cynthia Lummis proposed the Responsible Financial Innovation Act, which is a regulatory framework for digital assets that they claim "encourages responsible financial innovation, flexibility, transparency and robust consumer protections while integrating digital assets into existing law."[54] This framework takes a proactionary approach by, for instance, reduce regulatory burdens and by protecting certain participants from liabilities they otherwise might have been subject to. As discussed in Section II, some have argued that DAOs should be subject to limited liability combined with more or less immunity for the members to enable these windfalls.[55]

There are also arguments for a more precautionary approach. DAOs are characterized by complexity.[56] While some risks are known, others may emerge from unknown unknowns. When it comes to DAOs, certain validation mechanisms may negatively impact society, such as crime facilitation, environmental harm due to energy usage and e-waste, and financial instability. A fictional example in the artificial intelligence literature is the risk of some unstoppable algorithm subverting all resources into producing paper clips.[57] Both self-regulatory governance mechanisms and market governance have obvious shortcomings when it comes to protecting public interests. The incentives to take into account public interests may be lacking. Furthermore, the decentralized self-regulatory aspects of protocol development entail that protocol changes may be hard to change and coordinate when first implemented, even if reputational risks provide incentives for changes. Market governance by competitive forces may be prevented by, for instance, lock-in mechanisms benefiting incumbents with large networks. While "unstoppable" technologies are often framed as a benefit of DAOs, the risk of losing control is accepted as a risk of concern regarding artificial intelligence. Precautionary guided duties and responsibilities directed at reducing the risk of "losing control" in developing artificial intelligence may be equally applicable when it comes to the algorithms running DAOs.[58]

---

[54] https://www.gillibrand.senate.gov/news/press/release/-lummis-gillibrand-introduce-landmark-legislation-to-create-regulatory-framework-for-digital-assets (accessed March 2023).

[55] See *Coala*, Model Law for Decentralized Autonomous Organizations (DAOs) with Explanatory Comments, 2021.

[56] See, for instance, *Hacker, Philipp*, Corporate governance for complex cryptocurrencies? A framework for stability and decision making in blockchain-based organizations, 2019.

[57] See *Bostrom, N.*, Superintelligence: Paths, Dangers, Strategies, 2016.

[58] For legal approaches to liability for algorithms, *Tjong Tjin Tai, Eric*, Liability for (Semi) Autonomous Systems: Robots and Algorithms, Research Handbook on Data Science and

Duties of care implied by civil liability serve several functions in aligning risky activity with public policy. From an economic perspective, a major hypothesis is that transaction costs often prevent efficient resource allocation, such as the allocation of risk, through voluntary agreements. Hence, a major role of law is to reduce transaction costs or, if not possible, replicate the outcomes as if they were reached by agreement (as if transaction costs were not prohibitive). For instance, transactions are not feasible in cases of more or less random interaction, such as in tort situations. There is a question of how legal liabilities should be allocated to promote efficient behavior in these situations. A basic premise is that some behaviors can provide both benefits and harms, and the risk (probability and magnitude) of harm can be reduced by incurring costly efforts. As long as efforts to reduce risk cost less than the reduced risk, such efforts should be incurred.[59] A negligence standard should implement this trade-off. A strict liability regime (no-fault liability) also aligns the overall activity level with public policy, as the risk-taker will internalize the cost of harm in the choice of activity level. However, strict liability may discourage potential victims from taking measures to reduce risk. Hence, it is not evident that a strict liability regime would be superior for liability for DAOs.

The threat of liability from violating duties of care will give incentives to mitigate risks and to truthfully explore potential risks in managing legal risks. It is easy to theoretically argue about the potential risks and benefits of DAOs. Almost anyone can create a theory where DAOs result in dystopias or utopias and support such arguments with more or less valid mechanisms and pseudoscience. Legal liability can incentivize developers and operators to base their behavior on credible evidence and valid mechanisms informing the consequences of their activities. To the extent duties of care are connected to the information of risks provided in whitepapers and other documentation provided, a duty of care provides incentives to provide and reveal truthful information. High standards of care and potentially strict liability are crucial for a precautionary approach.

The downside of a too high standard of care is that they might ineffectively provide incentives to take too many precautions and ultimately reduce the level of beneficial innovative activity. How much chilling effect a duty of care depends on the cost of exercising care and the potential utility of DAOs. Many measures to exercise care are low-cost, such as providing truthful information

Law (Edward Elgar, 2018), 2018, 55–82, *Abbot, R/Borges, G/Dacoronia, E/Devillier, N/Jankowska-Augustyn, M/Karner, E* u.a., Liability for Artificial Intelligence and other emerging digital technologies. Report from the Expert Group on Liability and New Technologies–New Technologies Formation, European Union, 2019 and *Beckers, Anna/Teubner, Gunther*, Three liability regimes for artificial intelligence: algorithmic actants, hybrids, crowds, 2021.

[59] See *Schäfer, Hans-Bernd/Müller-Langer, Frank*, Strict liability versus negligence, 2009 for elaboration.

and informing about known risks. When it comes to utility, it can be incorporated into the determination of duties of care. Developers and operators of DAOs that can demonstrate valid public utility potentials ex-ante could be subject to a lower standard of care if unknown risks materialize. Such a lower standard of care can be implemented as a rebuttable presumption. By being a rebuttable presumption, developers, and operators will have a burden of proof in justifying that they should be subject to a lower standard of care. This means that they will have to demonstrate evidence of public utility beyond theories.

To promote due care in the operation of a DAO, a residual liability approach is a possible policy option. Such a residual liability involves a residual "strict liability" for DAOs to the extent that those harmed have exercised due care themselves to protect themselves from harm. This will provide users with incentives to take due care and operators of DAOs to nudge users into taking due care. Such type of liability has been proposed for liability for robots.[60] Residual liability could also divide the liability allocation between protocol developers and validators. For instance, protocol developers could hold the residual strict liability. To make sure that traditional approaches to causal responsibility, as described in Section V, do not bar risk mitigation, legislation could ensure that innovative concepts of causality or participating in risky activity as such could be bases for liability.

Efficient risk mitigation can also guide the division of labor between regulation and private litigation. There are several reasons why private litigation, for instance, through tort law, has shortcomings compared to public enforcement.[61] One is information asymmetries. Specialized government entities may have more information on risks compared to private litigants. Furthermore, ex-ante enforcement tools may be more accessible to regulatory agencies as it is generally more difficult to privately litigate risks ex-ante before they are materialized. Also, insolvency risks may prevent the deterrent effect of ex-post private remedies (moral hazard). Finally, the harm from materialized risks may be spread among many victims, each lacking sufficient incentives to litigate. Adequate mechanisms for class actions can remedy the latter issue. Still, for many public policy objectives such as financial stability and environmental protection, the losses are spread over so many victims that private enforcement is inadequate. However, public enforcement does not exclude private enforcement. Efficient enforcement can benefit from both. Enforcement efficiency may also guide

---

[60] See *Guerra, Alice/Parisi, Francesco/Pi, Daniel*, Liability for robots II: an economic analysis, Journal of Institutional Economics 2022, 553–568.

[61] See *Faure, Michael/Visscher, Louis/Weber, Franziska*, Liability for Unknown Risks–A Law and Economics Perspective, Journal of European Tort Law 2016, 198–227 for a further discussion of the literature. See also *Posner, Richard A*, Economic analysis of law, 2014 and *Østbye, Peder*, Rational Antitrust Analysis. An inquiry into antitrust assessment principles and procedures, 2013.

practical issues. For instance, certain influential operators of a DAO may be out of jurisdictional reach for sanctions or hide behind several layers of anonymity. For efficiency reasons, less influential but known operators within a jurisdiction may be more efficient targets for sanctions.

VII. Is "code is law" a good policy?

Despite the arguments presented in the previous sections some seem to think that self-governance of DAOs is sufficient. Techno-liberalists often argue for a "code is law" approach to liability for DAOs. It is argued that the legal system is somehow redundant as the systems themselves are complete in distributing duties and allocating risks. Law should then be guided by "caveat emptor," which is Latin for "let the buyer beware," leaving justice to the self-regulatory mechanisms of a DAO. However, caveat emptor is not a generally accepted principle in law. For instance, consumers are not generally allowed to waive their rights, and crime victims cannot generally agree to crimes that harm them. Hence, such an approach lacks coherence with the law.[62] Furthermore, the victims of the activity of a DAO may be others than those who have accepted risks, and the activity may, more generally, interfere with public policies such as consumer protection, environmental protection, crime prevention, and financial stability. Participants in a DAO seem unsuitable to accept these risks, including systemic risks, on behalf of everyone else. It would be quite a coincidence if "caveat emptor" was aligned with the general objectives of civil liability. Hence, a general "code is law" approach seems inconsistent with high-level civil liability goals.

VIII. Concluding remarks

This paper has explored the DAO and civil liability nexus and discussed whether a specialized civil liability regime is required for this nexus to produce outcomes in line with the high-level goals of civil liability. It is found that specialized rules or, at least, some novel interpretations of law may prove necessary to maintain responsibility for DAO-organized activities (in an efficient manner) and for aligning DAO-organized activities with public policies. It is also briefly

[62] Are there any of features DAOs that give merits to applying "caveat emptor"? In some aspects, there are merits to such a stance, for instance, when it comes to certain attacks. In decentralized systems, the protocol is the primary self-regulatory tool to protect against attacks. If legal liability substitutes for this self-regulatory mechanism, this might chill the incentives to develop robust and secure protocols and the incentives for users to select DAOs providing such protocols. However, in general, there are also many counter-arguments.

argued that a "code is law" approach is not likely a good policy choice. Adequate civil liability for DAO-organized activities is a crucial element in fostering responsible innovation.

Decentralized autonomous organisations (DAOs) and knowledge attribution*

João Serras de Sousa

ABSTRACT This article addresses the problem of knowledge attribution to DAOs. Firstly, it is emphasised that DAOs, although decentralised autonomous organisations which rely on blockchain technology and smart contracts, are also forms of organisation of people that imply a risk of knowledge fragmentation due to the division of labour. Therefore, even if the problem of knowledge attribution has been studied mainly concerning legal persons, the principles of knowledge attribution apply to all forms of organisation that can lead to a fragmentation of knowledge and ultimately to DAOs (I.).

To fully understand who has the power to decide how and when a DAO acts, it is then addressed the internal decision-making process of a DAO (II.) and how decisions are externally executed (III.).

The problem of knowledge attribution is then specifically addressed by considering relative and absolute knowledge provisions and DAOs' actions based on smart contracts (IV.) or through a legal wrapper (V.).

I. Knowledge attribution to Decentralized Autonomous Organisations ("DAOs")?

DAOs were first described as a blockchain phenomenon in *Christopher Jentzsch*'s white paper dated 2016.[1] A DAO enables an automated organisation, management, and decision-making in associations of people without the use of conventional schemes of a corporate form and, particularly, a centralised management structure:[2] to sum up, a new form of organisation which relies on

---

* This article was the basis of the Author's speech on "DAOs and Knowledge Attribution" at the International Conference on DAO Regulation 2023 on 20 April 2023.

The opinions presented in this article are provided according to the Portuguese legal system. Therefore, the provisions quoted in the text belong – if not otherwise mentioned – to the Portuguese Civil Code ("CC"). In any event, the legal effects associated with knowledge, particularly in civil law legal systems, are similar.

[1] *Jentzsch*, Decentralized autonomous organisation to automate governance – final draft, available at lawofthelevel.lexblogplatformthree.com (20.04.203). On *Jentzsch*'s white paper see, for example: *Mann*, NZG 2017, 1014–1020, 1015–1016; *Rolo*, RDT 1-1 (2019), 33–87, 48 ff.

[2] *Linardatos*, Autonome und vernetzte Aktanten im Zivilrecht, 2021, 40–41; *Filippi/Wright*, Blockchain and the law – the rule of code, 2018, 136.

blockchain technology and smart contracts as their primary (or exclusive) form of organisation.[3]

DAOs are, therefore, entities made up of a multitude of smart contracts.[4]

The main objective of DAOs is to avoid abusive and contractual-breaking behaviours by the members of the organisation (in the traditional sense: shareholders or directors), which is to be prevented by contractual or legal stipulated obligations being automatically executed by the DAO – i.e., by its underlying algorithm – as soon as the prerequisites for the predetermined conditions are met.[5]

A DAO is put into operation by implementing a code in a blockchain network (e.g., ethereum). To be able to operate, the DAO must be provided with capital[6] – in blockchain-based systems, capital is collected via virtual means of payment, so-called cryptocurrencies (e.g., ether or bitcoin).[7] An interested investor can send this capital to an address within the blockchain assigned to the DAO (i.e., the DAO's smart contract address) – comparable to a bank account.[8] In return, the investor receives the so-called token – investment token or utility token – from the DAO, to which are attached various[9] rights (namely, ownership, voting rights, rights to share in DAO's profits, or the right to be engaged on the DAO's decision-making process). The percentage of the voting or participation rights attached to the token can be based on the paid-in capital – in a manner comparable to a conventional share.[10] All tokenholders manage the DAO according to a consensus or majority principle; directors are not appointed.[11]

Whether it makes sense to speak about the knowledge of a DAO may be the first raised question: as put forward, a DAO is a decentralised autonomous organisation which relies on blockchain technology and smart contracts. By intuition, the first reaction is to answer negatively: ultimately, a DAO is just a line of code laid on blockchain, and epistemologically speaking, knowledge is under-

---

[3] *Filippi/ Wright* (fn. 3), 136.

[4] *Mann* (fn. 2), 1015; *Linardatos* (fn. 3), 41; *Filippi/Wright* (fn. 3), 136.

[5] In this sense, *Jentzsch* (fn. 2), 1. It's a key feature that is frequently highlighted: see, inter alia, *Rolo* (fn. 2), 48–49; *Linardatos* (fn. 3), 41.

[6] *Linardatos* (fn. 3), 41.

[7] The legal nature of cryptocurrencies is not decisive for the objectives of this paper; for a legal perspective, see, inter alia, *Engrácia Antunes*, ROA 81 I/II 2021, 119ff.; Id., A moeda – Estudo jurídico e económico, 2021, 177ff.; *Rolo*, in: Ataíde/Fidalgo/Rocha, Estudos de Direito do Consumo, VI, 2022, 1–35, also available at ssrn.com (20.04.2023); *Langenbucher*, AcP 2018, 385–429, 385ff.

[8] In this sense, *Linardatos* (fn. 3), 42.

[9] *Filippi/Wright* (fn. 3), 136–137.

[10] *Linardatos* (fn. 3), 42. As conventional shares, tokens are also freely transferable.

[11] *Mann* (fn. 2), 1017.

stood as a specifically human capacity to maintain a kind of "relationship" with matters of fact.[12]

However, civil law is autonomous in the conceptualisation of knowledge and its attribution: the concept of knowledge and its attribution is always a problem of interpretation of (a) specific rule(s).[13] In the case at hand: DAOs consist of a smart contract conceptualised as an *organisation*[14] of people. With *Biyan Mienert*:

> "[...] DAOs can be described as a new type of permanent *organisation* consisting of a program code stored, decentralised and executed at blockchain".[15]

Some describe – however fallaciously – DAOs as the "first company without people".[16] This description is misleading since natural persons are also involved in DAOs, just not in the central management of the organisation.[17] As a – even if particular – form of organisation, DAOs are a form of cooperation of people that imply a risk of knowledge fragmentation due to the division of labour.

In recent years the problem of knowledge attribution has been studied mainly concerning legal persons. DAOs are often qualified as civil partnerships, but in most jurisdictions, the consequences are similar: "no *legal personality* and therefore *no legal capacity*, and *unlimited joint and several liability for token-holders*".[18] In Portugal DAOs can be qualified as civil partnerships ("*sociedades civis puras*") according to articles 980.º ff. CC,[19] being recognised by most legal scholars as legal persons or rudimentary legal persons ("*pessoas rudimentares*").[20] But even if civil partnerships were not to be considered legal persons, the principles of knowledge attribution apply "to all forms of organisation that can

---

[12] *Brendel*, Wissen, 2013, 29.

[13] In this direction, *Fatemi*, NJOZ 2010, 2637–2642, 2637.

[14] See *Rolo* (fn. 2), 56. On the same direction: *Filippi/Wright* (fn. 3), 148 ("a DAO is a particular kind of decentralized organization that is neither run nor controlled by any person but entirely by code"); *Wright/Filippi*, Decentralized blockchain technology and the rise of lex cryptographia, 2015, 1–58, available at ssrn.com (20.04.2023), 3 (describing DAOs as "organisations [that can] re-implement certain aspects of traditional corporate governance using software").

[15] *Mienert*, Dezentrale autonome Organisationen (DAOs) und Gesellschaftsrecht, 2022, 4 (emphasis added).

[16] *Grassegger*, Die erste Firma ohne Menschen, Zeit Online, 2016, available at www.zeit.de (20.04.2023).

[17] *Mienert*, Rdi 2021, 384–392, 384, fn. 4; *Mienert* (fn. 16), 4, fn. 13, 55.

[18] *Rolo* (fn. 2), 71.

[19] In this direction, with further details, *Teixeira*, in Madalena Perestrelo de Oliveira/Rolo, Decentralised Autonomous Organisations (DAOs) in various jurisdictions: from old rules to innovetive approaches, 2023, 11–23, 15 ff.

[20] *Menezes Cordeiro*, Tratado de direito civil, IV, 5ft ed., 2019, 912 ff.; *Menezes Leitão*, Direito das obrigações, III, 11th ed., 2016, 233 ff. Similarly also, *Caetano*, O Direito 99 (1967), 85–110, 100 ff.; *Castro Mendes*, Direito Civil – Teoria Geral, I, 1978, 313; *Ascensão*, Direito civil – Teoria geral, I, 2nd ed., 2000, 309 ff.; *Fernandes*, Teoria geral do direito civil, I, 6th ed., 2012, 512 ff.; denying the legal personality of civil partnerships, *Lima/Varela*, Código Civil

lead to a fragmentation of knowledge".[21] That is indisputably the case with DAOs.

II. DAOs' decision-making process

Knowledge is always deemed legally relevant in the context of an action (or an omission). In short, it is an accessory element of conduct:[22] legal consequences are always related to the fact that the agent acts despite his knowledge (or "duty"[23] to know) of specific facts.[24]

Therefore, the most basic knowledge attribution case to organisations is that of attribution of the knowledge of members of the corporation governing bodies.[25] Basically, because organs make legal persons capable of acting. This is particularly the case of the executive board, but it is also true for the general meeting (the shareholders) and the supervisory board within the framework of their legal or statutory powers and duties.[26] Because organs act on behalf of the legal person to enable it to participate in legal transactions, it becomes necessary to attribute their knowledge to the legal person.[27]

In the specific case of DAOs, as put forward, directors are not appointed. In addition to the collective body consisting of all members – the tokenholders –, there is typically no executive board with decision-making powers.[28]

This means that – if knowledge is legally relevant in the context of an action – to consider the problem of knowledge attribution, it is necessary to analyse the decision-making process of a DAO, to determine, concretely, who has the power to decide *when* and *how* a DAO *acts*.

anotado, II, 4th ed., 2010, 287–288; *Carlos Mota Pinto*, *Teoria geral do direito civil*, 4th ed., 2005, 295–296.

21 *Medicus*, in: Karlsruher Forum 1994 – Möglichkeiten der Wissenszurechnung 1994, 4–16, 12; in the same direction, for example, *Taupitz*, in: Karlsruher Forum 1994 – Möglichkeiten der Wissenszurechnung 1994, 16–30. In German case law: BGH of 2 February 1996 – V ZR 239/94, 1341.

22 In Germany, for example, *Faßbender*, Innerbetriebliches Wissen und bankrechtliche Aufklärungspflichten, 1998, 32ff., maxime, 39 ("*verhaltensakzessorisches Element der Rechtsordnung*"); in Italy, *Campobasso*, L'imputazione di conoscenza nelle Società, 2002, 141–142 ("*principio di accessorietà del sapere*"). In Portuguese: *acessoriedade do conhecimento*.

23 In most cases, the so-called "duty of knowledge" cannot be qualified as a legal duty on a technical sense. It can also be a "burden" ("*ónus material*"; "*Obliegenheit*").

24 *Grigoleit*, ZHR 181 (2017), 160–202, 177, 178, 198. Expressly following *Grigoleit*'s view, *Rachlitz*, Wissen – Vorsatz – Zurechnung, 265ff., 268, 375.

25 See *Gomes/Gonçalves*, A imputação de conhecimento às sociedades comerciais, 2017, 105.

26 *Seidel*, Die wertende Wissenszurechnung, 2021, 187.

27 *Seidel* (fn. 27), 187.

28 *Aufderheide*, WM 6 (2022), 264–271, 269.

The decentralised nature of a DAO is expressed by the fact that DAOs do not provide for a management that implements the internal decision-making of the organisation and represents it externally, but rely on automated implementation also vis-à-vis third parties.[29] How this will formation takes place depends on the underlying smart contract;[30] the governance protocol of a DAO can be freely programmed.[31] A simple example[32] is a proposal-based governance system with a yes/no majority for proposals required for approval and execution. Proposals can be, for example, about investing the tokens owned by the DAO and the votes can be weighted according to the initial contribution or the reputation[33] of each tokenholder.[34] The smart contract is independently and automatically executed if a specific majority is reached. From a technical point of view, it is not necessary for management to act independently of the internal decision-making process, neither internally nor externally.[35]

The decision-making process of the DAO is usually carried out through various coordinated voting systems by its tokenholders. If DAOs are to be qualified as civil partnerships according to Portuguese law, then all the shareholders (*rectius*, tokenholders) have equal and separated management powers (article 985.º (1) CC). It is however expected that a majority of votes to approve a decision is provided in the DAO's white paper, which corresponds to a stipulation in the bylaws:[36] management decisions are – if so – to be taken by the majority of the tokenholders. It can thus be noted that the management of DAOs takes place in the form of voting by the shareholders' meeting.[37] Management is not, therefore, exercised for each co-partner (*rectius*, co-tokenholder) personally, but for all DAO's tokenholders in their collective relationship for the group or organisation (the DAO): their collective decisions are thus to be attributed to the

---

29 *Langheld/Haagen*, NZG 2021, 724–729, 727.

30 *Mann* (fn. 2), 1015; *Langheld/Haagen* (fn. 30), 727.

31 *Mienert* (fn. 16), 151.

32 For example, according to *Jentzsch* proposal, the organisation (named "the DAO") would be activated on the etherum blockchain structure and then would begin to raise capital. Users could then send ether to the organisation's smart contract address and in return receive the so-called tokens, which convey ownership and voting rights. These tokens were freely transferable once the DAO were already full initiated, and each tokenholder could then propose uses for the capital raised and the whole tokenholders would vote on these proposals. If a majority agrees with the proposal – which was, before put to a vote by tokenholders, reviewed by "curators" to protect the DAO from malicious actors –, the organisation's programme code would carry automatically the desired transaction (see *Jentzsch* (fn. 2), 1 ff.; and, inter alia, the description of *Mann* (fn. 2), 1014–1015; or *Rolo* (fn. 2), 48 ff.

33 Weighting the vote according to the reputation of the tokenholders is a way to try to solve the problem of lack of involvement by the tokenholders in the DAOs decision-making process (see, inter alia, *Mienert* (fn. 16), 157–158.

34 *Mienert* (fn. 16), 151.

35 *Langheld/Haagen* (fn. 30), 727.

36 In this direction for German law, *Mienert* (fn. 16), 189.

37 *Mienert* (fn. 16), 189.

DAO and the rights and obligations arising from its execution affect the collective assets.[38]

III. DAOs' external action

It is also required to address the way that tokenholders' decisions are executed by DAOs.

A DAO is an organisation that manages itself, operating solely with its bylaws, which are immutable on the blockchain and are not controlled by anyone. But a DAO is pure software: it has – at least not yet – the ability to manufacture a product, write code, develop hardware[39] or sweep the streets.[40] For that, the DAO needs actors in the physical world. DAOs do it, traditionally, in two different ways.

Firstly, DAOs can turn to the so-called contractors[41], who develop products or supply services.[42] This is done in the form of smart contracts supplemented by natural language descriptions. Therefore, as a rule, the proposal is written in natural language together with a corresponding programmed smart contract that defines the relationship between the DAO and the contractor, the contractual obligations, and the terms of execution.[43] Discussions around the proposal – held between the tokenholders – can take place on-chain or off-chain via a service chosen by the DAO (e.g., discussion forums).[44]

Smart contracts are, in this case, used as a tool for the execution of tokenholders resolutions[45]. When used as a tool for entering into legal transactions with third parties, smart contracts are to be qualified as declarations of intent which have their origin in the tokenholders' vote and are transmitted by the algorithm of the DAO:[46] the if-then conditions used to programme smart contracts are, in this case, true contracts (the so-called smart legal contracts)[47] implemented by the DAO itself.[48_49]

---

[38] *Mann* (fn. 2), 1018; *Mienert* (fn. 16), 189.

[39] *Jentzsch* (fn. 2), 1; *Linardatos* (fn. 3), 42; *Mienert* (fn. 16), 202.

[40] *Mienert* (fn. 16), 202.

[41] *Jentzsch* (fn. 2), 2; *Linardatos* (fn. 3), 42; *Mienert* (fn. 16), 202.

[42] For example, building a wiki, coordinating a marketing campaign, or manufacturing products: see *Mienert* (fn. 16), 202-203.

[43] *Mienert* (fn. 16), 203.

[44] *Mienert* (fn. 16), 203.

[45] *Mienert* (fn. 16), 189.

[46] *Mann* (fn. 2), 1018.

[47] *Ana Perestrelo de Oliveira*, Smart contracts, risco e codificação da desvinculação ou modificação negocial, 2023, 22.

[48] *Mann* (fn. 2), 1018; *Mienert* (fn. 16), 189.

[49] Smart contracts can then serve as a functional contractual equivalent (i.e., the code is equivalent to the use of natural language) by providing for the "obligations' programme" or

As a result of my short description of the DAOs internal operation, it is then possible to establish that the concrete terms of the execution of the smart contract are predetermined – *rectius*, pre-programmed: the code is – or must be – designed according to the proposal made by the (a) tokenholder(s) and the (non) execution decision is made by the tokenholders, who vote the proposal that is automatically executed in case of approval. As *de Filippi* and *Wright* clearly state when addressing DAOs: "[p]eople still be responsible for creating the software that fuels the decentralized organisation. Humans will still have the power to dictate how these systems operate: their initial protocols, objectives, and goals; and the value systems that will determine their choices and decisions".[50] Thus: the execution of the smart contract can be ultimately considered an act of those responsible for its conception and concrete design. The tokenholders are supposed to decide, and despite the possible large numbers of participants, the organisation and management of a DAO are still strongly personalised.[51]

In addition to the possibility of DAOs entering into contractual relationships with third parties directly via smart contracts, a legal person – e. g., a company – can also be interposed as a kind of trustee who acts externally for the DAO (often referred to as a legal wrapper).[52] This is so because it still can be problematic for traditional companies to interact with a DAO on a business basis if it does not have a physical address, and especially concerning regulatory restrictions (e. g., for the company accounts).[53] With a legal wrapper, DAOs are, therefore, able to link the digital world to the physical world of contractors.[54]

This company is strictly distinguished from a possible company of the investors – i. e., the tokenholders – because, ultimately, they cannot control it:[55] it is a "sub-DAO" through which the DAO engages with third parties, holds assets (including, e. g., intellectual property rights) and raises funds. It is then said that – as far as this construction is disclosed to third parties – claims and liabilities arise exclusively to the legal wrapper.[56]

---

serve any other broader purposes by allowing to automate any process within the blockchain infrastructure (such as controlling, monitoring, and documenting the exchange of services or the implementation of the DAOs). Regarding the legal qualification of smart contracts – emphasising that they are not necessarily deemed as contracts – see, inter alia, *Schrey/Thalhofer*, NJW 2017, 1431–1436, 1431; *Möslein*, ZHR 183 (2019), 254–293, 264; *Teichmann*, ZfPW 2019, 247–272, 269; *Mienert* (fn. 16), 40, 49-50; *Ana Perestrelo de Oliveira* (fn. 48), 20ff.

50 *Filippi/ Wright* (fn. 3), 155.

51 In this direction, *Aufderheide* (fn. 29), 269.

52 See *Mann* (fn. 1), 1018; *Mienert* (fn. 16), 204.

The DAO – founded in 2016 by *Jentzsch* – used this construction: the developers founded a Swiss limited liability company with the name "DAOLink" to create an entity with which the business partners of The DAO could enter into agreements.

53 *Mienert* (fn. 16), 204.

54 *Mienert* (fn. 16), 204.

55 In this direction, *Mann* (fn. 2), 1018.

56 *Mann* (fn. 2), 1018.

In this case, the legal wrapper – and more specifically, its executive organs – are responsible for day-to-day decision-making and business management, whereas DAOs' tokenholders make key decisions (e.g., decisions regarding profit sharing and new investments). So, after the approval of a proposal within the DAO, tokenholders instruct the legal wrapper, which is then responsible for the execution of the approved proposals on behalf of the DAO.[57]

With this structure, the tokenholders lose a key advantage of a DAO: they can no longer rely solely on self-execution through smart contracts. Instead, they must rely on the integrity and loyalty of the trust's directors.[58]

IV. Knowledge attribution in the context of action through smart contracts

Already bearing in mind the internal and external terms of the action of a DAO, one can now consider the terms in which knowledge can be attributed to DAOs. Knowledge can be relevant in a variety of normative places.[59]

Considering the specificity of DAOs and their action based on smart contracts, the problem of knowledge attribution will be analysed in the context of the legal framework of error/mistake in the declaration (article 247.° CC) and fraud/dolus (article 253.° CC). As already put forward, knowledge is deemed to be legally relevant in the context of an action (or an omission): we will, therefore, consider the knowledge of the tokenholders because they make DAOs capable of acting.

Considering the case of action based on smart contracts, it is essential to bear in mind that while obligations are automatically executed – and the smart contract is executed exactly how it is programmed to be executed –, it is not guaranteed that the code or its concrete design matches the will of the contracting parties.[60]

It is, therefore, possible to have a divergence between the proposal made in natural language (wet code) – made by a tokenholder and discussed in the DAO's forum and passed on to the agreement proposal – and the smart contract code (dry code) – proposed both in the context of the DAO and to the third party.[61]

---

[57] Similarly, *Mann* (fn. 2), 1018.

[58] *Mann* (fn. 2), 1018.

[59] For example, in cases where the beginning of a time limitation period is dependent of knowledge of certain facts, in the legal framework of protection of justified expectations, as a cognitive element of wilfulness/*dolus* ("*dolo-culpa*"), in the legal framework of the duties of information, in the interpretation of declarations of intent, etc. See, for example, in Germany, *Medicus* (fn. 22), 4–5.

[60] *Ana Perestrelo de Oliveira* (fn. 48), 56.

[61] With reference to the possibility of divergence between natural language and code, *Ana Perestrelo de Oliveira* (fn. 48), 56 ff.; and *Gatteschi/Lamberti/Demartini*, in: DiMatteo/Can-

As DAOs can act and participate in legal transactions, knowledge provisions must apply to them. It is, consequently, necessary to ask if there is knowledge or a "duty" to know accessory to the DAO's action. The answer is affirmative if there is knowledge or a duty to know some facts by those who make and approve the proposal (i. e., the tokenholders).

This raises another problem: transactions on the blockchain are made pseudonymously,[62] which makes it to be extremely difficult – if not impossible – to track the tokenholders and, therefore, their knowledge. It is, therefore, necessary to resort to the rules of known experience and ask: should tokenholders, acting with due care, have known the divergence between the dry code and the wet code?

In the case at hand, let us assume the tokenholders, if acting with due care, should have known the divergence – and its essentiality[63] for the counterparty[64] – between the proposal and the code supporting the smart contract. The attributed "duty" to know or knowledge of the essentiality of the tokenholders

---

narsa/Poncibò (ed.), The cambridge handbook of smart contracts, blockchain technology and digital platforms, 2019, 37–58, 55.

[62] See, for example, *Ana Perestrelo de Oliveira* (fn. 48), 69.

[63] Essential to the declarant (i. e., the DAO's counterparty) can be any elements: core elements of the agreement (object, content, or other main aspects), surrounding elements (accessory matters of the object, incidental clauses, or other peripheral factors), and elements relating to the parties (identity, quality, their function etc.). See, *Menezes Cordeiro*, Tratado de direito civil, II, 4th ed., 2017, 848–849.

[64] The criterion for assessing the essentiality of the error is subjective (see *Menezes Cordeiro* (fn. 63), 849). Being the transaction entirely developed on the blockchain, it must be verified whether, in view of the discrepancy between the natural language (wet language) and the code (dry language), it can be assumed that the divergence was essential for the counterparty's decision to enter into the agreement. We are therefore facing one of those cases in which, by virtue of the nature of the transaction and the circumstances of its conclusion, certain elements cannot fail to be considered essential (considering this possibility, *Menezes Cordeiro* (fn. 64), 849).

Additionally, it should be borne in mind that to allow the annulment of the transaction, the counterparty's error must be excusable (in this direction, *Ascensão*, Direito civil – Teoria geral, II, 2nd ed., 2003, 139–143; *Galvão Telles*, Manual dos contratos em geral, 4th ed., 2010, 87–89; *Carvalho*, ROA 52 I (1992), 169–182, 177). This is not, at any case, the understanding of the majority of the Portuguese legal doctrine: inter alia, *Correia*, Erro e interpretação na teoria do negócio jurídico, 2nd ed., 1968, 293 ff.; *Carlos Mota Pinto* (fn. 21), 510–512; *Lima/Varela*, Código Civil anotado, I, 4th ed., 2010, 233; *Paulo Mota Pinto*, Declaração tácita e comportamento concludente no negócio jurídico, 1995, 406 ff., fn. 440; Id., in: Estudos em homenagem ao Prof. Doutor Inocêncio Galvão Telles, IV, 2003, 43–139, 81–85; *Castro Mendes*, Teoria geral do direito civil, II, 1995, 129; *Fernandes*, Teoria geral do direito civil, II, 5th ed., 2010, 210–211; *Vaz Tomé*, in: Fernandes/Proença, Comentário ao Código Civil – Parte geral, 584, para. 4; *Moreira da Silva*, Da responsabilidade pré-contratual por violação dos deveres de informação, 2003, 97–98; *Menezes Cordeiro* (fn. 64), 850–851; Id., in: Menezes Cordeiro, Código Civil comentado, I, 2020, 735, para. 16; *Pita*, in: Prata, Código Civil anotado, 2nd ed., 2019, 336; *Hörster/Moreira da Silva*, A parte geral do Código Civil português, 2nd ed., 2019, 628, para. 964; *Miranda Barbosa*, Falta e vícios da vontade, 2020, 101–105; Id., Lições de teoria geral do direito civil, 2021, 772. This is, however, not the place to discuss the topic.

to the DAO may be legally relevant in the context of the legal framework of error in the declaration (article 247.º CC). In this case, the will of the counterparty is correctly formed:[65] it is based on the natural language accompanying the smart contract code that defines the relationship between the DAO and the contractor, the contractual obligations, and the terms of execution.[66] However, at the time of the will exteriorisation, a failure emerges from the discrepancy between the natural language and the code in such a way that the declaration does not match the will of the third party.[67] Therefore, the agreement is voidable because there are grounds for considering that the DAO knew or should not have been unaware of the essentiality, for the counterparty, of the element on which the mistake was based (article 247.º CC).[68] The DAO is, therefore, exposed to annulment pursuant to article 247.º CC[69] and pre-contractual (reckless) liability according to article 227.º CC.[70]

It is also possible that only positive knowledge is relevant in the context of a knowledge provision.[71] As already put forward, transactions on the blockchain are made pseudonymously, thus being extremely difficult to track the tokenholders and their positive knowledge of certain facts. However, this is not a

---

[65] In this direction, *Menezes Cordeiro* (fn. 64), 848.

[66] We are therefore considering the hypotheses – which seem most relevant – in which the natural language overlaps the code, and the latter has only the role of an (automatic) externalisation of a previously formed will. Considering this and other possibilities, *Ana Perestrelo de Oliveira* (fn. 48), 56 ff.

In the case referred to in the text, the "corrective intervention of the legal system" is made through the legal framework of the error in the declaration (article 247.º CC).

[67] Again, *Menezes Cordeiro* (fn. 64), 848.

[68] The DAO (or the tokenholders) can in any case prove that they were not or should have not been unaware of the divergence between the natural language and the code.

[69] Which is a "relative knowledge provision" ("*norma de conhecimento relative*"; "*relative Wissensnorm*"), as, in addition to positive knowledge, the "duty" of knowledge is also legally relevant. The terminology is again proposed, in Germany, by *Grigoleit* (fn. 25), 169 ff.; Id., in: Grigoleit, Aktiengesetz, 2nd ed., 2020, AktG § 78, para. 28.

It could also be used a different terminology: "constructive knowledge" or "constructive notice" provisions – i. e., where, respectively, *(i)* knowledge of circumstances that would indicate the facts to an honest and reasonable person or *(ii)* knowledge of circumstances that would put an honest and reasonable person on inquiry are deemed relevant, being the person treated *as if* she knew (see, for example, *Bant*, in: Bant, The culpable corporate mind, 2023, 231–253, 239–240).

[70] Which is a "fault provision" ("*norma de culpa*"; "*Verschuldensnorm*") – as opposed to "simple knowledge provisions" ("*norma de simples conhecimento*"; "*einfachen Wissensnormen*"). This terminology is used by *Rachlitz* (fn. 25), 80, 353, *passim*.

Fault provisions are also knowledge provisions in a broad sense, since, as put forward (fn. 59), knowledge also plays a role in the domain of intent/*dolus* ("*dolo-culpa*"): the legal consequences in both types of knowledge provisions are yet different (see fn. 75).

[71] Thus, being qualified as an "absolute knowledge provision" ("*norma de conhecimento absoluta*"; "*absolute Wissensnorm*"). The terminology is again proposed, in Germany, by *Grigoleit* (fn. 25), 169 ff.; Id. (fn. 70), AktG § 78, para. 28.

It coul also be used a different terminology: "actual knowledge" provisions. See, for example, *Bant*, (fn. 70), 239–240.

problem exclusive to DAOs, tokenholders, or performance in the blockchain domain. Also, in the case of individuals, there is the difficulty associated to proving an internal fact (i.e., positive knowledge).[72] The problem is somehow different, but it seems that it can be solved in a similar way.

As already mentioned above,[73] in the context of (absolute) knowledge provisions, it is "sanctioned" the fact that the agent acts despite (positively) knowing specific facts. There is, therefore, an "assimilation" between the fault provisions (wilful misconduct/*dolus*) and knowledge provisions: knowledge and will always are at stake. Strictly speaking: the concrete terms of legal relevance of positive knowledge and *dolus* differ.[74] However, the assessment related to the existence of positive knowledge or wilfulness ("*dolo-culpa*") is the same:[75] there is (eventual) wilfulness – and (eventual) knowledge – if, given the specific risk situation, there are reasons to assume that the agent concretely represented the possibility of a certain state of affairs (*cognitive element*) and complied with it (*wilful element*).[76] In short: we face, in both cases, a normative assessment and not a psychological one.

Applying this idea to the case presented above: positive knowledge of the tokenholders can be assumed if there is a notorious or evident disparity between the proposal (wet language) and the code (dry code) – e.g., a bug – in such terms that one have to conclude that the tokenholders intentionally made the counterparty incur in error or that, knowing the counterparty (potential) error, they concealed it[77] (article 253.º (1) CC).[78] This knowledge of the tokenholders is at-

---

[72] See, inter alia, *Menezes Cordeiro*, Da boa fé no direito civil, 1983, 514–516; Id., Tratado de direito civil, I, 4.ª ed., 2016, 966; Guichard, A representação sem poderes no direito civil português – A ratificação, II, 2009, 889; Trindade, A prova de estados subjetivos no processo civil – presunções judiciais e regras de experiência, 2016, 53 ff.

[73] *Supra* II.

[74] In the simple knowledge provisions the addressee is "obliged" to adopt a conduct in conformity to his knowledge or "duty" to know certain facts. In the event of failure to do so, the consequences may be summed up as a weakening of his legal position: non-performance merely entails a disadvantage or failure to obtain an advantage (which cannot be seen as a penalty). Therefore, the addressee is not subject – as in fault provisions – to enforcement or a request for compensation for non-performance.

[75] In this direction, *Rachlitz* (fn. 25), 269–270.

[76] On eventual knowledge, see, inter alia, *Reichel*, Zeitschrift für das privat- und öffentliche Recht der Gegenwart 42 (1916), 173–262, 173 ff.; *Sallawitz*, Die tatbestandsmäßige Gleichsteillung von grobfahrlässiger Unkenntnis mit Kenntnis – Ein dogmatisches und praktisches Problem des Privatrechts, 1973, 50 ff.; *Medicus* (fn. 22), 6; *Buck*, Wissen und juristische Person – Wissenszurechnung und Herausbildung zivilrechtlicher Organisationspflichten, 2001, 58 ff.

[77] On the normativisation of *dolus eventualis*, see in Germany, *Roxin*, in: FS Hans-Joachim Rudolphi, 2004, 243–257, 255; *Roxin/Greco*, Strafrecht – Allgemeiner Teil, I, 5th ed., 2020, 551, para. 31; in Portugal, *Menezes Cordeiro*, *Tratado de direito civil*, VIII, 2016, 467; *Palma*, Direito Penal – Parte Geral – A teoria geral da infração como teoria da decisão penal, 5th ed., 2020, 146 ff.; *Dias*, Direito Penal – Parte geral, I, 2nd ed., 2007, 371 ff.

[78] The DAO (or the tokenholders) can in any case prove that they had no positive knowledge of the divergence between the code and the natural language.

tributable to the DAO, thus being exposed to annulment under article 253.º CC and to (wilful) pre-contractual liability under article 227.º CC.

One key characteristic of smart contracts is that the code cannot be modified or deleted by default.[79] There is, thus, a problem related to the fact that blockchain runs on a distributed network of independent nodes with no centralised authority: a litigant seeking to enjoy the performance (in case of breach) or to destroy the contractual effects (in case of voidability) may have – it is said – no way to enforce an execution[80] regarding performance or restitution in kind (i.e., on-chain). That is the reason why it is said that "[i]n many ways, smart contracts are not different from today's written agreements [...]. Where traditional legal agreements and smart contracts begin to differ is in the ability of smart contracts to enforce obligations using autonomous code".[81]

There are, however, a few ways to "destroy"[82] the effects of the executed (and voidable) smart contract. Firstly, a contract can be "deleted" by removing the code and its internal state (storage) from its address – being the remaining ether in the contract transferred to the previously codified account – if the so-called "selfdestruct" functionality is added to the smart contract code by its author.[83]

When the selfdestruct functionality is not programmed, the best way to achieve restitution in kind (in accordance with article 289.º (1) CC) seems to be the introduction reverse transaction on the blockchain. The prerequisite for this is that the transaction's recipient executes it again with a reversed sign and thus transfers back the sent tokens, for example. The disadvantage, in this case, is that the sender is dependent on the recipient's cooperation: as the owner of his private key, only the recipient can carry out the (reverse) transaction.[84] A state court can, however, order the DAO to introduce the reverse transaction and

---

[79] *Antonopoulos/Wood*, Mastering ethereum, 2018, 129; *Mienert* (fn. 16), 37.

[80] *Werbrach/Cornell*, Duke Law Journal 67 (2017), 313–382, 332. The Authors emphasise that determining exactly how powerless a court is would depend on the system. Smart contracts are, however, autonomous in nature, which means that promises memorialised in a smart contract are, by default, more complex to terminate than those memorialised in a traditional legal agreement. Because no single party controls a blockchain, there may not be a way to halt the execution of a smart contract: smart contracts are "executed in a distributed manner by all nodes supporting the underlying blockchain-based network, without relying on an intermediary operator or a trusted middleman" (*Filippi/Wright* [fn. 3], 74).

[81] *Filippi/ Wright* (fn. 3), 74. In the same direction, *Möslein*, in: Braegelmann/Kaulartz, Rechtshandbuch Smart Contracts, 2019, 81–98, 84–85, para. 6.

[82] In this article we are concerned with the annulment of the agreement. But the ideas developed in the text also proceed for termination (for termination see, in Portugal, *Ana Perestrelo de Oliveira* [fn. 48], 80 ff.).

Identifying various possibilities for introducing changes to the blockchain, *Saive*, DuD 42-12 (2018), 764–767, 766.

[83] *Antonopoulos/Wood* (fn. 80), 129; *Mienert* (fn. 16), 37.

[84] *Saive* (fn. 83), 766; *Ana Perestrelo de Oliveira* (fn. 48), 82.

impose a periodic penalty payment (according to article 829.º-A CC) if it fails to do so.[85]

Introducing forks is also theoretically possible to seek restitution in kind if a DAO refuses to cooperate. In this case, the majority of the participants would have to be convinced that a specific transaction is faulty: a new block would be inserted, and the blockchain would split and the retroactively modified by "undoing" the undesirable transactions of blocks.[86] It is, however, correctly emphasised that the use of forks aiming the restitution in kind must be difficult on a public[87] blockchain[88]: it is only adequate to systematic failures and thus to rare cases where the integrity of blockchain is breached.[89]

As a last resort, the failing party (*in casu*, the DAO) can be forced to pay the litigant the corresponding value off-chain (article 289.º (1) CC) or to pay a compensation off-chain (article 798.º CC).

V. Knowledge attribution in the context of action through a legal wrapper (sub-DAO)

The legal wrapper does not fall under the organisational responsibility of the DAO, being legally and organisationally independent; this fact for itself should prevent the attribution of the legal wrapper's knowledge to the DAO. As said above: the legal wrapper, as an entity, is strictly distinguished from the DAO.[90]

In addition to the – not doubtful – cases where an (authorised) agent has representative powers ("*representação voluntária*"), where his knowledge is to be attributable to the principal directly under article 259.º (1) CC, it is possible – as in German case law and literature has been already stated regarding § 166 BGB (1) – to consider that article 259.º (1) of CC is conceived as an expression of a general principle not necessarily limited to (authorised) agency relationships in a strict sense: a person who engages someone else to carry out a task is attributed the knowledge which the person so engaged acquires in the process.[91] For-

[85] In this direction, *Ana Perestrelo de Oliveira* (fn. 48), 88–89; in Germany, applying § 888 (1) ZPO, *Spindler/Wöbbeking*, in: Braegelmann/Kaulartz, Rechtshandbuch Smart Contracts, 2019, 135–146, 143, para. 30.

[86] See, for example, *Tai*, in: DiMatteo/Cannarsa/Poncibò, The cambridge handbook of smart contracts, blockchain technology and digital platforms, 2019, 80–101, 82.

[87] On a private blockchain, the central authority could initiate the introduction of the fork (*Saive* (fn. 83), 766).

[88] *Spindler/Wöbbeking* (fn. 86), 142, para. 30. Addressing the introduction of forks as a "non-realistic" hypothesis, *Ana Perestrelo de Oliveira* (fn. 48), 83.

[89] *Pasa/DiMatteo*, in: DiMatteo/Cannarsa/Poncibò, The cambridge handbook of smart contracts, blockchain technology and digital platforms, 2019, 334–358, 354.

[90] *Supra*, III.

[91] Inter alia, *Rademacher*, in: Jansen/Zimmermann, Commentaries on European Contract Laws, 2018, 224; *Stumpf*, BB 2021, 2056–2062, 2060.

mulating differently: a person who delegates the handling of their own affairs to a third party on their own responsibility – even outside a representative relationship – must allow the knowledge obtained in this context to be attributed to them[92]. This is intended to prevent the principal from benefiting from knowledge fragmentation emerging from the division of labour.[93]

Attribution of knowledge is, therefore, also possible outside and between different organisations/persons/companies. In the specific case of the attribution of knowledge of the service provider to the principal, a "representative-like" self-responsible function is required within the scope of duties of the principal.[94] Nonetheless, the exact rage of auxiliaries whose knowledge is attributable is far from clear. There are no clear rules to determine whether the knowledge of third parties – not engaged in the principal's organisation – is to be attributed to the principal.[95] Unsurprisingly: it is often emphasised that the problem of knowledge attribution – even if considering the knowledge of a legal person's organs – "cannot be decided with logical and conceptual stringency, entailing rather an evaluative assessment".[96]

Even abstractly and always considering the need to address the specific case, it is possible to address the relationship that is traditionally established between the DAO and the legal wrapper.

Traditionally it is said that only simple management tasks can be delegated to subordinate management levels or entrusted to external service providers.[97] In

---

[92] In this direction, *Stumpf* (fn. 92), 2061; in German case law, see, for example: BGH of 25 March 1982 – VII ZR 60/81, 1586; or BGH of 14 January 2016 – I ZR 65/14, 3450.

Therefore, German case law applies the knowledge attribution principles not only considering subjects involved within a legal person/organisation based on the division of labour, but also to the involvement of "external" third parties, e.g., with an advisory function for the principal; thus, in some cases, the knowledge of facts possessed by lawyers can be attributed to the client as if it were his knowledge (BGH of 25 October 2018 – IX ZR 168/17, 117–118). Additionally, BGH has also already considered that the knowledge of a collection agency – which acts as creditor's receiving agent – is attributable to the creditor (BGH of 3 April 2014 – IX ZR 201/13, 1966; commented by Wilhelm, BB 2014, 1615–1619).

[93] In this direction, with multiple doctrinal references, BGH of 14 January 2016 – I ZR 65/14, 3450.

[94] *Stumpf* (fn. 92), 2061 ("*einer vertreterähnlichen eigenverantwortlichen Funktion des Dritten*").

[95] Expressly in this sense, *Rademacher* (fn. 92), 224.

[96] This statement is dated back to 1989 and was proclaimed by the BGH on 8 December 1989 – V ZR 246/87, 976. The statement is often reproduced by German legal doctrine: recently, see, *Seidel* (fn. 27), 56; following the idea in Portugal, *Gomes/Gonçalves* (fn. 26), 86.

[97] In this direction, *Liese*, Grenzen der Wissenszurechnung – Konzern und Outsourcing, 2019, 239 ff. Therefore, there are matters that, integrating the core of the management duty, are inalienable and cannot be delegated. In short, as appointed by Fleischer, this is the case of: *(i)* planning and control responsibility (definition of the strategic plan – long-term plan, main business areas, most relevant investment decisions and the duty to intervene at any time in the event of unforeseen disturbances during plan implementation); *(ii)* organisational responsibility (definition of the company's structural framework, through the delegation of powers and

the case of DAOs – due to their nature – it is likely that, given the interposition of a legal wrapper, some of these matters may be delegated. By adopting this course of action, it seems clear that the DAO is transferring managing functions to another natural or legal person that otherwise would have to be performed by the DAO using its own material or personal resources.[98] Shortly: DAO outsources management functions to the legal wrapper. Outsourcing is distinguished from mere service provision because it is not merely temporary or a short-term activity, and the service provider is independent in its execution[99] – as it can occur with contractors.[100]

Let us consider a case where a user pays a company to use its hardware or software, and the maintenance of the hardware or software is outsourced to a third-party company.[101] Generally speaking, a counterparty of a company – whose knowledge is internally split up – is protected against the company being able to invoke ignorance solely based on its organisational structure. And this is not limited to the company's employees or other auxiliaries falling inside its organisation.[102] For a counterparty, it makes no difference whether a company performs their obligations with the involvement of its own employees or a third-party: what truly matters is that the obligation is complied in accordance with the agreement.[103] Furthermore, for a counterparty, it is usually not recognisable whether a service – that the company is contractually is obliged to perform by itself – has been outsourced or if the service provider performs by itself.[104]

It seems appropriate to apply the principles of knowledge attribution to contractual constellations of service outsourcing if the situation is comparable to a company organisation.[105] Returning to DAOs and legal wrappers: we are not facing just outsourcing of performance related to a contractual obligation vis-à-vis a third party. The management duties themselves are outsourced to the legal wrapper: somehow, the DAOs organisation is being outsourced. The reasons to

division into functional sub-units, ensuring that the organisation adopter has the capacity to adapt to change); *(iii)* financial responsibility (ensuring forward-looking financial planning and financial audits); and *(iv)* responsibility for information (ensuring that the organisation of information is adequate to the company). This does not mean that they cannot be assisted in the execution of these tasks by other workers/auxiliaries, but rather that they are ultimately responsible for the decision regarding the execution of those tasks (*Fleischer*, ZIP 2003, 1–11, 5).

[98] See the definition of outsourcing offered by *Liese* (fn. 98), 317.

[99] *Liese* (fn. 98), 317.

[100] But contractors can act in a similar way to legal wrappers. In that case, remarks now made in the text seem to proceed entirely.

[101] Exemple offered by *Spindler/Schuster*, in: Recht der elektronischen Medien, 4th ed., 2019, BGB § 166, para. 6.

[102] *Spindler/Schuster* (fn. 102), para. 6; *Liese* (fn. 98), 261.

[103] *Liese* (fn. 98), 261.

[104] *Spindler/Schuster* (fn. 102), para. 6; *Liese* (fn. 98), 261.

[105] *Spindler/Schuster* (fn. 102), para. 6.

apply the attribution knowledge principles are reinforced, as the DAO is, in this case, organised in such a way that part of its "scope of action" ("*Aufgabenbereich*") is outsourced to a natural person or an independent legal entity.[106]

If, on the other hand, the attribution of knowledge were to be excluded in cases like this, the DAO itself would have on its own hands the chance to evade the attribution of knowledge by continually outsourcing tasks to the legal wrapper.[107] Denying knowledge attribution would then create an incentive to split knowledge and manipulate knowledge attribution.[108] Additionally, it would be contrary to the general sense of justice that companies – and DAOs – were allowed to avoid their knowledge responsibility by outsourcing, especially since this is often not recognisable to a counterparty.[109] In this respect, a counterparty would suffer considerable disadvantages compared to a counterparty benefiting from the performance of a service provider who performs himself.[110]

Therefore, in principle, the division of labour definition may also fit the outsourcing situation: outsourcing of corporate functions – and, mainly, management functions – is to be addressed as a sub-case of the division of labour, as the situation is not fundamentally different.[111] This being the case: the knowledge of the legal wrapper – a natural or legal person – is, in principle, attributable to the DAO in the context of its action on behalf of the DAO.

---

[106] In this direction BGH of 13 October 2000 – V ZR 349/99, 360 – by *obiter dictum* (the so-called "outsourcing case"). Seeking to develop the grounds for this decision of the BGH, *Liese* finds the material ground for the knowledge attribution in the outsourcing company's possibility to control the risk sphere newly created by outsourcing, since rights of instruction and control can be agreed between the outsourcing company and the service provider. In addition, the author correctly considers that in the case of outsourcing management tasks, the board of directors' duty to manage is modified to a duty of supervision and, furthermore, that it only can be attributed to the outsourcing company the knowledge acquired by the service provider within the framework of the agreed functions (*Liese* [fn. 98], 284 ff., maxime, 307–308).

[107] In this direction for traditional companies, *Buck* (fn. 77), 321.

[108] *Iro*, ÖBA 2 (2001), 112–124, 116.

[109] *Liese* (fn. 98), 262.

[110] *Spindler/Schuster* (fn. 102), 6.

[111] *Koller*, JZ 53-2 (1998), 75–85, 79.

For this reason, the grounds justifying knowledge attribution in the case of outsourcing are, in principle, the same as those for attributing knowledge held internally by the organisation. *Liese* does, however, rule out that reasons of traffic protection should be the basis for knowledge attribution in the event of outsourcing (*Liese* [fn. 98], 319).

The Nature of the DAO: Transaction Costs, MiCA and a Specific Legal Framework

João Vieira dos Santos

ABSTRACT This article aims to analyze DAOs through the lens of Ronald Coase's groundbreaking and famous paper "The Nature of the Firm", from 1937. From there, the article seeks elements in DAOs that may contribute to the establishment of a legal intervention and a specific legal framework for them. In that vein, the article takes the opportunity to analyse the EU's crypto-assets regulation, called MiCA and published recently, on 9 June 2023, with the aim to find out what solutions there might be for DAOs in this area.

I. The Nature of the Firm

The paper "The Nature of the Firm" (1937), from Ronald Coase, starts by confronting the economists' vision of the economic system as being totally coordinated by the price mechanism, without the need of any planning by individuals and assuming that the direction of resources is dependent directly on the price mechanism.

Coase states that within a firm, the mentioned description does not fit at all, and he includes a funny and clever remark by D.H. Robertson about this: "we find islands of conscious power in this ocean of unconscious co-operation like lumps of butter coagulating in a pail of buttermilk". Subsequently, Coase asks if it is argued that co-ordination could be done alone by the price mechanism, why is such organizations necessary? Why are there these "islands of conscious power"?[1]

Coase's task is to attempt to discover why a firm emerges at all in a specialized exchange economy and the main reason he found was the costs of using the price mechanism, or transactions costs. being the most obvious the cost of discovering what the relevant prices are.[2] Other transactions costs arise from negotiating and concluding separate contracts for each exchange transaction which takes place on a market.

---

[1] *Coase*, The Nature of the Firm. Economica, 4, 386-405, (1937), p. 391.
[2] *Coase*, The Nature of the Firm. Economica, 4, 386-405, (1937), p. 392.

In the other hand, by forming an organization and allowing some authority (an "entrepreneur") to direct the resources, certain transaction costs are saved. The entrepreneur has to carry out his function at less costs, taking into account the fact that he may get factors of production at a lower price than the market transactions which he supersedes, because it is always possible to revert to the open market if he fails to do this.[3]

With this premises, Coase defines firm as a system of relationships which comes into existence when the direction of resources is dependent on an entrepreneur; This dependency in the entrepreneur is justified by Coase in the uncertainty of the economic systems. Most contracts are incomplete. To forecast the consumers' needs it requires a lot of research. Therefore, when uncertainty is present and the task of deciding of that to do and how to do it takes the ascendancy over that of execution, the internal organization of the productive groups is no longer a matter of indifference or a mechanic detail. For Coase the centralization of the deciding and controlling function is imperative in a firm.[4]

II. What this have to do with DAOs?

In relation to DAOs, I think it is possible to make a parallelism on what was advocated by Coase. In the blockchain ecosystem, almost everything is based in the price mechanism, even mining and other validation processes, which are structured through economic incentives. These incentives work depending on the open market's price of the crypto-assets that are native to the protocol. Notwithstanding, DAOs emerge in the blockchain ecosystem like firms, as "islands of conscious power".

DAOs are thus able to reduce some transactions costs exist in the blockchain ecosystem that are also to discover what are the relevant prices and the individual negotiating, which is also a need in the blockchain ecosystem, despite all the automation. And DAOs also can be a tool to better decide and control what developments should take place in that ecosystem, without total dependence on the open market.

Other reason for a firm's high transaction costs is due to the 'costliness of ascertaining violations and the severity of punishment'. DAOs can mitigate this factor by enforcing rules through smart contracts, which strengthens the parties' confidence in the fulfilment of what has been agreed.[5]

---

[3] *Coase*, The Nature of the Firm. Economica, 4, 386-405, (1937), p. 293.

[4] *Coase*, The Nature of the Firm. Economica, 4, 386-405, (1937), p. 399.

[5] *Sims*, Blockchain and Decentralised Autonomous Organisations (DAOs): The Evolution of Companies? (November 1, 2019). 28 New Zealand Universities Law Review 423-458 , The University of Auckland Business School Research Paper, (2019) p. 17, available at: https://ssrn.com/abstract=3524674 (15.05.2023).

Of course, DAOs are different than firms. DAOs aim to end the need of the centralization of the deciding and controlling function that Coase finds imperative in firms. In legal terms, corporate structures require institutions like boards of directors and centralized management and for DAO's participants such formality defeats the point of DAOs since they do not accommodate fully decentralized environments built on trustless, much less pseudonymous, infrastructures.[6] This decentralisation entails costs, but DAOs seek to mitigate these through process automation, which may lead to a more efficient governance.

In the light of the above, I think these assumptions about DAOs can be good arguments for granting legal status to DAOs. I am not speaking about the reference to DAOs that existed in the Parliament version of MiCA,[7] which included only its definition and its definition DAOs were just a set of smart contracts. In my view, DAOs are more than that, DAOs are organizations. As António Garcia Rolo stated, "DAO is a smart contract conceptualised as an organization – very much like companies have been described as nexus of contracts, one can describe a DAO as a nexus of smart contracts or as a smart contract of considerable size and breadth"[8], and, as stated by Aaron Wright, "members rely on smart contracts as the primary glue to manage member-to-member transactions".[9]

Being true that DAOs are composed of smart contracts or systems of smart contracts, those smart contracts incorporate governance and decision-making rules for DAOs members[10]. The decentralising and disintermediating functions of distributed ledger technologies provide for the creation of open communities for the development of economic activities.

This means DAOs are durable and cohesive structures, this means DAOs are entities that comprise multiple (two or more) people acting towards a common goal,[11] this means DAOs are islands of conscious power that, like firms, help our economic system by reducing transactions costs. DAO are entities since they can be defined as something that exists separately from other things and

---

6 *Brummer/Seira*, Legal Wrappers and DAOs, 2022, p. 8, available at: https://ssrn.com/abstract=4123737 (12.05.2023).

7 Regulation (EU) 2023/1114 on markets in crypto-assets.

8 *Rolo*, Challenges in the Legal Qualification of Decentralised Autonomous Organisations (DAOs): The Rise of the Crypto-Partnership? (December 19, 2018). Revista de Direito e Tecnologia, Vol 1, no. 1, 33-87, Centro de Investigação de Direito Privado (CIDP) Research Paper No. 11, (2019), p. 56, available at: https://ssrn.com/abstract=3417900, (02.06.2023).

9 *Wright*, The rise of decentralized autonomous organizations: Opportunities and challenges,: 152-176, Stanford Journal of Blockchain Law & Policy 4.2, (2021), p. 155, available at: https://stanford-jblp.pubpub.org/pub/rise-of-daos/release/1 (20.06.2023).

10 *Reyes*, If Rockefeller Were a Coder, 87 Geo. Wash. L. Rev. 373, (2019), p. 387, available at: https://ssrn.com/abstract=3082915 (24.05.2023).

11 *Mondoh/Johnson/Green/Georgopoulos*, Decentralised Autonomous Organisations: The Future of Corporate Governance or an Illusion?, 2022, p. 4, available at: https://ssrn.com/abstract=4144753 (21.05.2023).

has a clear identity of its own.[12] Therefore, the legal status of DAOs must recognize them as organizations, promoting them as important economic actors in the blockchain ecosystem and in our society.

The *affirmative asset partitioning* and the *entity shielding* are the forms of legal intervention that can enhance the nexus of smart contracts we have already said that DAOs are. This legal intervention consists of a special rule of property law, attributing assets to a legal person and granting priority to its creditors.[13]

III. But what kind of legal intervention?

It might be thought that already we already have a legal intervention on DAOs in MiCA, since it is possible to interpret the reference of undertakings as an intention to include DAOs.[14]

This European Regulation lays down uniform requirements for the offer to the public and admission to trading on a trading platform of crypto-assets, as well as requirements for crypto-asset service providers, across the European Union. It has an extensive scope by defining the term crypto-asset broadly as "a digital representation of value or rights which may be transferred and stored electronically, using distributed ledger technology or similar technology".

Although, besides the non-fungible tokens being excluded, other exemptions exist in MiCA, mainly in public offers of crypto-assets, depending on a taxonomy that MiCA establishes, as there are different for each type of crypto-assets and they can be designed in a variety of ways and entail the ownership of a variety of rights, financial and non-financial.[15] Also, crypto-assets covered in European Union financial services legislation are excluded.

This exclusion and the taxonomy of crypto-assets covered in MiCA can be summarised as follows:

---

[12] *Riva*, Sven, Decentralized Autonomous Organizations (DAOs) as Subjects of Law – the Recognition of DAOs in the Swiss Legal Order. Master's Thesis, 2019, p. 29, available at: https://ssrn.com/abstract=3515229 (02.06.2023).

[13] *Schillig*, Some Reflections on the Nature of Decentralized (Autonomous) Organizations. King's College London Law School Research Paper Forthcoming, (2021), p. 27, available at: https://ssrn.com/abstract=3915843 (16.05.2023).

[14] *Rolo*, Out of Scope, Out of Mind, and Don't Say Decentralisation: Brief Remarks on the new MiCA Regulation, 2023, available at: https://europeanlawblog.eu/2023/05/23/out-of-scope-out-of-mind-and-dont-say-decentralisation-brief-remarks-on-the-new-mica-regulation/ (20.06.2023).

[15] *Zetzsche/Annunziata/Arner/Buckley*, The Markets in Crypto-Assets Regulation (MICA) and the EU Digital Finance Strategy, European Banking Institute Working Paper Series No. 2020/77, University of Luxembourg Law Working Paper Series No. 2020-018, University of Hong Kong Faculty of Law Research Paper No. 2020/059, (2020), p. 5, available at: https://ssrn.com/abstract=3725395 (14.05.2023).

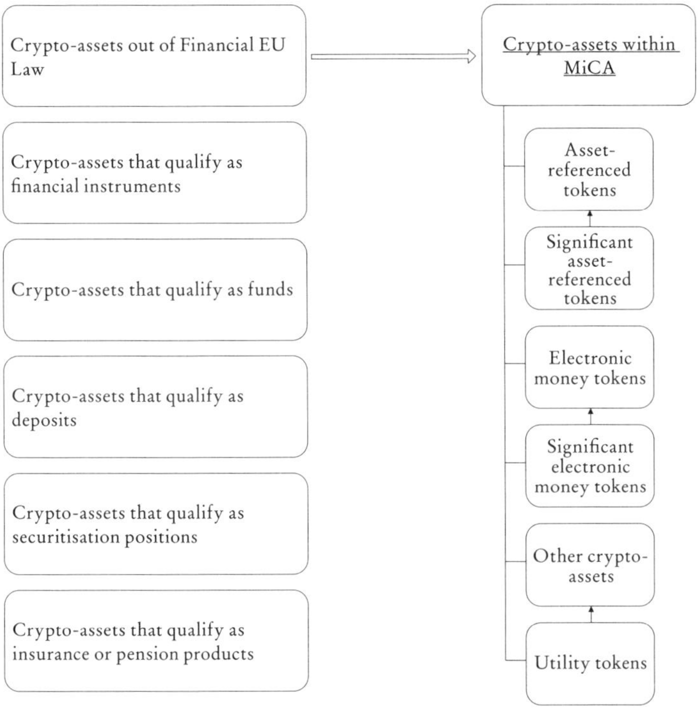

Two categories of crypto-assets were created for the so-called stablecoins: asset-referenced tokens and electronic money tokens. This distinction of stablecoins was made due to their widespread adoption and potential to be used as a payment method and a store of value.[16]

An asset-referenced token is a type of crypto-asset that is not an electronic money token and that purports to maintain a stable value by referencing another value or right or a combination thereof, including one or more official currencies. An electronic money token is a type of crypto-asset that purports to maintain a stable value by referencing the value of one official currency.

To respond to the risks for the financial stability that an asset-referenced token or electronic money token may pose if they reach a large scale in terms of market capitalisation, number and value of transactions and other factors, two sub-categories have been created in MiCA, significant asset-referenced tokens

[16] "[…] stablecoins have the potential to reach globally systemic dimensions from a financial stability perspective", *Zetzsche/Annunziata/Arner/Buckley*, The Markets in Crypto-Assets Regulation (MICA) and the EU Digital Finance Strategy, European Banking Institute Working Paper Series No. 2020/77, University of Luxembourg Law Working Paper Series No. 2020-018, University of Hong Kong Faculty of Law Research Paper No. 2020/059, (2020), p. 5, available at: https://ssrn.com/abstract=3725395 (14.05.2023).

and electronic money tokens. The rules foreseen in the draft regulation regarding these sub-categories of crypto-assets, deemed as significant, consist of additional obligations, such as remuneration policies, governance arrangements and the participation in a college of issuers chaired by EBA (European Banking Authority) that aims to facilitate the exercise of the supervisory tasks of this authority.

The remaining category of crypto-assets is delimited by the negative as they are composed of all crypto-assets covered by MiCA that are not asset-referenced tokens nor e-money tokens. Inside this catch-all category is the sub-category of utility tokens, a type of crypto-asset that is only intended to provide access to a good or a service supplied by its issuer.

This taxonomy guides us to how MiCA is structured. However, the subject of this regulation is mainly related to the disclosure requirements for the offering and admission to trading of crypto-assets and the authorisation and supervision of crypto-asset service providers and issuers of asset-referenced tokens and issuers of electronic money tokens.

As states in Article 2(1) of MiCA: "This Regulation applies to natural and legal persons and certain other undertakings that are engaged in the issuance, offer to the public and admission to trading of crypto-assets or that provide services related to crypto-assets in the Union".

Furthermore, the reference to "undertakings" is repeated in Articles 16, 18, 59 and 62, aimed at issuers of asset-referenced tokens and crypto-assets service providers. This intends to extent the subjective scope of MiCA to other entities that are not legal persons, but this is not a novelty. It is also laid down in Article 4(1) of MiFID[17] that: "Member States may include in the definition of investment firms undertakings which are not legal persons, provided that: (a) their legal status ensures a level of protection for third parties' interests equivalent to that afforded by legal persons; and (b) they are subject to equivalent prudential supervision appropriate to their legal form".

MiCA is not so restrictive, but the idea is surely the same that is to include some entities without legal personality from certain Member States. In this way, it seems far-fetched to us to consider that these references are intended to include DAOs. That might a reality only if any national law from a Member State starts considering DAOs as entities without legal personality in its jurisdiction, something that did not happen yet.

Notwithstanding, the scope of MiCA deals with decentralization by excluding the provision of services and the issuance of crypto-assets that is fully decentralized. As stated in recital 22: "This Regulation should apply to natural and legal persons and certain other undertakings and to the crypto-asset servic-

[17] Directive 2014/65/EU of the European Parliament and of the Council of 15 May 2014 on markets in financial instruments.

es and activities performed, provided or controlled, directly or indirectly, by them, including when part of such activities or services is performed in a decentralised manner. Where crypto-asset services are provided in a fully decentralised manner without any intermediary, they should not fall within the scope of this Regulation. This Regulation covers the rights and obligations of issuers of crypto-assets, offerors, persons seeking admission to trading of crypto-assets and crypto-asset service providers. Where crypto-assets have no identifiable issuer, they should not fall within the scope of Title II, III or IV of this Regulation. Crypto-asset service providers providing services in respect of such crypto-assets should, however, be covered by this Regulation".

Part of this recital does not make much sense because it includes issuers of crypto-assets from Title II, whereas this Title only applies to offerors and not issuers. Thus, this inconsistency will lead to problems when implementing the law.

However, the core issue is that it is not possible to determine, on the basis of MiCA, what is decentralised or not. Therefore, we will have to wait for the level 2 measures. For instance, it is unclear whether decentralisation only needs to be established on the infrastructural layer (i.e. at the level of the underlying blockchain-based network) or whether it also needs to be implemented at the governance level.[18]

MiCA will thus be a diploma to be considered by DAOs, but unfortunately it will not provide them with much legal certainty. This will require a broader and specific legal framework for DAOs in my view.

IV. How should a broad and specific DAOs legal framework look like?

An apparent example of where a European legislation on DAOs could draw inspiration from is the Council Regulation (EC) No 2157/2001 on the Statute for a European company (*Societas Europaea* or SE). This diploma creates a new type of entity and that is what is intended with DAOs. However, its purpose is to facilitate the reorganisation and cooperation processes of the companies the business of which is not limited to satisfying purely local needs and the formation of an SE shall be governed by the law applicable to public limited-liability companies in the Member State in which the SE establishes its registered office.

Thus, this regulation therefore simply provides rules on the models for conversion of limited public limited-liability companies into SEs, their governance (but not in great detail), their accounts and their liquidation. This limited scope

---

[18] *Hassan/De Filippi*, Decentralized Autonomous Organization, Internet Policy Review, 2197-6775, 10. 2, Alexander von Humboldt Institute for Internet and Society, Berlin, 2021, 1-10, (2020) p. 7, available at: https://www.econstor.eu/handle/10419/235960 (05.06.2023).

and the fact that an extra layer has been created over something that already exists in the legislation of the Member States, which hinders the uniform treatment of these entities, have meant that the diploma has not had a large following. By 21st August 2009, five years after the enter into force of this regulation, only 418 SEs have been registered.[19]

Regarding DAOs, its specific legal framework will necessarily have to be different purpose. First of all, because of because we are talking about a reality that is not yet regulated in any Member State. Second, because of the virtual dimension of DAOs, which implies that enforcement will only be effective in an enlarged jurisdiction, such as that of the EU.

In terms of content, the approach should be the same as that used in recent diplomas of the Digital Finance Package, i.e. risk-based. The first risks that are raised are obviously the cyber-risks and the financial risks of the funds allocated to each DAO. In this sense, it is necessary for a legal framework to provide for such organizational and capital requirements in order to grant legal status and limited liability to DAOs.

Another content that could be in a legal framework for DAOs could be something that benefits the reduction of transaction costs and promote this particularity of DAOs, as described above. Since it is in its nature, this can be done by determining the legal definition of DAO as an entity without management bodies and in which part of its governance or business activity is automated by smart contracts.

In this way, we avoid that other organisational constructs mischaracterize DAOs and undermine their benefits for reducing transaction costs. For instance, a DAO with a board of directors would have the same hierarchical structure[20] as a firm, so firms legal regime should applied and in that way this DAO should not be consider a DAO in legal terms.

Lastly, it is important to notice that if a DAO has a legal status and limited liability, it should be publicly registered, with a view to safeguarding creditors and differentiating itself from uncompliant DAOs. The tokenholders of a DAO should also be publicly registered, not only for anti-money laundering reasons, but also for the sake of legal certainty, for their own benefit and for that of their creditors.

In short, it seems to me that a first simple attempt at a legal framework in the EU would have to have these elements: legal definition of DAO; cyber risk and capital requirements; limited liability attribution; and public registration of DAOs and tokenholders.

[19] *Kadi*, Societas Europaea, 2009, p. 67, available at: https://ssrn.com/abstract=3799120 (06.06.2023).

[20] DAOs operate through public and distributed decision-making, *Bellavitis/Fisch/Momtaz*, The rise of decentralized autonomous organizations (DAOs): a first empirical glimpse, 2022, p. 3, available at: https://ssrn.com/abstract=4074833 (10.06.2023).

DeFi Attacks and the Role of DAOs*

Bianca Kremer and Kanye Ye Wang

Abstract Decentralized Finance (DeFi) represents an innovative alternative to the traditional financial system and is driven by blockchain technology. While it has witnessed significant growth, it has also been plagued by a range of security breaches, including hacks and other malicious attacks, leading to significant financial losses. By 2022, such attacks within the DeFi ecosystem amounted to an alarming $3.8 billion. Within this landscape, Decentralized Autonomous Organizations (DAOs), a pioneering model of bottom-up coordination, have emerged as both potential mitigators of risk and, paradoxically, potential attack vectors. In this paper, we explore the multifunctional role of DAOs within DeFi attacks. We examine their proactive involvement in preventing, mitigating, and responding to such attacks, while also being susceptible targets. Through case studies involving DAOs, we provide insights into how DAOs operate in DeFi.

I. Introduction

Decentralized Finance (DeFi) is an alternative to the traditional financial system and offers a rich array of services.[1] It is built using blockchain technology and supported by smart contracts. Ethereum, a leading programmable blockchain, hosts both DeFi incarnations of traditional financial services, such as exchanges, trading, lending, derivatives, banking, and a plethora of novel and innovative financial products, including stablecoins, flash loans, and more.[2]

---

* Thanks to Ding Feng for valuable research assistance. We thank Professor Kevin Werbach for valuable feedback on the initial draft. We are grateful to the organizers of the Lisbon DAO Regulation Conference for inviting us to share and test our preliminary ideas. This article is based on our presentation at the Lisbon DAO Observatory's DAO Regulation Conference held in April 2023. This article was made possible due to the support of the Wharton Blockchain and Digital Asset Project and the grant from the University of Macau (File no. APAEM/SG/0005/2023).

[1] See e.g., *Coelho-Prabhu*, A Beginner's Guide to Decentralized Finance (DeFi), Coinbase, 2020, https://www.coinbase.com/de/blog/a-beginners-guide-to-decentralized-finance-defi (26.07.2023) ("Imagine a global, open alternative to *every* financial service you use today – savings, loans, trading, insurance and more – accessible to anyone in the world with a smartphone and internet connection."). See also *Zetzsche et al.*, Decentralized Finance, Journal of Financial Regulation, 2020, 6, 183.

[2] See https://ethereum.org/en/defi (13.07.2023) ("DeFi is a collective term for financial products and services that are accessible to anyone who can use Ethereum – anyone with an

The DeFi ecosystem has seen substantial growth, especially during 2020 and 2021. DeFi projects now hold a total value of close to 50 billion USD (total value locked, TVL), reaching its peak of close to 180 billion USD in mid-2022 before entering a bear market.[3] However, it is impossible to ignore the significant number of hacking incidents that occurred during this period. Indeed, 2022 was the worst year for DeFi in terms of hacks, with losses totaling 3.8 billion USD according to Chainalysis reports.[4] These attacks often exploit vulnerabilities in the code or the governance system of DeFi protocols, in a way that harms the protocol or its users. Additionally, numerous risk events shook the market in 2022, such as the Terra Luna crash.[5] The wider crypto ecosystem, especially centralized finance (CeFi) saw the collapse of Three Arrows Capital,[6] the bankruptcy of the crypto exchange FTX,[7] and the financial failure of Silvergate and Silicon Valley Bank (SVB), which were banks that supported crypto startups.[8]

In face of potential malicious attacks and various risks, a robust governance system is vital for DeFi projects to be successful. One of the fastest growing bottom-up governance models in DeFi are so-called Decentralized Autonomous Organizations (DAOs). While the concept of DAOs was initially theorized in the 1990s, it gained significant attention when Ethereum co-founder Vitalik Buterin wrote a blog post about it on ethereum.org.[9] Though early experiments

internet connection. With DeFi, the markets are always open and there are no centralized authorities who can block payments or deny you access to anything.", "There's a booming crypto economy out there, where you can lend, borrow, long/short, earn interest, and more. Crypto-savvy Argentinians have used DeFi to escape crippling inflation.").

[3] See https://defillama.com/ (13.07.2023).

[4] See https://blog.chainalysis.com/reports/2022-biggest-year-ever-for-crypto-hacking (13.07.2023).

[5] See e.g., *Liu et al.*, Anatomy of a Run: The Terra Luna Crash, National Bureau of Economic Research, Working Paper 31160, 2023, https://www.nber.org/papers/w31160 (13.07.2023) (explaining that a variety of factors led to the collapse and incentivizing market participants to stay vigilant and actively monitor the system, "The complexity of the system made it difficult even for insiders to understand the buildup of risk. Finally, we draw broader lessons about financial fragility in an environment where a regulatory safety net does not exist, pseudonymous transactions are publicly observable, and market participants are incentivized to monitor the financial health of the system.")

[6] See *Lee et al.*, How Three Arrows Capital Blew Up and Set Off a Crypto Contagion, Bloomberg, 2022, https://www.bloomberg.com/news/features/2022-07-13/how-crypto-hedge-fund-three-arrows-capital-fell-apart-3ac (13.07.2023).

[7] See *Reif*, The Collapse of FTX: What Went Wrong with the Crypto Exchange?, Investopedia, 2023, https://www.investopedia.com/what-went-wrong-with-ftx-6828447 (25.08.2023). See also Chaturvedi, Crypto's Horrible, No Good, Very Bad Year, Investopedia, 2022, https://www.investopedia.com/cryptos-horrible-no-good-very-bad-year-6835076 (13.07.2023).

[8] See *Morris*, A Tale of 2 Banks: Why Silvergate and Silicon Valley Bank Collapsed, Yahoo Finance via CoinDesk, 2023, https://finance.yahoo.com/news/tale-2-banks-why-silvergate-174002150.html (13.07.2023).

[9] See *Buterin*, Ethereum Blog 2014, https://blog.ethereum.org/2014/05/06/daos-dacs-das-and-more-an-incomplete-terminology-guide (13.07.2023).

like “The DAO” in 2016 were pivotal,[10] it was not until the DeFi boom of 2020 that DAOs truly began to proliferate.[11] DAOs are essentially self-governing entities that operate on a set of rules encoded in smart contracts, without the need for traditional intermediaries or centralized authorities. DAOs can have various purposes and goals, such as investing in start-ups, managing a stablecoin, or buying digital art.

Most major DeFi platforms employ DAOs, and if they do not, DAOs are often seen as a promising direction for the evolution of DeFi, as they embody the ethos of decentralization and empower users to have a voice and a stake in the protocols they use. Indeed, DAOs are highly popular within the DeFi ecosystem. According to Chainalysis reports, among various Web3 sectors, DeFi boasts the highest concentration of DAOs.[12] Noteworthy examples include Uniswap DAO, Lido DAO, MakerDAO, and CurveDAO, some of the largest entities in this space. This is no surprise as DAOs emerged as a way to manage resources and coordinate activities when DeFi skyrocketed in 2020, a period often referred to as “DeFi summer”.[13]

DAOs play an important role in the DeFi ecosystem. They serve as entities managing governance systems for DeFi protocols, enabling collective decision-making and coordination among participants. However, the functionalities and operations of DAOs can also be susceptible to various attacks, with consequences potentially reverberating throughout the DeFi ecosystem.

Governance attacks are typically aimed at exploiting the decision-making processes of DAOs. Bad actors might manipulate votes to make decisions favorable to them, oftentimes utilizing flash loans to acquire substantial voting power temporarily. This form of attack focuses primarily on the governance structure and procedures, rather than on the underlying smart contract vulnerabilities.

Direct vulnerabilities in the smart contracts of DeFi services could lead to loss of funds or other exploitable scenarios independent of DAO governance attacks. Hackers may take advantage of flaws in the code and drain funds or manipulate contract interactions for their benefit. Other types of attacks are, e.g., bridge attacks, which involve exploiting vulnerabilities in the bridges con-

---

[10] See e.g., *Morris*, The DAO Hack: How a $60M Ethereum Attack Shaped Crypto History, 2023, https://www.coindesk.com/consensus-magazine/2023/05/09/coindesk-turns-10-how-the-dao-hack-changed-ethereum-and-crypto (13.07.2023).

[11] *Gogel et al.*, Decentralized Autonomous Organization Toolkit Insight Report, World Economic Forum in Collaboration with the Wharton Blockchain and Digital Asset Project, 2023, 4, https://www3.weforum.org/docs/WEF_Decentralized_Autonomous_Organization_Toolkit_2023.pdf (13.07.2023).

[12] See https://www.chainalysis.com (13.07.2023).

[13] *Gogel et al.*, Decentralized Autonomous Organization Toolkit Insight Report, World Economic Forum in Collaboration with the Wharton Blockchain and Digital Asset Project, 2023, 4, https://www3.weforum.org/docs/WEF_Decentralized_Autonomous_Organization_Toolkit_2023.pdf (25.08.2023).

necting different blockchains or layer 2 solutions, affecting the interoperability and functionality of DeFi services, potentially leading to loss of funds and data integrity issues.

DAOs can actively work to prevent, mitigate, and respond to the various forms of attacks mentioned above by enforcing rigorous code audits, implementing robust governance mechanisms, and establishing responsive frameworks to detect and handle vulnerabilities and breaches.

Given the rising prominence and economic influence of DAOs in the DeFi ecosystem, there is an increasing need to understand these entities better. DAOs have become critical players in shaping the economic landscape of decentralized finance, affecting how value is created, distributed, and exchanged. Therefore, our research aims to investigate what role DAOs play in DeFi attacks. Understanding the interplay between DeFi and DAOs can give valuable insights into the stability and governance of the DeFi ecosystem, offering actionable strategies to bolster its security and resilience. These findings can inform subsequent research questions aimed at addressing the challenges of regulating DeFi and DAOs.

To address our research question about the role of DAOs in DeFi attacks, we conduct empirical studies, beginning with an examination of projects in the attack dataset provided by Zhou et al.,[14] which consists of 181 DeFi attacks that occurred on Ethereum and Binance Smart Chain between April 30, 2018, and April 30, 2022. Excluding duplicate attacks, we find 169 unique instances. Among these, 92 projects featured a DAO or voting mechanism, 72 did not, and 5 were inconclusive. We then examine the response measures adopted by DAOs against attacks, along with specific instances of governance attacks targeting DAOs.

This paper is structured as follows. Part I introduces DeFi and DAOs and offers some background information. Part II delves into the risks of the DeFi ecosystem and the role DAOs play in this complex landscape. Part III delivers the findings of our empirical analysis and interprets the results in the context of our present discussion. Part IV brings our discussion to a close with concluding remarks.

II. DeFi, its Risk Landscape and The Role of DAOs

This Part introduces the phenomena of DeFi, DeFi risks and DAOs. Section 1 outlines the features of DeFi. Section 2 explores DeFi risks, highlighting risk categories and real-world examples. Section 3 defines DAOs, while Section 4 examines their role within the DeFi landscape.

---

[14] *Zhou et al.*, SoK: Decentralized Finance (DeFi) Attacks, Cryptology EPrint Archive, 2022.

1. Features of DeFi

DeFi protocols represent a noteworthy innovation in financial systems, challenging traditional financial models by utilizing smart contracts, and offering decentralized alternatives to traditional financial services.[15] Some even suggests that the convergence of DeFi and web3 could potentially lead to notable changes in future financial infrastructures.[16] Web3 is a term used to describe the evolution of applications on the internet, aiming for decentralized architectures built on technologies such as blockchain and smart contracts. While the original internet was designed for peer-to-peer communication, web3 aims to extend this decentralization to include user data ownership, financial transactions, and more. DeFi can be considered a significant application of the web3 vision, seeking to create more open, transparent, fair, and inclusive financial systems that empower users and communities over traditional intermediaries.[17]

DeFi platforms enable users to access and exchange financial assets without relying on intermediaries, which increases the efficiency of transactions and potentially reduces costs.[18] One key feature of DeFi protocols is their non-custodial nature; unlike traditional financial institutions, these platforms do not hold or manage users' funds. Instead, users retain complete control over their assets, stored in their own digital wallets, which interact directly with the smart contracts.

Typically, users do not need to provide any personal information or credentials to access or use DeFi protocols. Furthermore, the open source and permissionless nature of DeFi protocols allow anyone to audit the code and join or leave the network at will, increasing financial inclusion and offering opportunities to a more diverse range of participants.

DeFi platforms are often championed as catalysts for financial democratization, aspiring to extend financial services to the unbanked or underbanked, thus allowing more inclusive participation in financial activities beyond the confines of traditional banking infrastructures. This inclusivity potentially empowers

---

[15] *Schär*, Decentralized Finance: On Blockchain- and Smart Contract-Based Financial Markets, Federal Reserve Bank of St. Louis Review 103 no. 2, 2021, 153-74.

[16] See *Gapusan*, DeFi: Who Will Build The Future of Finance?, Forbes 2021, https://www.forbes.com/sites/jeffgapusan/2021/11/02/defi-who-will-build-the-future-of-finance/ (25.08.2023).

[17] See e.g., *Zetzsche et al.*, Decentralized Finance, Journal of Financial Regulation, 2020, 6, 183 ("Despite technological limitations of the Bitcoin design, particularly in terms of speed and scalability, DeFi enthusiasts argue that the cryptoanarchist vision which was part of the motivation for Bitcoin is now attainable: the democratization of finance.", "DeFi enthusiasts go beyond technical decentralization. For them, DeFi offers governance structures they perceive as the 'democratization' of finance, while incuments might well view such structures as 'anarchy'.")

[18] *Deshmukh et al.*, Decentralized Finance (DeFi) Policy-Maker Toolkit, World Economic Forum in Collaboration with the Wharton Blockchain and Digital Asset Project, 2021, 6, https://www3.weforum.org/docs/WEF_DeFi_Policy_Maker_Toolkit_2021.pdf (25.08.2023).

individuals in developing regions, or those marginalized from mainstream financial systems to access savings, lending, and investment opportunities previously unavailable to them. However, despite its potential and the advocacies for its democratizing role, the discourse around DeFi's actual effectiveness in making finance more inclusive is ongoing, with varying perspectives on DeFi's capacity to deliver on its promises. While DeFi may reduce the risk of fund misuse or mismanagement by eliminating central authorities, there are numerous other risks inherent in DeFi.

2. DeFi Risks

Despite its many promised advantages, it's crucial to acknowledge that DeFi also presents its own set of challenges and risks, many of which are not yet fully understood. Researchers like Carter and Jeng,[19] point out that these risks are understudied,[20] making the mitigation of these challenges a pressing issue. They also argue that as DeFi becomes mainstream, it will be paramount for regulators and industry to understand the risks that DeFi poses for society and the economy.[21]

Various organizations and researchers have proposed classifications for these risks, providing a framework to comprehend and address them. We will introduce some DeFi risk categories and offer examples of real-life incidents in the DeFi space.

a) DeFi Risk Categories

In a report published in February 2023, the Financial Stability Board (FSB), an intergovernmental body responsible for monitoring and making recommendations about the global financial system, outlined key vulnerabilities associated with DeFi.[22] These vulnerabilities include operational fragilities, liquidity and maturity mismatches, leverage, interconnectedness, concentration, and complexity, as well as other risks like market integrity issues and cross-border regulatory arbitrage. Given the FSB's role in assessing global financial risks, these findings serve as a crucial point of reference for understanding the challenges posed by DeFi's rapid evolution.

Other models and risk categorization offer valuable insight. In Zhou et al.'s threat model taxonomy, DeFi incidents are described as "a series of actions that

---

[19] *Carter/Jeng*, DeFi Protocol Risks: The Paradox of DeFi, Regtech, Suptech and Beyond: Innovation and Technology in Financial Services, RiskBooks 2021, 36.

[20] *Carter/Jeng*, DeFi Protocol Risks: The Paradox of DeFi, Regtech, Suptech and Beyond: Innovation and Technology in Financial Services, RiskBooks 2021, 1.

[21] *Carter/Jeng*, DeFi Protocol Risks: The Paradox of DeFi, Regtech, Suptech and Beyond: Innovation and Technology in Financial Services, RiskBooks 2021, 1.

[22] Financial Stability Board, The Financial Stability Risks of Decentralized Finance, 2023, https://www.fsb.org/2023/02/the-financial-stability-risks-of-decentralised-finance/(25.08.2023).

result in an unexpected financial loss to one or more of the following entities: (i) users; (ii) liquidity providers; (iii) speculators; or (iv) operators".[23] Further subcategories for DeFi incidents distinguish between "attacks" and "accidents", whereby in the former an "attacker" may take advantage of vulnerabilities in either the smart contract, the DeFi protocol design or auxiliary service layers and in the latter proactive adversaries may "not explicitly [be] involved".[24] The lines dividing "attacks" and "accidents" may not always be clear cut.

WEF's and Wharton BDAP's DeFi Policy-Maker Toolkit[25] presents five DeFi risk categories: financial,[26] technical,[27] operational,[28] legal compliance,[29] and emergent.[30] The report distinguishes several related risks in each of these five broader risk categories. Some risks, like liquidity risk, are analogous to those encountered in conventional finance, whereas others are entirely new such as smart contract failures, MEV[31] or flash loans.[32]

---

[23] *Zhou et al.*, SoK: Decentralized Finance (DeFi) Attacks, Cryptology EPrint Archive, 2022, 4.

[24] *Zhou et al.*, SoK: Decentralized Finance (DeFi) Attacks, Cryptology EPrint Archive, 2022, 4 ("For example, a user's fund may become permanently locked in a contract due to unintentional coding mistakes.").

[25] WEF/Wharton BDAP, Decentralized Finance (DeFi) Policy-Maker Toolkit, Whitepaper 2021, https://wifpr.wharton.upenn.edu/wp-content/uploads/2021/06/DeFi-Policy-Maker-Toolkit-Final.pdf (25.08.2023).

[26] See WEF/Wharton BDAP, Decentralized Finance (DeFi) Policy-Maker Toolkit, Whitepaper 2021, 14. Financial risks involve potential fund loss due to market volatility, counterparty defaults, liquidity crunches, or market manipulation.

[27] See WEF/Wharton BDAP, Decentralized Finance (DeFi) Policy-Maker Toolkit, Whitepaper 2021, 15 et seq. Technical risks pertain to software failures or attacks, such as those affecting smart contracts or miners, which may result in DeFi service disruptions or significant financial losses like the 2016 DAO exploit.

[28] See WEF/Wharton BDAP, Decentralized Finance (DeFi) Policy-Maker Toolkit, Whitepaper 2021, 16 et seq. Operational risks are human-system failures or challenges, including maintenance, upgrades, or governance issues, that can cause difficulties in implementing changes or make DeFi services vulnerable to malicious attacks.

[29] See WEF/Wharton BDAP, Decentralized Finance (DeFi) Policy-Maker Toolkit, Whitepaper 2021, 18. Legal compliance risks are associated with illicit activities or regulatory evasion through DeFi, potentially involving money laundering or market manipulation via pseudonymous identities, challenging regulatory enforcement.

[30] See WEF/Wharton BDAP, Decentralized Finance (DeFi) Policy-Maker Toolkit, Whitepaper 2021, 18 et seq. Emergent risks represent systemic instability due to the interaction and scaling of DeFi components, creating potentially complex financial instruments that may cause widespread impacts like a flash loan attack.

[31] MEV, or Miner/Maximal Extractable Value, refers to the measure of the profit a miner (or validator etc.) can make through their ability to arbitrarily include, exclude, or re-order transactions within the blocks they produce. In blockchain ecosystems, especially in Ethereum, MEV has become a prominent issue as it can lead to various forms of exploitation or unfair advantage, impacting the fairness and security of the network. For more on MEV, see https://ethereum.org/en/developers/docs/mev (25.08.2023).

[32] See Knowledge at Wharton, The Opportunities and Dangers of Decentralizing Finance, 2021, https://knowledge.wharton.upenn.edu/article/opportunities-dangers-decentralizing-finance/ (25.08.2023). Flash loans are uncollateralized loans that are borrowed and repaid

Carter and Jeng[33] categorize DeFi risks in five broad risk factors. The first is the risk arising from DeFi's interconnections with the traditional financial system, including bank failures, regulatory actions, and market illiquidity that could impact associated stablecoins or fiat currencies. Additionally, the operational risks deriving from the underlying blockchains are considered, with potential pitfalls such as consensus failures, protocol interventions, and miner or validator manipulation, all of which could compromise the security or functionality of DeFi systems.

The study further highlights the vulnerabilities tied to the usage of smart contracts in DeFi. These encompass technical glitches, oracle attacks, and excessive leverage which can affect the contracts' code or logic. Moreover, governance and regulatory risks pose threats of administrative key abuse, governance attacks, tainted liquidity, or pseudo-equities that might weaken the control mechanisms or legitimacy of DeFi protocols. Lastly, scalability challenges in the form of high transaction fees, low throughput, or network congestion are recognized, which could negatively impact the overall performance and accessibility of DeFi platforms.

These are just some among several risk categorization efforts undertaken across various groups. Multiple models like Zhou et al.'s threat model taxonomy, the WEF's and Wharton BDAP's DeFi Policy-Maker Toolkit, the model presented by Carter and Jeng, and the Financial Stability Board's report have sought to categorize and shed light on these potential pitfalls. These encompass both familiar risks as well as newer, technology-specific risks.

Understanding risks associated with smart contracts and governance mechanisms is important due to their central role in the functioning of DeFi platforms, and any glitches or malicious attacks can have serious consequences. The operational risks deriving from the underlying blockchains such as consensus failures and protocol interventions are equally important, as they can compromise the security or functionality of DeFi systems.

In conclusion, while all the models presented offer valuable insights, FSB's taxonomy provides a comprehensive framework that is globally attuned, making it particularly relevant. However, assimilating insights from the various taxonomies will allow for a more nuanced and holistic understanding of the risks in the DeFi landscape, enabling the development of robust solutions and informed policymaking.

---

within the same transaction, allowing users to execute complex arbitrage or manipulation strategies without upfront capital.

33 *Carter/Jeng*, DeFi Protocol Risks: The Paradox of DeFi, Regtech, Suptech and Beyond: Innovation and Technology in Financial Services, RiskBooks 2021, 6 et seq.

b) Examples of Real-World DeFi Incidents

One of the most prominent and controversial incidents in the history of DAOs and DeFi protocols was the hack of The DAO in 2016, arguably not only the first DAO but also the first attempt at creating a DeFi mechanism. The DAO developers wanted to leverage the technology for a new way of funding and governing decentralized applications (DApps) on the Ethereum blockchain. Additionally, this was also a first attempt to realize Vitalik's concept of a DAO. The DAO was powered by smart contracts, which are self-executing agreements encoded in computer code. It raised over 150 million USD worth of ether (ETH), the native cryptocurrency of Ethereum, in a crowdfunding campaign, considered as one of the largest crowdfunding campaigns of its time,[34] and it attracted thousands of investors from around the world.

However, things took a dark turn when an unknown attacker exploited a re-entrancy bug in The DAO's smart contract code and drained over 50 million USD worth of ether from the fund. This was a devastating blow for The DAO and its investors, and it sparked a heated debate in the Ethereum community about how to deal with the situation. Some argued that code is law, and that the attacker should be allowed to keep the stolen funds, as they were acting within the rules of the smart contract. Others argued that code is not law, and that the funds should be returned to investors. This led to a proposal to conduct a hard fork[35] on Ethereum to undo the attack.

The hard fork proposal was put to a vote by the Ethereum community, and it received majority support. However, not everyone agreed with the hard fork, and some decided to stick with the original version of Ethereum that did not reverse the attack. This resulted in two separate blockchains: Ethereum and Ethereum Classic. Ethereum Classic maintained the original history of transactions, while Ethereum created a new history that erased the attack.

This was a significant event that had major implications for DeFi and Ethereum. It exposed some of the risks and challenges of building decentralized applications on smart contracts, such as security vulnerabilities, governance issues, ethical dilemmas, and community conflicts. It also raised questions about the immutability and censorship-resistance of blockchains.

---

[34] However, it's important to note that despite its initial fundraising success, The DAO did not manage to successfully fund projects that reached fruition. Additionally, while it attracted thousands of investors from around the world, subsequent crowdfunding efforts, have since surpassed it in scale.

[35] A hard fork is a radical change to a blockchain protocol that creates a permanent divergence from the previous version of the protocol. A hard fork requires all nodes or users to upgrade to the latest version of the protocol software. Those who do not upgrade will be left behind on an incompatible network.

After the DAO hack of 2016, the landscape of DeFi has continued to evolve and expand. Along with this growth, unfortunately, have come several notable instances of security breaches and attacks.

For instance, in 2017, an attacker exploited a vulnerability in the smart contract code of Parity, a popular Ethereum wallet, and stole 32 million USD worth of ether from several DeFi projects that used Parity as their wallet provider.[36] Another example is the 2018 attack on Bancor, a decentralized exchange, where an attacker compromised a wallet used by the platform and stole 23.5 million USD worth of ether, Bancor's BNT, and Pundi X's NPXS tokens from the platform.[37]

Some of these attacks also involve the use of flash loans, which are loans that are borrowed and repaid within the same transaction. Flash loans allow users to access large amounts of liquidity without collateral, but they also enable attackers to manipulate prices and exploit arbitrage opportunities. For example, in 2022, an attacker used flash loans to exploit Cream Finance, a lending protocol, and stole 130 million USD worth of cryptocurrency from the platform.[38]

In May 2023 the Tornado Cash DAO[39] was attacked by an unknown entity that managed to gain full control over its governance state via a malicious proposal granting it more than a million votes.[40] The attacker then submitted a proposal to undo their attack and return governance control back to the community.[41] The attacker's motives were unclear, but some speculated that they were trying to manipulate the price of TORN or test the security of the protocol.

Each highlighted incident reveals distinct vulnerabilities and challenges within DeFi, contributing uniquely to the evolution of this space. The DAO Hack in 2016 triggered philosophical debates and led to structural changes in Ethereum. The 2017 Parity and 2018 Bancor attacks illuminated critical security vulnerabilities in wallet software and decentralized exchanges, emphasizing the need for robust security protocols across diverse applications and platforms. Cream Finance's 2022 exploit unveiled the risks associated with innovative

[36] See *Zhao*, $30 Million: Ether Reported Stolen Due to Parity Wallet Breach, Coindesk, 2017, https://www.coindesk.com/markets/2017/07/19/30-million-ether-reported-stolen-due-to-parity-wallet-breach/ (25.08.2023).

[37] See *Russell*, The crypto world's latest hack sees Bancor lose $23.5M, TechCrunch, 2018, https://techcrunch.com/2018/07/10/bancor-loses-23-5m breach (25.08.2023).

[38] See *Copeland*, Ethereum DeFi protocol Cream Finance hacked for more than $130 million, The Block 2022, https://www.theblock.co/post/122241/ethereum-defi-protocol-cream-finance-hacked-for-115-million (25.08.2023).

[39] Tornado Cash is a privacy-preserving protocol that allows users to send anonymous transactions on Ethereum. The Tornado Cash DAO is distinct from the Tornado Cash mixer. In 2022, the Tornado Cash mixer was sanctioned by OFAC.

[40] See *Sarkar*, Attacker hijacks Tornado Cash governance via malicious proposal, Coindesk, 2023, https://cointelegraph.com/news/attacker-hijacks-tornado-cash-governance-via-malicious-proposal (25.08.2023).

[41] See *Nwaokocha*, Tornado Cash governance control set to be restored as voters approve proposal, Coindesk 2023, https://cointelegraph.com/news/tornado-cash-governance-control-set-to-be-restored-as-token-votes-approve-proposal (25.08.2023).

DeFi instruments like flash loans, stressing the substantial financial repercussions of such vulnerabilities. Finally, the 2023 Tornado Cash DAO incident spotlighted the complexities and potential frailties in decentralized governance, emphasizing the diverse motivations behind such attacks. Each incident can serve as a lesson to refine governance and security frameworks in DeFi and their DAO ecosystems.

3. What are DAOs?

DeFi and DAOs are not just new technologies. They are new modes of organizing and governing economic activity. They challenge the existing legal and regulatory frameworks that have been designed for a different world – a world of centralized intermediaries, custodial services, and jurisdictional boundaries.

DAOs and DeFi protocols are new dynamic phenomena that do not always correspond to traditional notions of corporations, legal contracts, assets, or financial services. Moreover, DAOs and DeFi protocols may change over time, as they evolve through governance decisions, code updates or forks.

There is no universally accepted or standardized definition of DAOs and DeFi protocols, as various stakeholders may have different perspectives. For example, developers may focus on the technical features and functionalities, while regulators may be more interested in the legal implications and consequences of DeFi and DAOs.

A possible definition for DAOs is that they are a new form of internet-native organization represented by rules and decision processes encoded via blockchain technology using smart contracts. DAOs, in essence, can be seen as blockchain-based, open-source systems that operate through smart contracts and are governed by token holders' consensus, primarily to achieve a democratic governance structure that guides the developmental trajectory of the platform.

In a DAO, the process typically consists of a set of programmed rules or protocols allowing members to propose, discuss, and vote on decisions and changes related to the project.[42] Users typically become members by purchasing or earning tokens related to the DAO. These tokens usually represent voting power within the organization. DAO members can submit proposals for changes, new features, developments, or any other modifications to the organization or its governing protocols. Any submitted proposals are subject to discussion and scrutiny by the community, allowing for a thorough examination of their merits and disadvantages. This can occur on various platforms such as forums, chat groups, or other communication channels associated with the DAO.

Finally, members vote on proposals using their tokens, where one token may represent one vote. However, different models and voting structures exist. Some

---

[42] See e.g., snapshot, which is a popular voting service, https://snapshot.org (25.08.2023).

DAOs may have a quorum requirement, meaning a minimum number of votes is needed for the proposal to go through. If a proposal receives enough support (meets the required quorum and receives more affirmative than negative votes), the proposed changes are either automatically executed by the smart contract or are taken forward for implementation. The specifics of how a proposal is executed can vary depending on the rules encoded in the DAO's smart contracts.

4. DAOs in the DeFi Ecosystem

As new internet-native modes of organization, DAOs can be seen as a new form of organizational structure that challenges traditional models.[43] DAOs are designed to enable collective decision-making and coordination among participants. They thus enable communities to coordinate their activities in a more open and transparent way, minimizing trust. DAOs in the DeFi space play three key roles. First, they decentralize decision-making, allowing participants to shape the direction of DeFi protocols directly, without traditional intermediaries. Second, they promote innovation, providing a platform for creating and testing new DeFi products and services. They facilitate resource sharing and foster partnerships across different DAOs and protocols. Lastly, DAOs may encourage inclusivity by allowing anyone with internet access and a compatible digital wallet to join, thereby giving interested users the opportunity to benefit from and contribute to DeFi protocols. Nevertheless, the realization of these key benefits is not always guaranteed. Issues can arise when governance becomes concentrated in the hands of a select few, undermining the principle of decentralized decision-making. Similarly, if DAOs and DeFi protocols do not offer genuine opportunities for user involvement, the potential for inclusivity can be significantly diminished.

By transitioning control and ownership to the broader community, developers may wish to distance themselves from the purview of regulatory scrutiny and legal responsibility, not only in the U.S. but across various jurisdictions worldwide. For example, bZx Protocol developers stated that the creation of a DAO would insulate the Protocol "from regulatory oversight and accountability for compliance with U.S. law,"[44]. However, this may not always be the case, as some DAOs have faced legal challenges and lawsuits from users and/or regulators.

[43] See e.g., Ethereum Foundation, Decentralized autonomous organizations (DAOs), https://ethereum.org/en/dao (25.08.2023).

[44] See *Drylewski et al.*, Court Ruling Could Affect the Future Direction of DAOs, Insights, Skadden, Arps, Slate, Meagher & Flom LLP 2023, https://www.skadden.com/insights/publications/2023/04/court-ruling-could-affect-the-future-direction-of-daos (25.08.2023).

III. Empirical Analysis

We investigate real-world DeFi attacks to examine the involvement of DAOs. The dataset[45] consists of 181 DeFi attacks that happened on Ethereum and Binance Smart Chain (BSC) between April 30, 2018, and April 30, 2022 (four years). These attacks were reported on internet websites, predominantly Rekt News,[46] SlowMist,[47] PeckShield,[48] and Medium.[49]

1. Method

This Section describes the method and findings of the empirical analysis conducted in this study.

a) Data Collection

To examine the involvement of DAOs in DeFi attacks, we analyzed whether the 169 projects in the attack event dataset[50] (totaling 181 attack events, with some projects attacked multiple times) used DAOs or similar voting mechanisms for governance. We used three information channels to make this determination:

1. We looked for information or subpages related to "Governance", "Vote", or "DAO" on the official project website.
2. We used Twitter's advanced search function to find tweets of exploited projects containing the keywords: "Governance," "vote," or "DAO" within a timeframe from one month before the attack event to one month after.
3. We searched Google for content containing the keywords "project name" + "Governance," "vote," or "DAO".

After uncovering attacked projects with DAOs, we selected the ten most recent ones from the dataset for case studies, in order to examine the way in which DAOs are involved in attacks.

b) Findings

Ultimately, we found that out of the 169 attacked projects, 92 had a DAO or a similar voting governance mechanism, 72 did not adopt a DAO, and 5 projects were inconclusive due to broken official website links and deactivation of Twitter accounts.

---

[45] *Zhou et al.*, Sok: Decentralized finance (defi) attacks, Cryptology ePrint Archive 2022.
[46] rekt. https://rekt.news/ (25.08.2023).
[47] SlowMist Hacked, https://hacked.slowmist.io/en/ (25.08.2023).
[48] PeckShield, https://peckshield.medium.com (25.08.2023).
[49] Medium, https://medium.com (25.08.2023).
[50] *Zhou et al.*, Sok: Decentralized finance (defi) attacks, Cryptology ePrint Archive 2022.

More than half of the attacked projects have DAOs or some form of voting and governance mechanism, a fact that underscores the widespread acceptance and adoption of DAOs within the DeFi ecosystem. However, it's important to note that the existence of a DAO within an attacked project does not necessarily imply that the DAO directly participated in handling and responding to the attack.

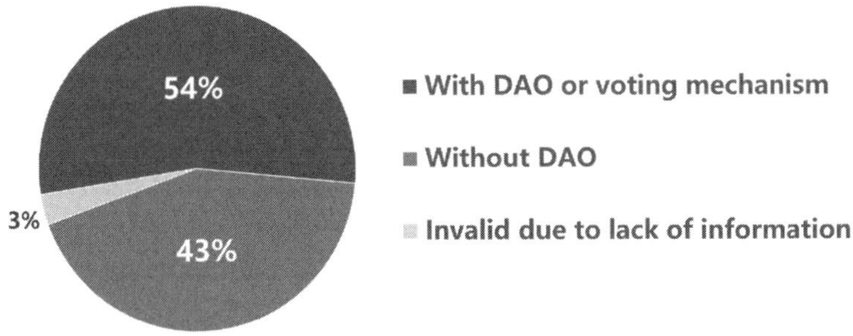

Figure 1. Breakdown of attacked DeFi projects based on the presence of DAOs or voting mechanisms

2. Systematizing DAO Involvement in DeFi Attacks

In DeFi, DAOs shape the dynamics of community-driven governance mechanisms and protocols. The governance vote is indeed the overt function of DAOs, as it permits participants to propose, discuss, and implement changes; however, the scope of DAOs extends beyond governance. They inherently encapsulate functions related to the management, organization, and security of DeFi platforms, rendering them pivotal in sustaining the platform's integrity and operational flow.

This Section delineates the involvement of DAOs in DeFi attacks, with a focus on their roles and responses either before, during, or after the attack, providing a systematic analysis on how the characteristics and functionality of DAOs are intertwined with the attack vectors and mitigation measures of DeFi platforms. A nuanced understanding of DAO participation is indispensable, as it sheds light on the implications of their decisions and interventions on the security and resilience of DeFi ecosystems.

We selected the six most recently attacked projects within the data set that had a DAO governance system, which are:

1. Yearn Finance[51]
2. Beanstalk Farms[52]

[51] YearnFinance, https://yearn.finance (25.08.2023).
[52] Beanstalk Farm, https://beanstalk.farm (25.08.2023).

3. Badger-DAO[53]
4. Bancor DAO[54]
5. Value DeFi[55]
6. PiDAO[56].

For each project, we visited its corresponding governance page, looked at all proposal themes from the inception of the DAO organization to March 2023, and summarized and organized these themes.

Organizational Level
Personnel Management Governance Mechanism Updates Treasury Pool Management
Project Level
Modifying Protocol Parameters Version Updates
Community Level
Event Organization Inter-project Collaboration

Table 1: Types of Proposals in DAOs

We have summarized the recurring proposal themes in DAOs into three levels: Organization Level, Project Level, and Community Level (see Table 1).

The Organization Level refers to adjustments in the governance mechanisms and personnel structure of the DAO organization itself. For example, Yearn Finance's YIP-61[57] and YIP-62[58] proposals aim to address governance enhancements within the DAO, while BeanStalk Farms Proposal BFP-65[59] focuses on making hiring decisions and is thus concerned with personnel management. The Project Level primarily involves the management of protocol parameters

[53] Badger DAO, https://badger.com (25.08.2023).

[54] BancorDAO, https://forum.badger.finance (25.08.2023).

[55] ValueDeFi, https://valuedefi.io (25.08.2023).

[56] PiDAO, https://www.pidao.finance (25.08.2023).

[57] YearnFinance, YIP-61: Governance 2.0 – Proposals, https://gov.yearn.fi/t/yip-61-governance-2-0/10460 (25.08.2023).

[58] YearnFinance, YIP 62 Contribute to the nomic foundation, https://gov.yearn.fi/t/yip-62-change-two-multisig-signers/10758 (25.08.2023).

[59] Beanstalk Farm, Proposal: BFP-65: Hire Beasley and Pay Retroactively (snapshot.org), https://snapshot.org/#/beanstalkfarms.eth/proposal/0xe8564cb73e098193fcc6470a1216a7192b9edce093422864f48e1ffc2b01f78a (25.08.2023).

and version updates, which are essential for the smooth operation of the DeFi protocol. The Community Level involves collaboration and communication between different protocols, such as Bancor DAO's whitelist updates,[60] as well as the organization of activities within the user community, as seen in BancorDAO's BIP 34.[61]

When confronting attack incidents, the resolutions put forth by DAOs in the form of e.g., emergency responses and post-incident rectifications, may focus on any of the proposal levels, from Organizational, to Project and Community Levels.

Proposals emerging at the Community Level are chiefly characterized by user compensation and the institution or allocation of White Hat bounties. BadgerDAO, for example, created an ambitious restitution plan.[62] In contrast, the proposals at the Project Level are designed to mend and enhance the protocol coding subsequent to an attack. For instance, BeanStalk initiated a proposal for a thorough re-audit of its smart contracts.[63]

A hybrid Community and Organizational level proposal took place after Inverse Finance suffered an attack in April 2022. A proposal was put to the vote to form a risk working group.[64] Shortly after the execution of this proposal, another proposal was put to the vote to fully compensate users affected by the April attack.[65]

These varied responses show the adaptive nature of DAOs in steering through crises and in assuring the sustained progression of the project, thereby accentuating their resilient attributes.

---

[60] See BancorDAO, https://gov.bancor.network/t/proposal-to-determine-whitelisting-status-of-sbtc-on-bancor-v3/3680, see also https://vote.bancor.network/#/proposal/0xf68058a221c25f02c1438680b9c9174176ed4c472113bb869ac30139c1191327 (25.08.2023).

[61] BancorDAO, BIP 34: Meme Competition for WenDIGG – BIP, Badger Improvement Proposals, https://forum.badger.finance/t/bip-34-meme-competition-for-wendigg/2728 (25.08.2023).

[62] See *Thurman*, After $130M Hack, Badger's Restitution Plan Tests Limits of DAO Governance, Coindesk 2021, https://www.coindesk.com/tech/2021/12/16/after-130m-hack-badgers-restitution-plan-tests-limits-of-dao-governance/ (25.08.2023).

[63] See BFP-66: Hire Halborn to Perform Audit, April 22, 2022, https://snapshot.org/#/beanstalkfarms.eth/proposal/0x54fad9c756daa38bb4bafadbee2cea6cb98f380fe2d6a62fdf723d0b15430d42 (25.08.2023). The Beanstalk DAO also wanted to strengthen the governance structure by switching to a community-run multisig wallet custodied by nine Beanstalk community members until a more resilient governance mechanism was developed, audited and implemented. See Brandy Betz, Beanstalk Stablecoin Protocol "Barn Raise" aims to restore $77M in lost funds, Coindesk 2022, https://www.coindesk.com/business/2022/06/02/beanstalk-stablecoin-protocol-barn-raise-aims-to-restore-77m-in-lost-funds/ (25.08.2023).

[64] See Inverse Finance, Proposal To Form a Risk Working Group, 2022, https://www.inverse.finance/governance/proposals/mills/22; see also https://forum.inverse.finance/t/proposal-to-form-a-risk-working-group/119/1 (25.08.2023).

[65] See Inverse Finance, Proposed Make-Good For Users Affected by April 2, 2022 Price Manipulation Incident, 2022 https://www.inverse.finance/governance/proposals/mills/28 (25.08.2023).

Table 2 beneath shows the different forms of involvement throughout distinct phases of an attack, each illustrated with pertinent incidents.

Category	Time	DAO's Role	Example
DeFi Attack Response Mechanism	Before an Attack	Preventive measures	Fei FIP82[66]
	During an Attack	Emergency DAOs	Curve Emergency DAO[67]
	After an Attack	Rescue Plans, Future Risk Proofing	InverseFinance Proposal 28[68]
DAO Attack	N/A	DAO as Target	Beanstalk BIP18/19[69]

Table 2: Involvement of Decentralized Autonomous Organizations (DAOs) in DeFi Attacks

This section analyzes how DAOs engage with DeFi security incidents, exploring their strategies to impact, mitigate, or resolve breaches. It highlights DAOs' critical roles in shaping security frameworks within the DeFi ecosystem.

a) Before an Attack

DAOs within DeFi platforms allow for a collective approach towards risk management and security. DAOs, as part of their governance functionality, regularly propose Improvement Proposals (IPs) to preventively address potential security breaches and bolster the platform's defenses. These IPs are pivotal as they act as a collective resolution mechanism that aims to identify and mitigate risks related to security vulnerabilities, thus serving as an integral component in safeguarding the DeFi ecosystem from prospective attacks.

In our case studies, the emphasis on IPs is not just tangential; rather, it holds significance in fortifying platforms through diverse strategies such as establishing Bug Bounty programs, procuring services of audit firms, and refining governance structures. These Improvement Proposals are strategic initiatives that exemplify the proactive stance of DAOs in enhancing the resilience and security robustness of DeFi platforms.

---

[66] Fei, FIP-82: Governance Enhancements, https://snapshot.fei.money/#/proposal/0x463fd1be98d9e86c83eb845ca7e2a5555387e3c86ca0b756aada17a11df87f2b (25.08.2023).

[67] Curve Emergency DAO, https://dao.curve.fi/emergencymembers (25.08.2023).

[68] See Inverse Finance Governance Proposals, https://www.inverse.finance/governance/proposals (25.08.2023).

[69] BIP18: Beanstalk Exploit – A Simplified Post-Mortem Analysis, https://medium.com/coinmonks/beanstalk-exploit-a-simplified-post-mortem-analysis-92e6cdb17ace (25.08.2023).

A notable example is the Fei Protocol's "Governance Enhancement" initiative, proposed on March 9, 2022.[70] This initiative was not a simple amendment; it represented a paradigmatic shift aiming to overhaul the existing Optimistic Approval process by adopting a Council approach. In essence, the proposition involved the establishment of a Tribal Council entrusted with proposing and approving governance actions. This alteration was not trivial; it was designed to mitigate prevalent issues such as voter apathy, lack of community context, and barriers to participation like gas fees by ensuring a streamlined and inclusive governance process. The significance of shifting to a Council approach composed of Tribe DAO community members lies in its ability to provide a structured, organized, and transparent governance model. Unlike non-DAO DeFi or traditional financial (TradFi) protocols, which often are centralized and lack community-driven governance mechanisms, the Tribe DAO community Council approach enables a collective, consensus-driven governance model. This is instrumental in addressing and resolving potential discrepancies, conflicts, and risks, allowing for a more agile and responsive decision-making process. In the Tribal Council model, a collective body has the responsibility to thoroughly deliberate upon, scrutinize, and assess the proposed actions, ensuring that every decision is well-informed, balanced, and reflective of the community's interests and needs. This approach follows the Liquid Representative Democracy model, which aims to be more democratic and inclusive, allowing for a diverse range of perspectives and inputs to be considered.

Regrettably, a conspicuous absence of comprehensive emergency plans was observed across the studied projects. This lack of preemptive planning to address potential losses and impacts on the project's ecosystem due to hacker attacks underscores a critical vulnerability. It highlights the necessity for DAOs to not only concentrate on enhancing governance structures but also to develop robust contingency plans to effectively navigate and mitigate the repercussions of unanticipated security breaches.

The initiation of Improvement Proposals by DAOs and the shift towards more structured governance models, like the Tribal Council approach, signify the proactive and strategic efforts made within the DeFi sector to curb potential threats and vulnerabilities. However, the general lack of emergency plans reveals a critical gap that needs careful attention and calls for a holistic approach to security and risk management that combines proactive risk mitigation with strategic response mechanisms.

---

[70] Fei, FIP-82: Governance Enhancements, https://snapshot.fei.money/#/proposal/0x463fd1be98d9e86c83eb845ca7e2a5555387e3c86ca0b756aada17a11df87f2b (25.08.2023).

b) During an Attack

DAOs facilitate community-driven governance within DeFi ecosystems. While their decentralized nature offers an avenue for collective decision-making, the challenges associated with this decentralization become palpable during security breaches or attacks, where the urgency and immediacy of responses are imperative to mitigate losses. Thus, an important aspect to examine is how DAOs, traditionally reliant on community consensus, reconcile the need for swift actions during emergencies with the principles of decentralized governance.

An example that illustrates such a reconciliation is Curve's Emergency DAO.[71] Structured as a specialized arm within the project's overall DAO, the Emergency DAO is configured with nine members who are democratically elected by CurveDAO. This entity is vested with unparalleled authority during crisis scenarios where the risk of losing funds is imminent. In such instances, the Emergency DAO holds the prerogative to suspend all project functionalities, sparing only the withdrawal feature.

The embodiment of such an emergency mechanism is emblematic of a strategic resolution to counterbalance the inherent limitations of DAOs in terms of response agility. Given that DAOs necessitate public voting for decision-making, this often becomes a bottleneck during crisis scenarios, impeding the immediate execution of countermeasures. Curve's Emergency DAO, by circumventing the prolonged deliberations associated with public voting, ensures a timely intervention, thereby mitigating the potential escalations of the attack's impacts.

However, the inception of such an emergency mechanism also beckons a slew of controversies and debates surrounding the ethos of decentralization intrinsic to DAOs. The empowerment of a select group with elevated privileges during emergencies sparks discussions on the paradox of centralization within decentralized entities. This duality brings forth crucial questions about the sanctity of decentralization in DeFi projects and opens dialogues on the extent to which concessions on decentralization are justifiable in the pursuit of security and operational stability.

This mechanism reflects a tradeoff between decentralized governance and the necessity for instantaneous decisions during crises. Addressing this point, it is imperative to understand that the incorporation of mechanisms like the Emergency DAO doesn't inherently negate the principles of decentralization. Rather, it acts as a pragmatic adaptation to the operational exigencies that demand immediate resolutions.

In essence, the deployment of such mechanisms is an acknowledgment of the varying demands of different operational scenarios within DeFi platforms. It is a nuanced approach aimed at preserving the foundational ethos of decentraliza-

[71] Curve Emergency DAO, https://dao.curve.fi/emergencymembers (25.08.2023).

tion while ensuring the adaptability and responsiveness of the system in the face of unforeseen security breaches. The quest here is about fostering a harmonious coexistence between decentralization and the imperative for swift, decisive actions in critical situations.

The implementation of emergency response mechanisms like Curve's Emergency DAO encapsulates the ongoing endeavors to refine and optimize the governance structures within DeFi ecosystems, addressing the intrinsic tensions between decentralized governance and the necessity for quick, effective responses during security incidents. This dialectic between centralization and decentralization in DeFi DAO governance models is reflective of their pursuit to reconcile operational efficiency with foundational principles.

c) After an Attack

The aftermath of an attack on DeFi platforms involves a meticulous response management to contain and rectify the damages incurred. It is within this critical juncture that DAOs play an important role in orchestrating comprehensive response strategies. These strategies span across multiple facets including devising immediate rescue plans, formulating equitable user compensation frameworks, implementing security rectifications, and conceptualizing long-term enhancements for bolstering the project's security. All these elements are integral to re-establishing operational normalcy and rebuilding user trust post-attack.

Illustrative of such post-attack management is the approach adopted by Inverse Finance following a price manipulation attack on its oracle.[72] The community-led governance system was swift in proposing a series of counteractive measures aimed at restoring stability and mitigating further damages. On April 3rd, 2022, Inverse Finance's governance community introduced Proposal 19, suggesting a substantial reduction of INV rewards for several assets to re-establish DOLA DEX liquidity, followed by a sequence of additional proposals targeting different aspects of the platform's recovery and user compensation.[73]

Proposal 19 articulated a specific strategy focusing on restoring liquidity by altering the reward dynamics for various assets, showcasing a precise and targeted approach to liquidity management post-attack. Subsequently, Proposal 20, introduced on April 4th, was aimed at curtailing the burgeoning bad debt by temporarily setting the rates for several assets to zero, a necessary measure to arrest the daily increment of $20,000 in bad debt.[74] The unanimous approval of

---

[72] Inverse Finance, https://www.inverse.finance (25.08.2023).

[73] See Inverse Finance, Proposal 19, https://www.inverse.finance/governance/proposals/mills/19 (25.08.2023).

[74] See Inverse Finance, Proposal 20, https://www.inverse.finance/governance/proposals/mills/20 (25.08.2023).

this proposal underscores the community's consensus on the urgency and importance of such immediate interventions.

Beyond immediate interventions, Inverse Finance also emphasized addressing the impacts on its user base. Proposal 28, unveiled on May 8th, delineated a comprehensive compensation plan, signifying the DAO's commitment to uphold user interests and ensure equitable redressal for those affected by the attack.[75] This proposal manifested the holistic approach of Inverse Finance, combining immediate mitigative actions with long-term user-centric solutions, portraying a balanced and responsible post-attack management strategy.

Moreover, the series of proposals tabled by Inverse Finance also highlighted the importance of fortifying the project's security framework to preclude future incidents. This included considerations for conducting fresh audits and establishing more robust bug bounty programs, reflecting a forward-looking approach that seeks to intertwine immediate recovery with sustained resilience.[76] The integration of such measures is indicative of the DAO's resolve to continually refine and enhance the platform's security posture, emphasizing a progressive and proactive stance in aftermath management.

The involvement of DAOs in the aftermath of an attack can serve as the nexus for initiating multifaceted response strategies based on the communities' wishes. Inverse Finance exemplifies the diverse and comprehensive approach necessitated post-attack, balancing immediate interventions with user compensation and long-term security enhancements. The unanimous and swift adoption of multiple proposals shows the collective resolve of the community to restore operational stability and fortify the platform against future vulnerabilities. It underscores the inherent strength of decentralized governance in merging diverse insights to forge cohesive recovery and enhancement pathways, essential for sustaining trust in the evolving DeFi landscape.

d) Special Case of DAO Attacks

While DAOs play an important role in defining and implementing the governance structures of various DeFi platforms, their inherent design mechanisms are not immune to exploitation. The DAOs' public and transparent nature, coupled with the possibility of flaws in their governance structures or smart contract implementations, can render them susceptible to malevolent attacks. Intruders, exploiting price manipulations of governance tokens or leveraging logical vulnerabilities, can ingeniously pass and execute malicious proposals, potentially

---

[75] See Inverse Finance, Proposal 28, https://www.inverse.finance/governance/proposals/mills/28 (25.08.2023).

[76] See e.g., Inverse Finance, Proposal 32 on additional funding for security related services, https://www.inverse.finance/governance/proposals/mills/32 (25.08.2023).

leading to severe financial ramifications and undermining the treasury governed by the DAO.

A glaring instance of such vulnerabilities being exploited occurred in the attack on the yield farming protocol, Beanstalk Farms, in April 2022.[77] The attacker manipulated the protocol's democratic governance mechanism by creating two deceptive proposals, BIP18 and BIP19, under the guise of philanthropic intents. BIP18, disguised with the humanitarian cause of "donating to Ukraine," was a mere empty shell, harboring no content or real intention to donate. In contrast, BIP19 was a more intricate deceptive proposal, designed with a contract that benefited the attacker while maintaining the façade of contributing to Ukraine. This incident unraveled the potential of exploiting the DAO's transparent and open mechanism for malevolent gains and emphasized the need for meticulous scrutiny and verification of proposals.

Similarly, the incident involving Tornado Cash[78] underscored the critical vulnerabilities in DAO governance, where a malicious actor, through a meticulously crafted governance proposal, seized control over both the DAO and the protocol.[79] This unscrupulous control enabled the malefactor to withdraw tokens from the governance contract and even launder money through the protocol.[80] Although control was subsequently relinquished, the exploitation highlighted some methods by which attackers could manipulate decentralized governance mechanisms to their advantage.

These incidents serve as stark reminders of the potential exploitations that can permeate through DAOs. The subversion of governance mechanisms by leveraging manipulative and deceptive proposals emphasizes the need for robust validation mechanisms and heightened vigilance within the community. The adaptability and resilience of DAOs are contingent on the continuous refinement of their governance structures, aiming to strike a balance between openness and security. The assimilation of multi-layered validation processes, rigorous auditing of smart contracts, and the integration of advanced security protocols are imperative to bolster the resilience of DAOs. Enhanced community awareness and participation in governance mechanisms can act as additional safeguards against deceptive proposals, ensuring the integrity and credibility of

---

[77] BIP18: Beanstalk Exploit – A Simplified Post-Mortem Analysis, https://medium.com/coinmonks/beanstalk-exploit-a-simplified-post-mortem-analysis-92e6cdb17ace (25.08.2023).

[78] Tornado Cash has reportedly been used by North Korean hacking group Lazarus Group to launder at least 450 million USD. The mixing service has been sanctioned by OFAC and some of its smart contract addresses were put on the OFAC list.

[79] See *Malwa*, Tornado Cash DAO Attacker Starts to Move Ether, TORN Tokens, Coindesk 2023, https://www.coindesk.com/tech/2023/05/25/tornado-cash-dao-attacker-starts-to-move-ether-torn-tokens/ (25.08.2023).

[80] See *Mutunkei*, Hacker drops control over Tornado Cash as they use it to wash stolen funds, Crypto News 2023, https://crypto.news/hacker-drops-control-over-tornado-cash-as-they-use-it-to-wash-stolen-funds (20.06.2023)

the decentralized governance model. These combined efforts will be instrumental in preserving the ethos of decentralization while mitigating the risks associated with potential exploitations and vulnerabilities in DAOs.

IV. Conclusion

Our research aimed to investigate the roles of DAOs in the Decentralized Finance ecosystem, focusing on their roles in an illustrative data set of attacks that plagued the ecosystem and DAOs' responses to such exploits. DeFi, a disruptive innovation in the financial world, reached considerable growth with a Total Value Locked (TVL) peaking at around 180 billion USD in 2022, despite suffering a series of significant setbacks, including relentless hacking incidents and other financial risks.

We find that of 169 attacked DeFi projects in our data set, 92 had a DAO or voting mechanism, highlighting the critical presence and influence of DAOs in the DeFi space. DAOs are not just a concept but are practical components in the management and governance of DeFi projects. Our empirical analysis revealed vulnerabilities both in the direct functionalities of DeFi services and the governance systems managed by DAOs. Attackers exploited these vulnerabilities to manipulate outcomes or drain funds, proving that the underlying smart contract and governance mechanisms are critical points of concern.

Bad actors often exploit governance systems by manipulating votes to pass favorable decisions, revealing the need for stronger, more secure governance structures that can resist malicious actors and ensure the integrity of collective decision-making processes. DAOs, despite being susceptible to attacks, have actively worked on enforcing rigorous code audits and implementing robust governance mechanisms. They are the frontline defense in preventing and mitigating various forms of attacks and are pivotal in establishing responsive frameworks for detected vulnerabilities and breaches.

The interrelation between DeFi and DAOs is intricate, with DAOs shaping the economic landscape of decentralized finance. Understanding this interplay gives valuable insights into the stability, governance, and future developments of the DeFi ecosystem.

Our findings underscore the importance of strong, resilient DAOs for the security, stability, and growth of the DeFi ecosystem. DAOs must focus on enhancing their governance structures and decision-making processes to counteract attacks effectively. Rigorous and frequent code audits, robust governance models, and proactive vulnerability detection and management are crucial to maintaining integrity and user trust.

Enhanced security measures and continuous improvements in governance systems will not only prevent the exploitation of vulnerabilities but will also ensure the sustainable development of DeFi projects, helping them to realize their full potential in revolutionizing the financial sector.

Furthermore, the evolving nature of DAOs and their increasing economic influence necessitate further research. Subsequent studies should address the regulatory challenges surrounding DeFi and DAOs, aiming to create a more resilient and inclusive financial ecosystem.

In conclusion, DAOs, with their decentralized and transparent nature, are integral components in the realization of the promises of DeFi, acting as the guardians of decentralization and user participation. While they are vulnerable to attacks and exploitations, their continuous improvement and adaptation are essential in overcoming these challenges and ensuring the development of a secure and stable DeFi ecosystem.

The Case for Taxing DAOs

Challenges, Methods, and Impossibility

António Rocha Mendes

Abstract The article explores the rationale for imposing taxes on decentralized autonomous organizations (DAOs) while highlighting the unique challenges posed by their lack of centralized structure and geographical location. Despite similarities to traditional corporations, the decentralized nature of DAOs complicates taxation within existing frameworks designed for entities with identifiable locations. The first section argues for taxing DAOs based on principles of equality and the ability to pay, emphasizing parallels with traditional business operations and the need for income tax on generated profits.

The second section delves into the challenges of taxing DAOs within the current international tax system, considering the limitations of existing frameworks for brick-and-mortar businesses and the complexities introduced by the digital economy. The article anticipates increased scrutiny of DAOs in the future despite their stateless and decentralized operation. The third section proposes potential methods for taxing DAOs' income, evaluating the feasibility of taxing the DAO directly or its participants. However, enforcing taxation on participants in different sovereign countries poses significant challenges, requiring international cooperation and effective audit mechanisms. In conclusion, the article acknowledges the compelling case for taxing DAOs but emphasizes the inadequacy of current tax systems for entities operating in a decentralized manner, presenting a complex issue that demands innovative solutions within the global regulatory landscape.

I. The Case for Taxing DAOs

We believe there is a strong case to tax DAO's profits.

Let's start with the general principle of equality between the members of the community. This requires that the tax burden (revenue used to fund public services, infrastructure, social programs, defense, and other essential functions of government) be shared equally among them. This means, in practice, that everyone must contribute, but that the contribution should be based on the capacity of each member of the community. In technical words, taxes should be borne equally by those with the same ability to pay (horizontal equality), but unequally by those with different ability to pay, in proportion to this difference (vertical equality).

The need to raise resources from the members of the community and the obligation to share the burden equitably forced governments to: (i) find manifestations of the community members' ability to pay (what is taxed), and (ii) define who pays the tax (the taxpayers).

1. Manifestations of the Ability to Pay (Taxing Business Profits)

The first task is to find manifestations of the ability to pay that justify the transfer of private resources to the public sphere. The relevant manifestations of the ability to pay are to be found in the different phases of the wealth cycle: in its creation (income), in its maintenance (assets), and upon its destruction (consumption). Income taxes are taxes on the creation of wealth.

Business enterprises consist of factors of production organized by entrepreneurs for profit. Economically, profits are income and represent the creation of wealth to the entrepreneur. Profit is, therefore, identified by the tax system as a manifestation of the entrepreneur's ability to pay. This is why business profits are subject to income tax.

Similarly to other forms of organizations, DAOs' purpose might be carrying out a business enterprise for profit. The business income may result from providing services, earning transaction fees, or holding assets that appreciate. Successful businesses will generate profits. If a certain government has decided to tax business profits, there are no reasons to exempt the DAO's profits from income tax.

2. Who Pays the Tax (Taxpayers)

The second task is to define who should pay the tax on the business profits. The issues here are: (i) should some business organizations (entities) be taxed separately from its owners and, if so, (ii) which should be taxed autonomously?

a) Does it make sense to tax entities?

To answer this question, we must first understand what business entities are and why they are autonomous from their owners.

Let's start with the simple case of sole proprietorship. Sole proprietors of businesses are the owners of the enterprise's assets. It is the individual proprietor that owns the business assets and that carries out the business activity. The business profits are integrated into their individual income.

However, modern business is mostly carried out by large groups of owners, not sole proprietors. In most businesses (think of listed entities or even DAOs), the owners and the business assets are patrimonial and functionally separated. The business is an autonomous economic unit, separated from its owners, that is susceptible to being the legal owner of its assets, activities, and income. These forms of business organizations are generally referred to as "business entities".

The tax system recognizes this functional and patrimonial autonomy. As a result, business entities have tax personalities, i.e. they are taxpayers in their own capacity. The recognition of the separation of owners and businesses, through the "interposition" of an entity, is the first reason why business entities are autonomously subject to tax.

It is true that, sooner or later, all the business profit realized by these entities will be appropriated by their owners, which usually occurs through its distribution (in the case of companies via dividends). So, why not wait until such distribution to tax the business profits?

The reason is that the "interposition" of the entity causes a tax deferral effect for the owners, which has serious consequences in terms of equality and government revenue. If the owners kept the profits in the entity, the tax would be indefinitely postponed. This would incentivize businesses to retain profits at the entity level, even if they could be employed in more profitable investments.

b) Does it Make Sense to Tax All Entities Autonomously?

So, now that we know that it makes sense to tax entities autonomously, the question is if it makes sense to treat all forms of business entities equally.

The fact is that not all business organizations separate the business from the owners. That separation varies according to the specific circumstances of the business and the agreement between the owners. And that effect has little connection to the legal form of the business or its legal personality. The interposition of a business entity with legal personality does not necessarily mean that there is a high degree of separation between the entrepreneur and the business, just as such a relevant separation may well exist as an effect of a depersonalized entity (think of investment funds, where all the investors are co-owners of the investment assets but have no control over them).

Shareholders in listed companies, for instance, acquire and hold their shares as a financial investment, with a view only to obtaining dividends or capital gains. These shareholders are not seeking a vehicle for carrying out their own business activities. They have little influence over the company's business decisions or the timing of the appropriation of its profit. These powers are concentrated in the management body of the company, often controlled by a small but compact core of shareholders. In these cases, there is a large gap between the owners and the business.

The opposite is professional partnerships, owned by a small number of partners united by close professional or personal relationships, who use a simple partnership agreement as a mere instrument for the joint exercise of their business or professional activity. In this case, the business or professional activity of each of the shareholders is of fundamental importance and, in practice, reflects their inseparable connection with the company. Here, unlike in the previous case, the shareholders exercise effective decision-making power over the destinies of the company, including the moment of appropriation of the respective profits. The business and the income of the company are intertwined with the business activity and the income of the shareholders. Due to this extreme proximity, entrepreneurs and the company form an economic unit, which may justify the disregard of the entity for tax purposes, in the sense that its activities and income are directly attributed to the shareholders.

For this reason, most tax systems tax the income of corporations as per se entities and partnerships as "pass-through" entities, meaning that the business profits are directly attributed to the owners for tax purposes.

3. There is a Case for Taxing the DAO

A surprising (to someone, not a tax practitioner) aspect of analyzing any DAO for tax purposes is that it can be a taxable entity[1]. In some sense, it appears like a disembodied creation floating in cyberspace, with no apparent form. Take the original DAO, for instance. Its group of investors intended to consult together to decide on investments, to make the investments, and to share in the profits. They, and those on the Ethereum blockchain, ultimately worked together to resolve the problem created by a rogue investor. Despite the disclaimers in the material presenting the original DAO to potential investors, the structure operated very much like a partnership contract[2].

DAOs are, by definition, sufficiently separated from their owners. They "own" assets in the blockchain and their profits are not immediately paid to the participants. A collective decision, through consensus mechanisms, and token-based governance is required for that and any other purpose that affects the DAO (such as protocol upgrades, funding for projects, changes in rules, or adjustments to token economics).

In addition, although DAO's purpose and structure are not inherently tied to being either for-profit or non-profit, most operate with the goal of generating a profit and distributing it among its token holders or stakeholders. The profits might come from various sources, such as revenue generated by products or services offered by the DAO, investment activities, or other business ventures. It seems clear that these profits, like any other business profits, are manifestations of the ability to pay taxes.

[1] *Shakow*, The Tax Treatment of Tokens: What Does It, 2017, 1387
[2] *Shakow*, The Tao of the DAO, 2018, 11

Based on the above considerations, in our opinion, there is a strong case for taxing DAOs. They are autonomous entities that may generate taxable income.

II. The Challenges to Tax DAO's Income

Having a strong case does not mean that taxing the DAO will be an easy task, or even feasible under the current tax system.

The international tax system is built on a combination of domestic tax laws, bilateral and multilateral agreements, and international organizations that help establish guidelines and standards for taxation.

Each country has its own set of domestic tax laws that determine how income taxes are levied on individuals, businesses, and other entities within its borders. On top of this domestic structure, countries enter bilateral tax treaties with each other to establish rules for taxing cross-border activities.

According to this international tax order, in cross-border situations, the jurisdiction where the business owner is domiciled has the right to tax its worldwide profits and the country where the income is sourced has the right to tax the portion of the foreign entity's income that was generated in its territory.

The problem, insofar as taxing DAOs is concerned, is that the international tax system assumes that businesses are not only owned by individuals or entities that have a domicile in a specific country, and that their income may be pinpointed to a certain jurisdiction.

However, that is not how the global economy has evolved and technology has advanced.

1. Challenges of the Digital Economy

With the rise of digital technology and the growth of multinational corporations, the international tax system has faced many challenges. Digital businesses operate globally without a significant physical presence in each market they serve. This has led to debates about how to tax their profits, as traditional tax rules were not designed to address such scenarios. In addition, the digital economy relies heavily on data, and there are debates about how data should be treated in terms of taxation and value creation.

Also, multinational corporations, including digital giants, have been accused of using complex structures to shift profits to low-tax jurisdictions, minimizing their tax liabilities in higher-tax countries. This practice is known as base erosion and profit shifting (BEPS).

In response to these challenges, efforts have been made to update and reform the international tax system to better capture the realities of the modern economy, including the BEPS Project (launched to address the challenges of profit shifting and tax avoidance); the Digital Services Tax (levied on revenue generated from certain digital services, which sparked international debates and concerns about double taxation); and the Pillar One/Pillar Two Initiative (that addresses the allocation of taxing rights for digital businesses and establish a global minimum tax to prevent profit shifting).

2. DAO Specific Challenges

However, taxing DAOs is one step further from the complexity of taxing digital companies. These new taxes and initiatives, even if implemented, will not be sufficient to impose taxes on DAOs profits.

The main difference between digital business and business in the blockchain is that the first happens (digitally through the internet) between traditional legal entities, all of them domiciled in certain jurisdictions. The discussion is focused on where the income is sourced and where the business entities are really located, particularly because some companies are "redomiciled" to low-tax jurisdictions, but their customer base remains in high-tax countries.

The DAO, however, completely eludes this discussion. Contrarily to digital companies, the DAO is not domiciled anywhere, it operates based on blockchain technology and smart contracts, without employees, physical presence, or even legal status. DAOs are code. The DAO "exists" in cyberspace.

III. The Methods to Tax DAO's Income

In theory, there are two approaches to tax DAOs income: (i) tax the DAO directly, as a business entity; or (ii) tax its participants (often referred to as members or token holders).

1. Taxing the DAO's Income Directly

As we discussed, under current international tax rules, only two countries are entitled to tax business profits. The country of the entity's domicile, which in practice is where the entity is managed (entitled to tax the entity's worldwide profits); and the income source country (that may tax income produced within its borders).

This system has been in place since the 1960s and has been extremely efficient at taxing traditional brick-and-mortar businesses. Traditional brick-and-mortar businesses have physical operations, such as storefronts, factories, and offices, within specific jurisdictions.

Even digital taxation proposals try to conform to these principles. The discussion is being focused on shifting the primary taxing rights from the place of management to where the income is sourced, or at least creating a tax apportionment system based on the location of the client base and business assets.

Both current and digital taxation rules are completely inappropriate for taxing DAOs. First, the DAO does not have a place of incorporation, a registered seat, or a location where it is effectively managed. It does not have a domicile under the existing taxation principles. The DAO functions in a decentralized manner, without a central governing authority or traditional hierarchical structure. DAO's decision-making and coordination among participants are totally automated and are often carried out through consensus mechanisms or voting protocols among participants. DAOs are designed to execute predefined rules and actions automatically, without the need for intermediaries.

In addition, DAOs' don't have employees, they don't have offices or stores and most of their business happens in the blockchain. Its participants and "customers" are identified through pseudonyms. This makes it impossible to identify a source country for its revenue.

In practice, this means that, from the perspective of the existing taxing principles, DAOs are aliens inhabiting cyberspace. And as such it is impossible to tax unless a totally innovative tax system is created.

But, even if such a system was created, it would be virtually impossible to enforce it. If a DAO was required to pay taxes somewhere, or to some global organization, the fact is that in a truly "autonomous" DAO those who developed it and promoted it no longer have any power to control it. There would be no one responsible for filing the forms and returns required by the tax system and no one to be responsible for paying the taxes. If the DAO would fail to report income and pay taxes, the reality is that there is no one to blame and no one to collect penalties from.[3]

2. *Taxing the Participants*

We think that the only possible alternative to tax DAO's profits is imposing such tax at the level of the participants. From a policy perspective, the participants could be taxed: (i) currently on the DAO's profits (similarly to a pass-through partnership); (ii) on receipt of rewards, dividends, or tokens, and (iii) on the realization of gains on the exchange of tokens[4].

Taxing the participants is possible because, contrary to the DAO, they do not live in cyberspace, but rather in sovereign countries. They could therefore be subject to reporting obligations, to disclose their holdings, any transactions,

---

[3] *Shakow*, The Tao of the DAO, 2018, 15

[4] Some DAO participants might stake tokens or participate in governance decisions. The tax implications of staking, rewards earned from staking, and participation in governance mechanisms could also be subject to tax. But technically this would not be the DAOs income but rather personal income of the participants.

and other activities related to the DAO. Failure to report those accurately could lead to penalties that would be obviously enforceable on the participant.

This is not an easy task though. It is very difficult for governments to have mechanisms to effectively audit the participants that reside in their country. One way of getting some control would be to force cryptocurrency exchanges to make available the identities of those trading on them. To a significant degree, entities running wallet applications (where most cryptocurrency investors store their holdings) already require anti-money laundering/know-your-customer checks upon sign-up[5].

To be effective, this system would require that all nations charge exchanges with the responsibility of knowing who their customers are. If customers trading on exchanges realize that their identities will be made known to tax authorities, it would make hiding behind a blockchain more and more difficult. Whether such a level of international cooperation could be achieved is certainly not clear. But this solution assumes that we can locate exchanges in a jurisdiction. If exchanges can themselves operate solely in cyberspace, with no connection to any jurisdiction, governments will need to find another way of dealing with the DAO phenomenon[6].

IV. Conclusion

There is a clear case to tax DAO's profits. Their business profits are manifestations of an ability to pay taxes and DAOs are, generally, business entities separated from their owners.

However, the reality is that pure blockchain entities do not conform to the international tax system, under which countries are entitled to tax business profits based on the entity's place of management and on the source of income.

These criteria to allocate taxing powers to one jurisdiction do not work with DAOs. They are stateless and their income, mostly generated in the blockchain, cannot be attributed to any jurisdiction. For this reason, no government in the world can claim jurisdiction to tax their income.

The alternative to taxing the DAO directly would be to tax their participants. They don't live in cyberspace and may therefore be subject to reporting obligations to disclose their holdings, transactions, and other activities in their country of residence. Failure to comply with those obligations could be penalized.

However, the reality is that in public blockchains, despite the transactions being transparent and traceable, the participants are often pseudonymous, identified only by their public keys. This makes enforcement of tax rules virtually

[5] *Shakow*, The Tao of the DAO, 2018, 21
[6] *Shakow*, The Tao of the DAO, 2018, 21

impossible, until governments hypothetically force all exchanges and wallet applications with the responsibility of knowing who their customers are, and customers trading on exchanges realize that their identities will be made known to tax authorities. The level of international coordination required to achieve this will not happen soon.

Some DAOs will adjust to the "real" world and create business entities outside the blockchain to comply with the requirements of certain jurisdictions (in particular, having in mind the concerns of their participants). But the majority will most likely remain as it is for a long time.

There is no tax on the DAO's income in sight.

Laws Applicable to International Smart Contracts and Decentralized Autonomous Organizations (DAOs)

Luís de Lima Pinheiro

Abstract International contracts, legal persons and other external organizations raise choice-of-law problems. Should smart contracts and DAOs in general be considered international? Are the choice-of-law rules in force for State courts and for arbitral tribunals appropriate for the determination of the applicable laws? To provide replies to these questions the present essay starts by general introductions to smart contracts and DAOs and also outlines the Private International Law framework of these realities. Solutions for difficulties on the application of the choice-of-law rules in force and more flexible approaches to address them are proposed.

I. Introduction to Smart Contracts

Smart contracts are one of the new realities of the internet world, with which many legal professionals, scholars and law students are not yet familiar. Therefore, in a study on determining the law applicable to international smart contracts, it is advisable to start with an introduction to these realities. It is not about examining their substantive regime or even identifying all of their regulatory problems, but only about making the object of my study intelligible and delimiting its scope.

There are multiple concepts of smart contract that have been adopted by authors and accepted in some States' legislations.

According to the most widespread concept, the smart contract is a computer program that operates based on distributed ledger technology, namely the blockchain, and which allows the automatic performance of certain obligations when certain facts occur[1].

---

[1] See Cardozo Blockchain Project "Smart Contracts" & Legal Enforceability, 2018, 4-5, at https://cardozo.yu.edu/sites/default/files/2020-01/smart_contracts_report_2_0.pdf (22.08.2023), 2; *Miguel Asensio*, EAPIL Blog 19/6/2019; *Id.*, Conflict of Laws and the Internet, 2020, n. 6.63 et seq.; *Lima Pinheiro*, in: Anna Carolina Pinho (ed.), Discussões sobre Direito na Era Digital, 2021, 503, 503; *Perestrelo de Oliveira,* Smart Contracts, Risco e Codificação da Desvinculação ou Modificação Negocial – Os Falsos Dilemas da Inter-relação Lei-código nos Contratos Empresariais, 2023. See further *Ramos Alves*, in: António Menezes Cordeiro, Ana Perestrelo de Oliveira and Diogo Pereira Duarte (eds.-), FinTech II. Novos Estudos sobre Tecnologia Financeira, 2019, § 5.1

Distributed ledger technology consists of digital records that are shared simultaneously by a network of operators. They are distributed because the record is held by each of the network operators (or nodes) and each copy is simultaneously updated with new information. Distributed ledger technology uses a consensus technique to ensure that each node complies with the record.[2]

In blockchain networks, anyone can create an "account", using a public address (public key) and a password (private key). To carry out a transaction, a network user searches for the public key of another user and introduces his private key. In this way the transaction is "authenticated", since it cannot be denied by the party that entered its private key.[3] The user's identity on certain platforms or types of transactions may not be known or may be difficult to know because users may use pseudonyms.[4]

Understood in this sense, smart contracts can either be employed for the performance of the contract's obligations, or part of them, or for compensation in the event of a breach of contract or of other voluntary or involuntary obligations.

For example, the smart contract can be used to automatically compensate passengers for a canceled or delayed flight. The computer program can, in this case, be designed in such a way that, once the cancellation or delay is verified, the affected passengers are identified and the amount of compensation transferred to their bank accounts. This not only saves the resources needed to manage claims, but also facilitates obtaining compensation.[5]

Smart contracts have been widely used for complex financial transactions, such as loans made by banking syndicates and derivatives, as well as for copyright license agreements. As we will see later, they also provide the basis for DAOs (*infra* IV).

As a contractual instrument, the smart contract offers the advantage of eliminating or reducing the risk of non-performance, since the execution of the contract no longer depends on human intervention.

When the smart contract is used as a contractual instrument, it presupposes that the parties reach an agreement on the contractual clauses raised by them.[6] This agreement can, in general terms, be formalized both in natural language and in machine language (also called a "hybrid agreement"), i.e., computer code, or in machine language only. On the other hand, the agreement may be

---

2 See *ISDA and Linklaters*, Whitepaper Smart Contracts and Distributed legal – A Legal perspective, 2017, 7, at www.isda.org/2017/08/03/smart-contracts-and-distributed-ledger-a-legal-perspective/ (22.08.2023); *Law Commission*, Advice to Government. Smart Legal Contracts, 2021, n. 2.22 et seq.

3 See Cardozo Blockchain Project "Smart Contracts" & Legal Enforceability, 2018, at https://cardozo.yu.edu/sites/default/files/2020-01/smart_contracts_report_2_0.pdf, 2.

4 *Law Commission*, Advice to Government. Smart Legal Contracts, 2021, nos. 3.19 et seq.

5 See also *Rey*, Redes – Revista Eletrônica Direito e Sociedade 7/3, 2019, 96.

6 See *Martiny*, IPRax 2018, 553, 555.

concluded prior to the insertion of clauses in the distributed ledger platform (off-chain smart contract) or be concluded on the platform itself (on-chain smart contract).[7]

In other words, as a contractual instrument, the smart contract can be used to conclude a contract on a distributed ledger platform or as a measure of performance of a contract entered into in natural language, where the insertion of clauses in a distributed ledger platform already integrates the performance of the contract.

However, it is also possible that formalizing the contract in machine language constitutes a conventional form stipulated by the parties who are only bound after the insertion of the clauses in the distributed ledger platform (as provided in Art. 223 of the Portuguese Civil Code.[8]

A different problem is that of knowing whether an agreement formalized only in machine language meets the requirement of legal form prescribed by a given legal order.

In the case of a dispute, the parties will have to reach an amicable agreement, namely a settlement, or resort to a judicial or arbitration means of dispute resolution. In both cases, it may be necessary to reverse some of the effects of the smart contract, for example, through the restitution of automatically performed payments. This reversal can be effected through a new computer program (reverse transaction) and therefore automatically (on-chain), or through acts performed outside the distributed ledger platform and therefore not automatically (off-chain).

What distinguishes the contract based on a smart contract from a traditional contract is the fact that the contract clauses, or part of them, are transcribed in machine language and that the performance of the contract, or part of it, does not depend on human performance. While in a traditional contract the parties may not perform the contract, or suspend its performance, naturally subjecting themselves to the consequences of non-performance, in a contract supported by a smart contract the performance is computer programmed and the program is executed by the operators of the distributed ledger platform.[9]

The contract supported by a smart contract may or may not be a case of electronic contracting, i. e., in which declarations of will are transmitted through technological means. This will happen in the vast majority of cases.

The contract supported by a smart contract may or may not be associated with automatic contracting. In automatic contracting, the declaration is made through a machine, for example, a vending machine. In this case, according to

---

[7] See *Durovic and Janssen*, in: Dimatteo/Cannarsa/Poncibò (eds.), The Cambridge Handbook of Smart Contracts, Blockchain Technology and Digital Platforms, 2019, § 4.3

[8] See also *Rey* (fn. 5) 103-104.

[9] See also Cardozo Blockchain Project "Smart Contracts" & Legal Enforceability, 2018, at https://cardozo.yu.edu/sites/default/files/2020-01/smart_contracts_report_2_0.pdf,, 4-5.

the prevailing opinion, there is an offer to the public that the buyer accepts when activating the machine.[10] Automatic contracting may or may not be electronic. If it is, we may speak of computer contracting.[11]

According to Portuguese and German laws, the electronic declaration is attributable to the person who programmed or had the computer programmed.[12]

When concluding certain contracts supported by a smart contract, there is an offer of goods or services on a distributed ledger platform that allows the automatic performance of the contract with the acceptance of any person. According to the same laws, this offer should, in principle, be qualified as an offer to the public.[13] Acceptance is received by the offeror at the time it is entered into the distributed ledger platform.[14]

It may also happen that both declarations are made using machines, namely computers, programmed for this purpose. Taking one more step, the computer can be programmed in such a way as to allow it to learn from the data given to it and to make decisions that result not only from the input introduced by the programmer, but also from this learning. These are, therefore, contracts concluded with the intervention of autonomous artificial intelligence systems in which the declarations of will are not precisely determined by the programmer.

The expression "smart contract" could suggest a relationship with artificial intelligence. However, this relationship is not necessary. In the case of a contract supported by a smart contract, what is automatic is the performance which also happens in certain cases of automatic contracting that cannot be considered smart contracts because the contractual clauses are not inserted into a distributed ledger platform.[15] Therefore, the term "smart contract" is misleading.

Finally, the smart contract may cover the entire performance of the contract, which is called on-chain, or involve the performance of non-automatic acts, which are called off-chain.

To obtain the information needed to perform the program, smart contracts use so-called oracles. Oracles are external data sources that transmit information to a computer program.

---

[10] See *Oliveira Ascensão*, Direito Civil. Teoria Geral, vol. II – Acções e Factos Jurídicos, 2nd ed., 2003, 472-273; and *Menezes Cordeiro*, Tratado de Direito Civil, vol. II – Parte Geral/ Negócio Jurídico, 2021, 343-345 (with reference to the theory of automatic offer). See further *Pais de Vasconcelos*, 7th ed., 2012, 413-414.

[11] Cf. *Neuner*, Allgemeiner Teil des Bürgerlichen Rechts, 12nd ed., 2020, § 32 n. 38.

[12] Cf. *Menezes Cordeiro* (fn. 10) 347, and *Neuner* (fn. 11) § 30 n. 39.

[13] Cf. *Braegelmann/Kaulartz*, Rechtshandbuch Smart Contracts, 2019, Ch.VIII, n. 19. For a convergent view, regarding contracts concluded in digital platforms in general, *Costa e Silva*, in: Direito da Sociedade da Informação, vol. IV, 289, 2003, 295 et seq. See Art. 32(1) of the DL no. 7/2004, of 7/1 (Electronic Commerce Law) on online offer of goods and services.

[14] Cf. *Braegelmann/Kaulartz* (fn. 13) n. 20.

[15] See also *Ribeiro de Faria*, Revista de Direito Civil 2020, 723, 726, remarking that that this also occurs with devices for repossession of vehicles sold with retention of title used in the USA.

Oracles can be of three types:

- software oracles that allow information to be extracted online (for example, meteorological information);
- hardware oracles that allow objects to be tracked in the physical world (for example, the arrival of an aircraft); and
- oracles associated with natural or legal persons who verify the occurrence of certain facts (for example, a smart contract in which the sale price of a car is paid when it is delivered without defects, the mechanical assessment being entrusted to an expert.[16]

In a broader sense, a smart contract can be understood as the set formed by the contract and the computer program used in its performance. It is in this sense that, in the next sections, I will refer to smart contracts.

It is also clear that, in this sense, the smart contract is not a contractual type, but a contract that uses a certain technology for performance and, eventually, conclusion. The characterization of the contractual type will fundamentally depend on the economic function and the content of the rights and obligations stipulated by the parties. This could be, for example, a sales contract, an insurance contract, a copyright license agreement or a financial derivative.

Regarding DAOs (*infra* IV-VI), I will again refer to smart contracts in the strict sense of computer programs, but I will argue that DAOs also have a contractual dimension and, therefore, these computer programs also support a contractual relationship. Nevertheless, the common purpose nature of this contract and its connection with an organization introduces specificities that are relevant for the determination of its governing law (*infra* VI).

The present essay deals only with international smart contracts and DAOs. I will start by pointing out the Private International Law framework of these contracts (II), then go on to determine the law applicable to these contracts when they are not covered by unified substantive law (III). I will then turn to DAOs, starting with an introduction (IV), followed by the outline of their Private International Law framework (V) and by the determination of the applicable laws (VI), and ending with some brief final remarks (VII).

The Private International Law issues involved will be addressed under the general choice-of-law rules of the European Union, the Transnational Arbitration Law, and the special Portuguese choice-of-law rules of arbitration. However, I will also refer to the special Spanish choice-of-law rules of arbitration and to the Brazilian general choice-of-law rules and special choice-of-law rules of arbitration, as it seems to me that many of the problems identified in the Portuguese legal order, as well as the solutions proposed to address them, will also be of interest to the Spanish and Brazilian legal orders.

---

16 See *Rey* (fn. 5) 109, and *Armo*, in: Jiménez Blanco/Espiniella Menéndez (eds.), Nuevos Escenarios del Derecho Internacional Privado de la Contratación, 683, 2021, 686.

II. Smart Contracts and Private International Law

Smart contracts fall under Private International Law when they have relevant contacts with more than one sovereign State. The Internet, in general, is characterized by its ubiquity and a high rate of transnational relationships. Nevertheless, the fact that the internet is a global network does not mean that all contracts entered into over the internet or that use platforms for their automatic performance are international.

This transnationality is reinforced in blockchain networks by the multiple localization of the nodes.[17] The relevance of storing records or the location of operators of the distributed ledger platform in different countries can, then, raise doubts. According to some authors, since the blockchain is essentially transnational, any relationship based upon the blockchain is transnational.[18]

However, only some contacts with States are relevant for the purposes of Private International Law. Furthermore, it is today commonly understood that the location of the servers is not relevant for choice-of-law purposes regarding relationships established through the internet. Also, the multiple localization of the nodes does not trigger the transnationality of the relationships based upon blockchain, because they do not have an objective connection with the parties nor do they convey specificity to the performance of the contract.[19]

I believe that the most relevant internationality criterion for smart contracts is a subjective criterion: the location of the parties in different countries. The internationality of the contract can also result from the place of performance. The automatic performance of the contract does not mean that all acts are carried out online and, therefore, internationality can also result from the place of performance. Internationality may also result from a close connection between the smart contract and a multi-localized contract or from the fact that it is an operation that is carried out in an international market, as is often the case with financial operations on derivatives.

In any case, bearing in mind the difficulty in determining the location, and even of the identity of parties, I believe that the internationality of the smart contract can be presumed. The same will be advocated regarding most DAOs (*infra* V).

Like all international contracts, the international smart contract poses specific problems of determining the competent jurisdiction, determining the applicable law and, eventually, recognizing foreign judgments and awards.

---

[17] Cf. *Audit*, R. crit. 2020/4, 669, 678, stresses the immateriality and the decentralization specific of the blockchain.

[18] Cf. *Guillaume*, in: Kraus/Obrist/Ha (eds.), Blockchains, Smart Contracts, Decentralised Autonomous Organisations and the Law, 2019, 59; *Audit* (fn. 17) 672.

[19] For a different view, *Braegelmann/ Kaulartz* (fn. 13) § 12 n. 5 and 13.

With regard to the competent jurisdiction, it is necessary to verify whether or not there is a valid arbitration agreement. If so, the competent jurisdiction is a transnational arbitral tribunal. Otherwise, it is necessary to determine the internationally competent State jurisdiction or jurisdictions. The present essay will not deal with the resolution of this problem, but it cannot fail to consider the difference between the general choice-of-law system, applicable in the first place by the State courts, and the arbitration choice-of-law rules, which governs the determination of the applicable law to the merits by the transnational arbitration tribunals in the strict sense, or international commercial arbitration tribunals.

The present essay will also not deal with the problem of recognition of foreign judgments and awards rendered in relation to smart contracts.

The need for legal regulation of smart contracts seems evident today. Initially, some voices were heard expressing the view that the self-enforceability of smart contracts would dispense with legal regulation and the intervention of jurisdictional means of dispute resolution. However, it is clear that this is not the case. The law must regulate, namely, the formation of the smart contract, its validity pre-requisites and its interpretation and integration. Smart contracts may even give rise, with particular frequency, to certain disputes, such as those resulting from programming errors or the refund of payments in the event of revocation of contracts concluded by consumers.[20] The intervention of State courts or arbitration tribunals will be necessary, as already noted, when disputes arising from smart contracts are not resolved amicably.

This does not mean, however, that legal regulation cannot, to some extent, be provided by autonomous sources, such as customs or rules created by autonomous entities that administer distributed ledger platforms. This autonomous regulation could play an important role, especially in relations between enterprises.[21]

When the smart contract is international, it cannot be assumed that it is subject to the substantive law of the forum. It is necessary to determine the applicable law. The determination of the law applicable to smart contracts does not only operate through the general choice-of-law system and the transnational arbitration choice-of-law rules. Certain smart contracts may fall within the scope of application of unified substantive law, especially by international conventions that regulate certain types of contracts.

---

[20] See *Meyer*, Stopping the Unstoppable – Termination and Unwinding of Smart Contracts, 2020, on ssrn.com, 6 et seqs., mentioning the possibility of programming the automatic restitution in case of revocation.

[21] See *Lima Pinheiro*, Reflections on Internet Governance and Regulation with Special Consideration of the ICANN, 2016, on ssrn.com, B., and Algumas reflexões sobre a governação e a regulação da internet, CyberLaw by CIJIC 3 (february 2017). 136-145, B.

This is the case of the Vienna Convention on the International Sale of Goods, to which Portugal, Spain and Brazil are parties. It should be noted that, for the purposes of this Convention, the concept of goods includes software.[22]

In the European Union (hereinafter referred to as the EU), other instruments may also apply, such as Reg. (EC) No. 261/2004, of 2/11/2004, Establishing Common Rules on Compensation and Assistance to Passengers in the Event of Denied Boarding and of Cancellation or Long Delay of Flights, a situation in which, as noted (I), smart contracts can find a field of use. In the same space, there are instruments for harmonizing the laws of Member States that may be relevant to the discipline of smart contracts, as is the case of the Directive on Electronic Commerce, regarding smart contracts concluded over the internet,[23] and the Directive on Abusive Clauses, in relation to contracts concluded with consumers.[24]

From the point of view of the Portuguese legal system, there is still the possibility of applicability of the regime of standard contractual clauses to be considered.[25] This regime is applicable not only to contractual clauses characterized by generality and rigidity, but also to pre-drafted individual clauses that the addressee cannot influence. Once these pre-requisites are met, the regime covers clauses drawn up by third parties.

Therefore, the regime of standard contractual clauses may be applicable to clauses encoded in machine language on smart contract platforms that are rigid.[26] For this purpose, the contract needs to be governed by Portuguese law or, in consumer relations, it must present a close connection with Portuguese territory or with the territory of another EU Member State (Art. 23).

As for the inclusion of these clauses in individual contracts, this regime may also be relevant based on the addressee's habitual residence in Portugal, if it appears from the circumstances that it would not be reasonable to determine the effect of his or her conduct in accordance with the law applicable to the contract (Art. 10(2) of Reg. no. 593/2008 on the Law Applicable to Contractual Obligations, hereinafter Rome I Regulation).

On the other hand, even when the smart contract is not covered by an instrument of unification of substantive law, the determination of the applicable law is not limited to issues that generally fall under the scope of the law applicable to the contract, namely formation of consent, interpretation and integration, substantial validity and obligations resulting from the contract.

---

[22] Cf. *Schlechtriem/Schwenzer*, Commentary on the UN-Convention on the International Sale of Goods (CISG), 4th ed., 2016, Art. 1, n. III.

[23] Transposed to the Portuguese legal order by DL no 7/2004, of 7/1.

[24] Those diretives have been ammended Dir. (EU) 2019/2161. See, in the Portuguese legal order, the standard clauses regime provided by DL no 446/85, of 25/10, ammended by DLs nos 220/95, of 31/8, 249/99, of 7/7, and 323/2001, of 17/12.

[25] See previous footnote.

[26] Cf. *Braegelmann/Kaulartz* (fn. 13) Ch. VIII n. 21.

First of all, there are legal issues concerning the relationship between the parties and the operators of the distributed ledger platform, which I will not address here.

Other issues are subject to autonomous connections, i. e., they are not covered by the *lex contractus*. This is the case, in particular, of the capacity of the parties, the form of the contract and the protection of personal data. With regard to these issues, it is important to resort to other bilateral conflict rules (capacity, form) or to instruments that establish their spatial scope of application through unilateral conflict rules (General Data Protection Regulation, in the EU, General Law for Data Protection, in Brazil).

I will not be examining these autonomous connections, but I would like to call attention to the importance that choice-of-law rules on formal validity can assume for smart contracts. In the EU, the Rome I Regulation establishes, as a general rule, alternative connections aimed at favoring the formal validity of the contract (Art. 11(1) and (2)). However, regarding contracts with consumers covered by Art. 6 of the Regulation, it is provided the application of the law of the consumer's habitual residence (Art. 11(4)).

One issue that arises is whether a smart contract that is not based on a document written in natural language satisfies the requirement of written form prescribed by several regimes on contracts with consumers.

In the EU, pre-contractual liability arising out of dealings prior to the conclusion of a contract is the subject of another instrument: Regulation no. 864/2007 Regarding the Law Applicable to Non-Contractual Obligations (Art. 12). This is another issue that will not be addressed in this essay.

Finally, smart contracts may also raise questions of proof, namely admissibility as a mode of proof and probative force.

The admissibility of modes of proof is subject to the choice-of-law rule provided in Art. 18(2) of Rome I Regulation, according to which a "contract or an act intended to have legal effect may be proved by any mode of proof recognised by the law of the forum or by any of the laws referred to in Article 11 [formal validity] under which that contract or act is formally valid, provided that such mode of proof can be administered by the forum".

The probative force remained outside the scope of this Regulation;[27] in the Portuguese legal order, this issue must be assessed according to Portuguese substantive law.[28] In both cases, is also relevant for smart contracts Regulation EU no. 910/2014 on Electronic Identification and Trust Services for Electronic Transactions in the Internal Market (Arts. 25 et seq.).

---

[27] Cf. *Giuliano/Lagarde*, Rapport concernant la convention sur la loi applicable aux obligations contractuelles, *JOCE* C 282, 31/10, 1980, 37.

[28] Cf. *Lima Pinheiro*, Direito Internacional Privado, vol. II – Direito de Conflitos/Parte Especial, 4th ed., 2015, 32-33, with further references.

III. Law Applicable to International Smart Contracts

1. *Lex cryptographia?*

Regarding the law applicable to contracts in the context of blockchain networks , it has been argued that these networks are an independent legal space of a new type and that they are governed by the rules of their computer code, regardless of any national law, a *lex cryptographia.*[29]

This is an obvious parallel to previous theses favorable to the new *lex mercatoria*, as an autonomous law of international business,[30] and to the *lex informatica*, as an autonomous law of internet relationships. However, here there are some additional factors of autonomy:

- transactions automatically performed in blockchain networks, namely transactions based upon some smart contracts, do not require a conduct of a party or court enforcement for their performance;
- the disputes involved can, up to a certain point, be settled by dispute resolution mechanisms operating within the framework of the blockchain network;
- State control of blockchain networks and transactions is particularly difficult.

Some of the arguments opposed to this opinion do not strictly concern the contractual relationship and do not take into account the different degree of State regulation required by business-to-business relationships and to business-to-consumer or non-professional investors relationships.[31] Other arguments, such as the limitation of the scope of these rules, would not prevent them from operating in coordination with the State rules that are applicable to issues outside their scope.

Although I believe that determination of the rules applicable to smart contracts and DAOs have to be mainly based upon the choice-of-law rules in force for State courts and arbitration tribunals, I think that we should pay attention to the autonomous processes of rule creation that can occur in blockchain networks, and that we should not completely exclude the possibility of these rules being chosen by the parties to the merits of a dispute submitted to arbitration and that falls under their scope.

---

[29] See *Mayer*, *NJW* 1996, 1782, 1790; *Kraus/Obrist/Hari/Guillaume* (fn. 18) 71 et seq.; *De Filippi/Wright*, Blockchain and the Law: The Rule of Code, 2018, 193 et seq.

[30] See *Lima Pinheiro*, Direito Internacional Privado, vol. I – Introdução e Direito de Conflitos/Parte Geral, 3rd ed., 2014, § 6, with further references.

[31] See namely *Audit* (fn. 17) 676-677; *Drögemüller*, Blockchain-Netzwerke und Krypto-Token im Internationalen Privatrecht, 2023, 347-348. Liability regarding third parties of external organizations or insolvency matters do not fall within the scope of the law applicable to the contract.

Deference to autonomous rules has advantages, namely from the point of view of the restraint required in the exercise of States'jurisdiction to prescribe in order to avoid regulatory conflicts or conflicts of duties for the addresses of such regulations.

2. *General choice-of-law rules*

When talking about the law applicable to smart contracts, it is important to bear in mind the meaning of the relevant smart contract for this purpose. As I pointed out earlier (I), not all computer programs for the automatic performance of obligations are intended for the performance of contractual obligations or even of voluntary obligations. In determining the applicable law, the computer program should not be considered in isolation, rather the overall relationship in which it operates. It is this relationship that is the object of characterization for the purposes of selecting the choice-of-law rule that designates the applicable law.[32] The present essay deals only with cases in which the relationship qualifies as *a* contractual relationship or, more complexly, as a DAO (*infra* V-VI).

The choice-of-law rules concerning obligational contracts were unified in the EU, first by the Rome Convention on the Law Governing Contractual Obligations and then by the Rome I Regulation.

Pursuant to art. 12(1)(b) of the Rome I Regulation, the scope of the law applicable to the contract includes the performance of obligations arising therefrom and, therefore, the computer program used for its automatic performance is covered by the contractual statute.[33]

The Rome I Regulation establishes a general regime for determining the law applicable to the contract and a special regime for consumer contracts, which aims to protect the consumer. Let us start with the general rule.

The freedom of choice of the law applicable to obligational contracts is today a principle of Private International Law common to the overwhelming majority of national systems.[34] In the Rome I Regulation, this principle is enshrined in no. 1 of Art. 3.

---

[32] Cf. *Martiny* (fn. 6) 559-560. See also *Zimmermann*, IPRax 2018, 566, 568.

[33] See also *Zimmermann* (fn. 32) 569.

[34] Cf. *Lando*, RCADI 189, 1984, 223, 284; *Ferrer Correia*, RLJ 1990, n. 3787 to 3789; *Vischer* RCADI 232, 1992, 9, 139, considers that the freedom to choose the applicable law can be considered as a general principle of law; but refers to *Rigaux*, RCADI 213, 1989, 7, 234, when this author points out that the problem is not so much the principle itself, as its scope and limits. Strictly speaking, there has been some resistance to this principle by Latin American States – see *Fernández Arroyo* (ed.), Derecho Internacional Privado de los Estados del Mercosur, 2003, 1015 et seq. According to the Preamble of the Resolution of the *Institut de Droit International* on the Autonomy of the Parties in International Contracts Between Private Persons or Entities, adopted in the session of Basel (1991), the "autonomy of the parties is one of the fundamental principles of private international law". It should be remarked that, in the

Art. 3 of the Rome I Regulation establishes no limits as to the State legal orders that can be designated. It is common ground that the chosen law does not need to have an objective connection with the contract and, according to widely held understanding, there are no other limits to the freedom to choose State or local law.[35]

The rules on the formation of consent and the formal validity of the contract also apply to agreement on the applicable law (Arts. 10 and 11 *ex vi* Art. 3(5)). Thus, the formation of consent on the applicable law is governed, in principle, by the designated law. In the most common contracts for the provision of goods and services, it should be considered sufficient, under Portuguese law, that consent is expressed through an exchange of email messages or, as is more frequent, through a mouse click on a field or icon on an internet page that expresses acceptance of the general terms accessible via a hyperlink or in an a pop-up window and that can be saved on the hard drive of the adherent's computer or printed by him.

It is also necessary to take into account the relevance granted to the law of the habitual residence of the contracting party under the terms of Art. 10(2). If the agreement on the applicable law constitutes a standard contractual clause, its inclusion in the contract will be assessed, primarily by the chosen law; if the question is answered in the affirmative by the chosen law, the addressee may also invoke, based on Art. 10(2), the law of his or her habitual residence to demonstrate that he or she has not agreed, if it appears from the circumstances that it would be unreasonable to determine the effects of his or her conduct according to the chosen law.[36]

Portuguese law, freedom of choice of the applicable law was already adopted, in 1888, by Art. 4(1) of the Commercial Code.

[35] With regard to the Rome Convention, it follows from *Giuliano/Lagarde* (fn. 27) n. 4 of Art. 3, that the risk of evading mandatory provisions through *dépeçage* was considered in the preparatory work, the experts understanding that this risk would be neutralized by the provisions of Art. 7. This comment, made with regard to partial references, applies *a fortiori* to the (minor) risk of evasion by means of a global designation. *Lando* (fn. 34) 292, further states that the possibility of including the "principle of *fraus legis*" was raised, and not implemented, by the experts, and infers from the commentary on Art. 16, in which it is emphasized that "public order does not intervene, abstractly and globally, against the law designated by the convention", the exclusion of the application of the public policy to cases of *fraus legis*. The Explanatory Memorandum of the Proposal for the Rome I Regulation seems to point in the same direction when it states that "fraud of the law" is covered by paragraphs 4 and 5 of Art. 3, which correspond in the Regulation to paragraphs 3 and 4 of Art. 3. See further references in *Lima Pinheiro* (n. 16) n. 658.

[36] See *Frada de Sousa*, Conflito de Clausulados e Consenso nos Contratos Internacionais, 1999, 245 et seq. Art. 5 of the above mentioned Resolution of the *Institut de Droit International* on the Autonomy of the Parties in International Contracts Between Private Persons or Entities, after admitting, in its no. 1, that the "applicable law may be designated by general conditions of contract, to which the parties have agreed", add, in its no. 2, a substantive rule, according to which this "agreement must be expressed in writing, or in a way which conforms with practices established by the parties, or in accordance with trade custom known to them".

Under the provision of the 2nd part of paragraph 1 of Art. 3 of the Regulation, the consent of the parties to the designation of the applicable law may be expressed expressly or tacitly.

The choice of applicable law presupposes an agreement between the parties. A simple computer program for automatic performance of obligations does not allow this to occur. Therefore, the agreement has to be stipulated off-chain[37] or at least complemented by natural language comments.[38] Normally, it will constitute a clause of the contract that uses the program for its performance, concluded off-chain, but it could also be an autonomous agreement. Of course, this does not prevent the choice of applicable law from being made on an electronic platform, provided that this is compatible with the form required for the contract.[39]

The choice of the law that is applicable to the smart contract is highly recommended, not only because of the difficulties that may arise in determining the applicable law in the absence of choice, which are discussed below, but also because smart contracts are only subject to specific regulation in a few national systems: it may be convenient to choose one of these systems, even if it has no objective connection with the contract.

The choice of the applicable law excludes, in principle, mandatory rules of the law of the forum or of third laws, but the applicability of certain mandatory rules is safeguarded by Art. 3(3) and (4) of the Rome I Regulation regarding contracts "located" in the same State or in several EU Member States, as well as by Art. 9, regarding the "overriding mandatory provisions" of the State of the forum and certain "overriding mandatory provisions" of the State of performance of the contract.

In the absence of a valid choice of applicable law, the Rome I Regulation establishes primary connections based on a specific criterion (Art. 4(1) and (2)) accompanied by the relevance of the general criterion of the closest connection within the framework of an escape clause (Art. 4(4)) or to establish a subsidiary connection (Art. 4(4)).

This solution is inspired by case law of the TCE regarding the choice of court clause inserted in the standard contract form proposed by one of the parties – cf. *Jayme*, L'autonomie de la volonté des parties dans les contrats internationaux entre personnes privées. Rapport définitif, Ann. Inst. dr. int. 64-I 1991, 62, 72 et seq.

See further, regarding the cases of battle of forms, Art. 6(1)(b) of the Hague Principles on Choice of Law in International Commercial Contracts (2015), and the critique of *Lando*, in: Mélanges Hans Van Loon, 299, 2013, 307-309.

[37] For this view, see *Braegelmann/Kaulartz* (fn. 13) § 12 n. 17.

[38] See *Law Commission*, Advice to Government. Smart Legal Contracts, 2021, n. 7.71 et seq.

[39] See *Lima Pinheiro*, ROA 66 2006, 131 (= in: Direito da Sociedade da Informação, vol. VII, 363, 2008, Spanish version in Estudios de Deusto 54/2 2006, 151), I.A, and in: Estudos em Homenagem a Agostinho Pereira de Miranda, 219, 2019 (=Revista de Direito Civil 2018, 743), II.A.

The primary connection is mainly based on the doctrine of characteristic performance: the contract is, in principle, governed by the law of the habitual residence of the debtor of the characteristic performance.[40] In contracts whose function is the exchange of a thing, the use of a thing or the provision of a service for a pecuniary amount, the characteristic performance consists of the delivery of the thing, the allowance of the use of the thing or the provision of the service.

However, the Rome I Regulation does not limit itself to adopting this doctrine to establish the primary connection. With regard to a certain number of contracts, the Regulation materializes this doctrine (sale, provision of services, franchising and distribution), which proves to be useful in cases where determination of the characteristic performance is controversial. This is the case with franchising and distribution contracts, which are subject to the law of the habitual residence of the franchisee and distributor (Art. 4.(1)e and (f).[41]

Contracts that do not appear in the typology contained in paragraph 1, or that are "mixed contracts", in the sense of being covered by more than one type, are governed by the law of the habitual residence of the debtor of the characteristic performance (Art. 4(2).[42]

Often, smart contracts do not correspond to one of the types referred to in Art. 4(1). This is the case of contracts for the sale of cryptocurrency and auctions that are carried out through blockchain. It is also the case of contracts underlying DAOs (*infra* IV and VI).

Cryptocurrency sales contracts are not considered to be sales of goods. They are subject to the rule of art. 4/2.[43]

In auction sale contracts carried out via blockchain, it is not usually possible to determine the location of the auction due to the decentralization of the blockchain. The situation may be different when the blockchain is centrally administered.[44] In this case, it is conceivable that the law of the habitual residence of the

[40] See, with further development, *Galvão Teles*, O Direito 127 1995, 71, 108 et seq., and in: Estudos de Direito Comercial Internacional, vol. I, Lima Pinheiro (ed.), 63, 2004, 85 et seqs.; and *Lima Pinheiro*, Direito Comercial Internacional, 2005, 117 et seq.

[41] The Explanatory Memorandum of the Commission's Proposal [6] states that these solutions "are based on the fact that Community law seeks to protect the franchisee and the distributor as the weaker parties". See, for a critical view, *Borges Morais*, Themis 11 2011, 279, 306 et seqs.

[42] Recital 19 states that "In the case of a contract consisting of a bundle of rights and obligations capable of being categorised as falling within more than one of the specified types of contract, the characteristic performance of the contract should be determined having regard to its centre of gravity". The meaning of this passage raises doubts. It seems that it has in mind the cases in which the debtor of the characteristic performance would be the party A, before one of the types involved, and the party B before another of the types involved.

[43] Cf. *Martiny* (fn. 6) 561 and *Zimmermann* (fn. 32) 569.

[44] For this view, *Braegelmann/Kaulartz* (fn. 13) § 12 n. 27; see, on the modalities of central administration of the blockchain network, *Zimmermann* (fn. 32) 569.

network administrator will apply. The term 'auction' should be understood, in line with Art. 2(b) of the Vienna Convention on the International Sale of Goods, as a public and publicly announced sale upon acceptance of the highest bid by the auctioneer. Article 4(1)(g) of the Regulation in Rome I only includes auctions organized by private parties.[45] In any case, it seems that many of the so-called auctions on the internet are not auctions in the legal sense because there is no formal acceptance of the highest bid, which therefore qualifies them as mere sales of goods, if they have as object things that may be considered goods.[46] If the bidders are consumers, the special regime for contracts with consumers, discussed below, is applicable.[47]

According to Art. 4(3) of the Regulation, where "it is clear from all the circumstances of the case that the contract is manifestly more closely connected with a country other than that indicated in paragraphs 1 or 2, the law of that other country shall apply".

According to one opinion, this escape clause does not normally operate in relation to smart contracts, due to the fact that, through the blockchain network, they have a multiplicity of contacts with several States.[48] This opinion does not seem to me to be entirely correct, because similarly to what was noted with regard to the internationality of these contracts (II), I understand that the places where the records are stored or the location of the operators of the distributed ledger platform are not, in principle, relevant. The most relevant connecting factors for the materialization of the escape clause are the location of the parties, the place of off-chain performance, the language of the contract concluded in natural language, the reference of this contract to provisions of a given legal order or the use of terms and expressions characteristic of this legal order (which, however, do not allow a tacit designation to be inferred), and the functional link that the contract establishes with another contract governed by a certain law.

The subsidiary operation of the general criterion of the closest connection is, above all, conceivable with respect to those contracts in which it is not possible to individualize a characteristic performance (Art. 4(4)). This is what happens with the barter contract and with most contracts for a common purpose (for example, with most joint venture contracts).[49] This also applies to contracts underlying DAOs which, as we will see, are contracts for a common purpose (*infra*

---

45 Cf. *Magnus/Mankowski/Magnus*, Rome I Regulation. Commentary, 2017, Art. 4 n. 143.

46 See *Magnus/Mankowski/Magnus* (fn. 45) Art. 4 n. 652.

47 For this view, but referring to all internet auctions, *Magnus/Mankowski/Magnus* (fn. 45) Art. 4 no. 654.

48 For this view, *Braegelmann/Kaulartz* (fn. 13) § 12 n. 26.

49 See *Lima Pinheiro*, Contrato de Empreendimento Comum (Joint Venture) em Direito Internacional Privado, 1998, 1215 et seq.

IV and VI). If contracts in which payment is made through cryptocurrency are characterized as barter contracts, they will be subject to this provision.[50]

Naturally, determining the closest connection can be problematic in relation to certain international smart contracts, especially contracts concluded and performed on-chain between parties located in different countries.

Most of the rules contained in Art. 4 refer to the law of the habitual residence of one of the parties.

In international contracts, it is very common for one of the parties, or both, to enter into the contract in the exercise of a professional activity. This poses the question of the relevance of their establishment. It is also common for legal persons to intervene, who do not exactly have a residence, but a seat (registered or of administration) and, normally, an establishment (or a main establishment and one or more secondary establishments).

Art. 19 of the Rome I Regulation seeks to answer these questions by determining that:

- "the habitual residence of companies and other bodies, corporate or unincorporated, shall be the place of central administration" ((1) § 1);
- "The habitual residence of a natural person acting in the course of his business activity shall be his principal place of business" ((1) § 2).

Paragraph 2 adds that where "the contract is concluded in the course of the operations of a branch, agency or any other establishment, or if, under the contract, performance is the responsibility of such a branch, agency or establishment, the place where the branch, agency or any other establishment is located shall be treated as the place of habitual residence".

The place of habitual residence is also, in principle, relevant for contracts concluded through the internet. However, it should be added that the party who, in the preliminary dealings or in the contract, declares to have habitual residence or relevant establishment in a given country cannot later claim the falsehood or inaccuracy of this statement.[51]

The Directive on Electronic Commerce provides that Member States must ensure that the supplier of goods, as well as the provider of online services, both indicate to the beneficiary the geographical address where he or she is established (Art. 5(1)(b)). In the Portuguese legal order, this provision was transposed to Art. 10(1)(b) of DL no. 7/2004, of 7/1 (hereinafter referred to as the Electronic Commerce Law).

With regard to legal bodies, although Art. 19(1) refers to the place where the central administration of the provider is located, the location cognoscible by the

[50] Cf. *Martiny* (fn. 6) 561.

[51] See *Lima Pinheiro* (fn. 39 [2006]) 26 and 34; *Magnus/Mankowski/Lima Pinheiro* (fn. 45) Art. 19 n. 14 and 43; and *Carrascosa González*, La ley aplicable a los contratos internacionales – el reglamento Roma I, 2009, 332.

beneficiary in contracts concluded through the internet is normally the place of establishment that is indicated by the provider. In the absence of a statement about the place of establishment, its location can be inferred from a geographical indication contained in the domain name. If this indication is also missing, and that location is not otherwise cognoscible with reasonable diligence by the beneficiary,[52] resort shall be made to the subsidiary connection of Art. 4(4) (law of the country with which the contract has the closest connection).

With regard to natural persons acting in the exercise of a professional activity, if the place of establishment cannot be determined with reasonable diligence by the beneficiary, resort shall also be made to the subsidiary connection.

Thus, the subsidiary criterion of the closest connection must also operate when the habitual residence of the relevant party to establish the connection with the smart contract pursuant to Art. 4(1) and (2) is not cognoscible with reasonable diligence by the other party.[53]

The special regime for contracts with consumers applies to international contracts concluded between a person who acts in the context of his or her commercial or professional activities and a consumer, i. e., a person who does not act in the exercise of a professional activity.

Pursuant to Art. 6(1), this regime is applicable when there is a connection between the activity of the professional and the country of habitual residence of the consumer. The professional must:

- pursue his commercial or professional activities in the country where the consumer has his habitual residence, or
- by any means, direct such activities to that country or to several countries including that country,

and the contract must fall within the scope of such activities.

Let us see what the special regime for determining the law applicable to contracts with consumers consists of.

Art. 6(2) of the Regulation establishes a limit to the principle of freedom of choice of the law applicable to the contract. Indeed, this provision determines that the choice by the parties of the applicable law cannot have the consequence of depriving the consumer of the protection afforded to him or her by mandatory provisions of the law of the country in which he or she is habitually resident.

In the absence of choice by the parties of the applicable law, Art. 6(1) of the Regulation provides a deviation from the connection established by Art. 4.

---

52 In case that the place of central administration or the place of the relevant secondary establishment is not known, the place of the registered office may be considered, if it is known by the beneficiary – see *Magnus/Mankowski/Lima Pinheiro* (fn. 45) Art. 19 n. 43.

53 Cf. *Magnus/Mankowski/Lima Pinheiro* (fn. 45) Art. 19 n. 43; *Martiny* (fn. 6) 558; *Braegelmann/Kaulartz* (fn. 13) § 12 n. 28 and 41.

Art. 4 often leads to the application of the law of the country in which the provider of goods or services is established. By virtue of Art. 6(1), the contract with a consumer will be governed by the law of the country in which the consumer has his or her habitual residence.

In the case *Verein für Konsumenteninformation I* (2016),[54] the Court of Justice of the European Union understood that, under the Directive on Unfair Terms (Dir. 93/13/EEC), a standard contractual clause stipulating that the contract concluded with a consumer is governed by the law of the Member State in which that professional is seated is abusive insofar as it misleads that consumer, giving him or her the impression that only the law of that Member State is applicable to the contract, without informing him or her that he or she also benefits from the protection provided by the mandatory provisions of the Law that would be applicable in the absence of this clause.[55]

It follows, from this judgment, that choice-of-law clauses are subject to the general control of the rules transposing the Directive on Unfair Terms, within the scope of application of this Directive (consumer contracts).

According to Art. 12(2) of the Rome I Regulation, the law of the country where the obligation is performed must be taken into account as to the manner of performance and the steps to be taken in the event of defective performance. By the term 'manner of performance' it is understood the measures that, according to the contract or the *lex contractus*, are necessary for the its performance and do not concern the content of the obligation.[56] This rule does not mean that the modes of performance are entirely subject to the law of the place of performance. One should apply the *lex contractus*, but take into account the law of the place of performance.[57] In the case of the performance of an on-chain smart contract, the manner of performance is governed exclusively by the *lex contractus*. Art. 12(2) may already have a useful meaning for a smart contract involving off-chain performance.

Although a smart contract can, in certain cases, be seen as a performance measure prescribed by an underlying contract, it should not be considered a manner of performance for the purposes of Art. 12(2) of the Rome I Regulation, because what is at stake are external performance procedures that are mandatorily conformed by the law of the place of performance, to which digital processes are unrelated.

---

54 ECJ 28/7/2016 [ECLI:EU:C:2016:612].

55 What is for the national court to determine in the light of all the relevant circumstances (para. 71).

56 Cf. *Reithmann/Martiny/Martiny*, Internationales Vertragsrecht. Das internationale Privatrecht der Schuldverträge, 9th ed., 2022, n. 3.219; *Staudinger/Magnus*, Internationales Vertragsrecht. Neubarbeitung 2011, Art. 12 n. 81; and *Magnus/Mankowski/Ferrari* (fn. 42) Art. 12 n. 38.

57 Cp., regarding this issue, *Reithmann/Martiny/Martiny* (fn. 56) n. 3.221; Staudinger/MAGNUS (fn. 56) Art. 12 n. 93; and *Magnus/Mankowski/Ferrari* (fn. 45) Art. 12 n. 41

The foregoing examination demonstrates, in my view, that the general choice-of-law rules in force in the Portuguese legal order regarding obligational contracts are, to a certain extent, appropriate to determine the law applicable to smart contracts. The place of conclusion of the contract and the place of its performance are not primarily relevant and, therefore, there is no reason to distinguish contracts concluded and/or performed on-chain from those concluded and/or performed off-chain in terms of determining the applicable law.[58]

I have already alluded to the problem raised by cases, frequent in contracts through the Internet, in which the habitual residence of one of the parties is not known with reasonable diligence by the other party. Recourse to the subsidiary connection may not be possible in borderline cases, in which no links relevant to the determination of the closest connection are determinable. In an even more extreme hypothesis, the identity of one of the parties may not be known with reasonable diligence by the other party, with consequences for access to jurisdictional protection. This can occur in cases of pseudonymity of blockchain accounts.

In cases where it is not possible to materialize the connecting factor of the primary connection or the subsidiary connection, it has been held that one has to resort to the application of the substantive law of the forum (Arts. 23(2) and, by analogy, 348(3) of the Portuguese Civil Code). A more flexible approach in determining the applicable law, such as that provided by the Transnational Arbitration Law (*infra* 3), would allow for a more satisfactory solution, at least in these cases. I will return later to this issue (3).

Regarding Brazilian law, Art. 9 of the Law of Introduction to the Norms of Brazilian Law (hereinafter referred to as LINDB), determines that in order to characterize and govern the obligations, the law of the country in which they are constituted will apply. The obligation resulting from the contract is deemed to have been constituted in the place where the offeror resides (§ 2). The law does not expressly allow the choice of applicable law by the parties and its admissibility divides the authors.[59] Case law is also not entirely conclusive on this point. However, there is a decision by the Superior Court of Justice in 2016 that does allow this choice, although only in *obita*, i. e., on considerations that do not form part of the reasons for the judgment.[60]

With regard to contracts with consumers, the courts tend to favor the Brazilian Consumer Protection Code over the foreign governing law.[61]

[58] For the same view, *Braegelmann/Kaulartz* (fn. 13) § 12 n. 41 and fn. 144.

[59] See *Dolinger*, Direito Internacional Privado. Parte Geral, 11st ed., 2014, 350; *Araujo*, Direito Internacional Privado. Teoria e Prática Brasileira, 8th ed., 2019, 372 et seq.; *Basso*, Curso de Direito Internacional Privado, 6th ed., 2020, 366 et seq.; *Mazzuoli*, Curso de Direito Internacional Privado, 5th ed., 2019, 143 et seq. and 421 et seq.

[60] REsp. 1.280.218/MG, 12/8/2016, https://stj.jusbrasil.com.br/jurisprudencia/373068518/recurso-especial-resp-1280218-mg-2011-0169279-7/inteiro-teor-373068520.

[61] See *Nadia de Araujo* (fn. 59) 378.

It was proposed that Art. 9 of LINDB be amended in order to allow freedom of choice of the applicable law and to establish a special regime for contracts with consumers.[62]

Meanwhile, the Mercosur Agreement on the Law Applicable in Matters of International Consumer Contracts (2017) was adopted. Pursuant to its main rule (Art. 4 – contracts concluded by the consumer in the Contracting state of his or her domicile), there is freedom of choice, but the choice only prevails if the chosen law is more favorable to the consumer than the law of his domicile. Additionally, the choice is limited to the law of the consumer's domicile, the law of the place of conclusion or performance or the law of the provider's seat. If a valid choice is lacking, the law of the Contracting State where the consumer has his or her domicile is applicable.

Therefore, the direction in which Brazilian law is evolving points to a convergence with Portuguese law and the abovementioned considerations on the choice of law applicable to smart contracts and on the problems in determining the habitual residence of one of the parties may be of interest under present and future Brazilian law.[63]

3. Arbitration choice-of-law rules

Transnational arbitration is the normal mode of dispute resolution in international business. Recourse to State courts is marginal. The advantages of resorting to arbitration with respect to international smart contracts are largely common to those found in relation to other international contracts.[64]

With regard to smart contracts, there is also the possibility of using arbitration as an oracle (*supra* I) which, in the face of controversies arising from relevant facts, allows for the suspension of its automatic performance and the introduction of modifications to the performance program.[65] For example, the program can be formulated in such a way that, in case of notification of a dispute, performance is suspended until there is a decision by the arbitrator. The decision can trigger a restart of the previously programmed performance or be converted into a modification of the automatic performance program.

[62] See *Nadia de Araujo* (fn. 59) 379 et seq., *Maristela Basso* (fn. 59) 376.

[63] See, on the difficulties that may arise in determining the offeror's residence, from the perspective of Brazilian Private International Law, *Garcia*, in: Direito Internacional Privado – negócios e novas tecnologias, Campos Monaco, Camargo e Smith Martins (eds.), 2021, n. 4.

[64] Regarding these advantages, see *Lima Pinheiro*, Arbitragem Transnacional. A Determinação do Estatuto da Arbitragem, 2005, Introdução I.

[65] See *Bourque/Ling Tsui*, in: Scientia Nobilitat. Reviewed Legal Studies, 4, 2014, 10; *Durovic*, Law and Autonomous Systems Series: How to Resolve Smart Contract Disputes – Smart Arbitration as a Solution, University of Oxford – Faculty of Law, Blog 1/6/2018, at https://www.law.ox.ac.uk/business-law-blog/blog/2018/06/law-and-autonomous-systems-series-how-resolve-smart-contract-disputes (22.08.2023); and *Shehata*, Smart Contracts & International Arbitration, 2019, on ssrn.com, 9-10.

Arbitrators enjoy broad autonomy in the determination of the law applicable to the merits of the case, namely because the control by State courts of the law applied by arbitrators is quite limited and the main systems, when they do not abdicate from issuing any directive on the determination of the applicable law by the arbitrators, fully enshrine the principle of freedom of choice and provide, in the absence of a designation of the applicable law by the parties, flexible criteria for the determination of the applicable law that leave a wide margin of appreciation to the arbitrators.

Furthermore, transnational arbitration courts are not exclusively subject to a particular national system.[66] Arbitrators are not bound to exclusively apply the choice-of-law rules of a given State.

The combination of these factors results in the determination of the law applicable to the merits of the case being mainly governed by rules and principles specific to Transnational Arbitration Law.[67] Solutions adopted by the consulted national systems interact with these autonomous rules and principles and can only be properly understood in their light.

Hence, it is justified, in this matter, to start by studying the solutions of the Transnational Arbitration Law and then assess to what extent its application is limited by State guidelines.

Solutions provided by the Transnational Arbitration Law result mainly from the practice of arbitral tribunals, which embodied certain principles that are now part of the legal conscience of the arbitral community, and from the rules of institutionalized arbitration centers, which employ criteria for determining the applicable law that are different from those generally followed by State courts and adopted in national choice-of-law systems.

Thus, the principle of freedom of choice is understood, within the framework of this Transnational Law, as allowing the parties to refer to State law, to Public International Law, to *lex mercatoria*, to rule models such as the UNIDROIT Principles of International Commercial Contracts, to "general principles" or to *ex aequo et bono* considerations.[68] In the practice of arbitral tribunals, the use of non-State decision criteria is relatively frequent.

---

[66] See *Lima Pinheiro* (fn. 64) 29 et seq. and 234 et seq., with further references. For the same view, *Galgano* and *Marrella*, Diritto del commercio internazionale, 2nd ed., 2007, 264, and *Brito*, in: Est. Miguel Galvão Teles, vol. II, 27, 2012, 43. The authors that advocate the subjection of arbitration to the law of the State of its seat hold a contrary view – see references in *Lima Pinheiro* [*loc cit.*], to which shall be added *Mankowski*, in: Fest. Bernd von Hoffmann, 1012, 2011, 1013 et seq.

[67] This conception, that I already advocated in Contrato de Empreendimento Comum (Joint Venture) em Direito Internacional Privado (fn. 49) 630 et seq., was adopted by the Supremo Tribunal de Justiça in its ruling of 11/10/2005, proc. 05A2507 [at www.dgsi.pt]. See also *Brito* (fn. 66) 43-44.

[68] Cf. the case law referred by *Dasser*, Internationales Schiedsgerichte und Lex mercatoria. Rechtsvergleichender Beitrag zur Diskussion über ein nicht-staatliches Handelsrecht, 1989, 180 et seq., and, namely, *Schlosser*, Das Recht der internationalen privaten Schiedsgerichts-

The choice of the rules of law applicable to the merits of the case is particularly important with respect to smart contracts, first of all, for the same reasons that were mentioned in relation to general choice-of-law rules (2). The greater freedom allowed by the choice-of-law rules of arbitration increases the possibilities of choosing the most appropriate decision criteria for smart contracts, including the possibility of conflictual references to some rules that develop within the platforms on which they are concluded and/or performed.

The legal nature of the rules that develop within blockchain networks depend on their object and sources. Code provisions can be formulated by the person or entity administrating the blockchain infrastructure, and which does not represent its users, who only adhere to these provisions. They can then be considered standard contractual clauses. These rules can also be formed based on the collective autonomy or on the trade practices of users, and are not limited to contractual provisions stipulated between the platforms' administrators and their users. It is in this second case that a conflictual reference seems plausible.

Naturally, the choice of fragmentary rules that do not govern all aspects of the contract does not dispense with the use of other decision criteria that are necessary in deciding the dispute.

The parties' reference to State law shall be understood, in the absence of an indication to the contrary, as a reference to the substantive law of that State. In this sense, Art. 28(1) of the UNCITRAL Model Law on International Commercial Arbitration, Art. 52(1) of the Portuguese Voluntary Arbitration Law (hereinafter LAV) and Art. 34(2) § 1 of the Spanish Law on Arbitration. Of course, nothing prevents the parties from making a global reference to the law of a State, which includes its choice-of-law rules (as expressly results from the aforementioned provisions).

In the omission of the parties, there are no clearly established rules of Transnational Arbitration Law for determining the applicable law.

The most significant trend that has been displayed in arbitration case law and in arbitration center rules adopts the criterion of the rules of law most appropriate for the dispute.

This trend is echoed in French, Dutch and Spanish legislation, according to which the dispute must be decided in accordance with the rules of law that the arbitrator considers appropriate (Art. 1511(1) of the French CPC, Art. 1054 of the Dutch CPC and Art. 34(/2) § 2 of the Spanish Arbitration Law). The same

barkeit, 2nd ed., 1989, 532-533; *De Ly*, International Business Law and Lex Mercatoria, 1992, 290; *Stein*, Lex Mercatoria. Realität und Theorie, 1995, 138; *Derains*, in: The Practice of Transnational Law, Berger (ed.), 43, 2001, 41; and *Blackaby/Partasides*, Redfern and Hunter on International Arbitration, 7th. ed., , 2023, n. 3.124 et seq. See also Preamble of the UNIDROIT Principles on International Commercial Contracts and respective comment no. 4a. My opinion, already advocated in Contrato de Empreendimento Comum (Joint Venture) em Direito Internacional Privado (fn. 49) 1020 et seq., was adopted by the Supremo Tribunal de Justiça in its ruling of 11/10/2005, proc. 05A2507 [at www.dgsi.pt].

was true, in the Portuguese legal order, with the LAV of 1986, which ordered the application of the most appropriate law to the dispute (Art. 33(2)).[69]

The idea of appropriation allows for a balancing of interests and consideration of the specific content of the legal issues to be resolved.[70] In determining the applicable law, the arbitrators must take into account the links that the disputed relationship establishes with the different countries, although they can also consider the content of the respective laws.[71]

Assessment of the content of the laws in question should not be based on the subjective preference of the arbitrators. The idea of appropriation for the dispute postulates an objective assessment of the content of the laws in question, depending on the existence of legal rules applicable to the case, the degree of development of this legal regime and its suitability in view of the current needs of the trade[72], its correspondence to the legal culture that most influenced the contract in dispute and the consequences of its application on the validity of the contract.

Arbitral tribunals cannot be governed solely by autonomous rules and principles. They must take into account the guidelines for determining the applicable law issued by States that have particularly significant links with arbitration or where the awarding may foreseeably have to be enforced.

Portuguese and Spanish law have a special regime for determining the applicable law in international arbitration (Art. 52 LAV and Art. 34(2) of the Spanish Arbitration Law).

Under Portuguese law, international arbitration is understood to be that which, taking place in Portuguese territory (Art. 61 LAV), "puts international business interests at stake" (art. 49 LAV).

Under Spanish law, arbitration will be international not only when the dispute affects the interests of international business, but also when the parties are domiciled in different States at the time of conclusion of the arbitration agreement and when the place of arbitration, the place of performance of a substantial part of the obligations of the disputed relationship or the place with which it has a closer relationship is located outside the State where the parties have their domiciles (Art. 3(1) of the Spanish Arbitration Law).

Art. 52(1) LAV allows parties to choose, without any restriction, the "rules of law" to be applied by the arbitrators. The replacement of "law", which appeared in the 1986 LAV, by "rules of law", aligns Portuguese law with UNCITRAL

---

[69] See *Batiffol*, in: Études Berthold Goldman, 1-13, 1982, and *Gaillard*, in : J.-cl. dr. int. 1996, n. 133.

[70] See *Magalhães Collaço*, in: Droit international et droit communautaire. Actes du colloque. Paris 5 et 6 avril 1990, 55, 1991, 64.

[71] See *Batiffol* (fn. 69), *Gaillard* (fn. 69) n. 133, and *Fouchard/Gaillard/Goldman*, Traité de l'arbitrage commercial international, 1996, 889-890.

[72] Cp. the critical remarks of *Moura Ramos*, Da Lei Aplicável ao Contrato de Trabalho Internacional, 1991, 578 et seq.

Model Law, and cannot be deprived of a useful meaning. Indeed, this reference to "rules of law" has been understood as not limiting the broad freedom conferred to the parties by Transnational Arbitration Law.[73] This expressly adopts the solution that I defended before the LAV of 1986.[74]

Spanish Arbitration Law also allows parties to choose, without any restriction, the "legal norms" applicable to the merits of the case (Art. 34(2) § 1). The Preamble of the law clarifies that this formula must be understood in the sense that the choice is not limited to a certain State order, and may also have as its object common rules of international trade (no. VII). At least some authors point to the same interpretation that I defended regarding Portuguese law.[75]

Art. 52(2) of the 2011 LAV, however, came to provide that, in the absence of designation by the parties, the arbitral tribunal applies the law of the State with which the object of the dispute presents a closer connection. This solution approximates the Portuguese law to UNCITRAL Model Law, but represents a step backwards in relation to the provisions of the 1986 LAV, which followed the trend in which Transnational Arbitration Law was evolving, and does not seem to meet the needs of international trade. Indeed, the provision does not allow arbitrators to designate non-State law nor to take into account the substantive content of the State laws in question.[76]

The disadvantages of this solution also seem clear when it comes to smart contracts. The possibility that, in determining the law applicable to the merits of the case, the arbitrators could take into account the content of the laws in question and apply non-State rules is important in the case of a new and complex matter, which is only subject to specific regulation in a few State systems.

In borderline cases where it is not possible to determine which State has the closest connection with the object of the dispute, Portuguese choice-of-law rules of arbitration do not offer a solution. It seems particularly clear that it is preferable to apply the most appropriate law to the dispute rather than resorting simply to Portuguese substantive law.

If we accept that, in the case of *i*mpossibility of determination of the closest connection, there is a gap in both general choice-of-law rules and arbitration choice-of-law rules, the gap should be filled according to the methodology

---

[73] For the same view, *Moura Ramos*, BFDUC 88 2012, 583, 595; *Brito* (fn. 66) 44; *Moura Vicente*, Rev. Int. de Arbitragem e Conciliação 5 (2012) 37, 45-46; *Barrocas*, Lei da Arbitragem Comentada, 2013, Art. 52 n. 4; and *Esteves de Oliveira* (ed.), Lei da Abitragem Voluntária Comentada, 2014, Art. 52 n. 4. Cp. *Menezes Cordeiro*, Tratado da Arbitragem. Comenário à Lei 63/2011, de 14 de dezembro, 2015, Art. 52 n. 30 and 115.

[74] Cf. *Lima Pinheiro* (fn. 49) § 19 D and (fn. 64) § 25.

[75] See *Calvo Caravaca/Carrascoza González*, Tratado de Derecho Internacional Privado, 2020, XX n. 313.

[76] For the same view, *Brito* (fn. 66) 46, *Moura Vicente* (fn. 73) 47, and *Esteves de Oliveira* (ed.) (fn. 73) Art. 52 n. 6-7. For a different view, *Menezes Cordeiro* (fn. 73) Art. 52 n. 115.

adopted by the law and legal science. Normally, there is a margin of appreciation that allows for the search for appropriate solutions.

Pursuant to Art. 10 of the Portuguese Civil Code and main Portuguese authors, the first resort should be made to legal analogy, secondly, to general principles and, lastly to a solution created "within the spirit of the system". It seems that the analogy with Art. 348(3) of the Portuguese Civil Code that concerns cases of impossibility of determining the content of the applicable foreign law, is limited. In particular, it does not seem justified where there are solutions that are more appropriate to the problem of impossibility of materialization of the connecting factor from the point of view of choice-of-law justice. The general choice-of-law principles provide a solution for the gap in this particular case. However, there are system values that can be relevant for the creation of a solution "within the spirit of the system", namely, in the present case, the appropriateness. This value is inherent to the idea of connecting justice and, more widely, to all conflictual justice and requires that, in the determination of applicable law, due account is taken of the legal matter concerned and of the circumstances of the case.[77] Therefore, it is arguable that applying the rules most appropriate to the issue is a sound solution also from a *de iure condito* point of view.

Even if the law designated by the parties or, in its omission, chosen by the arbitrators, is a State law, it constitutes a rule adopted by the international unification of Transnational Arbitration Law, by the rules of arbitration centers and by the arbitral case law that the arbitral tribunal, in contractual matters, must always take into account the provisions of the contract and trade usages. Portuguese and Spanish law, like German and French law,[78] expressly establish the autonomous relevance of usages in "international commercial arbitration" (Art. 52(3) LAV and Art. 34(3) of the Spanish Arbitration Law). Therefore, practices generally observed in blockchain platforms should be taken into account regardless of the law applicable to the merits of the case.

The general choice-of-law rules, examined above (2), are applicable to arbitrations that, having legally relevant contacts with more than one State, are not "international" in the sense of Art. 49 LAV, i. e., do not put international trade interests at stake.[79] This is the case of arbitration of disputes arising from international contracts with consumers. This understanding was adopted in Art. 14 of L no. 144/2015, of 8/9, which transposed Directive 2013/11/EU on Alternative Dispute Resolution for Consumer Disputes into the Portuguese legal order.

---

[77] See *Lima Pinheiro*, Choice-of-Law Justice, 2020, on ssrn.com (Portuguese version in: Direito Internacional e Comparado: Trajetória e Perspectivas. Homenagem aos 70 anos do Professor Catedrático Rui Manuel Moura Ramos, Campos Monaco/Loula (eds.), vol. I, 411, 2021, III.C.

[78] Cf. Art. 1051/4 ZPO and Art. 1511(2) French CPC.

[79] Cf. *Isabel de Magalhães Collaço* (n. 70) 60 in fine-61. See further *Menezes Cordeiro* (fn. 73) Art. 52 n. 111.

Indeed, this provision, based on Art. 11 of the Directive, refers to Art. 5 of the Rome Convention on the Law Applicable to Contractual Obligations and Art. 6 of the Rome I Regulation.

To conclude, let us briefly examine Brazilian Arbitration Law. Art. 2. This law provides that the parties may freely choose the rules of law that will be applied in the arbitration process, provided there is no violation of good customs and public policy (§ 1), and clarifies that the parties may agree that the arbitration be carried out based on the general principles of law, on usages and customs and on international business rules (§ 2).

It therefore seems that Brazilian law does not limit the scope that the principle of freedom of choice has according to Transnational Arbitration Law.[80]

The silence of the Law regarding the law applicable to the merits of the case in the omission of the parties can certainly be understood in different ways, but I believe that an understanding that conforms to the best trends of Transnational Arbitration Law should be favored.

IV. Introduction to DAOs

According to one of the first definitions of a DAO, "[it]is a particular kind of decentralized organization that is neither run nor controlled by any person, but entirely by code". It can be based on one or more interacting smart contracts, but generally is based on a set of interacting smart contracts.[81] This definition is not completely accurate, as we will see, but can serve as a starting point.

What distinguishes a DAO from a mere smart contract is the fact that a DAO has some form of organization, either internal or external.[82]

When the DAO operates on blockchain, it is also based upon a decentralized software program that runs in the blockchain, and that allows the programming of the smart contracts on which the DAO is based.[83]

It is often assumed that a DAO is not managed by a person or a limited group of persons in view of the fact that all decisions are taken by its members through a code protocol. As a matter of fact, the management of most DAOs is decen-

[80] See also *Straube/De Souza/Gagliardi*, in: Arbitragem Comercial. Princípios, Instituições e Procedimentos, Basso/Pasquot Polido (eds.), 2013, 156; *Basso* (fn. 59) 372 and 379; *Pereira Dias*, in: Manual de Arbitragem Internacional Lusófona, *Monteiro Pires/Pereira Dias* (eds.), vol. I., 2020, 186-187.

[81] Cf. *De Filippi/Wright* (fn. 29) 148.

[82] See also *Guillaume/Riva*, Blockchain Dispute Resolution for Decentralized Autonomous Organizations: The Rise of Decentralized Autonomous Justice, See also *Guillaume/Riva*, 2022, on ssrn.com, 3-4.

[83] See *Mienert*, Dezentrale autonome Organisationen (DAOs) und Gesellschaftsrecht, 2022, 33-34.

tralized. However, this does not happen, or does not happen entirely, in the case of all DAOs.

It was recently stated that certain decisions on DAO management can be taken by autonomous systems based upon artificial intelligence.[84] The present essay will not be dealing with the specific issues that can arise when decentralized organizations and artificial intelligence are combined.

DAOs are very heterogeneous. They may pursue different purposes, carry out different activities, and have different types of organization.

First of all, they can have completely different purposes. Normally they pursue an economic purpose, but they can also pursue a non-economic purpose. The economic purpose can be a shareable profit resulting from a common activity, in a strict sense, or, more widely, a direct economic advantage for the parties involved.

The activity of DAOs often has a certain degree of permanence, but can also be limited to a specific act, such as raising funds for an investment project or a charity action.[85]

Their organization can be internal or external, at least according to the organization's visibility by third parties.

Furthermore, a DAO can be based upon a public or a private blockchain and upon a permissioned or a permissionless blockchain.

From a legal point of view, DAOs can be incorporated with the intervention of public bodies belonging to one State, and then registered, or unincorporated, as is mostly the case. Since the purposes and activities of DAOs can be different, the corporate form and the way they operate can also differ quite significantly and can correspond to human-run version of organizations that have the same type of purpose and carry out the same type of activity.[86]

DAOs can have a legal personality that is independent from the personality of their members, or, as often happens with unincorporated DAOs, they can be deprived of legal personality.

Although their management is often decentralized, DAOs can also by managed by members' representatives or by an external entity. In certain cases, these representatives or this external entity can hold only part of the powers that are normally held by the management of a company or other external organization, making it difficult to draw a line between central management and decentralized governance.

---

[84] See *Mienert* (fn. 83) 53.

[85] See *De Filippi/Wright* (fn. 29) 148; *Anderson*, DAO – Decentralized Autonomous Organizations for Beginners: The Ultimate Beginner's Guide, 2021, 20-21; *Mienert* (fn. 82) 56 et seq., referring several DAOs examples and modalities.

[86] See *Audit* (fn. 17) 69, points out that it also does not require employees; *Anderson* (fn. 83); *Madalena Perestrelo de Oliveira, António Garcia Rolo, João Vieira Santos* e *Ana Nunes Teixeira*, Boletim da Ordem dos Advogados 35 2022, 66, 66.

DAOs also involve different categories of actors. Let us consider the most relevant for our analysis.

Often a DAO is promoted by a group of developers who create the code for the smart contracts on which it is based.

Interested parties become members of the DAO by acquiring a digital representation of their membership, a certain type of token. These tokens can be of different types and confer different powers.

Thirdly, we have the validators, who operate validating nodes and maintain the network by creating new blocks to be added to the chain.[87]

Finally, we can still have a person or entity who is entrusted with the management of the blockchain infrastructure and who administrates the respective protocol.

The ideal DAO operates only within a blockchain network, even when its activity includes the provision of goods and services to third parties. However, if the smart contracts on which the DAO is based include off-chain performance, there is a need for human intervention.[88] Additionally, other circumstances can occur that require human intervention besides the taking of decisions by the members according to the code protocol, such as changes of the code to correct programming errors or preventing or reverting illegal exploitations of code vulnerabilities.

Although DAOs are projected to operate, as far as possible, according to the provisions that are codified in smart contracts, as I pointed out above (I), the law has to govern the formation of the contract and its requisites of validity, as well as its interpretation and gap filling.

In the case of DAOs, vulnerabilities caused by programming errors can lead to misappropriation of assets as happened in the famous hacking case of "The DAO" and the corresponding issue of the right to fork, i. e., the right to change the code.

Normally, DAOs have both a contractual and an organizational dimension.

Setting aside the possibility of relationships in which there is no intention of legal binding and where there is no external organization with legal relevance, DAOs can be prone to internal conflicts (between a DAO and its members or among its members concerning the DAO's operation) as well as external conflicts (between a DAO or its members and third parties) that must be governed by legal rules.

---

[87] Through either proof-of-work or, increasingly, proof-of-stake consensus mechanisms – see *Schillig*, 2022, on ssrn.com. These validating nodes are, therefore, mining nodes in the sense referred by *Artzt/Richter* (eds.), Handbook of Blockchain Law: A Guide to Understanding and Resolving the Legal Challenges of Blockchain Technology, 2020, 152-154. On the mining process, see further *Colin*, in: Les blockchains et les smart contracts *à l›épreuve du droit*, Cotiga-Raccah/Jacquemin/Poullet (eds.), 2020, 19..

[88] See also *Anderson* (fn. 84) 34-35.

The pseudonymity of a DAO's members and the decentralization and immateriality of the blockchain can set limits for the application of law and for resorting to State courts. However, as far as possible, these disputes shall be settled according to rules of law and enforced by dispute resolution mechanisms that apply these rules in order to avoid situations of denial of justice.[89]

The contract between DAO members can be considered, from a legal science viewpoint, as a contract for a common purpose.[90] Depending on the circumstances of the case and of the applicable law, it can be substantively characterized in different ways, namely as a "society" (for example, a civil society in Portuguese law, a partnership or a memorandum of association of a company in a Common Law system or a *BGB Gesellschaft* in German law), a joint venture or a consortium.

Another problem is the nature and characterization of the relationship with the developers who did not become members, as well as with the validators and with the administrator of the blockchain infrastructure. I cannot enter into an examination of these relationships.[91]

We have reached, therefore, the point where applicable rules should be determined. This determination requires not only the characterization of relationships with regard to a given legal order and the interpretation and application of its substantive provisions, but also, often, the solution of choice-of-law problems to be provided by Private International Law.

V. DAOs and Private International Law

As stressed above (II), a choice-of-law problem in the sense of Private International Law results from relevant contacts of the relationship with two or more sovereign States. If there are no relevant contacts with more than one State, the law of this State is directly applicable.

However, difficulty in determining the residence, nationality or seat of the members of a DAO, and even their identity, should be taken into account. Therefore, the transnationality of a DAO that does not limit its membership to persons located in the same State should also be presumed. The location of the developers or of the managing representatives or external entity can also be relevant as a transnational factor. The same can be said of a close connection with an international market, namely financial markets. Furthermore, the place of incorporation can be of some relevance, but it may not be enough if all the elements of the DAO are clearly localized in one State.

---

[89] See *Guillaume/Riva* (fn. 82) 16.

[90] For the view that the contract can be considered as a cooperation contract, also *Drögemüller* (fn. 31) 114-115.

[91] See *Mienert* (fn. 83) 106 et seq.

There is some specificity in choice-of-law problems regarding DAOs.

On one hand, the pseudonymity of a DAO's members can make it difficult or even impossible to materialize connecting factors related to their location.[92]

On the other hand, members may voluntarily submit to the provisions codified in the network computer code that the members expressly or implicitly accept by participating in the network.[93]

I have already stated (*supra* III), that the legal nature of the provisions codified in blockchain networks depend on their object and sources. I would like to add that the code provisions can be formulated not only by the person or entity administrating the blockchain infrastructure, but also by the developers or by an entity managing the DAO. Even if the members only adhere to these provisions, they display important differences in relation to traditional standard clauses where these also govern the relations between the members of the DAO that have accepted them, and this can be of relevance to the applicability of legal rules for standard clauses and to the determination of their legal nature. It is also conceivable that the code provisions are formulated by representatives chosen by the DAO's members, and are, therefore, an expression of their collective autonomy.

I refer to what was previously exposed regarding the relevance of the *lex cryptographia* for the regulation of international DAOs (*supra* III.1).

Since DAOs have both a contractual and an organizational dimension, the choice-of-law rules for contracts and for legal persons come into play.

If the DAO is incorporated as a legal person, the choice-of-law rules on legal persons apply. These choice-of-law rules pursue not only the interests of the members of the DAO and of the legal person itself, but also the interests of third parties dealing with the DAO and of legal commerce in general.

These choice-of-law rules are applicable to the acquisition of personality; capacity; internal affairs; liability of the DAO, as well as of its organs and members regarding third parties; "representation" of the DAO by its organs; and the transformation, dissolution and extinction of a DAO.

They do not cover contractual or tort liability regarding third parties, which are governed by the laws applicable to contractual and non-contractual obligations.

The main solutions provided by these choice-of-law rules are incorporation theory, which subjects the legal person to the legal order according to which it was incorporated, and seat theory, which subjects the legal person to the law of the place of the seat of its administration. With regard to incorporation theory, as it is understood in Common Law countries, the decisive factor is the place where public bodies perform the acts that trigger the acquisition of legal personality.

---

[92] See *Drögemüller* (fn. 31) 36.

[93] See *Drögemüller* (fn. 31) and 114-115 regarding blockchain networks in general.

Portuguese law adopts seat theory (Art. 33 of Portuguese Civil Code), but does not only give relevance to the registered seat regarding commercial companies (Art. 3(1) Commercial Companies Code), as also it is advocated that it should be presumed that the administration seat is located in the place of the registered seat, which normally coincides with the place of incorporation.[94] Furthermore, incorporation theory applies to foundations (Arts. 2(1) and 5 of Foundations Law[95]).

Spanish law is more differentiated. In principle, it refers to the law of the nationality of the legal person (Art. 9.11 of the Spanish Civil Code). Some authors and recent case law point towards the incorporation theory regarding companies.[96] The law of domicile applies, in principle, to associations, although associations with foreign domicile that carry out their main activities in Spain are also subject to Spanish law.[97] Spanish law applies to foundations that carry out their main activity in Spain and the law of domicile to other foundations.[98]

Brazilian law adopts incorporation theory (Art. 11 of the Law of Introduction to the Rules of Brazilian Law).

In romangermanic family systems, the assumption prevails that entities without legal personality that have an external organization are subject directly or by analogy to choice-law rules on legal persons. Regarding Portuguese law, the best opinion seems to be that these choice-of-law rules apply analogically where there are sufficient reasons for this to occur, and to the extent that is justified by the analogy.[99]

Choice-of-law rules on contracts play a role regarding DAOs, not only when they do not have an external organization, but also, according to the best opinion, even if these DAOs are directly or by analogy subject to choice-of-law rules on legal persons. Regarding special connections relevant for partial issues and pre-contractual liability, I refer to my previous remarks (*supra* II). The considerations that follow concern only the determination of the *lex contractus*.

Choice-of-law rules on contracts that are more relevant for DAOs fundamentally pursue the interests of the parties involved and are, therefore, based upon freedom of choice of the applicable law (Art. 3 of Rome I Regulation, Art. 41 of the Portuguese Civil Code) and Art. 52(1) LAV). In the absence of a valid choice of law by the parties, these rules provide for the application of the law of the State with which the contract is most closely connected (Art. 4(3)and(4) Rome I

---

94 See *Lima Pinheiro*, Direito Internacional Privado, vol. II – Direito de Conflitos/Parte Especial, t. I – Introdução, Pessoas Singulares e Coletivas e Princípios Gerais de Direito dos Estrangeiros, 5th ed., 2023, § 59 B and D, with further references.

95 Adopted by L no. 24/2012, of 9/9.

96 See *Calvo Caravaca/Carrascosa González* (fn. 75) n. 44.

97 Op. cit., n. 121.

98 Op. cit., n. 122.

99 See *Lima Pinheiro* (fn. 94) § 58 B.

Regulation, up to a certain point Art. 42(1) of the Portuguese Civil Code and Art. 52(2) LAV).

In my opinion, choice-of-law rules on contracts are applicable to the contract of common purpose underlying the DAO.[100] However, two points should be made. Firstly, this is without prejudice to mandatory rules concerning the contract provided by the law applicable to the DAO's organization. Secondly, as the Rome I Regulation seems to exclude from its scope of application contracts that directly institute entities with external organization subject to an institutional regime (Art. 1(2)(f)), the choice-of-law rules relevant in this case are those provided in Arts. 41 and 42 of the Portuguese Civil Code. In the case of a valid arbitration agreement, the choice-of-law rule is provided by Art. 52 LAV.

These choice-of-law rules are, in principle, applicable to the formation, validity, interpretation and gap filling obligations created by the contract and consequences of non-performance.

Regarding the right to fork, it seems that the law governing the contract should be applied as long as the law governing the external organization does not claim applicability. If there is a person or entity who is entrusted with the administration of the blockchain infrastructure, it seems that the law applicable to the relationship between the DAO, or its members, with this person or entity should also be taken into account, but I believe that the stance of the laws previously mentioned cannot be ignored.

In any case, three observations should be made in this regard.

First of all, the principles and values underlying choice-of-law rules on contracts and choice-of-law rules on legal persons are, to a certain extent, different and, therefore, contrarily to some proposals, determination of the law applicable to DAOs with external organization should not be based exclusively on one of them.

Notwithstanding, the coincidence of the law applicable to the DAO contract with the law applicable to the DAO organization is desirable, since it promotes substantive harmony and avoids many problems of delimitation among issues governed by each of the laws and of coordination of these laws.

Furthermore, proprietary issues of DAO tokens, namely those that can be characterized as securities, also raise a choice-of-law problem. These issues include, for example, the determination of the effects of the tokenholder's right with regard to third parties, with the exclusion of those effects that are subject to the external organization's governing law.[101] I will not be dealing with these issues in the present essay.

---

[100] Cp. *Mienert* (fn. 83) 82-85, understanding that in most cases DAOs are external organizations; and in general, regarding the relationship between the participants in a blockchain network, *Drögemüller* (fn. 31) 113 et seq.

[101] See *John*, in: Fest. 40 Jahre IPRG, Heindler (ed.), 405-423, 2020, 413 et seq.; *Aigner*, ZfRV 2020, 211, 218-220; *Wendehorst*, EGBGB Art. 43, in: Münchener Kommentar zum

VI. Laws Applicable to International DAOs

As previously mentioned (V), choice-of-law rules on contracts have a role to play in the determination of the law applicable to DAOs, as well as choice-of-law rules on legal persons regarding DAOs with an external organization.

Regarding choice-of-law rules on contracts, choice of law by the parties involved should be strongly recommended. However, abstracting of the possibility of an implicit submission to code rules relevant in arbitration, an off-chain agreement seems to be required[102] or, at least, a complement by commentaries in natural language (see *supra* III.2).[103]

As previously stated, in the absence of a valid choice of law by the parties, these choice-of-law rules provide for the application of the law of the State with which the contract is most closely connected (Art. 4(3) and (4) Rome I Regulation, up to a certain point Art. 42(1) CC and Art. 52(2) LAV). Determining the closest connection with the contract is highly problematic in most DAOs in which the members are located in multiple States or in situations where it is difficult or even impossible to know where they are located.

Links that can be used to establish the closest connection do not only consist of members' habitual residence or seat that can be cognoscible through reasonable diligence by other members, but also:

- the habitual residence or seat of a person or entity that has some power of administration of the DAO;
- the place of incorporation of the incorporated DAO;
- the registered address or seat of a registered representative of the DAO;
- the habitual residence or seat of the developers;
- the seat of the entity that administrates the blockchain infrastructure;
- the language of the underlying contract concluded in natural language; and
- the reference to a law, particular provisions or concepts of a law contained in any off-chain agreement or on the website of the developers that, however, does not amount to a valid choice of law by the parties.

If these links are not available or do not allow for the determination of the closest connection because they do not point clearly to a given State, as can often happen, it has been held that Portuguese Private International Law will lead to the application of the *lex fori* (by analogy with Art. 348(3) CC of the Portuguese

---

BGB, 8th ed., , 2021, n. 306 et seqs.; *Yang*, When Jurisdiction Rules Meet Blockchain: Can the Old Bottle Contain the New Wine?, 2022, on ssrn.com, 49 et seq.

[102] For this view, *Braegelmann/Kaulartz* (fn. 13) § 12 n. 17.

[103] See *Law Commission*, Advice to Government. Smart Legal Contracts, 2021, n. 7.71 et seq.

Civil Code).[104] The same position is held in the context of Spanish Private International Law.[105]

In contrast, the Transnational Arbitration Law (above III.3), allows for the application of the rules most appropriate to the dispute. This flexible approach would seem more satisfactory than resorting to the *lex fori*, also given the fact that Portuguese substantive law does not contain specific provisions on DAOs.

As previously stated (*supra* III.3), if we accept that, in the case of impossibility of determination of the closest connection, there is a gap in both general choice-of-law rules and arbitration choice-of-law rules, it is arguable that the application of the rules most appropriate to the issue is sound also from a *de iure condito* point of view.

Regarding choice-of-law rules on legal persons, the first assertion is that corporate DAOs should be governed by the law of the State of incorporation, understood in the previously mentioned terms (V). This is even true, in principle, regarding a system based upon the seat theory, such as the Portuguese, for many reasons among which I will mention the following:

- incorporation with the intervention of public bodies is always governed by the law of place of incorporation;[106]
- it should be presumed that the seat of administration is located in the same place as the registered seat, which is normally in the State of incorporation, namely to protect the trust of third parties;[107]
- Portuguese law gives relevance to the place of the registered seat towards third parties regarding commercial companies and to the incorporation theory regarding foundations (*supra* V);[108]
- the great majority of DAOs are not centrally managed, and therefore, there is gap that should be filled according to the principle of freedom of choice and the values of legal certainty and foreseeability.[109] This points to incorporation theory.

In most cases, DAOs are unincorporated and, therefore, the law applicable to external organization should be determined, in my opinion, by a subsidiary connecting factor that is as close as possible to incorporation theory: the law according to which, in an externally visible manner, its constitution was guided (see also Art. 154 (1) *in fine* of Swiss Private International Law Act).

[104] See *Marques dos Santos*, ROA 2000, 647, 667; and *Lima Pinheiro* (fn. 30) § 29 B. In result, also *Baptista Machado*, Lições de Direito Internacional Privado, 2nd ed., 1982, 251.

[105] See *Fernández Rozas/Sánchez Lorenzo*, Derecho Internacional Privado, 12nd ed., 2022, n. 130.

[106] See *Lima Pinheiro* (fn. 94) § 59 C.

[107] Op. cit., § 59 B and D.

[108] Op. cit., § 59 D.

[109] See *Lima Pinheiro* (fn. 77) III.C.

A choice of law in an off-chain agreement or a reference to the applicable law on the developers' website could be relevant in this regard. Taking a step further, a choice of the law applicable to the DAO's organization should be allowed, as far as cognoscible with reasonable diligence by third parties.[110]

If unequivocal determination of this law is impossible, the subsidiary solution would be the application of the law of the seat of administration.

However, these solutions are often unavailable. On one hand, because the constitution of an unincorporated DAO is often not guided by any law, or this guidance is not externally visible. On the other hand, because the great majority of DAOs do not have a central administration in the sense required by seat theory.[111]

In exceptional cases, in which participation in the DAO is limited to persons located in one State, and admitting that despite this a choice-of-law problem arises, the seat of administration may be deemed to be situated in this State.

In normal cases, we have to resort to other connecting factors to fill the gap.

If there is a person or entity with some powers to administer the DAO, or, if not, a registered representative of the DAO, or, if this is not the case, a person or entity entrusted with the administration of the blockchain infrastructure, his or her registered address or its registered seat can provide the necessary point of reference for third parties and consequently operate as the relevant connecting factor.[112]

As a last resort, if there is no point of reference for third parties, instead of applying the *lex fori*, it seems preferable, with regard to the internal affairs of the external organization, to apply the law governing the DAO contract, and with regard to liability involving third parties, the law governing each contractual or non-contractual relationship with a third party.[113]

The flexible approach of the rules most appropriate to the dispute that is allowed by Transnational Arbitration Law could again constitute a better solution for these hard cases.

---

110 See also *Mienert* (fn. 83) 86-87, less clearly regarding cognoscibility by third parties.

111 For the same view, *Zimmermann* (fn. 32) 568; *Audit* (fn 17) 693; *Guillaume/Riva* (fn. 82) 9. The nationality or residence of the group of tokenholders with sufficient voting rights to determine the activity of the DAO has been suggested as a relevant connecting factor – see *Oliveira/Rolo/Santos/Teixeira* (fn. 85) 69, but this solution does not assure the required point of reference to third parties.

112 See also the remarks of *Mienert* (fn. 83) 95 et seq. For this purpose, it is also conceivable that the habitual residence of a person may operate as the relevant connecting factor in lack of a registered address, but the issue raises doubts.

113 For this view, in any case of impossibility of materialization of the traditional connecting factors, see *Zimmermann* (fn. 32) 570 et seqs.

VII. Final Remarks

International smart contracts and DAOs are new dimensions of the challenge that the Internet has posed to Private International Law, due to the weakening of the spatial ties of the relationships that are established within it. It is now not just a matter of contracts that are concluded through the internet, but also contracts that tend to be performed on chain in distributed ledger platforms with multi-located operators and organizations that tend to be managed and operate in these platforms.

In principle, it is possible to respond to this challenge with choice-of-law techniques, but, in hard cases, more flexible standards for the determination of the applicable law, such as those that are practiced in transnational arbitration, prove to be more appropriate to the specificity of these relationships rather than the traditional solutions adopted by general choice-of-law rules (i.e., choice of law rules applied by State courts).

In extreme cases, such as the identity of one of the parties not being known with reasonable diligence by the other party, it is not only Private International Law that does not provide an answer to the legal regulation of the smart contract or of the DAO, it is the legal protection itself that comes into crisis.[114]

The analysis I have carried out certainly does not provide an answer to all issues regarding the determination of the laws applicable to smart contracts and DAOs, even if limited to the *lex contractus* and the law governing external organizations. My goal was merely to make a first approach to these issues, more concerned with identifying the problems and suggesting possible solutions rather than offering definitive conclusions.

---

[114] See also *Audit* (fn. 17) 689.

Index of Subects

Index of Contributors

Axelsen, Henrik, Ph.D. Fellow, Department of Computer Science, University of Copenhagen

Boura, Marta, Ph.D. Candidate, Guest Lecturer, Faculty of Law, University of Lisbon; Researcher at the Lisbon Research Centre for Private Law (CIDP); Researcher of the Lisbon DAO Observatory Research Project; Lawyer

Garcia Rolo, António, Ph.D. Candidate, Guest Lecturer, Faculty of Law, University of Lisbon; Researcher at Lisbon Research Centre for Private Law (CIDP): Co-Principal Investigator of the Lisbon DAO Observatory Research Project; Legal Advisor at the Bank of Portugal

Guillaume, Florence, Full Professor, Faculty of Law, University of Neuchâtel (Switzerland), Director of the LexTech Institute (lextechinstitute.ch)

Jensen, Johannes Rude, Research Coordinator – Financial Transparency Group, Department of Computer Science, University of Copenhagen

Kremer, Bianca, Dr. iur. (HSG), Senior Fellow, Wharton Blockchain and Digital Asset Project, The Wharton School, University of Pennsylvania

de Lima Pinheiro, Luís, Full Professor, Faculty of Law, University of Lisbon

Mienert, Biyan, Dr., General Counsel at LUKSO, Attorney-at-law (Germany)

Möslein, Florian, Prof. Dr., LL.M. (London), Full Professor, Faculty of Law, Philipps-Universität Marburg; Director, Institute for Law and Regulation of Digitalisation (www.irdi.institute)

Østbye, Peter, Dr. Philos., University of Oslo; Norges Bank

Ostrovski, Daniel, Ph.D. Candidate, Faculty of Law, Philipps-Universität Marburg

Perestrelo de Oliveira, Madalena, Prof. Dr., Professor, Faculty of Law, University of Lisbon; Researcher at Lisbon Research Centre for Private Law (CIDP); Co-Principal Investigator of the Lisbon DAO Observatory Research Project; Legal Counsel

Rocha Mendes, António, LL.M., Boston University School of Law; Head of Tax at CS' Associados, Lawyer

Ross, Omri, Associate Professor, Department of Computer Science, University of Copenhagen

Serras de Sousa, João, Researcher at Lisbon Research Centre for Private Law (CIDP); Researcher at Lisbon DAO Observatory Research Project; Guest Lecturer, Faculty of Law, University of Lisbon; Lawyer at PLMJ Advogados, SP, RL

Vandy, Nathan, M.A., Ph.D. Candidate, Université Paris II Panthéon-Assas; Head of Decentralisation at DappRadar

Vieira dos Santos, João, Ph.D., Professor, Faculty of Law, Lusófona University; Legal Advisor, CMVM – Portuguese Securities Market Commission

Wang, Kanye Ye, Dr. sc ETH Zurich, Assistant Professor, Department of Computer and Information Science, Asia-Pacific Academy of Economics and Management, University of Macau

Wray, Christopher, M.A. Oxford University; Barrister; Legal Graph Company Limited